VIRGIL

AENEID

BOOK XI

EDITED BY
SCOTT MCGILL
Rice University, Houston

CAMBRIDGE
UNIVERSITY PRESS

CAMBRIDGE
UNIVERSITY PRESS

Shaftesbury Road, Cambridge CB2 8EA, United Kingdom

One Liberty Plaza, 20th Floor, New York, NY 10006, USA

477 Williamstown Road, Port Melbourne, VIC 3207, Australia

314–321, 3rd Floor, Plot 3, Splendor Forum, Jasola District Centre, New Delhi – 110025, India

103 Penang Road, #05–06/07, Visioncrest Commercial, Singapore 238467

Cambridge University Press is part of Cambridge University Press & Assessment, a department of the University of Cambridge.

We share the University's mission to contribute to society through the pursuit of education, learning and research at the highest international levels of excellence.

www.cambridge.org
Information on this title: www.cambridge.org/9781107416789

DOI: 10.1017/9781107775527

First published 2020

A catalogue record for this publication is available from the British Library

Library of Congress Cataloging-in-Publication data
NAMES: Virgil, author. | McGill, Scott, 1968 – editor, writer of added commentary.
TITLE: Aeneid : Book XI / edited by Scott McGill.
OTHER TITLES: Aeneis. Liber 11. Latin (McGill) |
Cambridge Greek and Latin classics.
DESCRIPTION: Cambridge, United Kingdom : Cambridge University Press, 2020. |
Series: Cambridge Greek and Latin classics | Includes
bibliographical references and index. | Introduction and notes in
English, with text in Latin.
IDENTIFIERS: LCCN 2019045615 | ISBN 9781107071339 (hardback)
SUBJECTS: LCSH: Aeneas (Legendary character) – Poetry. | Latini (Italic
people) – Poetry. | Trojans – Poetry. | LCGFT: Poetry. | Epic poetry.
CLASSIFICATION: LCC PA6803.B31 M34 2020 | DDC 873/.01–dc23
LC record available at https://lccn.loc.gov/2019045615

ISBN 978-1-107-07133-9 Hardback
ISBN 978-1-107-41678-9 Paperback

CONTENTS

PREFACE

Commentaries are links in a chain, connected to the predecessors from which they draw and, if they are successful, to the successors that draw from them. Two important predecessors for this book are K. W. Gransden's and Nicholas Horsfall's commentaries on *Aeneid* 11. Gransden's is the earlier Cambridge green and yellow on book 11, a thin volume of sparse, uneven notes; Horsfall's is one of his several exhaustive, magisterial Brill commentaries on the *Aeneid* that cast a looming shadow over any later commentator. I have tried to tread a middle path between Gransden and Horsfall by providing a more thorough commentary on *Aeneid* 11 than Gransden while keeping things trimmer than Horsfall. The guiding principle has been to produce a book that is both useful and readily useable for students and scholars alike.

When I embarked on this project, I felt like Ornytus in *Aeneid* 11, who fails to make the transition from hunter to fighter and is consequently out of place on the battlefield and ill-adapted to war; the transition I had to make was to learning to write a commentary, and I struggled to find my way. Any success that I have had in adapting to this new mode of writing depends significantly upon the good offices of others. The series editors Philip Hardie and Stephen Oakley have earned my deepest gratitude for their careful attention and patience. I must also thank my colleague Ted Somerville at Rice, who helped to clarify several details in book 11, particularly in matters of grammar and syntax. Alexander Hardie, Nicholas Horsfall, and Richard Tarrant answered questions that I periodically sent at aporetic moments, and for that I am grateful. Finally, my students in a Virgil seminar at Rice offered valuable feedback on a draft of the commentary. I appreciate the chance to have been their *discipulus* as well as their *magister*, and this book is better because of them.

ABBREVIATIONS

The names and titles of classical authors and texts are generally abbreviated in accordance with *OLD* for Latin and LSJ for Greek. Latin authors and works not included in *OLD* are cited according to the conventions in *OCD*. Journal titles are abbreviated according to the practice of *L'Année philologique.*

A–G	A. Mahoney, ed., *Allen and Greenough's new Latin grammar* (Newburyport, MA 2001)
EV	*Enciclopedia Virgiliana* (Rome 1984–91)
G–L	B. L. Gildersleeve and G. Lodge, *Gildersleeve's Latin grammar,* 3rd edn (London 1895)
GLK	H. Keil, ed., *Grammatici Latini,* 8 vols. (Leipzig 1857–80)
H–S	J. B. Hofmann and A. Szantyr, *Lateinische Syntax und Stilistik* (Munich 1965)
K–S	R. Kühner and C. Stegman, *Ausfürliche Grammatik der lateinischen Sprache, zweiter Teil* (Hanover 1971)
NLS	E. C. Woodcock, *A new Latin syntax* (London 1959)
OLD	P. G. W. Glare, ed., *Oxford Latin dictionary* (Oxford 1968–82)
TLL	*Thesaurus linguae Latinae* (Leipzig 1900–)
VE	R. F. Thomas and J. M. Ziolkowski, eds., *The Virgil encyclopedia,* 3 vols. (Malden, MA 2014)

INTRODUCTION

1 SUMMARY OF *AENEID* 11

Aen. 11 divides into three sections.[1] It opens in the calm after the storm, on the morning after the ferocious fighting in *Aen.* 10 between the Trojans and the Latin forces. That clash saw Turnus killing Pallas, Aeneas' furious rampage on the battlefield in response to Pallas' demise, and the deaths of Lausus and his father, the exiled Etruscan tyrant Mezentius. The first section of book 11 centres on the funerals for the dead on both sides of the war (1–212); Aeneas agrees to a twelve-day truce to allow for preparations and for burial. Pallas is a principal figure: Aeneas mourns over him and prepares a cortège that returns him to his native Pallanteum and his father, the king Evander. The second section (225–444) comprises a Latin council. Venulus first reports to the assembly, which includes King Latinus and Turnus, on the failure of his mission to convince Diomedes, now settled in Italy, to join with the Latins and fight the Trojans.[2] In the wake of that bad news, Latinus, a Latin demagogue named Drances, and Turnus give speeches presenting very different visions for how to proceed with the war. The third section finds the Trojans and Italians resuming hostilities after the truce has ended (445–915). Neither Aeneas nor Turnus figures in the fighting. Instead, the predominant warrior is a woman in the Latin forces, the Volscian Camilla.

An outline of the action in *Aen.* 11 will help to orient readers by filling out the above summary:

1. Funerals
   - i. At dawn, Aeneas erects a trophy to Mars from Mezentius' spoils (1–11), encourages his lieutenants (12–21), and calls for funeral rites for his fallen soldiers, with an emphasis on Pallas (22–8)
   - ii. Aeneas mourns Pallas (29–58)
   - iii. Aeneas leads the preparation of Pallas' cortège and bids him a final farewell (59–99)
   - iv. Latin envoys, led by Drances, seek a truce to bury the dead, which Aeneas grants (100–32)
   - v. Trojans and Latins prepare pyres (133–8)
   - vi. Pallas' cortège arrives in Pallanteum; Evander laments over him and calls upon Aeneas to avenge his death (139–81)

[1] Virgil was partial to triadic divisions within books and in the overall structure of *Aen.*; see Gransden, *Aen.* 8, Intro. pp. 6–7 and Hardie, Intro. p. 9.

[2] Lines 213–24 form a brief pendant to the Latin funerals; the passage describes the suffering and unrest in Latinus' city that follows upon them.

- vii. The Trojan funerals (182–202)
- viii. The Latin funerals (203–12)
- ix. The inhabitants of Latinus' city grieve over the dead. Some criticise the war and Turnus; fanned by Drances, sentiment rises for him to fight Aeneas in single combat. Others defend Turnus, laying bare divisions in the city (213–24)

2. The Latin Council
   - i. News comes that Diomedes will not join the Latin war effort. Latinus summons a council, at which Venulus reports on the mission to Diomedes (225–95)
   - ii. Latinus proposes seeking a peace treaty with the Trojans and lays out possible terms (296–335)
   - iii. Drances advises peace in a polemic against Turnus (336–75)
   - iv. Turnus answers Drances' attack and counters Latinus' proposal (376–444)

3. Battle
   - i. Word reaches the Latins that the Trojans have mobilised for battle; the unprepared Latins prepare hastily and chaotically; Turnus eagerly leaves the council and takes command (445–97)
   - ii. Camilla approaches Turnus with a battle plan; Turnus gives her command of the cavalry and departs to set an ambush (498–531)
   - iii. The goddess Diana tells the nymph Opis the story of Camilla's early life, including how the girl entered into her service, laments Camilla's entry into war, and sends Opis to avenge her death (532–96)
   - iv. The cavalry fight is joined (597–647)
   - v. Camilla's *aristeia* (648–724)
   - vi. Jupiter stirs the Etruscan Tarchon to resist; Tarchon exhorts his troops and charges; they follow his example; Arruns stalks Camilla (725–67)
   - vii. Camilla blindly pursues the spoils of the Trojan fighter Chloreus; Arruns fatally strikes her with a spear-throw; with her death, the battle begins to turn in favour of the Trojan side (768–835)
   - viii. Opis kills Arruns (836–67)
   - ix. The Trojans/Etruscans rout the Latins, who are slaughtered at the gates of Latinus' city (837–95)
   - x. At the news of the cavalry disaster, Turnus leaves his place of ambush, barely missing his chance to attack Aeneas and the Trojans; night falls before Turnus and Aeneas can join battle (896–915)

2 BOOK 11 WITHIN THE *AENEID*

Content in *Aen.* 11 connects it to *Aen.* 5. Both books prominently feature funeral rites; in the fifth book, Aeneas puts on funeral games for his father Anchises (5.104–603). As part of those games, the Trojan youth, led by Aeneas' son Ascanius, perform *the lusus Troiae* (5.545–603), a quasi-military exercise on horseback (cf. 5.585 *pugnae . . . simulacra*). This anticipates the cavalry fight in *Aen.* 11, the only such fight in the poem. Other smaller correspondences further connect the books.[3] The parallels between books 5 and 11 create symmetry in the architecture of the poem; Virgil aligns the penultimate book of his epic with the penultimate book of its first half.

Symmetrical, too, are the deaths at or very near the conclusions of *Aen.* 10, 11, and 12. In each one, a prominent warrior on the Italian side falls – Mezentius in the tenth book, Camilla in the eleventh, and Turnus in the twelfth. These are major events in the narrative arc of *Aen.* 10–12; over the course of the books, the Trojans move inexorably, though not easily and without cost, towards victory in their war against the Italians. With the first two deaths, Trojan victory grows that much more inevitable; with Turnus', it is assured. The triumph completes the re-enactment and reversal of the Trojan War that is essential to 'Virgil's *Iliad*', the story of the war in Italy in the second half of the *Aeneid*.[4] The Trojans turn from vanquished to victors, thus escaping from their past of defeat, trauma, and dislocation, and remake themselves by fighting and winning a new war. In doing so, they refute the stigma of eastern softness and prove themselves strong enough to defeat hardy Italians.[5] This makes them worthy westerners, back on their truly native Italian soil,[6] and with a future as Italians rather than as Trojans (12.821–40).

Virgil evokes the Trojan War recurrently in *Aen.* 7–12, thereby creating a complex web of associations with Homer. In book 11, Pallas corresponds to Patroclus, Achilles' dear companion whom Hector kills and strips of armour (*Il.* 16.818–63). Achilles calls for Patroclus' funeral at *Il.* 22.378–94; he then commands his Myrmidons to join with him in mourning the dead man at *Il.* 23.1–34, and he arranges and takes part in Patroclus' funeral at *Il.* 23.108–257. Hence Aeneas, who sees to Pallas'

[3] Thus Latinus' convening of the Latin council parallels 5.42–71, where Aeneas summons men to a meeting and addresses them. Both books also feature gifts from Dido (5.571–2, 11.72–5), and they open with transitional *interea* in their first line (as does *Aen.* 10).

[4] Gransden 1984, Anderson 1990, Quint 1993: 65–83.

[5] On the cultural stereotype of the Trojans' eastern weakness and effeminacy, voiced by their enemies in *Aen.*, see 145n., 9.598–620 with Hardie's note, and Thomas 1982: 98–9.

[6] See 353n., 7.122, 8.36–9.

funeral and mourns over him, stands as another Achilles. This is part of the process in the second half of *Aen.* through which Aeneas wrests the identity of Achilles away from Turnus, an *alius Achilles* at 6.742 and 9.742. Virgil is too rich a poet and thinker, and too creative with Homer, to limit things to a one-to-one correspondence between Aeneas and Achilles; Aeneas takes on other Homeric identities both from the vantage points of other characters in *Aen.* and in the third-person narrative, via intertextual engagement with Homer.[7] But his identification with Achilles is a driving feature of the second half of the poem, and book 11 contributes significantly to that.[8] Aeneas, the defeated, exiled wanderer of the first half of the epic, turns into Aeneas, an invincible and vengeful Achilles-like warrior on ancestral land, in the second half.[9]

Aeneas' identification with Achilles adds resonance when Evander, mourning over his son upon the arrival of the cortège in Pallanteum, lays upon Aeneas the obligation to meet and kill Turnus in order to avenge Pallas (11.176–80). The prospect of Turnus' death is the only thing that keeps the king alive now that his darkest fears for his son have been realised (cf. 8.578–83). The established connection between Aeneas and Achilles implies that Aeneas will succeed in killing Turnus, as Achilles kills Hector to avenge Patroclus' death. This foreshadows the concluding climax of the poem, where Aeneas is finally able to slay Turnus (12.940–52). At the same time, Evander's words are a hinge point in the development of the revenge theme that begins with Turnus' killing of Pallas and ends with the poem. When Aeneas hears of Pallas' death in *Aen.* 10, he thinks of Evander, his hospitality, and the pledge of alliance and good faith that the king and he made (10.515–17).[10] It becomes immediately clear that Aeneas feels in the death of Pallas the sting and shame of having failed to honour his bond with Evander and his duty to him to look after his son, and that this fuels his rage at Pallas' killing. (Aeneas makes this still more evident in his lament over Pallas at 11.42–58, to which we will return below.) The obligation that Evander then places on Aeneas in book 11 is a way for him to atone for that failure, at least partly.

[7] Thus in *Aen.* 11, Latin maidens liken Aeneas to Paris (see 484n.), while in the third-person narrative, he is equated with Diomedes (see 477–85n.).

[8] Along with the correspondences between Aeneas' response to Pallas' death and Achilles' to Patroclus', other major parallels are that Aeneas and Achilles both possess divinely crafted armour (see 8.370–453, 608–731), including shields that are the subjects of lengthy ecphrases, and that both are absent from battle for a period (for Aeneas, in *Aen.* 9).

[9] This means that Turnus becomes a Hector figure. Like Aeneas, however, Turnus contains other Homeric identities; in book 11, a major one is Paris (see 355–6n., 359n., 442n., 486–91n., 492–7n, 494n.).

[10] See Harrison's note on 10.516–17.

Evander is not the only person in *Aen.* 11 to call for Aeneas and Turnus to face off. At 11.220–1, Drances declares among the people of Latinus' city that 'Turnus alone is challenged, alone is summoned to battle' (*solumque uocari* | . . . *solum posci in certamina Turnum*) by Aeneas. This misrepresents Aeneas' words as he addressed the Italian embassy that came to him to seek a truce: Aeneas spoke in hypothetical terms and said that Turnus ought to have challenged him in single combat to settle the Italian conflict with the Trojans (11.116–18). Drances seeks to make the hypothetical real: members of the Latin public, unhappy with Turnus, bitterly complained that he should fight on his own to decide the war (11.218–19), and Drances, inveterately hostile to Turnus (see 11.12–13 and 11.336), fans the sentiment so that support for it grows and pressure on Turnus mounts. In the subsequent Latin council, Drances challenges Turnus directly to take on Aeneas in single combat (11.370, 374–6). In response, Turnus partly takes the bait, claiming that he would gladly fight Aeneas singly (11.438–42).

Because it introduces and advances the idea that Aeneas and Turnus should wage single combat, *Aen.* 11 plays a pivotal role in advancing the epic towards its climax. As the book progresses, the duel moves from the realm of the hypothetical and ever closer to reality. The action in the book is also decisive in the progress of the war towards the Latin defeat that Turnus' death seals. It opens in the aftermath of a major Trojan victory in *Aen.* 10; it closes with the Trojan forces routing the Latins and with Turnus squandering any chance for victory by leaving his place of ambush. Italian fortunes go from bad to worse over the course of book 11, and the situation at its conclusion is so dire that, at the start of *Aen.* 12, Turnus is left with no choice but to propose that he fight Aeneas alone to settle the conflict.

3 AENEAS

Aeneas appears only in the first scenes of book 11 up to 121 and at the very end of the poem, when he and his forces pass by Turnus' place of ambush.[11] At his first appearance in the book, he is very different from the Aeneas in *Aen.* 10. Upon receiving news of Pallas' death, he savagely rages on the battlefield, and as book 10 closes, he taunts the stricken Mezentius before plunging his sword into Mezentius' throat. Now, at the start of book 11, Aeneas no longer storms in fighting fury. The battle of

[11] His actions are also briefly reported (446), and other characters refer to him, notably Evander in his lament over Pallas (170–1, 176–80), Diomedes in his speech to the Latin embassy (282–92), and Drances and Turnus in their speeches to the Latin council (355, 374–5, 399–400, 438–40, 442). Drances addresses him, moreover, at 122–31.

Aen. 10 is over. At dawn on the next day, Aeneas grieves silently for the dead, especially Pallas, as he displays characteristic *pietas* – dutifulness to family, country, and the gods – by offering a trophy to Mars, or a tree trunk decked with Mezentius' spoils.[12] *Aen.* 11 is the only book to open with the start of a new day. This creates a break with the previous book that is appropriate to the sharp change in mood and the sharp change in Aeneas, now quite unlike the berserker he had been in *Aen.* 10. His are the responsibilities that follow after the fight, and, as a good general, he solemnly shows concern for his fallen troops and for his religious duty to give thanks for victory. At the same time, Aeneas' responsibilities necessarily include the continuing war effort. Hence, when addressing his lieutenants after erecting his trophy (11.14–28), he exhorts them to prepare materially and psychologically for the next stage in the conflict, while also ordering them to see to funerals for the dead, starting with Pallas.

Aeneas' pious handling of Mezentius' spoils pointedly contrasts with Turnus' handling of Pallas': after killing the boy, Turnus strips him of his baldric and wears it himself (10.496–500). There is also a contrast with Mezentius, who at 10.774–6 impiously vows his son Lausus as a living trophy of Aeneas – i.e. he will strip Aeneas and have Lausus don his armour. Wearing, or even wanting to wear, enemy spoils constitutes sacrilege in *Aen.*, and those who do so meet bad ends.[13]

While Aeneas at the start of book 11, piously honouring Mars in the quiet of dawn, differs from the enraged Aeneas on the previous day's battlefield, traces of the fighter remain. A material reminder are the spoils of Mezentius; they drip with blood, and the breastplate is pierced twelve times (11.8–10). The condition of the breastplate raises an important question: did Aeneas honour the dying Mezentius' plea to guard his body from the fury of his former subjects (10.903–6)? Because Aeneas stabbed Mezentius in the throat (10.907), and because Virgil gives no sign that the numerous blows to the breastplate came from an opponent in battle, the indication is that Aeneas refused Mezentius' suppliant appeal and allowed the Etruscans to abuse the corpse.[14] An intertextual clue points to the same conclusion. Virgil models Aeneas' subsequent speech (11.14–28) on

[12] I find no signs of tree violation, and hence of impiety, in Aeneas' erection of the trophy; see 5n.

[13] Katz, *VE* III.1212. Aeneas not only erects a trophy here but also at 10.541–2 has Serestus carry away the armour from the fallen Haemonides for a trophy to Mars. Pallas, meanwhile, vows a trophy to Father Tiber from the spoils of Halaesus (10.423). Trophies decked with the arms of Pallas' victims are carried in his cortège (11.83–4). We can reasonably imagine that these were later dedicated to a god or gods.

[14] Lyne 1989: 113, Anderson 1999: 198–9.

Il. 22.378–94. Just before that passage in Homer (22.371), it is said of the Greeks, 'No one drew near to him [Hector] without dealing him a wound' (οὐδ' ἄρα οἵ τις ἀνουτητί γε παρέστη). If this interpretation is correct, it colours the picture of Aeneas in the scene. As he displays quiet piety at the coming of the new day, he handles enemy arms that forcefully recall the unpitying warrior of *Aen.* 10. The rejection of Mezentius' appeal is itself no surprise.[15] But the harm done to Mezentius' corpse still lends his death a viciousness that extends to Aeneas, who allows the violence. This, in turn, serves as a reminder of the bitter harshness with which Aeneas treated Mezentius as he prepared to kill him (cf. 10.900 (Mezentius to Aeneas) *hostis amare, quid increpitas mortemque minaris?*). Aeneas' asperity there is part of his wider demonstration of raw Achillean μῆνις, 'wrath', in *Aen.* 10 after the death of Pallas.

That Aeneas remains, in part, the ferocious warrior of *Aen.* 10 is more apparent during the preparations for Pallas' cortège. Aeneas adds to the procession bound men, to kill them as offerings to Pallas' shades: *uinxerat et post terga manus, quos mitteret umbris | inferias, caeso sparsurus sanguine flammas* (11.81–2). These are the eight men that Aeneas had captured at 10.517–20 in his first flush of rage at Pallas' death for the purpose of sacrificing them to the boy. The human sacrifices derive from *Il.* 21.26–32 and 23.175–83; in the first passage, Achilles takes twelve men as blood-price (ποινή) for Patroclus, and in the second he kills them. Aeneas' dedication of human sacrifices constitutes a moment of atavistic violence, where he matches Achilles in his primal desire for retribution. The contrast with his dedication of spoils, his concern for his fallen soldiers' funerals, and his words to his men at the opening of the book shows vividly that piety and savagery coexist in him. He is at once an ideal Roman general, observant to the gods and full of sympathetic care for his troops, and a raging, vengeful Homeric warrior pursuing a non-Roman form of violence – for human sacrifice was not an accepted practice in Virgil's Rome.[16] Virgil makes his hero no 'pale paragon',[17] but rather a complicated character with unsettling traits to go along with his exemplary, proto-Roman features.

[15] Aeneas rejects all suppliant appeals on the battlefield in *Aen.* 10 (10.523–36, 554–60, 595–601); such rejections are conventional in epic. A further question is whether Aeneas granted the other part of Mezentius' plea at 10.904 and 906, that Aeneas allow him to be buried with his son Lausus. Given Aeneas' apparent rejection of Mezentius' plea to protect his corpse from the Etruscans, and given his behaviour with other suppliants in *Aen.* 10, we can plausibly assume that he did not. This would depart from the *Iliad*, since Achilles ultimately returns the body of Hector to Priam and Troy.

[16] See 81–2n. See also Panoussi 2009: 34 on Aeneas' human sacrifice as a perversion of proper ritual.

[17] Harrison on 10.510–605.

The interpretation of Aeneas' turn to human sacrifice grows more complicated because of his relationship to Augustus. As Richard Tarrant writes, 'Although Aeneas is an independent character and not an allegorical substitute for Augustus, the connections between the two are so strong that the view taken of one must inevitably colour one's view of the other.'[18] In this case, the urge to connect Aeneas' behaviour to Augustus is strong because Augustus (when still Octavian) was said to have performed human sacrifices to the shade of Julius Caesar after the siege of Perusia in 41–40 BCE.[19] The story clearly originates from hostile sources and is unlikely to be true.[20] But it is altogether plausible that Virgil knew it when he wrote the *Aeneid* in the 20s BCE, since it presumably emerged in the immediate aftermath of the Perusine War and circulated as a piece of anti-Octavian slander in the contentious years of the 30s. Therefore, Virgil could have wanted Aeneas, who pursues atavistic violence, to call to mind Octavian, who, according to rumour, did the same.[21] At the very least, because Aeneas is so identified with Augustus, it is difficult to separate his savagery from the emperor; certainly it would be intellectually dishonest to identify only Aeneas' good traits (e.g. *pietas, iustitia, uirtus*) with Augustus and none of his problematic ones.

But even though Aeneas' human sacrifice casts some shadow over him and Augustus, the reason for it partly relieves the savagery.[22] Aeneas' relationship with Pallas is assimilated to the *contubernium*, in which an aristocratic father placed his son in the care of an army commander on active service; the commander acted *in loco parentis* and instructed his charge in the business of war.[23] To restate an earlier point, Aeneas' rage at Pallas' death comes from his sorrow and shame at his inability to meet his responsibility towards his *contubernalis*. Because of this, he fails to live up to *fides*, his good-faith obligation to Pallas' father Evander.[24] *Fides* was a cardinal element in social and political affairs in Virgil's Rome.

[18] Tarrant, Intro. p. 24.
[19] See Suet. *Aug.* 15, Dio 48.14.4, and App. *Civ.* 1.541–2, with Alessio 1993: 168–9.
[20] At least literally; it is entirely possible that the story about human sacrifice distorts how Octavian killed ring-leaders of the war and prisoners.
[21] So Farron 1985. This implies that Virgil claimed the freedom to allude to a topic that was controversial to Augustus, and hence that the poet did not think himself limited to panegyric praise, despite his ties to the emperor, including via the patronage of Maecenas. It would not necessarily have required defiant or subversive bravery to do so; to judge by other evidence (Suet. *Aug.* 51 and 54–5), Augustus tolerated independence of thought in the 20s.
[22] So Tarrant, Intro. p. 26–7.
[23] Cf. 8.515–17, and see Serv. ad 5.546, Williams 1983: 104.
[24] See, further, pp. 10–11 below.

It signalled both 'trust' and 'trustworthiness', and it implied privileges and responsibilities for both parties in a relationship. Failure to honour *fides* was a serious offence, because of the concept's moral and even religious character.[25] While Aeneas is un-Roman in offering up human sacrifices, therefore, he is deeply Roman in his motivation for that act. The picture is double-sided, as Aeneas succumbs to problematic rage and violence, but is driven to do so because he fails to live up to Roman ideals that he (anachronistically) values.[26]

Upon seeing off Pallas' cortège, with its human sacrifices, Aeneas receives the Latin embassy led by Drances (11.100–21). Not only does Aeneas grant the Latins the truce that they were seeking, but he also deplores the war and wishes that hostilities had never begun, preferring instead, as mentioned above, that he and Turnus had fought singly. For Aeneas, peace – i.e. an advantageous political settlement – is the aim and end of war.[27] Even more, he wishes that the Trojans and Latins could have arrived at peace without going to war in the first place. He bemoans the bloodshed and suffering, and he would like to undo it all.

Yet Aeneas' response to the embassy is not simply an expression of humane regret at the war. He also justifies the Trojan presence in Italy, stating that it is the work of Fate, and says that his fight is not with the Latin people but with Latinus, who created hostilities, because he left an alliance with the Trojans and joined with Turnus. Aeneas is correct about Fate; his comments on Latinus, meanwhile, are only partly true, since the king wanted to forge an alliance with the Trojans but was compelled to go to war.[28] Aeneas himself no doubt believes what he says. But he also speaks rhetorically, to persuade his listeners to see the conflict as he did. An overarching aim is to make the embassy sympathetic to Aeneas and the Trojans and to drive a wedge between it and its leadership, as well as to induce its members to go back and agitate to end the war and settle with the Trojans. This would be to the Trojans' benefit, since, having the upper hand in the war, they would be able to negotiate a favourable agreement. Still, Aeneas presumably does not view the matter as a zero-sum game and

[25] Fraenkel 1916, Hellegouarc'h 1963: 23–40, 275–6, Hölkeskamp 2004: 105–34, Burton 2011: 40–1.

[26] Something similar is observable in Octavian's human sacrifices: as offerings to Octavian's adoptive father Julius Caesar, the sacrifices become expressions of *pietas*, however misplaced. Cf. Tarrant, Intro. pp. 26–7: 'To the extent, therefore, that [Aeneas] provides a prism through which the actions of Octavian can be assessed, Virgil's characterization offers a way for even the horrors of the Perusine siege to be subsumed under the heading of *pietas*.'

[27] Bowra 1990: 375, Nisbet 1990: 388.

[28] See 114n.

has in mind a mutually satisfactory pact.[29] That would create conditions for the peace that he desires to take lasting hold.

4 AENEAS, PALLAS, AND EVANDER

The Latin embassy comes to Aeneas at an opportune moment for their request. Not only did he himself want to bury the Trojan dead, but he also had just come from Pallas' cortège; his grief must have made him sympathetic to their wish to prepare funerals for their own. Aeneas had been occupied with Pallas' death from the moment when, after addressing his lieutenants, he entered his tent and found Pallas' body laid out, surrounded by mourners. There he delivers a lament over the boy (11.42–58). The principal model for the passage is *Il.* 18.324–42, where Achilles grieves over the death of Patroclus. Comparison with that passage is instructive. Achilles begins with Patroclus' father Menoetius, stating that his promise to him to return Patroclus safe from the war had been in vain (*Il.* 18.324–7). He continues that he and Patroclus will share the fate of dying in Troy (*Il.* 18.328–32), and then devotes the rest of his speech to his plans for Patroclus' funeral. By contrast, Aeneas begins by briefly addressing Pallas (11.42–4) before turning to his father Evander for nearly the remainder of his lament (11.45–57). Aeneas feels affection for Pallas, although it could not have been especially deep, since he had only known him for a few days. He also recognises the boy's youth and beauty and registers the sadness of how death has swept them away.[30] But Pallas is secondary to Evander in Aeneas' attention and even in his grief.

As a quasi-father to Pallas in the *contubernium*, and as a father himself, Aeneas identifies with Evander and feels profound sympathy for him. But what really fuels his mourning is his aforementioned guilty sense that he has violated *fides* and failed to live up to his duty to the king. This is made explicit at 11.55, where Aeneas asks the rueful rhetorical question *haec mea magna fides?* – i.e. he bitterly suggests that by letting Pallas die, he failed to honour the pledge of *fides* that he made to Evander.

Does Aeneas really violate *fides*, or is this just his own guilt-ridden interpretation of events? At 8.169, Evander states that he joins with the Trojans in a *foedus*, or divinely sanctioned binding agreement (*iuncta est mihi foedere dextra*); Aeneas recalls this when he hears of Pallas death at 10.517

[29] This view is supported by *Aen.* 12.187–91, where Aeneas lays out the terms he will seek should he defeat Turnus in single combat: *sin nostrum adnuerit nobis Victoria Martem* | . . . | *non ego nec Teucris Italos parere iubebo* | *nec mihi regna peto: paribus se legibus ambae* | *inuictae gentes aeterna in foedera mittant.*

[30] See 29–41n.

(*dextraeque datae*). Evander alludes to the *foedus* again at 11.164, when he magnanimously refuses to blame the Trojans or their pact for Pallas' death. A *foedus* was based on *fides*. In entering into a *foedus*, therefore, Aeneas had entered into a relationship of *fides* – and significantly, he had done so with the king of Pallanteum, located at the future site of Rome (8.99–100, 8.337–61). It is obvious that a place to demonstrate his trustworthiness was in the *contubernium* with Pallas. Did that extend to keeping the boy safe in battle? Evander appears not to think so; he attributes Pallas' death to the hazards of war and Pallas' eagerness to fight for glory (11.152–5, 164–6). But Aeneas has a different sense of his responsibilities in the *contubernium*.[31] He demonstrates not only good proto-Roman (and proto-Augustan) regard for *fides* but also a rigorous, solemn understanding of its demands.

Aeneas attempts to make up in some small way for his failure of *fides* by preparing the great cortège that accompanies the dead Pallas back to Pallanteum and Evander. The procession is a grand spectacle with a beautiful, delicate boy at its centre; Virgil includes a simile comparing the corpse to a freshly cut flower, an image that, through allusion to Catullus, likens his death to a maiden's loss of virginity, thereby blurring gender boundaries and feminising Pallas (11.68–71).[32] At the same time, the cortège is an expression of masculine military identity and accomplishment, because it features elements of a Roman triumph: it contains spoils won by Pallas, processing troops, and captured enemy soldiers.[33] Despite his success on the battlefield before meeting Turnus, Pallas is of course no victor in the war.[34] Yet the cortège emphasises his martial achievements to honour both him and his father, as compensation for Aeneas' inability to return the living Pallas home victorious and as consolation to Evander.

Aeneas does not accompany the procession to Pallanteum; he walks only a short way before stopping and bidding a final farewell to Pallas and then returning to the Trojan camp (11.95–9). Those who do arrive in Pallanteum witness a wrenching scene: Evander rushes towards the procession, throws himself over the body of his son, and mourns his death (11.148–81). Pallas is one of several young people, notably Euryalus, Pallas, Lausus, Camilla, and Turnus, who die in the second half of the

[31] We might wonder, however, why Aeneas did not keep Pallas away from the thick of battle if he felt that his *fides* extended to keeping the boy safe.

[32] Cf. Catull. 62.43–7 as well as Catull. 11.22–4. For more on the erotic imagery around the dead Pallas, including on the issue of homoeroticism as it relates to him and Aeneas, see 29–41n.

[33] On the Roman triumph, see Versnel 1970 and Beard 2007.

[34] Cf. 11.91–2: *hastam alii galeamque ferunt; nam cetera Turnus | uictor habet.*

epic.[35] Irrespective of the side on which they fight, and irrespective of how necessary and justified their deaths might be, their fates are tragic because they are young; Virgil knows that every war has its awful cost in the budding lives that it snuffs out.

Evander offers a paternal perspective on the tragedy of premature death, lamenting that, in an unspeakable reversal of nature's course, he has over-lived and seen his son die before him. Evander develops and amplifies the theme of the mourning father begun in book 11 with Pallas' quasi-*pater* Aeneas. In addition, he recalls Mezentius in *Aen.* 10. A terrible Etruscan tyrant for most of his time in the poem, Mezentius becomes a sympathetic figure after his son Lausus falls defending him against Aeneas; crucial to the generation of sympathy is Mezentius' pitiful lament for his fallen child (10.846–56). But Evander is both a mourning father and a mourning mother when he laments over Pallas. His wife is dead, and in her absence, he takes on the role of a lamenting woman – the customary gender of mourners in epic – and, specifically within the *Aen.*, of Euryalus' mother in book 9 (9.481–97). Evander's maternal turn is another moment where Virgil complicates and blurs gender roles; gender and the crossing of gender lines are major preoccupations in book 11.[36]

It is in his lament that Evander calls upon Aeneas to avenge Pallas' death by killing Turnus, which Aeneas then does to close *Aen.* 12; that call places on Aeneas its own obligation of *fides.* To Virgil's late-antique commentator Servius, Aeneas' final act is a profile in piety. In the lead-up to it, Aeneas famously wavers and considers sparing Turnus' life in the face of Turnus' supplicatory speech: pleading for his life, Turnus acknowledges defeat, renounces his claim to Lavinia, and appeals to Aeneas' moderation, by calling on him not to pursue his hatred any further, and his piety, by evoking Turnus' aged father Daunus (12.931–41).[37] But Aeneas sees Pallas' baldric worn by Turnus, which stokes his terrible anger. He then takes vengeance on Turnus in Pallas' name (12.941–52). To Servius, Aeneas' wavering and his killing of Turnus both redound to his glory: *omnis intentio ad Aeneae pertinet gloriam: nam et ex eo quod hosti cogitat parcere, pius ostenditur, et ex eo quod eum interimit, pietatis gestat insigne: nam Euandri intuitu Pallantis ulciscitur mortem* (Serv. ad 12.940). Servius draws a straight line from the

[35] It is no accident that the first casualty of war mentioned in *Aen.* 7–12 is Almo, a *iuuenis* (7.532–3). Almo is identified as the eldest son of Tyrrhus; this detail suggests the loss to the father.

[36] Virgil treats the issue of gender most thoroughly in the character of Camilla; see pp. 22–4.

[37] My summary echoes Tarrant, Intro. p. 18.

obligation of *fides* that Evander places on Aeneas at 11.176–180 to the end of the poem, and he casts that final act as the pious fulfilment of his duty to the king.

Servius' is the interpretation of the smooth brow – an untroubled reading of what is in fact a complicated, difficult final scene. Its complexities have been well covered.[38] A fundamental question is whether Aeneas is justified in killing Turnus, a sympathetic suppliant, and so a candidate for *clementia*, or sparing forgiveness. Of the ways of vindicating Aeneas' act,[39] one is to follow Servius and to look to 11.176–80 – and in fact, those lines do justify the killing in Roman terms, since honouring *fides* was a cardinal virtue in Virgil's culture. Yet the matter is not as straightforward as Servius would have it. It would have been easy for Virgil to state, or to have Aeneas state, that the hero meets his obligation to Evander in killing Turnus, particularly after Turnus evokes his aged father Daunus; Virgil could have had Aeneas respond by recalling Pallas' aged father Evander and his responsibility to him. Instead, Aeneas rises to vengeance upon seeing the *cingula . . . | Pallantis pueri* (12.942–3). Virgil focalises *pueri* through Aeneas – i.e. this is how he sees Pallas. The noun indicates both affection and Aeneas' sense of quasi-parental responsibility.[40] At the same time, the use of *puer* could suggest Aeneas' thoughts of Pallas' *pater* Evander and, by extension, of the duty of *fides* that Aeneas had to him.

This, however, would be a very oblique allusion to Evander. Virgil does not provide tidy, blunt resolution in which Aeneas explicitly meets the obligation placed on him in book 11. Readers can recall that passage and use it to justify the death of Turnus. But establishing that link requires that we apply 11.176–80 to the conclusion in ways that Virgil, at least overtly, does not.[41] Aeneas refers to and identifies with Pallas, not Evander, when he strikes Turnus down, and he treats his killing of Turnus as an act of

[38] My understanding of the final scene has benefited particularly from Putnam 1965: 151–7 and 2012, Galinsky 1988, Stahl 1990, Tarrant, Intro. pp. 16–30. Concise and insightful are Gildenhard and Henderson, Intro. pp. 8–10.

[39] Tarrant, Intro. pp. 17–18 gives other justifications: '[Turnus] had agreed to a decisive single combat with A., and as the loser his life is forfeit . . . Although T. was not personally responsible for breaking the treaty [between the Latins and Trojans in *Aen.* 12] he had taken it upon himself to expiate its violation . . . Finally, T.'s death is demanded by V.'s own narrative, which has been anticipating it throughout [*Aen.* 12].' One could add that Turnus must die because, despite his virtues, he is on the wrong side of history, and he is endowed with a proud heroism that does not fit with the heroism of *Aen.*, defined by dutiful commitment to the common good.

[40] So Tarrant on 12.943. See also Esposito 2016.

[41] The plural *meorum* at 12.947 (*tune hinc spoliis indute meorum | eripiare mihi?*, 12.947–8) is of course to Pallas alone, not to him and Evander; the plural is poetic, and it occurs at least partly *metri gratia*, and perhaps for weighty effect (see 273n.).

personal vengeance for Turnus' crime against the boy (12.947–51).[42] Evander and the issue of *fides* remain below the surface, providing understood justification rather than openly driving the action.

5 THE LATIN COUNCIL

5.1 Diomedes

Despite the death of Pallas, Aeneas feels confident about the course of the war – understandably so, after the Trojan success in battle in *Aen.* 10. By contrast, Latin morale is low, and it sinks even lower when the embassy to Diomedes, sent at 8.8–17, returns with the news that he will not join with the Latin forces in fighting the Trojans. In response to that news, a despondent Latinus summons a high council, and he calls upon Venulus, the leader of the embassy, to deliver a report on the mission. Venulus' statement mainly comprises a quoted speech from Diomedes, in which he explains why he will not fight and tries to convince the Latins to seek peace with the Trojans.

The peaceable Diomedes comes as a surprise. In *Aen.* 10 (10.28–9), Venus anticipates that the Latin mission to Diomedes will be a success, and she laments that he rises up once more against the Trojans. Venus envisions the great fighter of the *Iliad* reprising his Homeric role and returning to challenge and even to defeat Aeneas and the Trojans.[43] But Diomedes defies her, and the reader's, expectations. His speech gives the reasons why. First, he now sees the Trojan War as a profanation, and he understands that he and other Greeks were punished after the war for their actions in Troy – he for wounding Venus when she came to save Aeneas from him in *Il.* 5 (5.334–51). The punishments come as the Greeks travel home and at their homecomings; Diomedes' account constitutes a compressed history of disastrous *nostoi*-stories, or stories of returns

[42] The manner in which Aeneas kills Turnus is another controversial issue: he returns to the atavistic rage of *Aen.* 10 at the sight of Pallas' baldric and cuts Turnus down in that emotional state – and his assertion that through his hand Pallas 'sacrifices' (*immolat*, 12.949) Turnus recalls his human sacrifices to Pallas (cf. 10.519–20 *inferias quos immolet umbris | captiuoque rogi perfundat sanguine flammas*). That Aeneas honours *fides* partly redeems his rage. But such emotion was of course unnecessary to showing good faith, and it remains just as problematic in the final scene as it was in *Aen.* 10. See, further, Gross 2003–4: 146–8; also Gaskin 1994.

[43] Venus also worries that Diomedes returns to wound her again (10.29–30), as he did in *Il.* 5 (more on this shortly). The Iliadic Diomedes appears twice in *Aen.* 1: Aeneas wishes that Diomedes, the 'bravest of the Danaan race' (*Danaum fortissime gentis | Tydide*, 1.96–7), had killed him in Troy (1.96–8), as Diomedes nearly did at *Il.* 5.297–317; and Diomedes is among the images of the Trojan War on the temple to Juno in Carthage, blood-stained and laying waste to the enemy camp on his sortie with Odysseus, described in *Il.* 10 (1.470–1).

after the war.[44] Given that one war with the Trojans brought terrible crime and punishment, Diomedes is disinclined to take part in another. Second, Diomedes describes Aeneas as a great warrior who equalled Hector in fighting prowess (while surpassing him in *pietas*); who joined with Hector to stave off the Greeks for ten long years; and who, if joined by two others like him, would have not only prevented Greek victory in Troy but also conquered Greece itself. Diomedes does not want to contend with such an opponent again, and he advises the Latins against challenging him as well.

Diomedes is of course speaking rhetorically; he aims to persuade the Latins not to go to war with the Trojans while also justifying his decision not to join the fight as a Latin ally.[45] This naturally shapes what he says and how he says it. Still, there is no sign that Diomedes tells the embassy anything he does not believe. His and his fellow Greeks' post-war ordeals have made him think about the Trojan War differently from when he was fighting it; they also lead him to oppose another engagement with the Trojans. His regard for the great warrior Aeneas departs from the 'facts' of the *Iliad*, where Diomedes was the superior fighter and nearly killed Aeneas. But this discrepancy is the product of the character's selective memory that recreates the past through the filter of later experiences and perspectives, rather than of deliberate misrepresentation. Now a weary, chastened veteran, Diomedes remembers the toil and difficulty of the Trojan War, not its triumphs. While he stresses Aeneas' excellence to impress on the Latins that they should not go to war against him, he thinks back on him as one of the formidable challenges of a hard struggle.

Diomedes' perspectives on the Trojan War and Aeneas constitute another way in which Virgil reverses the *Iliad*.[46] The great Greek will not arrive to re-enact the war. A central reason for this, that Aeneas is such a difficult foe, obscures Diomedes' success against him in *Il.* 5. Aeneas has now become a warrior whom Diomedes wants to avoid. This undoes his defeat at Diomedes' hand, thereby distancing him from his vanquished Homeric self and intimating that this is a different Aeneas from before, with victory now his destiny.

[44] The *Nostoi* was one of the poems of the epic cycle, or collection of poems dealing with events of the Trojan and Theban wars. It is unclear if Virgil relied on cyclic material (whether poems or summaries) or on elaborations of cyclic content in other texts; see Fantuzzi, *VE* 1.438 and below, pp. 20–1.

[45] On the rhetoric of Diomedes' speech, see Horsfall 1995: 187–8, Hardie 2012: 139–42.

[46] Papaioannou 2000, Fletcher 2006: 243–50, Chaudhuri 2014: 75–6. Cf. 12.896–907, where Turnus tries to play the role of Diomedes at *Il.* 5.302–10 and to wound Aeneas with a huge stone, but fails.

5.2 *Latinus*

The news from Venulus dismays the council, and an agitated murmur rises among its members. In response, Latinus gives a speech advising that the Italians come to terms with the Trojans. This is the start of the war-council proper, in which Latinus, Drances, and Turnus address the assembly and each other over the next steps to take in the war. War-councils are standard in epic; this is the only one in *Aen.*[47] Virgil models it on the βουλή, or select council, in the *Iliad*, although he imitates Homeric figures who speak in the ἀγορή, or general assembly.[48] The speeches of Latinus, Drances, and Turnus join with that of Diomedes to present a varied picture of the purposes, effects, and truth-value of rhetoric in the council scene, as well as of Virgil's use of the speeches to reflect and express character.

Latinus' speech is gloomy. He has recognised since *Aen.* 7 that the war against the Trojans runs contrary to the course of Fate and is doomed (see 7.249–74, 594–600). The battle in *Aen.* 10 and Venulus' report have only confirmed this. His address to the council displays his bleak outlook; he contends that the Latins wage an unholy war against an invincible foe and that the Latin situation is past hope. This is both an old, despairing king's honest assessment of how things stand and a rhetorical argument designed to get the council to see that peace is the only good option, and hence that it should accept Latinus' proposal to offer terms. Latinus is a weakened ruler, unable to dictate the course of action. He must persuade the council, and especially Turnus, to see things as he does; accordingly, he emphasises how dire the situation is, says nothing that might offend Turnus, and presents his proposal in a manner that might be most palatable.[49]

Latinus' vision of the situation and what it demands is at once personal, interested, and accurate. He sees things through the filter of his resistance to the war and his belief that the Trojans have come to Italy by Fate and are invincible, and he shapes his message to make the most persuasive case for peace he can. Yet he also sees what is in fact true: he is right that his side cannot win the war against a people who have arrived

[47] See 234n.

[48] Virgil perhaps also has as a model an ἀγορή in Apollonius Rhodius; see 302–35n. I am indebted to the discussion of the Latin war-council in Irene Peirano Garrison's forthcoming book *Eloquentia: Persuasion, Rhetoric and Roman Poetry*; I am grateful to her for sending me material from the book.

[49] 312n., 314n., 316–21n., 316n., 318–19n., 325n., 330n. I depart from Horsfall (App. II.472–3) and find no conflict between Latinus' proposal here and his offer of *hospitium* to the Trojans in book 7, which was short-circuited by the start of war. There is certainly no reason for Latinus not to try again to make peace.

at their fated homeland. What is more, the king advocates a peace that will be realised – indeed, that must be realised, because it is the design of Fate. While Latinus imposes his own interpretation on events, therefore, the position he takes is not deceived or deceptive. Instead, it accords with large, authoritative truths in the *Aeneid* and with the movement towards a fated peace, to which the epic's narrative tends.

5.3 Drances

After Latinus finishes, Drances takes the floor as another advocate for peace, and also as Turnus' enemy. A model for the character – by all appearances Virgil's invention – is the Trojan Antenor, who in a general assembly (ἀγορή) at *Il.* 7.348–53 calls for peace but is overruled; another is the Trojan Polydamas at *Il.* 18.249–83, who, also in an ἀγορή, advises that the Trojans cease fighting and return to their city, to Hector's chagrin.[50] A third Homeric model is the Greek Thersites, an odious common soldier and rabble-rouser hated by the Greek leadership that he often vilified. In a general assembly in *Il.* 2, Thersites calls for an end to the Trojan War while reviling Agamemnon for his insatiable greed for spoils (2.210–42), only to have an angry Odysseus rebuke him and strike him with his staff, to the delight of the gathered crowd (2.243–77). Virgil adapts Thersites to create in Drances an odious character of his own who calls for peace in opposition to a leader whom he hates and attacks, Turnus.[51] In an extended character sketch (11.336–41), Virgil attributes Drances' hatred of Turnus to jealousy and paints him as a cowardly demagogue, seditious and, it is suggested, corrupt.[52] At the same time, Drances is considered a 'not worthless adviser' (*consiliis habitus non futtilis auctor,* 11.339). While the litotes, or deliberate understatement, yields only grudging praise, Virgil still assigns Drances some slight virtue and value to go along with his unsavoury characteristics.

Drances' call for peace is simultaneously a snide, sly attack on Turnus – indeed, it is really more the latter than the former, and hence is more a kind of judicial accusation than a deliberative speech over the course of action to take.[53] His arguments for ending the war, and the measures he advises the Latins pursue to make peace with the Trojans, are designed to taunt and to provoke Turnus, as well as to stir sentiment against him. Particularly cutting to Turnus is Drances' accusation of cowardice when

[50] 336–75n., 338–9n., 355–6n., 376–444n., 390n., 393–8n., and 399n.

[51] 336–41n., 344n., 348n., and 369n. On Drances, see Highet 1972: 248–51 and 282–3, Burke 1978, Fantham 1999: 265–9, and Scholz 1999.

[52] On his apparent corruption, see 338n., on *largus opum.*

[53] Fantham 1999: 266.

he asserts that Turnus trusted to flight in battle (11.351); his contention that Turnus has been routed (11.366); and his statement that terms with the Trojans must include marriage to Latinus' daughter Lavinia (11.353–8), to whom Turnus considered himself engaged.[54] When Drances proposes that Turnus fight Aeneas singly to decide the war, moreover (11.370, 374–6), he believes that Turnus will lose if he fights or lose face if he refuses. Drances wants what is good for the Latins, but he wants even more what is bad for Turnus. The rhetoric of his speech moves in two directions, one to bring about peace and the other, more forcefully, to cause trouble for Turnus and to create opposition to him. The latter purpose aligns Drances' speech with political invective in ancient Rome, and particularly with that of the late Republic, through which Virgil had lived.[55] Virgil is indirectly critical of such speech, because he portrays Drances so negatively. He presents it as a tool of personal score-settling and partisan bickering, exploited by demagogic types to foment discord, even as Drances deliberates on a matter of public concern.

However ugly Drances' motives, he confirms in his speech that he is no worthless adviser. Drances wants peace with the Trojans principally because Turnus does not want it and because he assumes, correctly, that terms will include details extremely painful to Turnus. But his position is anything but aberrant. On the contrary, it aligns with the wishes of Latinus (and Aeneas) and with the designs of Fate. Drances is on the right, authorised side in the deliberation over the war. This complicates the representation of his rhetoric as well as of the character himself. In seeing the facts as they are and the Latin policy as it should be, but in giving the right advice for interested, impure reasons, Drances embodies the messiness of political rhetoric and political decision-making, and he exemplifies how sound counsel can come from unsound and even unprincipled sources. Virgil is critical of demagogic wrangling but, characteristically, he views the matter from more than one perspective and holds contradictory views in tension, by showing that ugly, destructive speech can contain useful, correct advice.

5.4 Turnus

Turnus, the final speaker in the war-council, divides his speech into three sections; the first and third respond to Drances and the second to Latinus.[56] Turnus is a young man who values action over words and fighting over speaking. Even so, he is able to deliver a well-organised,

[54] See 217n., 440n.
[55] Hardie 2012: 147–8.
[56] See, further, 376–444n.

forceful speech, and one that is over twice as long as that of Drances (sixty-seven to thirty-three lines). This dissolves the binary between deeds and words that Turnus himself establishes when he taunts Drances for being a brave talker while cravenly avoiding war (11.378–91), and when he scorns the council for deliberating while the Trojans prepare for battle (11.460–1). Epic heroism included the ability to fight and the ability to speak.[57] In the council, Turnus displays the latter but is desperate to show off the former; he is a person who feels that he expresses himself truly and fully in battle and who defines himself by his martial prowess.

Drances' speech hurts Turnus' heroic pride. In response, Turnus delivers a stinging rebuttal with a double purpose: to counter-attack and to defend himself, which gives his words a quasi-judicial character in his altercation with Drances.[58] The question of how to proceed in the war with the Trojans remains operative: in the first section of his speech, Turnus contends that he and, by extension, the Latins are in no way beaten, thereby suggesting that they should battle on, and in the third, he states that he would be willing to resolve the war by meeting Aeneas singly. But Turnus takes these positions while primarily fighting back against the detested Drances. He is not thinking rationally and deliberatively about what the situation demands, and his wounded sense of honour and his enmity towards Drances drive him headlong to anger, bitter mockery, defiance, and proud self-defence.[59]

Turnus' response to Latinus in the second section of his speech argues directly against Italian surrender and exhorts the council to continue the war. Turnus' resistance in the face of both Italian defeat in battle and Latinus' defeatism demonstrates traits that were ideals in Rome: manly bravery (*uirtus*), resilience in the face of hardship, hatred of dishonour, and desire for glory. The problem is that his idealism and code of heroism are misplaced and even delusional. In his pride and single-minded quest for victory, Turnus does not acknowledge the doom he faces. This is destructive for him, for the forces he commands, and for the king and city he serves. Turnus is willing to die fighting (11.440–2). But he is unwilling to make the necessary self-sacrifice of putting aside his warrior's pride and recognising that the Italians should, and indeed must, come to terms with the Trojans. His reading of the current situation and, consequently, his advocacy in the war-council to continue fighting are blinkered to the

[57] E.g. *Il.* 1.258, 9.53–4, 9.443.
[58] Fantham 1999: 271.
[59] Fantham 1999: 272.

point where he becomes myopic.[60] In contrast to Latinus and Drances, Turnus' slanted rhetoric is aligned with what is untrue. It is not that he sets out deliberately to deceive his listeners. Rather, he believes the false thing, viz., that his and Italian victory is still possible, but thinks that it is right, and he designs his hortatory rhetoric to get the council to view matters through the distorting lens that he does.[61]

6 CAMILLA

The Latin council ends without resolution: news arrives that the Trojans are on the march, and this dissolves the meeting before its members come to any decision.[62] Contending over what to do about the war, the Latins are unprepared to contend in renewed battle, and they must now scramble to get ready. Turnus warms immediately to the task, thrilling at the prospect of resuming war and the chance to prove that he was right to advocate fighting on.

One reason that Turnus gives in the council for continuing to fight is that the Italians still had excellent warriors on their side (11.429–33). Among them is Camilla, Queen of the Volscians. This is the first appearance of the female warrior since book 7, where she is the final figure in the catalogue of Italian fighters (7.803–17). Although celebrated there for her supernatural speed of foot, Camilla is a cavalry fighter in book 11. As Turnus prepares for the coming clash after departing from the council, Camilla rides up to him with an equestrian force and volunteers to advance out and meet the Trojan/Etruscan cavalry (11.498–506). The brave woman awes Turnus, who gives her command over the Italian cavalry. From this point until near the very end of book 11, the memorable Camilla dominates the narrative.[63]

Camilla is by all appearances Virgil's creation.[64] As a female warrior, she is an Amazonian figure, and she has similarities to the Amazon Queen Penthesilea, described at 1.490–3.[65] Critics have looked to Arctinus' *Aethiopis*, a poem of the Greek epic cycle that features the Amazons and

[60] For other interpretations of what the war-council reveals about Turnus, see Burke 1978 and Fantham 1999: 271–6, 278–9. On Turnus' character more broadly, see Schenk 1984.

[61] For other perspectives on the relationship between rhetoric and truth in *Aen.*, with a focus on the council-scene, see Hardie 2012: 126–48.

[62] It is tempting to think that the fractious meeting reflects Virgil's dark view of political debate in Rome, especially at the end of the Republic.

[63] Turnus, meanwhile, sits offstage in his place of ambush until 11.896; Aeneas is on the march offstage until 11.903.

[64] Horsfall 1988. See also Brill 1972. For a good introduction to Camilla, see Gildenhard and Henderson, Intro. pp. 22–30.

[65] See 648–63n., 649n., 652n., 662n., 762n., 803n.

their queen, as a source for Penthesilea and Camilla. Nicholas Horsfall, however, has convincingly argued that Virgil did not directly know Arctinus' epic, although he might have had access to an epitome.[66] Otherwise, Virgil's sources on the Amazons and Penthesilea – clearly models for Camilla – are obscure.

Camilla resembles another character in book 1 as well: Harpalyce, a virgin Thracian huntress of incredible speed to whom the disguised Venus is compared (1.316–17). Servius Danielis (ad 1.317) gives the story of Harpalyce, and details parallel those in Virgil's account of Camilla: both characters lived as children in the woods with their exiled fathers, and both were fed on mare's milk.[67] This could suggest that Virgil took an earlier account of Harpalyce, probably Hellenistic, as his model for Camilla.[68] Yet there is nothing to keep the opposite from being true: Virgil's Camilla could have been the model for the development of Harpalyce's story, which only occurs in post-Virgilian sources (Servius Danielis and Hyginus). Virgil's brief allusion to Harpalyce would have presented an invitation to fill in her tale, and Virgil's expansive treatment of the life of Camilla would have provided material for the account.[69]

A third female character in *Aen.* 1 contributes to the composite Camilla. This is Dido, better known, of course, for her starring role in *Aen.* 4. Dido and Camilla balance each other in *Aen.*: Dido is a prominent queen in the first half of the epic and Camilla in the second half, and both are significant obstacles to the fulfilment of Aeneas' and Trojan destiny.[70] It cannot be an accident that Dido, like Camilla, is associated with Penthesilea and Diana,[71] and that a goddess (Venus) tells her story (1.335–68), as Diana tells Camilla's. Virgil takes the associations with the Amazons and Diana adumbrated in the story of Dido and develops them with Camilla, and he varies his narrating goddess in book 1 with Diana in book 11.[72] As we will see, Virgil recurrently connects the two characters when treating

[66] Horsfall 1988: 46, Horsfall, App. 1. By contrast, La Penna 1988: 222 maintains that Virgil relied upon Arctinus' poem. See also Arrigoni 1982: 16–19.

[67] For Camilla with her exiled father in the woods, see 11.539–84; for Camilla's mare's milk, see 11.571–2. On Harpalyce, see also Hyg. *Fab.* 193, 252, 254.

[68] Austin on 1.317, La Penna 1988: 227.

[69] Horsfall 1988: 47. As Horsfall 2016: 56 notes, Harpalycus, the exiled father of Harpalyce, can then be understood to derive from Metabus, Camilla's father.

[70] Ramsby 2010: 13.

[71] See 1.490–7, where Aeneas turns from marvelling at the image of Penthesilea on Juno's temple in Carthage to seeing Dido, with the implication that his wonder at the Amazonian queen leads seamlessly to his wonder at Dido. See also 1.498–503, a simile comparing Diana and Dido.

[72] This assumes, uncontroversially, that Virgil produced *Aen.* 1 first and *Aen.* 11 later.

Camilla's death, thus putting that scene into intratextual dialogue both verbally and thematically with the Dido story.

It is likely that Virgil also took Atalanta, famed in myth for her ability to hunt and for her speed, as a model for Camilla.[73] Still another possible influence was Cloelia, the legendary Roman woman who swam across the Tiber to escape after Lars Porsena had taken her hostage.[74] Nor did Virgil limit himself to women when looking for material for Camilla. On the contrary, he links Camilla and Hippolytus, the virginal male devotee of Artemis.[75] Just maybe, too, he understood Camilla as the mirror reflection of the great Roman commander Camillus – she, the female defeated Volscian, and he, the male victor over the Volscians.[76]

6.1 Gender

Gender is a fundamental issue in the story of Camilla. Virgil is interested particularly in blurring the lines between male and female and in complicating gender norms. This begins with Camilla's father Metabus, who appears in Diana's inset story on Camilla's childhood. Metabus is an exiled king, driven from his throne because of his tyrannical ways.[77] He makes his escape from his city with Camilla but unaccompanied by a wife, who, presumably, has died. In her absence, he carries Camilla as a mother would when escaping into exile.[78] More strikingly, Metabus nurses his infant daughter (*nutribat*, 11.572) at the breast of a wild mare after he has settled with her into exiled life in the wild. Metabus, a fierce male warrior, crosses gender boundaries and turns partly female, compensating for the absence of Camilla's mother by taking on maternal roles.

From childhood, Camilla also mixes gender identities. Metabus dedicates Camilla to the service of Diana if the goddess allows them to escape their pursuers when fleeing into exile, and he honours that vow when things turn out well (11.557–66).[79] As a devotee of Diana, Camilla lives in a world defined by the female. Measured by civilised Roman norms, this is an anomalous femininity, marked by existence in the wild, a commitment

[73] Arrigoni 1982: 10, 18–19, 27–8, La Penna 1988: 227. Camilla is the primary model for Ovid's Atalanta in *Met.* 8; see Keith 2000: 31, with Fratantuono 2005.

[74] See 508n. Viparelli 2008: 15–23 argues for Cleopatra as another source for Camilla. I am not sure about this, although I suspect, with Trundle 2003: 171, that some first-century BCE readers anticipated Viparelli and thought of Cleopatra when encountering Virgil's Camilla.

[75] See 569n.

[76] Egan 2012: 22–3.

[77] In this, he resembles Mezentius. On this topic, see 532–96n.

[78] 544n.

[79] Camilla's name implies her status as a follower of Diana; see 543n.

to virginity, and a life devoted to the hunt. The last of these combines the feminine and the masculine, since hunting was fundamentally a male pursuit. Hence, when Camilla learns to hunt with *tela . . . puerilia* (11.578), she enters a world of dissolved gender binaries: her service to Diana is gynocentric, but she is a mix of the unconventional female and the male in it.

Camilla continues to confound gender binaries when she leaves Diana's service and, having become the Volscians' queen (Virgil does not tell us how), enters battle against the Trojans. Epic warfare is a quintessentially masculine arena,[80] as Turnus understands: *bella uiri pacemque gerent, quis bella gerenda* (7.443). Camilla is an exception to that rule, and one impressive enough to inspire Turnus himself to give her command over the Italian cavalry. When the battle begins, Camilla shatters gender stereotypes. In a thrilling *aristeia*, she excels in masculine warfare, so much so that she surpasses all the male forces in her fighting prowess.[81] Along the way, she confronts prejudice against her as a female warrior, and she emphatically answers and silences it by killing the men she faces.[82] The prejudice dismisses her as an aberrant, deficient Other intruding on a masculine world. By contrast, the narrative presents her both as a magnificent Other and as something familiar and native. Camilla is explicitly linked to the Amazons (11.650, 659–63), the quintessential Other of epic battle. Like them, she inhabits a space between male and female as a woman at home and formidable in masculine warfare. But whereas the Amazons come from the barbarian north of Thrace, Camilla belongs to Italy, and in the cavalry fight, she combines Amazonian traits with masculine Italian virtues of toughness, courage, and strength.[83]

The mix of genders in Camilla grows more complex as she approaches death. The Etruscan Arruns kills an unsuspecting Camilla when she is distracted by the gaudy arms and dress of Chloreus, an effeminate Phrygian priest of Cybele; she wants them as spoils, either to dedicate them or to wear them in the hunt (11.778–82).[84] Virgil describes Camilla's desire with the words *femineo praedae et spoliorum ardebat amore* (11.782). The wish for spoils is an epic norm for male warriors going back to Homer. But Camilla wants them in a particular gendered way, burning with a 'woman's passion' for them, i.e. with blind and wild desire. In this, she fits

[80] Keith 2000: 5–6.

[81] On the *aristeia*, see 664–724n.

[82] See 684–9, with 687n., and 705–24.

[83] Cf. Pöschl 1962: 118, on Camilla's *aristeia*: 'The full magnificence of Italian strength is shown.' See also Pyy 2010. Her Italian virtues are not, however, unalloyed; see p. 30, with West 1985: 22. See also 648–63n.

[84] On the Etruscan identity of Arruns, see see 759n.

the Greco-Roman stereotype that Virgil activates here of the emotional female, heedless and irrational to the point of disaster.[85] Thus Camilla's undoing is explicitly connected to her gender, which momentarily asserts itself with all its stereotyped baggage and with fatal consequences – and because the spoils she seeks are effeminate objects from an effeminate man, her gender identity tilts all the more towards the feminine. Camilla excels in the masculine role of warrior, but dies when she combines a typical epic desire, and hence a typical male desire, for spoils with female intensity of feeling.[86] There is disharmony in this combination, which reflects conflict within Camilla.[87] In the end, this masculine fighter is undone by a flash of emotion originating from an incompatible female self.

6.2 Hunting and War

Two Camillas die in book 11: the primitive maiden of the woods and the grand Volscian queen and soldier. Diana's inset speech creates that duality with its contrasting backstory to the main narrative. The speech varies the mood and delays the action with its fantastic tale about the young Camilla. But it is not a mere light interlude, and it serves significant narrative and thematic functions.[88] One is to raise the issue of the relationship between the hunt and war. Within the passage, Diana segregates Camilla's life as a huntress from her life as a warrior when she laments that the girl has left her service behind to go to battle (11.584–6). The war is a world apart from the hunt, and Camilla sheds one identity to take on another.

The gap between the hunt and battle opens again in a passage on Ornytus, one of Camilla's victims in her *aristeia*. Ornytus is a hunter who has not made the transition to fighter; this makes him no match for Camilla, who has successfully moved from the woods to the field of battle (11.677–89). That a transition was necessary implies, of course, a distinction between hunting and war. Later in the fight, when Camilla blindly chases Chloreus to win his spoils, perhaps to wear them while she hunts, there is an understood contrast between her identity as *uenatrix* (11.780)

[85] Anderson 1999: 208, Keith 2000: 28–30; for a different perspective, see Morello 2008: 53–5.

[86] This varies West 1985: 24. See also Reed 2007: 24, Lovatt 2013: 304. I resist West's argument (esp. pp. 24–5) that Camilla's feminine desire for spoils is part of a broader Virgilian critique of heroism and the nature of *uirtus*; in my interpretation, Virgil is interested here just in Camilla's character and the crossing of gender wires within her.

[87] Rosenmeyer 1960: 161.

[88] We have already seen one such function on p. 22.

and as *bellatrix* (7.805; cf. 1.493); Camilla might be imagining herself as a huntress when she should be thinking and acting as a warrior. This is another moment where Virgil distinguishes between the two defining pursuits of Camilla's life.

The relationship between hunting and battle in book 11, however, is not a simple oppositional one.[89] Several details show that to be the case. One is that Camilla wields *arma Dianae* (11.652) when fighting – i.e. she battles with the arrows and spears that she had used while a huntress in the goddess' service.[90] The arms are a bridge between the two arenas of bloodshed, and they suggest that the skills Camilla developed as a hunter were propaedeutic to combat; her life in the woods was separate from war, but it was not innocent of violence, and her ability to kill there translated to battle. Relevant is 7.817, where Camilla carries 'pastoral myrtle tipped with steel' (*pastoralem praefixa cuspide myrtum*). This is a rustic spear or javelin made of myrtle wood, which was adaptable to war – an apt symbol for the overlap between Camilla's hunting and martial selves, to which her *arma Dianae* also point.

Virgil further links hunting and warfare by repeatedly using hunting imagery in Camilla's battle scenes. In her encounter with Ornytus, he wears a wolf-head as a helmet, clearly a trophy from hunting (11.680–1).[91] Its unsuitability for war vividly exemplifies how he has failed to transform himself adequately into a fighter and, thus, points up the difference between hunting and warfare.[92] At the same time, the wolf-head connects the two activities, in that it renders Ornytus an animal for Camilla to pursue and kill. This establishes further continuity between the hunt and battle, which stands in tension with the distinctions between them that Virgil also draws. Camilla is engaged in a new and different form of hunting, at once similar to and different from her activities in Diana's service. That two-sided outlook abides at other points where Virgil uses imagery of the hunt for combat, including in Camilla's death scene, where she moves from hunter to hunted.[93]

89 La Penna 1988: 230–1. On hunting and war in *Aen.* generally, see Dunkle 1973.

90 Cf. 11.536, where Diana states that Camilla proceeds to war *nostris . . . armis.* See 11.575 and 578 for Camilla's arrows and spears as a (young) huntress, and, e.g., 11.649–50 and 11.652–4 for her arrows and spears in war.

91 This is part of a wolf-leitmotif in Camilla's battle scenes; see 664–724n.

92 Possibly, too, there is an allusion to Amazonian imagery; see 680–1n. Details in the story of the young Camilla also connect her to the Amazons (see 571n., 577n., 579n., 580n.). Hence the Amazonian warrior has Amazonian ties when still a huntress.

93 See 763n. and p. 27 below.

6.3 The Death of Camilla

Arruns, Camilla's killer, is unworthy of his victim. He is too cowardly to face her in open combat, and he consequently resorts to stealthy pursuit of her and to a spear-throw from an unseen distance.[94] His unworthiness lends a certain shabbiness to Camilla's death but at the same time points to her greatness, because it suggests that only a stealth attack against an inattentive Camilla could overcome her. In fighting prowess, she was too much for anyone else in the fray;[95] it took a momentary lapse, caused by her excessive, feminine passion, and a sly adversary to defeat her.

After striking Camilla with his spear-throw, Arruns successfully hides from the Volscians and other enemy fighters. But he does not escape Opis, dispatched by Diana to avenge Camilla's death. When Opis sees that Arruns has killed Camilla, she grieves momentarily but deeply over her death and then swoops down to shoot Arruns fatally with an arrow. The divine care that Diana and Opis show Camilla ennobles her death, by giving her a hero's special relationship to divinity. The sorrow over Camilla's fate that Diana displays in her inset story and that Opis expresses upon witnessing Camilla fall, moreover, establishes the model for how to respond to it. Readers are to follow the goddess and nymph in pitying the passing of this striking character. Camilla is an enemy of the Trojans, but she is cast in a sympathetic light.

In this, of course, Camilla resembles Dido in *Aen.* 4: Virgil treats the Carthaginian with sympathy by focusing on her suffering, even as he also makes it clear that she was not guiltless in her affair with Aeneas; that Aeneas had to leave her by the dictates of fate; and that, in her wrathful rage, she was increasingly dangerous to him and, more broadly, to the Trojan mission. But Dido is just one of the characters in *Aen.* to whom Virgil links Camilla's death.

6.3.1 Camilla and Dido

Echoes connect Camilla as she approaches death to Dido. Should Camilla wear Chloreus' trappings during the hunt, as she might imagine herself doing while she pursues him, she would resemble Dido when the Carthaginian goes hunting at 4.137–9.[96] Camilla has Dido's regal taste for fine things. Yet it is clear that this is not the time to indulge those tastes; Camilla might momentarily picture herself as a Dido, i.e. as a splendidly arrayed queen during a hunt, and this makes her unaware of the danger

[94] La Penna 1988: 238. See also 767n., 836–67n. Arruns' furtive cowardice overrides his excellence with the spear (760n.) as a defining trait.

[95] La Penna 1988: 236–8. Camilla, of course, does not live to battle Aeneas.

[96] 774–6n., 780n.

that she is in. The context of the Dido passage also suggests Camilla's doom. It was during the hunting expedition that Dido and Aeneas began their affair, which ended in the love-stricken, maddened Dido's suicide after Aeneas prepared to end their involvement and set sail for Italy. While Camilla's *amor* is of course not erotic,[97] it too renders the queen irrational and heedless and is fatal to her; the parallel with 4.137–9 is an intimation of that.

Virgil alludes to Camilla's heedlessness when he characterises her as *incauta* while she chases Chloreus (11.781). This recalls the deer to whom the love-stricken Dido is compared at 4.69–73, which wanders *incauta* (4.70) in the Cretan woods when hunted and fatally shot by a shepherd.[98] The echo implies that Camilla, like Dido, is the hunted, though she is unaware of it. Virgil joins the queens together not only as hunters but also as prey, and in doing the latter, he offers a further intratextual sign that Camilla's death is approaching.

When Camilla is then struck by Arruns' spear and lies dying, Virgil again conjures Dido through verbal parallels.[99] These include Camilla's final words to *Acca soror* (11.823), an obvious double for *Anna soror* (4.9), Dido's sister and confidante. The echoes tie together the two deaths of major female characters, deaths that are full of pathos even though the women are impediments to Aeneas' mission and Trojan destiny. But in her death scene, Camilla differs from Dido in her concern for public affairs, which the Carthaginian had let slip during her love affair with Aeneas; Camilla's last thoughts and words are on what Turnus needs to do in the battle now that she is dying (11.825–6).[100] Camilla resembles Dido in her susceptibility to *femineus amor*, irrational passion. Yet at the last moments of her life, she snaps back from it and returns to her role as a leader in the masculine world of war.

6.3.2 Camilla and Euryalus

Camilla's fatal desire for Chloreus' clothing and arms is comparable to Euryalus' desire for opulent spoils during his night-time attack, along with Nisus, on the sleeping Rutulians in book 9.[101] Euryalus carries off Rhamnes' trappings and sword-belt with golden studs as well as Messapus' crested helmet, and he proceeds to don the belt and helmet (9.357–66). Euryalus is attracted to the rich plunder, and his desire for it proves fatal

97 Virgil, however, eroticises Camilla's death by equating it with a bride's loss of virginity on her wedding night; see p. 28 and 803–4n.

98 Wilhelm 1987: 48.

99 See 805–6n., 823n., 825n., 829n., 841n.

100 Sharrock 2015: 167.

101 Keith 2000: 30.

to him, because the gleaming helmet gives him away as he and Nisus departs from the sortie (9.373–4), and because the burden of his spoils slows his movement (9.384–5). His fatal hunger for the spoils foreshadows that of Camilla. Both characters run to dangerous excess in their desire, and they fail to see the deadly consequences of their actions.[102] Still, Camilla and Euryalus are treated sympathetically; the two exemplify the sad waste of young life in war. As part of that sympathetic treatment, their deaths are mourned in the text – Camilla's by Diana and Opis, and Euryalus' by the narrator in an authorial apostrophe (9.446–9) and, as we have seen, by his mother.

6.3.3 Camilla and Pallas

The dead Camilla and the dead Pallas form bookends to *Aen.* 11. The two resemble each other as lamented young victims of war, whom Virgil links via intertextuality to Patroclus.[103] Highlighting their youth is the sexual imagery attached to their deaths. We saw earlier that a flower-simile equates Pallas' death to his loss of virginity (11.68–71). More graphically, Virgil likens the spear that kills Camilla to a phallic penetrator drinking her virgin blood and to a nursing child (11.803–4). As with Pallas – and as with Euryalus, whose death Virgil also equates, via a flower-simile, to lost virginity (9.435–7) – the image of Camilla's deflowering (implicity on her wedding night) implies that her death is premature; death both introduces her to adulthood and takes her adulthood away. But that image, coupled with that of motherhood, has deeper resonance, because of Camilla's devotion to virginity in Diana's service and because she is a manly woman in war. The point is not that she should have become a wife and mother in the normal way, which would suggest that her manner of death was a rebuke to the abnormality of her past life as a virgin huntress.[104] Instead, Virgil implies, with pathos, that the dead Camilla will never return to her life as a huntress; in addition, the imagery emphatically confirms how different her identity as a warrior was from her identity as a devotee of Diana. This is another example of the mixing of genders in Camilla's battle narrative. An Amazonian warrior who had so excelled in the masculine arena of war is strikingly made a woman at the moment of her death. This underscores that her success in male battle has come to an end.

When Camilla dies, the battle turns, and the Trojans, Etruscans, and Arcadians (i.e. Evander's forces) all advance together (*incurrunt densi simul omnis copia Teucrum | Tyrrhenique duces Euandrique Arcades alae,*

[102] Hardie, Intro. p. 26.
[103] See 785–93n., 794–835n.
[104] Fowler 1987: 166.

11.834–5). This unified movement of forces resembles the unified march of Trojans, Etruscans, and Arcadians in Pallas' cortège (*maesta phalanx Teucrique sequuntur | Tyrrhenique omnes et uersis Arcades armis*, 11.92–3). Each death unites the different groups comprising the Trojan allied forces; this is a step towards the broader unity in Italy that is an ideal in *Aen.*, once the conflict between the Trojan and Latin armies, presented as a civil war, comes to an end.[105] The civil war continues to rage as book 11 closes – indeed, it rages hideously, as the inhabitants of Latinus' city close the gates to their own soldiers, and the Trojan forces mercilessly attack. But after the deaths of Camilla and Pallas, there is an intimation of future Italian unity.

Another response to Camilla's death, Opis' killing of Arruns, creates a final tie between her and Pallas. That killing avenges Camilla; in so doing, it prefigures Aeneas' killing of Turnus to avenge Pallas. What happens near the end of *Aen.* 11 foreshadows what happens at the end of *Aen.* 12. Vengeance is a dish served twice in the concluding books.

6.3.4 Camilla and Turnus

With Camilla's death, the Trojan–Italian war and the epic are nearly over; with Turnus', they both come to an end. Virgil connects the two deaths directly by using the same line to describe them (*uitaque cum gemitu fugit indignata sub umbras*, 11.831 and 12.952, the last line of the poem). The repetition underscores the structural parallels between the two deaths: each ends the life of a great, young enemy warrior and obstacle to Trojan victory, and each is climactic in its respective book. In addition, the echo encourages readers to recognise how similar Camilla and Turnus are. Both have rugged, martial Italian virtues consistent with the military ideals of Rome; they are courageous, excellent soldiers, and they love the fight. Yet both are impetuous and even reckless on the battlefield, and both fail to exercise self-restraint and sober judgement at a crucial juncture in book 11: when the dying Camilla sends word to Turnus to come to reinforce the Italian cavalry, Turnus does just that, even though the course of action that might have led to Italian victory was for Turnus to remain in ambush.[106] On top of that, both have an egocentrism that at least stands in tension with concern for the public interest.[107]

A question that readers ask about Turnus can be asked about Camilla: did this young Italian have to die? In the narrative of the poem, she clearly did, to open further a path to Trojan victory, and as a link in the chain from Mezentius in book 10 to Turnus in book 12. But other things

[105] Fletcher 2014: 243–7.
[106] See 823–7n., 896–915n.
[107] See 505n., 510n., Tarrant, Intro. pp. 12–13.

imply the necessity of her death. One is her Volscian identity.[108] In Roman historiography, the Volscians were long enemies of Rome, unassimilable to its system of (imposed) peace and command. The implication is that Camilla would have likewise been an inveterate enemy of Aeneas and his successors had she lived, and a particularly ferocious and formidable one at that. What is more, her heroic code is out of step with the expectations for leadership in *Aen.* While Camilla certainly cares for her soldiers and her side, she is driven above all to excel and earn glory in the thrill of the fight; she is a volatile, charismatic warrior and commander, eager to win and to be seen winning, rather than an Aenean *dux*, defined and weighted by public duty, and fighting from a sense of that duty and for peace. All of this points further to someone who would clash with, and be a danger to, Aeneas' and the Trojans' pre-Roman/pre-Augustan order in Italy.[109] Camilla's death is treated with pathos. Yet that does not make it any less necessary. The attitude towards her is sympathetic but unsentimental; the defeated enemy is humanised instead of demonised, but she has to fall in the hard historical, political, and ethical calculi of the poem.

7 METRE

The commentary will fill out this discussion of the content of *Aen.* 11 by examining the substance of the book in localised detail. It will also deal extensively with matters of form and style,[110] including metre.[111] To aid in the understanding of the notes on metre, I provide here a brief overview of Latin dactylic hexameter and of Virgil's metrical practices.[112]

All metres in classical poetry are quantitative: they are based on the quantity of individual syllables. A syllable is long, or heavy, if it contains a long vowel or a diphthong, or if it contains a short vowel followed by

[108] On Camilla the Volscian, see Horsfall 1988: 43–4, Trundle 2003: esp. 173–4.

[109] Similarly, Ramsby 2010: 16, with Small 1959: 296. See also Lee 1979: 94–5 and 118. What I have said about Camilla's (Homeric) traits as warrior and leader can be applied to Turnus as well.

[110] On Virgil's style, see Jackson Knight 1944: 225–341, Horsfall 1995: 217–32, O'Hara 1997, Conte 2007: 58–122, and Dainotti 2015. Horsfall's Appendix II to his commentary (App. II.474–5) contains observations on the style of *Aen.* 11; he suggests that the book is not Virgil's richest on the stylistic level, but of course a much more thorough and systematic study than his appendix would be necessary to prove this. Horsfall also gathers examples of inconsistencies and infelicities in *Aen.* 11. In my view, these amount to little, and they are not enough to suggest that the book was written hastily or that it stands unrevised (a point with which Horsfall, it seems, would agree (App. II.475)).

[111] On Virgil's metre, see Cupaiuolo, *EV* II.375–9, Thomas, *VE* II.820–6, Duckworth 1969: 46–62, and Ross 2007: 143–52.

[112] Tarrant, Intro. pp. 37–42 is a model for my discussion. When other comments on style are not self-explanatory and require definitions of terms (mainly rhetorical figures), I provide them in the notes.

two or more consonants. When, however, the two consonants consist of a mute/plosive (*p, b, t, d, c, g*) followed by a liquid (*l* or *r*), poets can, and often do, regard the pair as a single consonant and, consequently, do not lengthen the preceding syllable. If a word ends in a vowel, a diphthong, or an *m* with an immediately preceding vowel, and the following word begins with a vowel, a diphthong, or an *h*, the first vowel or diphthong is elided, and the syllable takes the quantity of the second vowel or diphthong.[113]

The dactylic hexameter was the metre of Latin epic from Ennius' *Annales* (early second century BCE); Ennius' use of the metre derived from Greek epic. It is a line of six feet (Gk ἕξ, 'six'). Its first four feet can contain a dactyl (– ⏑⏑) or a spondee (– –), which substitutes for the dactyl. The fifth foot is almost always a dactyl,[114] and the sixth foot comprises a long vowel and a second syllable that can be long or short (*syllaba anceps*). The dactylic hexameter can therefore be notated this way:

– ⏕ – ⏕ ⏕ – ⏕ – ⏑⏑ – x

Word breaks are a significant feature of the dactylic hexameter line. A word break within a metrical foot is a *caesura*, while a word break coinciding with the end of a metrical foot is a *diaeresis*. Nearly every line will have one or more principal caesura, i.e. the main word break(s) within the line. More than 80 per cent of Virgil's lines have a word break in the third foot, and most of these constitute the principal caesura. The most common position for the caesura is after the initial long syllable of the third foot, as in, for instance, the first six lines of book 11. Principal caesurae can also occur in the second and fourth feet of the line; they are usually paired rather than single, in just the second or the fourth foot, as at 11.7 *Mezenti ducis exuuias, tibi magne tropaeum.*

The placement of caesurae is important to the issue of accentuation in the dactylic hexameter. The metrical stress of a foot (the *ictus*) falls on its first long syllable.[115] Hence in the opening line of book 11, the pattern of metrical stress is as follows: *Óceanum íntereá͘ surgéns Auróra relíquit.* But words themselves have their own natural accents. Words of two syllables are accented on the penult (i.e. the penultimate syllable); in words of more than two syllables, meanwhile, the penult receives the accent if it is long/heavy, and the antepenult (the previous syllable to the penult) receives it if the penult is short/light. In the first line of *Aen.* 11, there is thus a lack of

[113] The opposite of elision is hiatus, when a vowel is left unelided; see 31n.
[114] For exceptions to this rule, see 31n., 659n.
[115] Under the ictus, a short vowel can be lengthened in arsis, the first syllable of the foot that receives the metrical stress; see 69n., 111n., 323n., and 469n.

coincidence between metrical stress and word stress until the fifth and sixth feet. While correspondence between ictus and word accent varies from line to line, non-coincidence is significantly more common in the first four feet (especially in the fourth foot itself) throughout *Aen.*, while coincidence is the norm in the fifth and sixth feet. This indicates that tension between the two systems of stress was cultivated in the first two thirds of lines and resolved in the final third.[116] Caesurae contribute to the tension. A principal caesura in the third foot, if after a word of more than one syllable (as was customary), brings non-coincidence, because word stress cannot fall on the final syllable (as with *interea* at 11.1). So, too, principal caesurae in the second and fourth feet almost always result in non-coincidence (as at 11.7).

There are sixteen possible metrical patterns across the first four feet of a hexameter line. Virgil tends to vary them – although repeated patterns can themselves read very differently when we account for caesurae, elisions, and word order and length. Lines in which spondees predominate are more common; Virgil's favourite pattern in book 11, as in *Aen.* generally, is DSSS (D for dactyl, S for spondee). The second half of the epic is marginally more spondaic than the first half (56.29 per cent of feet in *Aen.* 1–6, 57.23 per cent in *Aen.* 7–12); while Virgil uses spondees more in his epic than in the *Ecl.* (50.76 per cent of feet), the numbers are not statistically significant enough to support the idea that Virgil continued to become more spondaic within *Aen.* in any meaningful way.[117]

In the large bulk of instances, the metrical patterns do not appear to have an expressive function. Yet expressiveness is possible. Thus the pattern DDDD or a preponderance of dactyls can reflect and underscore rapid movement and intensity of action.[118] Heavily spondaic lines, and especially those with an SSSS pattern, meanwhile, can indicate dark emotion, solemnity, or slow-moving, effortful exertion,[119] while juxtaposition of slow and rapid rhythms, including reversed patterns, can point up meaningful contrast or development of action.[120] Expressiveness, however, can be a difficult thing to determine and not easily separable from formal considerations.[121] An example comes in the last line of the book,

[116] Tarrant, Intro. p. 38. This is the case even if metrical stress was secondary to word stress, as is the current prevailing opinion among Anglophone classicists (Tarrant 38).

[117] Horsfall 1995: 235 gives the statistics. The *Georgics* are spondaic in 55.96 per cent of feet.

[118] See 137n., 623n., 710n., 638n., 746n., 756n., 810n., 875n.; for another possible use of dactyls, to suggest ease and languor, see 739–40n.

[119] See 53n., 99n., 147n., 209n., 238n., 294–5n., 370n., 481–2n., 826n., 860n.

[120] E.g. 872 and 875; see also 151n.

[121] The same is true of alliteration; see Fordyce's appendix to his commentary on *Aen.* 7 and 8. Expressiveness, however, is at times evident; see 16n., 44n., 151n., 182n., 192n., 200n., 209n., 277n., 330n., 348n., 361n., 381n., 454n., 470n., 614–15n., 625n., 673n., 705–6n., 714n., 745n., 753n., 843n., 845n., 875n., 877n.

an SSSS line: *considunt castris ante urbem et moenia uallant.* Virgil elsewhere uses the metrical pattern formally for closural effect, and this is clearly its function here.[122] But at this point in the book, after the terrible battle and the slaughter at the gates of Latinus' city, it is possible that the metre expresses heavy, gloomy exhaustion as well.

Virgil also seems on occasion to use elision for expressive effect.[123] Again, however, the presence of expressiveness is often not cut-and-dried, and consequently, there can often be disagreement over whether the metrical feature has expressive content. What is clear is how predominant elision is in book 11, as it is in *Aen.* on the whole; book 11 has the third-most elisions of any book in the poem (behind *Aen.* 2 and 3).[124] Elision is a crucial tool for Virgil to generate the metrical variety that is a hallmark of his technique.

8 THE TEXT

The text is based on Conte's 2009 Teubner edition.[125] It differs from Conte in the following places (for the sake of comparison, I also give the readings in Mynors' 1969 OCT edition):

Line	This Edition	Conte	Mynors
202	ardentibus	fulgentibus	ardentibus
256	mitto quae	mitto ea quae	mitto ea quae
830	arma relinquens	arma relinquunt	arma relinquens
854	fulgentem	laetantem	fulgentem

My text also differs from Conte's in its punctuation at vv. 18, 58, 70, 373, 734, and 737. I discuss departures from Conte at the relevant points in the commentary.

The *apparatus criticus* derives from Conte with a sprinkling of Mynors; it benefits from Conte's liberal citation of readings from the indirect tradition, especially Servius/DServius, Tiberius Claudius Donatus, and Macrobius. I follow Tarrant in his 2012 commentary on *Aen.* 12 in aiming to keep the

[122] See 99, 181, 202, 295. Virgil also has SSSS as an initial pattern for a narrative section or speech (108, 252, 336, 343, 522, 664). Tarrant, Intro. p. 41 observes that Virgil recurrently uses DSSS in initial and closural position in *Aen.* 12; I observe this to some degree in book 11 (124, 444, 468, 483, 617, 648, 663, 768, 785, 794, 836).

[123] See 51n., 58n., 140n., 166n., 219n., 392n., 401n., 451n., 462n., 503n., 564n., 609n., 612n., 632n., 879n. On the possible expressiveness of elision, see Winbolt 1903: 179–80 and Kenney 1967: 328.

[124] Horsfall 1995: 235.

[125] For good discussion of the Virgilian textual tradition and its problems, see Tarrant, Intro. pp. 45–7.

apparatus brief. To that end, I have adopted his use of φ to signify three or more manuscripts in the ninth-century tradition, but not the majority (rather than listing the individual manuscripts). I also take Tarrant as my model in using ac and c for readings of manuscripts before and after correction, respectively, rather than having Conte's wider range of sigla to denote particular sources for the corrections.

Manuscripts Cited

Capital Manuscripts

M	Florence, Biblioteca Medicea-Laurenziana plut. lat. 39.1 (codex Mediceus), late fifth century (before 494)
P	Vatican, Palatinus lat. 1631 (codex Palatinus), late fifth or early sixth century; missing 11.645–90
R	Vatican, Vat. lat. 3867 (codex Romanus), late fifth or early sixth century; missing 11.757–92
F	Vatican, Vat. lat. 322, late fourth or early fifth century; contains 11.858–95

Ninth-century Manuscripts[126]

a	Bern, Burgerbibliothek 172 + Paris BnF lat. 7929. Descended from R.
b	Bern 165
c	Bern 184
d	Bern 255 and 239 + Paris lat. 8093
e	Bern 167
f	Oxford, Bodleian Library Auct. F. 2.8
g	Paris lat. 7925
h	Valenciennes, Bibl. municipale 407 (389)
i	Vatican, Reginensis lat. 1669
j	Brussels, Bibl. Royale 5325–5327
k	Hamburg, Staats- und Universitätsbibliothek 52 in scrinio
n	Naples, Bibl. Nazionale Vind. lat. 6
r	Paris lat. 7926
t	Paris lat. 13043; missing 11.11–12, 952
u	Paris lat. 13044
v	Vatican, Vat. lat. 1570
x	Montepellier, Bibl. de la Faculté de Médecine H 253
y	Paris lat. 10307

[126] The sigla are those of Conte. Munk-Olsen 1982–9 dates three of the manuscripts (c (tentatively), n, and z) to the tenth century.

z	Paris lat. 7927
γ	Wolfenbüttel, Herzog-August Bibliothek Gud. lat. 2° 70. Closely related to P; I cite γ only when its readings differ from those of P.
ω	Consensus of all, or nearly all, ninth-century manuscripts
φ	At least three ninth-century manuscripts, but not the majority
recc.	Later manuscripts
codd.	Consensus of all manuscripts (or of all not otherwise mentioned)

Cited Sources in the Indirect Tradition

Diom.	Diomedes (fourth century), *Ars grammatica* (*GLK* I)
Don. *ad Ter.*	Aelius Donatus, *Commentum Terenti* (ed. P. Wessner, Leipzig 1902–5)
DSeru.	Servius Danielis (also known as Servius Auctus)
GLK	*Grammatici latini* (ed. H. Keil, Leipzig 1857–80)
Macrob.	Macrobius Ambrosius Theodosius (early fifth century), *Saturnalia* (ed. J. Willis 1963/1994, R. A. Kaster, Cambridge, MA 2011)
Non.	Nonius Marcellus (fourth century), *De compendiosa doctrina* (ed. W. M. Lindsay, Leipzig 1903)
Prisc.	Priscian of Caesarea (fifth/sixth century), *Institutiones grammaticae* (*GLK* II–III)
Probus	M. Valerius Probus (attrib.: fourth century?), *Instituta artium* (*GLK* IV)
Seru.	Servius (Maurus or Marius Servius Honoratus in some manuscripts, fourth/early fifth century), *Commentarii* (ed. G. Thilo, Leipzig 1881–7)
Tib.	Tiberius Claudius Donatus (fifth century?), *Interpretationes Vergilianae* (ed. H. Georgii, Leipzig 1905–6) (*Tib. in interpr.* refers to the reading found in or understood from a note, as distinguished from *Tib. in lemm.*, the heading to a note)

The author gratefully acknowledges permission to adapt the *apparatus criticus* of G. B. Conte (ed.), *P. Vergilius Maro: Aeneis.* Berlin and New York: Walter de Gruyter. 2009

P. VERGILI MARONIS
AENEIDOS
LIBER VNDECIMVS

P. VERGILI MARONIS
AENEIDOS LIBER VNDECIMVS

Oceanum interea surgens Aurora reliquit:
Aeneas, quamquam et sociis dare tempus humandis
praecipitant curae turbataque funere mens est,
uota deum primo uictor soluebat Eoo.
ingentem quercum decisis undique ramis
constituit tumulo fulgentiaque induit arma,
Mezenti ducis exuuias, tibi magne tropaeum
bellipotens; aptat rorantis sanguine cristas
telaque trunca uiri, et bis sex thoraca petitum
perfossumque locis clipeumque ex aere sinistrae
subligat atque ensem collo suspendit eburnum.
tum socios (namque omnis eum stipata tegebat
turba ducum) sic incipiens hortatur ouantis:
'maxima res effecta, uiri; timor omnis abesto,
quod superest: haec sunt spolia et de rege superbo
primitiae manibusque meis Mezentius hic est.
nunc iter ad regem nobis murosque Latinos.
arma parate, animis et spe praesumite bellum,
ne qua mora ignaros, ubi primum uellere signa
adnuerint superi pubemque educere castris,
impediat segnisue metu sententia tardet.
interea socios inhumataque corpora terrae
mandemus, qui solus honos Acheronte sub imo est.
ite,' ait 'egregias animas, quae sanguine nobis
hanc patriam peperere suo, decorate supremis
muneribus, maestamque Euandri primus ad urbem
mittatur Pallas, quem non uirtutis egentem
abstulit atra dies et funere mersit acerbo.'
Sic ait inlacrimans recipitque ad limina gressum,
corpus ubi exanimi positum Pallantis Acoetes
seruabat senior, qui Parrhasio Euandro

1–644 *MPR* 8 roranti *R* 21 segnisue M^{ac}*R*: segnisque $M^{c}\omega\gamma$ (sign- *P*φ, segne- *j*), *Tib.* 23 imo est M^{c} (imost M^{ac}) $\omega\gamma^{c}$ (*u. om.* γ), *Seru.*, *Tib.*: imo *PR* 24 qui *Macrob. 4.4.9* 30 exanime *My*: exanimis *R*φ: exanimum *Don. ad Ter. An. 234*

armiger ante fuit, sed non felicibus aeque
tum comes auspiciis caro datus ibat alumno;
circum omnis famulumque manus Troianaque turba
et maestum Iliades crinem de more solutae.
ut uero Aeneas foribus sese intulit altis,
ingentem gemitum tunsis ad sidera tollunt
pectoribus, maestoque immugit regia luctu.
ipse caput niuei fultum Pallantis et ora
ut uidit leuique patens in pectore uulnus
cuspidis Ausoniae, lacrimis ita fatur obortis:
'tene,' inquit 'miserande puer, cum laeta ueniret,
inuidit Fortuna mihi, ne regna uideres
nostra neque ad sedes uictor ueherere paternas?
non haec Euandro de te promissa parenti
discedens dederam, cum me complexus euntem
mitteret in magnum imperium metuensque moneret
acris esse uiros, cum dura proelia gente.
et nunc ille quidem spe multum captus inani
fors et uota facit cumulatque altaria donis;
nos iuuenem exanimum et nil iam caelestibus ullis
debentem uano maesti comitamur honore.
infelix, nati funus crudele uidebis!
hi nostri reditus exspectatique triumphi?
haec mea magna fides? at non, Euandre, pudendis
uulneribus pulsum aspicies nec sospite dirum
optabis nato funus pater. ei mihi, quantum
praesidium, Ausonia, et quantum tu perdis, Iule!'
Haec ubi defleuit, tolli miserabile corpus
imperat et toto lectos ex agmine mittit
mille uiros qui supremum comitentur honorem
intersintque patris lacrimis, solacia luctus
exigua ingentis, misero sed debita patri;
haud segnes alii cratis et molle feretrum
arbuteis texunt uirgis et uimine querno
exstructosque toros obtentu frondis inumbrant.
hic iuuenem agresti sublimem stramine ponunt:

41 abortis $\varphi\gamma^{ac}$ 51 exanimem *Rφ* 54 exoptatique *R* 57 ei *MPφ*, *Don. ad Ter. Ph. 178*: et *R*, *Tib.*: heu *ω* 60 agmine *Mωγ*, *Seru. hic et ad u. 92*, *Tib.*: ordine *PR*

qualem uirgineo demessum pollice florem
seu mollis uiolae seu languentis hyacinthi,
cui neque fulgor adhuc nec dum sua forma recessit,
non iam mater alit tellus uirisque ministrat.
tum geminas uestes auroque ostroque rigentis
extulit Aeneas, quas illi laeta laborum
ipsa suis quondam manibus Sidonia Dido
fecerat et tenui telas discreuerat auro:
harum unam iuueni supremum maestus honorem
induit arsurasque comas obnubit amictu,
multaque praeterea Laurentis praemia pugnae
aggerat et longo praedam iubet ordine duci;
addit equos et tela quibus spoliauerat hostem.
uinxerat et post terga manus, quos mitteret umbris
inferias, caeso sparsurus sanguine flammas,
indutosque iubet truncos hostilibus armis
ipsos ferre duces inimicaque nomina figi.
ducitur infelix aeuo confectus Acoetes,
pectora nunc foedans pugnis, nunc unguibus ora,
sternitur et toto proiectus corpore terrae;
ducunt et Rutulo perfusos sanguine currus.
post bellator equus positis insignibus Aethon
it lacrimans guttisque umectat grandibus ora.
hastam alii galeamque ferunt, nam cetera Turnus
uictor habet. tum maesta phalanx Teucrique sequuntur
Tyrrhenique omnes et uersis Arcades armis.
postquam omnis longe comitum praecesserat ordo,
substitit Aeneas gemituque haec addidit alto:
'nos alias hinc ad lacrimas eadem horrida belli
fata uocant: salue aeternum mihi, maxime Palla,
aeternumque uale.' nec plura effatus ad altos
tendebat muros gressumque in castra ferebat.
Iamque oratores aderant ex urbe Latina
uelati ramis oleae ueniamque rogantes:
corpora, per campos ferro quae fusa iacebant,

82 sparsuros γ^c *et fere* ω, *Tib.* flammam *Rnγ* 93 omnes *MP*ω, *Tib.*, *Probus 231.1*: duces *R*φ, *Seru. ad u. 92* 94 praecesserat *MPR*ω, *Tib.*: processerat γ^c 95 edidit *R*φ 101 rogantes *MP*ω, *DSeru.*: precantes *R*φ, *Seru. ad Aen. 10.31*, *Tib.*

redderet ac tumulo sineret succedere terrae;
nullum cum uictis certamen et aethere cassis;
parceret hospitibus quondam socerisque uocatis.
quos bonus Aeneas haud aspernanda precantis
prosequitur uenia et uerbis haec insuper addit:
'quaenam uos tanto fortuna indigna, Latini,
implicuit bello, qui nos fugiatis amicos?
pacem me exanimis et Martis sorte peremptis
oratis? equidem et uiuis concedere uellem.
nec ueni, nisi fata locum sedemque dedissent,
nec bellum cum gente gero: rex nostra reliquit
hospitia et Turni potius se credidit armis.
aequius huic Turnum fuerat se opponere morti.
si bellum finire manu, si pellere Teucros
apparat, his mecum decuit concurrere telis:
uixet cui uitam deus aut sua dextra dedisset.
nunc ite et miseris supponite ciuibus ignem.'
dixerat Aeneas. illi obstipuere silentes
conuersique oculos inter se atque ora tenebant.
Tum senior semperque odiis et crimine Drances
infensus iuueni Turno sic ore uicissim
orsa refert: 'o fama ingens, ingentior armis,
uir Troiane, quibus caelo te laudibus aequem?
iustitiaene prius mirer belline laborum?
nos uero haec patriam grati referemus ad urbem
et te, si qua uiam dederit Fortuna, Latino
iungemus regi: quaerat sibi foedera Turnus.
quin et fatalis murorum attollere moles
saxaque subuectare umeris Troiana iuuabit.'
dixerat haec unoque omnes eadem ore fremebant.
bis senos pepigere dies et pace sequestra
per siluas Teucri mixtique impune Latini
errauere iugis. ferro sonat alta bipenni
fraxinus, euertunt actas ad sidera pinus,

104 aere φ 110 pacem me] pacemne φ 113 relinquit φ 117 decuit mecum φ 122 tum] hunc M^{ac}: tunc M^{c} 126 iustitiaene *Pω, Seru.* iustitiane *MR, Prisc. saepius*: iustitiamne *r*; iustitiaene *et* iustitiane *agnoscit DSeru.* laborem $P^{ac}R\varphi$ 131 subiectare P^{ac}: subuectari φ troiane $M^{c?}R\varphi$ 134 siluam *M*

robora nec cuneis et olentem scindere cedrum
nec plaustris cessant uectare gementibus ornos.
Et iam Fama uolans, tanti praenuntia luctus,
Euandrum Euandrique domos et moenia replet,
quae modo uictorem Latio Pallanta ferebat.
Arcades ad portas ruere et de more uetusto
funereas rapuere faces: lucet uia longo
ordine flammarum et late discriminat agros.
contra turba Phrygum ueniens plangentia iungit
agmina. quae postquam matres succedere tectis
uiderunt, maestam incendunt clamoribus urbem.
at non Euandrum potis est uis ulla tenere,
sed uenit in medios. feretro Pallanta reposto
procubuit super atque haeret lacrimansque gemensque,
et uia uix tandem uoci laxata dolore est:
'non haec, o Palla, dederas promissa parenti,
cautius ut saeuo uelles te credere Marti.
haud ignarus eram quantum noua gloria in armis
et praedulce decus primo certamine posset.
primitiae iuuenis miserae bellique propinqui
dura rudimenta et nulli exaudita deorum
uota precesque meae! tuque, o sanctissima coniunx,
felix morte tua neque in hunc seruata dolorem!
contra ego uiuendo uici mea fata, superstes
restarem ut genitor. Troum socia arma secutum
obruerent Rutuli telis! animam ipse dedissem
atque haec pompa domum me, non Pallanta, referret!
nec uos arguerim, Teucri, nec foedera nec quas
iunximus hospitio dextras: sors ista senectae
debita erat nostrae. quod si immatura manebat
mors gnatum, caesis Volscorum milibus ante
ducentem in Latium Teucros cecidisse iuuabit.
quin ego non alio digner te funere, Palla,

139 uolans] mali *Tib. hic et ad Aen. 12.607* (*cf. Aen. 10.510*) 140 conplet M^{c} 142 at portis *'multa exemplaria' ap. DSeru.* 145 iungit *PRω* (iunget *c*): iungunt *Mbr, Tib.* 149 pallanta M^{c}*ix*^{c}: pallante M^{ac}*PRω*, *Seru.*, *Tib.* 150 procumbit *R* 151 uoci M^{c} P^{ac}*ω*, *Tib.*: uocis P^{c}*Ri*: 152 parenti] petenti *'alii' ap. DSeru.* 164 arguerem *Ru*γ^{ac} 168 iuuabit *Pω*, *Seru.*: iuuabat γ^{ac}: iuuare *R* 169 dignem *'alii' ap. DSeru.*

quam pius Aeneas et quam magni Phryges et quam
Tyrrhenique duces, Tyrrhenum exercitus omnis
magna tropaea ferunt quos dat tua dextera leto;
tu quoque nunc stares immanis truncus in armis,
esset par aetas et idem si robur ab annis,
Turne. sed infelix Teucros quid demoror armis?
uadite et haec memores regi mandata referte:
quod uitam moror inuisam Pallante perempto
dextera causa tua est, Turnum gnatoque patrique
quam debere uides. meritis uacat hic tibi solus
fortunaeque locus. non uitae gaudia quaero,
nec fas, sed gnato manis perferre sub imos.'
Aurora interea miseris mortalibus almam
extulerat lucem, referens opera atque labores:
iam pater Aeneas, iam curuo in litore Tarchon
constituere pyras; huc corpora quisque suorum
more tulere patrum, subiectisque ignibus atris
conditur in tenebras altum caligine caelum.
ter circum accensos cincti fulgentibus armis
decurrere rogos, ter maestum funeris ignem
lustrauere in equis ululatusque ore dedere.
spargitur et tellus lacrimis, sparguntur et arma,
it caelo clamorque uirum clangorque tubarum.
hic alii spolia occisis derepta Latinis
coniciunt igni, galeas ensesque decoros
frenaque feruentisque rotas; pars munera nota,
ipsorum clipeos et non felicia tela.
multa boum circa mactantur corpora Morti,
saetigerosque sues raptasque ex omnibus agris
in flammam iugulant pecudes. tum litore toto
ardentis spectant socios semustaque seruant
busta, neque auelli possunt, nox umida donec
inuertit caelum stellis ardentibus aptum.
Nec minus et miseri diuersa in parte Latini
innumeras struxere pyras, et corpora partim

172 ferant *PRφ* 173 armis *codd., Seru., Tib., Prisc. 16.11*: aruis *Heinsius, Bentley* 175 armis] ultra *Heinsius* 176 audite $P^{ac}R$ 202 ardentibus *MPω, Tib.*: fulgentibus *Rφ*

multa uirum terrae infodiunt auectaque partim
finitimos tollunt in agros urbique remittunt.
cetera confusaeque ingentem caedis aceruum
nec numero nec honore cremant: tunc undique uasti
certatim crebris conlucent ignibus agri.
tertia lux gelidam caelo dimouerat umbram:
maerentes altum cinerem et confusa ruebant
ossa focis tepidoque onerabant aggere terrae.
iam uero in tectis, praediuitis urbe Latini,
praecipuus fragor et longi pars maxima luctus;
hic matres miseraeque nurus, hic cara sororum
pectora maerentum puerique parentibus orbi
dirum exsecrantur bellum Turnique hymenaeos:
ipsum armis ipsumque iubent decernere ferro,
qui regnum Italiae et primos sibi poscat honores.
ingrauat haec saeuus Drances solumque uocari
testatur, solum posci in certamina Turnum.
multa simul contra uariis sententia dictis
pro Turno, et magnum reginae nomen obumbrat,
multa uirum meritis sustentat fama tropaeis.
  Hos inter motus, medio in flagrante tumultu,
ecce super maesti magna Diomedis ab urbe
legati responsa ferunt: nihil omnibus actum
tantorum impensis operum, nil dona neque aurum
nec magnas ualuisse preces, alia arma Latinis
quaerenda aut pacem Troiano ab rege petendum.
deficit ingenti luctu rex ipse Latinus;
fatalem Aenean manifesto numine ferri
admonet ira deum tumulique ante ora recentes.
ergo concilium magnum primosque suorum
imperio accitos alta intra limina cogit.
olli conuenere fluuntque ad regia plenis
tecta uiis. sedet in mediis et maximus aeuo

207 caedis] stragis *Rφ* (*cf. u. 384 et Aen. 6.504*) 208 nec^{2}] neque *Pc* 214 longe *fere* ω, *Tib.*, *'melius' iudice Seru.* 220 haec] et *P* 221 certamine *Rφ* 224 uirum] simul (*cf. u.* 222) M^{ac} 226 magna] magni *agnoscit Seru.*, *Diom. 413.26* (*cf. Aen. 8.9*) 228 neque] nec *R et fere* ω, *Seru.*, *Tib.* 230 petendum M^{c}φ, *Seru. hic et ad Aen. 10.628*, *DSeru. ad G. 4.484*: petendam $M^{ac}PR$ω, *Tib.* 235 limina] moenia *Rφ* 236 olli] ilico *φ* (illi *g*) ruuntque *Mbr*

et primus sceptris haud laeta fronte Latinus;
atque hic legatos Aetola ex urbe remissos
quae referant fari iubet, et responsa reposcit
ordine cuncta suo. tum facta silentia linguis,
et Venulus dicto parens ita farier infit:
  'Vidimus, o ciues, Diomedem Argiuaque castra,
atque iter emensi casus superauimus omnis,
contigimusque manum qua concidit Ilia tellus.
ille urbem Argyripam patriae cognomine gentis
uictor Gargani condebat Iapygis agris.
postquam introgressi et coram data copia fandi,
munera praeferimus, nomen patriamque docemus,
qui bellum intulerint, quae causa attraxerit Arpos.
auditis ille haec placido sic reddidit ore:
"o fortunatae gentes, Saturnia regna,
antiqui Ausonii, quae uos fortuna quietos
sollicitat suadetque ignota lacessere bella?
quicumque Iliacos ferro uiolauimus agros
(mitto quae muris bellando exhausta sub altis,
quos Simois premat ille uiros) infanda per orbem
supplicia et scelerum poenas expendimus omnes,
uel Priamo miseranda manus; scit triste Mineruae
sidus et Euboicae cautes ultorque Caphereus.
militia ex illa diuersum ad litus abacti
Atrides Protei Menelaus adusque columnas
exulat, Aetnaeos uidit Cyclopas Vlixes.
regna Neoptolemi referam uersosque penates
Idomenei? Libycone habitantis litore Locros?
ipse Mycenaeus magnorum ductor Achiuum
coniugis infandae prima inter limina dextra
oppetiit: deuictam Asiam subsedit adulter.
inuidisse deos, patriis ut redditus aris

243 diomedem *ω*, *DSeru.*: diomeden *MPRφ*, *Tib.*, *Macrob. 5.17.19* (*ut uid.*): diomede *f*; diomede 247 aruis *φ*, *Seru.*, *Tib.* 248 congressi *Rφ*, *Tib.* (*cf. u. 631*) 255 populauimus *Rφ* '*melius*' *iudice Seru.* 259 manus] damus *P*[c], *Tib.* 261 adacti *M*[c]*n*, *Tib.* 267 inter *Pφ*, *Macrob. 4.3.12 et 4.4.22*, *Tib.*: intra *MRωγ*[c], *Seru.* (*cf. u. 882*) 268 deuictam asiam *MPRφ*, *Tib.*, deuicta asia *ωγ*[c], '*melius*' *iudice Seru.* subsedit *M*[ac]*Pω*, *Seru. hic et ad Aen. 5.498*, *Arus.*: possedit *M*[c]*Rγ*[c], *Macrob. 4.4.22*, *Tib.*

coniugium optatum et pulchram Calydona uiderem?
nunc etiam horribili uisu portenta sequuntur
et socii amissi petierunt aethera pinnis
fluminibusque uagantur aues (heu, dira meorum
supplicia!) et scopulos lacrimosis uocibus implent.
haec adeo ex illo mihi iam speranda fuerunt
tempore cum ferro caelestia corpora demens
appetii et Veneris uiolaui uulnere dextram.
ne uero, ne me ad talis impellite pugnas:
nec mihi cum Teucris ullum post eruta bellum
Pergama nec ueterum memini laetorue malorum.
munera quae patriis ad me portatis ab oris
uertite ad Aenean. stetimus tela aspera contra
contulimusque manus: experto credite quantus
in clipeum adsurgat, quo turbine torqueat hastam.
si duo praeterea talis Idaea tulisset
terra uiros, ultro Inachias uenisset ad urbes
Dardanus et uersis lugeret Graecia fatis.
quidquid apud durae cessatum est moenia Troiae,
Hectoris Aeneaeque manu uictoria Graium
haesit et in decimum uestigia rettulit annum;
ambo animis, ambo insignes praestantibus armis,
hic pietate prior. coeant in foedera dextrae,
qua datur; ast armis concurrant arma cauete."
et responsa simul quae sint, rex optime, regis
audisti et quae sit magno sententia bello.'
   Vix ea legati, uariusque per ora cucurrit
Ausonidum turbata fremor, ceu saxa morantur
cum rapidos amnis, fit clauso gurgite murmur
uicinaeque fremunt ripae crepitantibus undis.
ut primum placati animi et trepida ora quierunt,
praefatus diuos solio rex infit ab alto:
   'Ante equidem summa de re statuisse, Latini,
et uellem et fuerat melius, non tempore tali
cogere concilium, cum muros adsidet hostis.

272 amissis P^{ac}: admissis *'nonnulli' ap. Seru.* 275 adeo] eadem *P* ex illo *om. R* superanda *R* 279 diruta *R* bellum *MPφ, Seru., Prisc. 8.26 et 10.12*: bellum est *Rω* 281 portastis *fere ω, Seru., DSeru. ad u. 243* 288 certatum M^{c} 294 regis] regum *R* (*cf. u. 353*) 300 trepida] rabida *R* (*cf. Aen. 6.102*) quierant *R* 304 obsidet *Mφ*

bellum importunum, ciues, cum gente deorum
inuictisque uiris gerimus, quos nulla fatigant
proelia nec uicti possunt absistere ferro.
spem si quam ascitis Aetolum habuistis in armis,
ponite: spes sibi quisque, sed haec quam angusta uidetis.
cetera qua rerum iaceant perculsa ruina,
ante oculos interque manus sunt omnia uestras.
nec quemquam incuso: potuit quae plurima uirtus
esse, fuit; toto certatum est corpore regni.
nunc adeo quae sit dubiae sententia menti
expediam et paucis (animos adhibete) docebo.
est antiquus ager Tusco mihi proximus amni,
longus in occasum, finis super usque Sicanos;
Aurunci Rutulique serunt et uomere duros
exercent collis atque horum asperrima pascunt.
haec omnis regio et celsi plaga pinea montis
cedat amicitiae Teucrorum, et foederis aequas
dicamus leges sociosque in regna uocemus:
considant, si tantus amor, et moenia condant.
sin alios finis aliamque capessere gentem
est animus possuntque solo decedere nostro,
bis denas Italo texamus robore nauis,
seu pluris complere ualent (iacet omnis ad undam
materies): ipsi numerumque modumque carinis
praecipiant, nos aera, manus, naualia demus.
praeterea, qui dicta ferant et foedera firmant
centum oratores prima de gente Latinos
ire placet pacisque manu praetendere ramos,
munera portantis aurique eborisque talenta
et sellam regni trabeamque insignia nostri.
consulite in medium et rebus succurrite fessis.'
  Tum Drances idem infensus, quem gloria Turni
obliqua inuidia stimulisque agitabat amaris,
largus opum et lingua melior, sed frigida bello
dextera, consiliis habitus non futtilis auctor,
seditione potens (genus huic materna superbum
nobilitas dabat, incertum de patre ferebat),

324 aliamque *MRω*: aliamue *Pφ*, *Tib.* 325 poscuntque *recc.* 335 fessis] uestris *P* 338 linguae P^{ac}, *DSeru.* 341 ferebat $MP^{c}\omega$, *Seru.*, *Tib.*: ferebant $P^{ac}R\varphi$

surgit et his onerat dictis atque aggerat iras:
'rem nulli obscuram nostrae nec uocis egentem
consulis, o bone rex: cuncti se scire fatentur
quid fortuna ferat populi, sed dicere mussant.
det libertatem fandi flatusque remittat,
cuius ob auspicium infaustum moresque sinistros
(dicam equidem, licet arma mihi mortemque minetur)
lumina tot cecidisse ducum totamque uidemus
consedisse urbem luctu, dum Troia temptat
castra fugae fidens et caelum territat armis.
unum etiam donis istis, quae plurima mitti
Dardanidis dicique iubes, unum, optime regum,
adicias, nec te ullius uiolentia uincat
quin natam egregio genero dignisque hymenaeis
des pater et pacem hanc aeterno foedere iungas.
quod si tantus habet mentes et pectora terror,
ipsum obtestemur ueniamque oremus ab ipso:
cedat, ius proprium regi patriaeque remittat.
quid miseros totiens in aperta pericula ciues
proicis, o Latio caput horum et causa malorum?
nulla salus bello: pacem te poscimus omnes,
Turne, simul pacis solum inuiolabile pignus.
primus ego, inuisum quem tu tibi fingis (et esse
nil moror), en supplex uenio. miserere tuorum,
pone animos et pulsus abi. sat funera fusi
uidimus ingentis et desolauimus agros.
aut si fama mouet, si tantum pectore robur
concipis et si adeo dotalis regia cordi est,
aude atque aduersum fidens fer pectus in hostem.
scilicet ut Turno contingat regia coniunx,
nos animae uiles, inhumata infletaque turba,
sternamur campis? etiam tu, si qua tibi uis,
si patrii quid Martis habes, illum aspice contra
qui uocat.'
Talibus exarsit dictis uiolentia Turni;

345 ferat *M*[c]*PRφ*, *Tib.*, *Prisc. 18.40*, *Non. 427.15*: petat *M*[ac]*ωγ*[c] 351 fuga *R* 353 ducique *γ*[ac] 356 iungas *M*[ac]*Pω*, *Tib.*: firmes *M*[c]*Rφ*, *Seru. hic et ad u. 363* 366 funere *P*[ac] fusi *M*[c]*Rωγ*[c], *Seru.*, *Tib.*: fusis *M*[ac]: fuso *P* 367 designauimus *Pb?* 369 et] aut *Mn* 373 sternemur *φγ*[c], *Tib.*

dat gemitum rumpitque has imo pectore uoces:
'larga quidem semper, Drance, tibi copia fandi
tum cum bella manus poscunt, patribusque uocatis
primus ades; sed non replenda est curia uerbis,
quae tuto tibi magna uolant, dum distinet hostem
agger moerorum nec inundant sanguine fossae.
proinde tona eloquio (solitum tibi) meque timoris
argue tu, Drance, quando tot stragis aceruos
Teucrorum tua dextra dedit passimque tropaeis
insignis agros. possit quid uiuida uirtus
experiare licet, nec longe scilicet hostes
quaerendi nobis; circumstant undique muros.
imus in aduersos: quid cessas? an tibi Mauors
uentosa in lingua pedibusque fugacibus istis
semper erit?
pulsus ego? aut quisquam merito, foedissime, pulsum
arguet, Iliaco tumidum qui crescere Thybrim
sanguine et Euandri totam cum stirpe uidebit
procubuisse domum atque exutos Arcadas armis?
haud ita me experti Bitias et Pandarus ingens
et quos mille die uictor sub Tartara misi,
inclusus muris hostilique aggere saeptus.
nulla salus bello? capiti cane talia, demens,
Dardanio rebusque tuis. proinde omnia magno
ne cessa turbare metu atque extollere uires
gentis bis uictae, contra premere arma Latini.
nunc et Myrmidonum proceres Phrygia arma tremescunt,
[nunc et Tydides et Larisaeus Achilles,]
amnis et Hadriacas retro fugit Aufidus undas.
uel cum se pauidum contra mea iurgia fingit,
artificis scelus, et formidine crimen acerbat.
numquam animam talem dextra hac (absiste moueri)
amittes: habitet tecum et sit pectore in isto.

378 drances semper *M* 381 distinet *Pω*, *Seru.*, *Tib.*: detinet *Mxz*: destinat *R* hostes *M*, *Prisc. 8.26* 382 agger *φγ*^{c}, *Tib.*, *Prisc. 8.26*: aggere *MPRω* (*cf. Aen. 10.144*) moerorum *MP*^{ac}*φ*: murorum *P*^{c}*Rω*, *Tib.*, *Prisc.* nec] et *P* 391 nequiquam armis terrebimus hostem *add. M*^{ac} (*del. M*^{c}) 393 arguit *M*^{ac}

nunc ad te et tua magna, pater, consulta reuertor.
si nullam nostris ultra spem ponis in armis,
si tam deserti sumus et semel agmine uerso
funditus occidimus neque habet Fortuna regressum,
oremus pacem et dextras tendamus inertis.
quamquam o si solitae quicquam uirtutis adesset!
ille mihi ante alios fortunatusque laborum
egregiusque animi, qui, ne quid tale uideret,
procubuit moriens et humum semel ore momordit.
sin et opes nobis et adhuc intacta iuuentus
auxilioque urbes Italae populique supersunt,
sin et Troianis cum multo gloria uenit
sanguine (sunt illis sua funera, parque per omnis
tempestas), cur indecores in limine primo
deficimus? Cur ante tubam tremor occupat artus?
multa dies uariique labor mutabilis aeui
rettulit in melius, multos alterna reuisens
lusit et in solido rursus Fortuna locauit.
non erit auxilio nobis Aetolus et Arpi:
at Messapus erit felixque Tolumnius et quos
tot populi misere duces, nec parua sequetur
gloria delectos Latio et Laurentibus agris.
est et Volscorum egregia de gente Camilla
agmen agens equitum et florentis aere cateruas.
quod si me solum Teucri in certamina poscunt
idque placet tantumque bonis communibus obsto,
non adeo has exosa manus Victoria fugit
ut tanta quicquam pro spe temptare recusem.
ibo animis contra, uel magnum praestet Achillem
factaque Volcani manibus paria induat arma
ille licet. uobis animam hanc soceroque Latino
Turnus ego, haud ulli ueterum uirtute secundus,
deuoui. solum Aeneas uocat? et uocet oro;
nec Drances potius, siue est haec ira deorum,
morte luat, siue est uirtus et gloria, tollat.'

410 magna *PRφ*: magne *Mω, Tib.* 412 semel] simul *P* 418 semel *M*[c]*ωγ, Seru., Tib.*: simul *M*[ac]*R*: semul *P* 422 suntque *Rb* illi *n, agnoscit Seru.* 425 uariusque *M*[c]*P*[c]*φ, Tib., Macrob. 6.2.16, Non. 380.40* 426 multosque *M*[c] 430 parua] tarda *i*[c]*x, Seru.* (*cf. G.* 2.52) 431 deiectos *φγ*[c] 439 induit *Pi*

Illi haec inter se dubiis de rebus agebant
certantes; castra Aeneas aciemque mouebat.
nuntius ingenti per regia tecta tumultu
ecce ruit magnisque urbem terroribus implet:
instructos acie Tiberino a flumine Teucros
Tyrrhenamque manum totis descendere campis.
extemplo turbati animi concussaque uulgi
pectora et arrectae stimulis haud mollibus irae.
arma manu trepidi poscunt, fremit arma iuuentus,
flent maesti mussantque patres; hic undique clamor
dissensu uario magnus se tollit in auras,
haud secus atque alto in luco cum forte cateruae
consedere auium piscosoue amne Padusae
dant sonitum rauci per stagna loquacia cycni.
'immo,' ait 'o ciues,' arrepto tempore Turnus,
'cogite concilium et pacem laudate sedentes;
illi armis in regna ruunt.' nec plura locutus
corripuit sese et tectis citus extulit altis.
'tu, Voluse, armari Volscorum edice maniplis,
duc' ait 'et Rutulos. equitem Messapus in armis
et cum fratre Coras latis diffundite campis.
pars aditus urbis firment turrisque capessant;
cetera, qua iusso, mecum manus inferat arma.'
Ilicet in muros tota discurritur urbe.
concilium ipse pater et magna incepta Latinus
deserit ac tristi turbatus tempore differt
multaque se incusat qui non acceperit ultro
Dardanium Aenean generumque asciuerit urbi.
praefodiunt alii portas aut saxa sudesque
subuectant. bello dat signum rauca cruentum
bucina; tum muros uaria cinxere corona
matronae puerique: uocat labor ultimus omnis.
nec non ad templum summasque ad Palladis arces
subuehitur magna matrum regina caterua

451 animo *Rφ* 455 in] ad *M* 461 ruant *e recc. Heinsius, Bentley* 463 maniplos *P* 464 equitem MP^{ac}*φ, Seru., Tib.* (*cf. u. 517*): equites P^{c}*Rω* 466 firment $M^{ac}R\omega\gamma^{c}$, *DSeru. ad u. 473, Tib.*: firmet M^{c}*Pgn* capessant $R\omega\gamma^{c}$, *Tib.*: capessat *MPn* 469 consilium $M^{ac}y\gamma^{c}$ pater ipse M^{ac} 471 qui] quod P^{c} ultro] ante *suspic. Mynors* 472 urbi] ultro *suspic. Mynors*

dona ferens, iuxtaque comes Lauinia uirgo,
causa mali tanti, oculos deiecta decoros.
succedunt matres et templum ture uaporant
et maestas alto fundunt de limine uoces:
‘armipotens, praeses belli, Tritonia uirgo,
frange manu telum Phrygii praedonis et ipsum
pronum sterne solo portisque effunde sub altis.’
cingitur ipse furens certatim in proelia Turnus.
iamque adeo rutilum thoraca indutus aënis
horrebat squamis surasque incluserat auro,
tempora nudus adhuc, laterique accinxerat ensem
fulgebatque alta decurrens aureus arce
exsultatque animis et spe iam praecipit hostem:
qualis ubi abruptis fugit praesepia uinclis
tandem liber equus, campoque potitus aperto
aut ille in pastus armentaque tendit equarum
aut adsuetus aquae perfundi flumine noto
emicat arrectisque fremit ceruicibus alte
luxurians, luduntque iubae per colla, per armos.
  Obuia cui Volscorum acie comitante Camilla
occurrit portisque ab equo regina sub ipsis
desiluit, quam tota cohors imitata relictis
ad terram defluxit equis; tum talia fatur:
‘Turne, sui merito si qua est fiducia forti,
audeo et Aeneadum promitto occurrere turmae
solaque Tyrrhenos equites ire obuia contra.
me sine prima manu temptare pericula belli,
tu pedes ad muros subsiste et moenia serua.’
Turnus ad haec oculos horrenda in uirgine fixus:
‘o decus Italiae uirgo, quas dicere grates
quasue referre parem? sed nunc, est omnia quando
iste animus supra, mecum partire laborem.
Aeneas, ut fama fidem missique reportant

480 mali tanti *M*^{c}*Pφ*, *DSeru.*, *Seru. ad Aen. 12.66*: mali tantis *M*^{ac}*bz*: malis tantis *Rω*: mali tanti *et* malis tantis *agnoscit Tib.* 483 praeses *M*^{ac}*P*^{ac}*Rφ*, *Seru.*, *Tib.*, *Diom. 446.29*: praesens *M*^{c}*P*^{c}*ω*, *Macrob. 5.3.10* 485 altis] ipsis *Macrob. 5.3.10* (*cf. u. 499*) 487 rutilum *Rφ*, *DSeru. ad Aen. 10.314*, *Gell. 2.6.22*, *Macrob. 5.10.11 et 6.7.18*: rutulum *MPω*, *Tib.* 503 turmis *R* 507 fixis *M*^{ac}*c*: fixos *γ*^{c} 510 supra] superat *M*^{ac}

exploratores, equitum leuia improbus arma
praemisit, quaterent campos; ipse ardua montis
per deserta iugo superans aduentat ad urbem.
furta paro belli conuexo in tramite siluae,
ut biuias armato obsidam milite fauces.
tu Tyrrhenum equitem conlatis excipe signis;
tecum acer Messapus erit turmaeque Latinae
Tiburtique manus, ducis et tu concipe curam.'
sic ait et paribus Messapum in proelia dictis
hortatur sociosque duces et pergit in hostem.
  Est curuo anfractu ualles, accommoda fraudi
armorumque dolis, quam densis frondibus atrum
urget utrimque latus, tenuis quo semita ducit
angustaeque ferunt fauces aditusque maligni.
hanc super in speculis summoque in uertice montis
planities ignota iacet tutique receptus,
seu dextra laeuaque uelis occurrere pugnae
siue instare iugis et grandia uoluere saxa:
huc iuuenis nota fertur regione uiarum
arripuitque locum et siluis insedit iniquis.
  Velocem interea superis in sedibus Opim,
unam ex uirginibus sociis sacraque caterua,
compellabat et has tristis Latonia uoces
ore dabat: 'graditur bellum ad crudele Camilla,
o uirgo, et nostris nequiquam cingitur armis,
cara mihi ante alias. neque enim nouus iste Dianae
uenit amor subitaque animum dulcedine mouit.
pulsus ob inuidiam regno uirisque superbas
Priuerno antiqua Metabus cum excederet urbe,
infantem fugiens media inter proelia belli
sustulit exilio comitem matrisque uocauit
nomine Casmillae mutata parte Camillam.
ipse sinu prae se portans iuga longa petebat
solorum nemorum: tela undique saeua premebant

519 tiburtique $M^{c?}P^{c}R\varphi$: tiburnique $M^{ac}P^{ac}\omega$, *Seru.*, *Tib.* 524 quo] quos *Rc*: '*legitur et* qua' *ap. Seru.* 526 *uersum ante 525 habet* φ in^{1}] e *Pf* (*cf. u. 877, Aen. 4.586, 7.511*): om. *R* 527 receptus $M^{ac}P\omega$, *Seru.*, *Tib.*: receptis γ^{ac}: recessus $M^{c}Rj$ 533 sacris sociaque *Re* 534 tristi *R* 538 subitoque M^{ac} mouet φ

et circumfuso uolitabant milite Volsci.
ecce fugae medio summis Amasenus abundans
spumabat ripis: tantus se nubibus imber
ruperat. ille innare parans infantis amore
tardatur caroque oneri timet. omnia secum
uersanti subito uix haec sententia sedit:
telum immane manu ualida quod forte gerebat
bellator, solidum nodis et robore cocto,
huic natam libro et siluestri subere clausam
implicat atque habilem mediae circumligat hastae;
quam dextra ingenti librans ita ad aethera fatur:
"alma, tibi hanc, nemorum cultrix, Latonia uirgo,
ipse pater famulam uoueo; tua prima per auras
tela tenens supplex hostem fugit. accipe, testor,
diua tuam, quae nunc dubiis committitur auris."
dixit, et adducto contortum hastile lacerto
immittit: sonuere undae, rapidum super amnem
infelix fugit in iaculo stridente Camilla.
at Metabus, magna propius iam urgente caterua,
dat sese fluuio atque hastam cum uirgine uictor
gramineo, donum Triuiae, de caespite uellit.
non illum tectis ullae, non moenibus urbes
accepere (neque ipse manus feritate dedisset),
pastorum et solis exegit montibus aeuum.
hic natam in dumis interque horrentia lustra
armentalis equae mammis et lacte ferino
nutribat teneris immulgens ubera labris.
utque pedum primis infans uestigia plantis
institerat, iaculo palmas armauit acuto
spiculaque ex umero paruae suspendit et arcum;
pro crinali auro, pro longae tegmine pallae
tigridis exuuiae per dorsum a uertice pendent.
tela manu iam tum tenera puerilia torsit
et fundam tereti circum caput egit habena
Strymoniamque gruem aut album deiecit olorem.
multae illam frustra Tyrrhena per oppida matres

552 ferebat *M*^{c} 554 huc *R*^{ac} 566 uellit] tollit *P* (*cf. G. 4.273*) 568 neque] nec *R* 570 hinc *P*^{ac} 574 armauit] onerauit *φ*, *Seru.* (*cf. Aen. 10.868*)

optauere nurum: sola contenta Diana
aeternum telorum et uirginitatis amorem
intemerata colit. uellem haud correpta fuisset
militia tali conata lacessere Teucros:
cara mihi comitumque foret nunc una mearum.
uerum age, quandoquidem fatis urgetur acerbis,
labere, nympha, polo finisque inuise Latinos,
tristis ubi infausto committitur omine pugna.
haec cape et ultricem pharetra deprome sagittam:
hac, quicumque sacrum uiolarit uulnere corpus,
Tros Italusque, mihi pariter det sanguine poenas.
post ego nube caua miserandae corpus et arma
inspoliata feram tumulo patriaeque reponam.'
Dixit; at illa leuis caeli delapsa per auras
insonuit nigro circumdata turbine corpus.
At manus interea muris Troiana propinquat
Etruscique duces equitumque exercitus omnis
compositi numero in turmas. fremit aequore toto
insultans sonipes et pressis pugnat habenis
huc conuersus et huc; tum late ferreus hastis
horret ager campique armis sublimibus ardent.
nec non Messapus contra celeresque Latini
et cum fratre Coras et uirginis ala Camillae
aduersi campo apparent, hastasque reductis
protendunt longe dextris et spicula uibrant,
aduentusque uirum fremitusque ardescit equorum.
iamque intra iactum teli progressus uterque
substiterat: subito erumpunt clamore furentisque
exhortantur equos; fundunt simul undique tela
crebra niuis ritu caelumque obtexitur umbra.
continuo aduersis Tyrrhenus et acer Aconteus
conixi incurrunt hastis primique ruinam
dant sonitu ingenti perfractaque quadrupedantum

587 acerbis] iniquis γ^c, *Tib.* (*cf. Aen. 2.257, 3.17, 10.380*) 592 italusue *φ*, *Seru.* 595 delapsa *Mφ*: demissa *PRω*, *Tib.*: dimissa *φ* 598 etrurique P^{ac}*dr*, *'quidam' ap. DSeru.* 601 conuersus *MPγ*: obuersus $R\omega\gamma^c$, *Tib.* 602 armis] hastis *P*, *e u. 601* 605 reductas M^{ac} 606 praetendunt M^{ac}*gz* 609 substiterat $M^cP\omega$, *Tib.* (-rant *φ*): constiterant M^{ac}: substituerant *R* 612 aduersis $P^{ac}\omega$, *DSeru.*, *Tib.*: aduersi MP^cR 613 ruina P^cn 614 sonitu $R\omega\gamma^c$, *Tib.*: sonitum *MPu* ingenti $MR\omega\gamma^c$, *Tib.*: ingentem *P*

pectora pectoribus rumpunt; excussus Aconteus
fulminis in morem aut tormento ponderis acti
praecipitat longe et uitam dispergit in auras.
  Extemplo turbatae acies, uersique Latini
reiciunt parmas et equos ad moenia uertunt;
Troes agunt, princeps turmas inducit Asilas.
iamque propinquabant portis rursusque Latini
clamorem tollunt et mollia colla reflectunt;
hi fugiunt penitusque datis referuntur habenis.
qualis ubi alterno procurrens gurgite pontus
nunc ruit ad terram scopulosque superiacit unda
spumeus extremamque sinu perfundit harenam,
nunc rapidus retro atque aestu reuoluta resorbens
saxa fugit litusque uado labente relinquit:
bis Tusci Rutulos egere ad moenia uersos,
bis reiecti armis respectant terga tegentes.
tertia sed postquam congressi in proelia totas
implicuere inter se acies legitque uirum uir,
tum uero et gemitus morientum et sanguine in alto
armaque corporaque et permixti caede uirorum
semianimes uoluuntur equi, pugna aspera surgit.
Orsilochus Remuli, quando ipsum horrebat adire,
hastam intorsit equo ferrumque sub aure reliquit;
quo sonipes ictu furit arduus altaque iactat
uulneris impatiens arrecto pectore crura:
uoluitur ille excussus humi. Catillus Iollan
ingentemque animis, ingentem corpore et armis
deicit Herminium, nudo cui uertice fulua
caesaries nudique umeri nec uulnera terrent:
tantus in arma patet. latos huic hasta per armos
acta tremit duplicatque uirum transfixa dolore.
funditur ater ubique cruor; dant funera ferro
certantes pulchramque petunt per uulnera mortem.

645–90 *M*γ *R*   616 actus P^r 619 uertunt] tendunt *b* (*cf. u. 871*)   624 procurrens $MP^r\varphi$, *Tib.*: procumbens $R\omega$ 625 terras *M* superiacit $M\omega\gamma^c$, *Seru.* (*superiacet* φ, *Tib.*): superlicit *P*: suberigit *R* unda $MPR\varphi$, *Tib.*: undam $\omega\gamma^c$, *Seru.*   628–30 *del.* P^r, *om.* γ^{ac} 629 tusci] teucri M^{ac} 637 relinquit φ 638 ferit $M^{ac}R$ 640 catillus φ: catthyllus *M*: catthillus *Pr*: cathillus $R\omega\gamma$: cathyllus *b* iollan $P^r\omega$: iollam $M^cR\varphi$, *Tib.*: ollam *v*   644 tantum *R*   645 fremit γ^{ac}: premit *b*

At medias inter caedes exsultat Amazon,
unum exserta latus pugnae, pharetratra Camilla,
et nunc lenta manu spargens hastilia denset,
nunc ualidam dextra rapit indefessa bipennem;
aureus ex umero sonat arcus et arma Dianae.
illa etiam, si quando in tergum pulsa recessit,
spicula conuerso fugientia derigit arcu.
at circum lectae comites, Larinaque uirgo
Tullaque et aeratam quatiens Tarpeia securim,
Italides, quas ipsa decus sibi dia Camilla
delegit pacisque bonas bellique ministras:
quales Threiciae cum flumina Thermodontis
pulsant et pictis bellantur Amazones armis,
seu circum Hippolyten seu cum se Martia curru
Penthesilea refert, magnoque ululante tumultu
feminea exsultant lunatis agmina peltis.
Quem telo primum, quem postremum, aspera uirgo,
deicis? aut quot humi morientia corpora fundis?
Eunaeum Clytio primum patre, cuius apertum
aduersi longa transuerberat abiete pectus:
sanguinis ille uomens riuos cadit atque cruentam
mandit humum moriensque suo se in uulnere uersat.
tum Lirim Pagasumque super, quorum alter habenas
suffosso reuolutus equo dum colligit, alter
dum subit ac dextram labenti tendit inermem:
praecipites pariterque ruunt. his addit Amastrum
Hippotaden, sequiturque incumbens eminus hasta
Tereaque Harpalycumque et Demophoonta Chromimque;
quotque emissa manu contorsit spicula uirgo,
tot Phrygii cecidere uiri. procul Ornytus armis
ignotis et equo uenator Iapyge fertur,
cui pellis latos umeros erepta iuuenco

650 denset $M^{c?}\varphi$, *DSeru.*: densat $M^{ac}\gamma R\omega$, *Tib.* 652 umeris *Re, Tib.* 653 in tergum si quando *b, Tib.* 654 fulgentia $R\varphi$ derigit $M\gamma^{ac}R$ (degerit *b*, adegerit *d*): dirigit $\gamma^{c}\omega$, *Tib.* 655 at] et γb 656 securim $M\gamma^{c}R\omega$, *Tib.*: securem $\gamma^{ac}y$, *Prisc. 7.53* 657 dia $M^{c}\gamma^{ac}\varphi$, *Seru. hic et ad Aen. 12.83, Tib.*: diua $M^{ac}\gamma^{c}\omega$: dura *Rc?* 658 bonas $M\gamma^{ac}r$, *Tib.*: bonae $\gamma^{c}R\omega$, *Seru.* 659 thermodontis $M\varphi$, *Seru.*: thermodoontis $\gamma^{c}R\omega$, *Tib.* 666 euneum *c, Seru.* 671 suffosso $M^{ac}\varphi$, *'alii' ap. Seru.*: suffuso $M^{c}R\omega$ (subfuso γ), *Seru., Tib.* 672 inermem $MR\varphi$, *Tib.*: inertem $\gamma\omega$, *DSeru.* 674 sequitur quem φ

pugnatori operit, caput ingens oris hiatus
et malae texere lupi cum dentibus albis,
agrestisque manus armat sparus; ipse cateruis
uertitur in mediis et toto uertice supra est.
hunc illa exceptum (neque enim labor agmine uerso)
traicit et super haec inimico pectore fatur:
'siluis te, Tyrrhene, feras agitare putasti?
aduenit qui uestra dies muliebribus armis
uerba redargueret. nomen tamen haud leue patrum
manibus hoc referes, telo cecidisse Camillae.'
  Protinus Orsilochum et Buten, duo maxima Teucrum
corpora, sed Buten auersum cuspide fixit
loricam galeamque inter, qua colla sedentis
lucent et laeuo dependet parma lacerto,
Orsilochum fugiens magnumque agitata per orbem
eludit gyro interior sequiturque sequentem;
tum ualidam perque arma uiro perque ossa securim
altior exsurgens oranti et multa precanti
congeminat: uulnus calido rigat ora cerebro.
incidit huic subitoque aspectu territus haesit
Appenninicolae bellator filius Auni,
haud Ligurum extremus, dum fallere fata sinebant.
isque ubi se nullo iam cursu euadere pugnae
posse neque instantem reginam auertere cernit,
consilio uersare dolos ingressus et astu
incipit haec: 'quid tam egregium si femina forti
fidis equo? dimitte fugam et te comminus aequo
mecum crede solo pugnaeque accinge pedestri:
iam nosces uentosa ferat cui gloria fraudem.'
dixit; at illa furens acrique accensa dolore
tradit equum comiti paribusque resistit in armis
ense pedes nudo puraque interrita parma.
at iuuenis uicisse dolo ratus auolat ipse
(haud mora) conuersisque fugax aufertur habenis

691–736 *MPR* 688 redargueret *MγRω, Tib.*: redarguerat *c*: redarguerit *Prisc. 10.10* 691 aduersum *fere ω* figit *fg, Tib.* 696 securim *MRωγ^c^, Tib.*: securem *Pγ^ac^* 703 aduertere *M^ac^*: uertere *Rb* 707 pugnaque *bd* 708 fraudem *M^ac^Ri, 'uera et antiqua lectio' iudice Seru.*: laudem *M^c^P^c^ω, Tib.*

quadrupedumque citum ferrata calce fatigat.
'uane Ligus frustraque animis elate superbis,
nequiquam patrias temptasti lubricus artis,
nec fraus te incolumem fallaci perferet Auno.'
haec fatur uirgo et pernicibus ignea plantis
transit equum cursu frenisque aduersa prehensis
congreditur poenasque inimico ex sanguine sumit:
quam facile accipiter saxo sacer ales ab alto
consequitur pinnis sublimem in nube columbam
comprensamque tenet pedibusque euiscerat uncis;
tum cruor et uulsae labuntur ab aethere plumae.
At non haec nullis hominum sator atque deorum
obseruans oculis summo sedet altus Olympo:
Tyrrhenum genitor Tarchonem in proelia saeua
suscitat et stimulis haud mollibus inicit iras.
ergo inter caedes cedentiaque agmina Tarchon
fertur equo uariisque instigat uocibus alas
nomine quemque uocans, reficitque in proelia pulsos.
'quis metus, o numquam dolituri, o semper inertes
Tyrrheni, quae tanta animis ignauia uenit?
femina palantis agit atque haec agmina uertit?
quo ferrum quidue haec gerimus tela inrita dextris?
at non in Venerem segnes nocturnaque bella,
aut ubi curua choros indixit tibia Bacchi.
exspectate dapes et plenae pocula mensae
(hic amor, hoc studium) dum sacra secundus haruspex
nuntiet ac lucos uocet hostia pinguis in altos!'
haec effatus equum in medios moriturus et ipse
concitat et Venulo aduersum se turbidus infert
dereptumque ab equo dextra complectitur hostem
et gremium ante suum multa ui concitus aufert.
tollitur in caelum clamor cunctique Latini
conuertere oculos. uolat igneus aequore Tarchon
arma uirumque ferens; tum summa ipsius ab hasta
defringit ferrum et partis rimatur apertas,

737–56 *M*γ *R* 720 ex] a *fere* ω (*cf. Aen. 12.949*) 728 inicit *R*ω: incitat *MP*φ, *Tib.*: incutit *Heinsius* 735 geritis *fere* ω, *Tib.* 738 exspectare *recc.* mensae] dextrae γ^{ac} 741 et ipse] in hostis γ (*cf. Aen. 2.511 et 9.554*) 742 turbidus] feruidus *Tib.* infert *M*ω, *Seru. ad u. 814*: offert γ*R*, *Tib.*

qua uulnus letale ferat; contra ille repugnans
sustinet a iugulo dextram et uim uiribus exit.
utque uolans alte raptum cum fulua draconem
fert aquila implicuitque pedes atque unguibus haesit,
saucius at serpens sinuosa uolumina uersat
arrectisque horret squamis et sibilat ore
arduus insurgens, illa haud minus urget obunco
luctantem rostro, simul aethera uerberat alis:
haud aliter praedam Tiburtum ex agmine Tarchon
portat ouans; ducis exemplum euentumque secuti
Maeonidae incurrunt. tum fatis debitus Arruns
uelocem iaculo et multa prior arte Camillam
circuit et quae sit fortuna facillima temptat.
qua se cumque furens medio tulit agmine uirgo,
hac Arruns subit et tacitus uestigia lustrat;
qua uictrix redit illa pedemque ex hoste reportat,
hac iuuenis furtim celeris detorquet habenas;
hos aditus iamque hos aditus omnemque pererrat
undique circuitum et certam quatit improbus hastam.
  Forte sacer Cybelo Chloreus olimque sacerdos
insignis longe Phrygiis fulgebat in armis
spumantemque agitabat equum, quem pellis aënis
in plumam squamis auro conserta tegebat.
ipse peregrina ferrugine clarus et ostro
spicula torquebat Lycio Gortynia cornu;
aureus ex umeris erat arcus et aurea uati
cassida; tum croceam chlamydemque sinusque crepantis
carbaseos fuluo in nodum collegerat auro,
pictus acu tunicas et barbara tegmina crurum.
hunc uirgo, siue ut templis praefigeret arma
Troia, captiuo siue ut se ferret in auro
uenatrix, unum ex omni certamine pugnae
caeca sequebatur totumque incauta per agmen
femineo praedae et spoliorum ardebat amore,

757–82 *Mγα* 755 obunco *Mγω*: adunco *Rφ*: abunco *φ* 759 fatis tum *φ* (fatis tantum *u*) 766 iamque] atque *γ* 768 cybelo *Maω*, *Seru.*, *Tib.*: cybele *φ*: cybeli *n*: cybelae *Macrob. 5.1.12* choreus *M*, *Macrob.* 774 umero *γ* (*cf. u. 652*) erat] sonat *γφ* (*cf. u. 652*) 781 incauta] incensa *φ* (*cf. Aen. 4.300*)

telum ex insidiis cum tandem tempore capto
concitat et superos Arruns sic uoce precatur:
'summe deum, sancti custos Soractis Apollo,
quem primi colimus, cui pineus ardor aceruo
pascitur, et medium freti pietate per ignem
cultores multa premimus uestigia pruna,
da, pater, hoc nostris aboleri dedecus armis,
omnipotens. non exuuias pulsaeue tropaeum
uirginis aut spolia ulla peto (mihi cetera laudem
facta ferent): haec dira meo dum uulnere pestis
pulsa cadat, patrias remeabo inglorius urbes.'
Audiit et uoti Phoebus succedere partem
mente dedit, partem uolucris dispersit in auras:
sterneret ut subita turbatam morte Camillam
adnuit oranti; reducem ut patria alta uideret
non dedit, inque Notos uocem uertere procellae.
ergo ut missa manu sonitum dedit hasta per auras,
conuertere animos acris oculosque tulere
cuncti ad reginam Volsci. nihil ipsa nec aurae
nec sonitus memor aut uenientis ab aethere teli,
hasta sub exsertam donec perlata papillam
haesit uirgineumque alte bibit acta cruorem.
concurrunt trepidae comites dominamque ruentem
suscipiunt. fugit ante omnis exterritus Arruns
laetitia mixtoque metu, nec iam amplius hastae
credere nec telis occurrere uirginis audet.
ac uelut ille, prius quam tela inimica sequantur,
continuo in montis sese auius abdidit altos
occiso pastore lupus magnoue iuuenco,
conscius audacis facti, caudamque remulcens
subiecit pauitantem utero siluasque petiuit:
haud secus ex oculis se turbidus abstulit Arruns
contentusque fuga mediis se immiscuit armis.
illa manu moriens telum trahit, ossa sed inter

783–92 *MPa* 793–857 *MPR* 784 conicit φ (*cf. Aen. 9.411 et 10.646*) 786 primis P^{ac}: primum *recc.* 789 aboleri $M^{c}P\omega$, *Tib.*: abolere $M^{ac}\varphi$ 792 ferant φ 794 uotis *j, Tib., Macrob. 5.3.7* partim *c, Tib.* 799 ut] ubi M^{ac} (*cf. Aen. 3.238, 4.474, G. 4.77*) 801 nec] neque φ, *Seru.* aurae *MPR*ω, *Tib.*: auras *di*, *'antiqua lectio' ap. Seru.* (*genitiuus singularis intellegitur*)

ferreus ad costas alto stat uulnere mucro.
labitur exsanguis, labuntur frigida leto
lumina, purpureus quondam color ora reliquit.
tum sic exspirans Accam ex aequalibus unam
adloquitur, fida ante alias quae sola Camillae
quicum partiri curas, atque haec ita fatur:
'hactenus, Acca soror, potui: nunc uulnus acerbum
conficit, et tenebris nigrescunt omnia circum.
effuge et haec Turno mandata nouissima perfer:
succedat pugnae Troianosque arceat urbe.
iamque uale.' simul his dictis linquebat habenas
ad terram non sponte fluens. tum frigida toto
paulatim exsoluit se corpore lentaque colla
et captum leto posuit caput, arma relinquens,
uitaque cum gemitu fugit indignata sub umbras.
tum uero immensus surgens ferit aurea clamor
sidera: deiecta crudescit pugna Camilla;
incurrunt densi simul omnis copia Teucrum
Tyrrhenique duces Euandrique Arcades alae.
At Triuiae custos iamdudum in montibus Opis
alta sedet summis spectatque interrita pugnas.
utque procul medio iuuenum in clamore furentum
prospexit tristi multatam morte Camillam,
ingemuitque deditque has imo pectore uoces:
'heu nimium, uirgo, nimium crudele luisti
supplicium, Teucros conata lacessere bello!
nec tibi desertae in dumis coluisse Dianam
profuit aut nostras umero gessisse pharetras.
non tamen indecorem tua te regina reliquit
extrema iam in morte, neque hoc sine nomine letum
per gentis erit aut famam patieris inultae.

818 leto] telo *'alii' ap. Seru.* 819 relinquit *c* 821 fida $M^{ac}R\omega\gamma^{c}$ fidam $M^{c?}P$ (fidem *b*), *Tib.* 822 quicum $MR\varphi\gamma^{c}$, *Tib.*: quacum $P^{c}\omega$ (quamcum γ) 826 urbe $MP^{c}\omega$, *Tib.*: urbi $P^{ac}R$ 830 relinquens $M^{c}P^{c}\omega$, *DSeru.*: relinquunt *'alii' ap. DSeru.*: relinquit M^{ac}: reliquit P^{ac} (*ut uid.*) *R* 834 concurrunt *Re* 835 tyrrhenumque *M* (*cf. u. 171*) 838 iuuenem medio P^{ac}: iuuenum medio γ^{ac} (iuuenem medio γ^{c}): medio iuuenem *b* furentem M^{c} (furente M^{ac}) $b\gamma^{c}$, *Tib. in interpr.* 839 multatam $\omega\gamma^{c}$: mulcatam $MPR\varphi$, *DSeru.* 844 pharetras $PR\omega$: sagittas $M\varphi$ 845 reliquit $MR\varphi$, *Prisc. 6.47*: relinquet $P\omega$: relinquit *r*, *Tib.* 846 neque] nec *Rn* numine φ (lum- *z*)

nam quicumque tuum uiolauit uulnere corpus
morte luet merita.' fuit ingens monte sub alto
regis Dercenni terreno ex aggere bustum
antiqui Laurentis opacaque ilice tectum:
hic dea se primum rapido pulcherrima nisu
sistit et Arruntem tumulo speculatur ab alto.
ut uidit fulgentem armis ac uana tumentem:
'cur' inquit 'diuersus abis? huc derige gressum,
huc periture ueni, capias ut digna Camillae
praemia. tune etiam telis moriere Dianae?'
dixit et aurata uolucrem Threissa sagittam
deprompsit pharetra cornuque infensa tetendit
et duxit longe, donec curuata coirent
inter se capita et manibus iam tangeret aequis,
laeua aciem ferri, dextra neruoque papillam.
extemplo teli stridorem aurasque sonantis
audiit una Arruns haesitque in corpore ferrum.
illum exspirantem socii atque extrema gementem
obliti ignoto camporum in puluere linquunt;
Opis ad aetherium pinnis aufertur Olympum.
　Prima fugit domina amissa leuis ala Camillae,
turbati fugiunt Rutuli, fugit acer Atinas,
disiectique duces desolatique manipli
tuta petunt et equis auersi ad moenia tendunt.
nec quisquam instantis Teucros letumque ferentis
sustentare ualet telis aut sistere contra,
sed laxos referunt umeris languentibus arcus,
quadrupedumque putrem cursu quatit ungula campum.
uoluitur ad muros caligine turbidus atra
puluis, et e speculis percussae pectora matres
femineum clamorem ad caeli sidera tollunt.
qui cursu portas primi inrupere patentis,
hos inimica super mixto premit agmine turba;
nec miseram effugiunt mortem, sed limine in ipso,

858–95 *FMPR* 852 dea] ea M^{ac} 854 fulgentem armis $M^{c}PR\omega$, *Tib.*: laetantem animis M^{ac} 855 dirige $\varphi\gamma^{c}$, *Tib.* 856 camilla *R* 860 et duxit] eduxit *bn*: adduxit *Macrob.* 5.3.2 861 tenderet *bd* 870 disiectique] defectique M^{ac} 871 equos *Pfg* aduersi φ 875 quadrupedumque $M^{ac}\varphi$ (quadrip- $M^{c}P\omega$): quadripedoque $F^{ac}R\varphi$, *Tib.*: quadripedemque F^{c} 877 e *om. FMbr* speculis] muris φ

moenibus in patriis atque inter tuta domorum
confixi exspirant animas. pars claudere portas,
nec sociis aperire uiam nec moenibus audent
accipere orantis, oriturque miserrima caedes
defendentum armis aditus inque arma ruentum.
exclusi ante oculos lacrimantumque ora parentum
pars in praecipitis fossas urgente ruina
uoluitur, immissis pars caeca et concita frenis
arietat in portas et duros obice postis.
ipsae de muris summo certamine matres
(monstrat amor uerus patriae), ut uidere Camillam,
tela manu trepidae iaciunt ac robore duro
stipitibus ferrum sudibusque imitantur obustis
praecipites, primaeque mori pro moenibus ardent.
  Interea Turnum in siluis saeuissimus implet
nuntius et iuueni ingentem fert Acca tumultum:
deletas Volscorum acies, cecidisse Camillam,
ingruere infensos hostis et Marte secundo
omnia corripuisse, metum iam ad moenia ferri.
ille furens (et saeua Iouis sic numina poscunt)
deserit obsessos colles, nemora aspera linquit.
uix e conspectu exierat campumque tenebat,
cum pater Aeneas saltus ingressus apertos
exsuperatque iugum siluaque euadit opaca.
sic ambo ad muros rapidi totoque feruntur
agmine nec longis inter se passibus absunt;
ac simul Aeneas fumantis puluere campos
prospexit longe Laurentiaque agmina uidit,
et saeuum Aenean agnouit Turnus in armis
aduentumque pedum flatusque audiuit equorum.
continuoque ineant pugnas et proelia temptent,
ni roseus fessos iam gurgite Phoebus Hibero
tingat equos noctemque die labente reducat.
considunt castris ante urbem et moenia uallant.

896–915 *MPR* 882 inter *FPω, Tib., Macrob. 4.3.12*: intra *MRφ* 892 uersus *R* 895 audent *M*[c]*γ*[c] *et fere ω, Seru.* (*cf. u. 884*) 901 poscunt *MPω, Seru., Tib.* (*cf. Aen. 4.614 et 8.512*): pellunt *R* 903 camposque *M*[ac] 908 ac simul] tum pater *PRφ* (*cf. u. 904*) 909 conspexit *b* 910 agnouit] conspexit *P* 911 aduentusque *Mjr, Tib.* (*cf. u. 607*) pedum] uirum *Tib.* flatumque *Rφ* 912 ineunt *M*[ac]*b* temptant *cgγ*

COMMENTARY

1–28 The book begins in the quiet of early morning, on the day after the fierce battle that dominates *Aen.* 10. The previous day's fighting casts a long shadow over *Aen.* 11; its casualties, including Pallas, are the focus down to 214, and central to the Latin debate over whether to surrender or to fight on (302–444) is the heavy reality of defeat in the engagement.

1 A high-poetic description of daybreak, repeated from 4.129. For other examples of repeated dawn formulae, see 3.589/4.7 and 4.584–5/9.459–60 (the second line in each = *G.* 1.447); very close are 4.119 and 5.65. On the whole, however, Virgil (hereafter V.) varies his descriptions of dawn; see Moskalew 1982: 66–72 and Traina on 12.113. This is the only book to begin with a temporal formula and at dawn. An apparent model is Furius Bibaculus fr. 7 Courtney *interea Oceani linquens Aurora cubile.* Cf., too, *Il.* 19.1–2 'now saffron-robed Dawn rose from the streams of Oceanus' (Ἠὼς μὲν κροκόπεπλος ἀπ' Ὠκεανοῖο ῥοάων | ὄρνυθ'). **interea** 'now', a loose transition to a new scene, with a change of subject and location. For this use of *interea,* common in V. and in epic generally, see Harrison on 10.1, Heinze 1993: 337 n. 31. On *interea* generally in V., see Kinsey 1979. **Aurora:** found twenty-five times in V., usually, as here, with light personification.

2–11 Aeneas (hereafter A.) demonstrates the cardinal virtue of *pietas* and, at daybreak, pays a vow to Mars (unrecorded in *Aen.* 10) by dedicating a trophy, i.e. a tree trunk hung with the spoils of a fallen enemy, from the arms of Mezentius (on whom see 7n.). On trophies in *Aen.*, see Nielson 1983: 27–31 and Malavolta, *EV* v*.296–7. A.'s dedication of the spoils to the god is consistent with Roman usage: 'You can dedicate your victim's arms to the gods in a *tropaeum*; you can hang them in a palace or temple; you can burn them in large quantities' (Horsfall 1995: 178).

2–3 quamquam et sociis dare tempus humandis | praecipitant curae 'although his concerns drive (him) to grant time for burying his allies'. This is the first occurrence in extant literature of *praecipito* with the infinitive (only here in V.); it is a variation on the infinitive with a verb of desiring. The ordinary construction of *cura* + inf. is also felt. Statius imitates at *Theb.* 1.679 *si praecipitant miserum cognoscere curae.* The plural *sociis . . . humandis* reflects A.'s concern for the burial of his fallen allies generally (cf. *socios* at 22), although the burial of Pallas is foremost in his thoughts (see 25–8). A. avoids pollution from contact with the dead before seeing to the burial of his comrades (cf. Serv. ad 11.2, Cilliers and Retief 2005). But V. does not suggest that this motivates A.; rather, he prioritises his *uotum* out of religious piety.

3 turbataque: *turbare* is a favourite verb, appearing forty-three times in *Aen.* (compared to nineteen times in Ovid's *Met.*) and twenty-six times in the final four books. V. makes varied use of it to describe the emotional disturbance of individuals and groups; here it conveys A.'s inner anguish, which he stifles while he attends to his religious duty. **funere:** probably 'death', as at 28, and probably with reference to Pallas; V. moves from A.'s concern for his fallen troops to the one death that especially occupies him. **mens est:** also at line-end at 8.400. V. has double final monosyllables thirty-two times in *Aen.* (and forty-seven times overall in his poetry); another example follows closely, at 16 (*hic est*). The pattern is found often in Lucretius (107 times), is avoided in Catul. 64, and appears widely in Augustan and first-century CE verse, most commonly in satire, followed by epic. Double final monosyllables are less harsh than single final monosyllables (see 373n.), in that there is a lighter clash of ictus, or metrical stress, and word accent at the end of the line than that which the single monosyllable creates; coincidence of ictus and accent in the final two feet is the norm (see Intro. p. 32). *est* at line-end tends not to have emphasis whether as part of a double monosyllable or on its own, including when unelided; this further mitigates the clash (Hough 1975: 18–19).

4 deum: an archaic form of the gen. pl.; V. uses the form with a limited group of gens. (*deum, diuum, superum, uirum, equum, iuuencum, socium, famulum*), with the adjs. *magnanimum* and *omnigenum*, and with some proper names. **primo . . . Eoo:** Gk *Eous* picks up on Lat. *Aurora* in the first line. For the combination of the two, cf. 3.588–9. **soluebat:** the verb for paying a vow (*OLD* 20b), also at 3.403 and *G.* 1.436. A descriptive imperfect showing action in progress; the pious A. was already seeing to his vow when daylight broke.

5 ingentem quercum: the spoils stripped from Mezentius are placed on an oak tree. The oak was closely associated with trophies; cf.10.421–3 and Liv. 1.10.5–6, where Romulus lays down the first Roman trophy, offered to Jupiter Feretrius, by an oak tree (sacred to Jupiter) on the Capitol. *ingens* is found 168 times in *Aen.* (never in *Ecl.*, thirty-one times in *G.*), with fourteen examples in this book; it fits well the larger-than-life quality of epic (although it is also a favourite of Livy's, who has it nearly 500 times). While sometimes a stopgap, here the adj. conveys epic scale, with an overtone of awe, and matches the great size of Mezentius and his arms (cf. 10.763–8). See, further, Quartarone 2011. **decisis undique**

ramis: the tree is a surrogate for Mezentius' body, and the violence done to it reflects the violence done to him. This is not tree violation, however (*pace* Hejduk, *VE* III.1293, 1303); there is no indication that the tree was sacred, and branches had to be lopped from trees in order for them to serve as trophies (cf. Suet. *Cal.* 45 *truncatis arboribus et in modum tropaeorum adornatis*). Cf. Lucr. 3.403–4 *caesis lacer undique membris | truncus.*

6 induit: sc. *quercui.* The oak is 'dressed' as if it were the body of the warrior. *in-duit* contrasts with *ex-uuias* in the next line. Cf. 10.775 *indutum spoliis . . . tropaeum.*

7 Mezenti ducis: Mezentius, the exiled Etruscan king. Introduced as a despotic villain and *contemptor diuum* (7.648), Mezentius is rendered sympathetic after his son Lausus dies in an attempt to save his father from A. (10.833–908). The transformation of Mezentius calls upon the reader to hold contradictory views simultaneously, in characteristic Virgilian manner: Mezentius is a wicked, impious despot and a grieving, pitiful old father (and, in the latter capacity, a precursor to Evander in this book). On Mezentius, see e.g. Burke 1974, Basson 1984, Gotoff 1984, Kronenberg 2005, and La Penna, *EV* III.510–15. There is a contrast between A.'s trophy and 10.774–6, where Mezentius sacrilegiously vows A.'s armour to Lausus, so that he might wear it as a 'living trophy', rather than to the gods. Cf., too, 10.862–3 (Mezentius to his horse Rhaebus) *aut hodie uictor spolia illa cruenta | et caput Aeneae referes.*

8 bellipotens = Mars; cf. 10.542 [*arma Serestus*] *lecta refert umeris tibi, rex Gradiue, tropaeum.* Mars is 'the natural dedicatee of war-spoils' (Harrison on 10.542); the god was also the recipient of *spolia secunda,* or spoils won by a Roman officer (not the general) from an enemy commander (see Austin on 6.859). Cf. Sil. 10.547–8 (arms dedicated to Mars) *at tibi, bellipotens, sacrum, constructus aceruo | ingenti mons armorum surgebat ad astra.* Attempts (Henry 1989: 106, Fratantuono ad loc., tentatively) to make Minerva the dedicatee (cf. Stat. *Theb.* 2.716), thus reading *magnae* or *magna* for *magne* at 7, are unconvincing. *bellipotens* is an example of the enjambment of a single word followed by a syntactical pause, a very common pattern in V.; the effect is to place strong emphasis on the word. The rare compound adj. is found before V. only at Enn. *Ann.* 198 Sk. (Achilles and Ajax) *bellipotentes sunt magis quam sapientipotentes.* **rorantis sanguine cristas:** *cristas* is a synecdoche (part for the whole) for 'crested helmet'. Mezentius' crest is of horsehair at 10.869 *aere caput fulgens cristaque hirsutus equina;* the horsehair crest is Homeric (*Il.* 3.336–7, 6.494–5, 11.41–2, 15.480–1, 16.137–8, 19.382, *Od.* 22.123–4; see Hollis on Ov. *Met.* 8.25) and heroic (S. *Ant.* (Adrastus) 116 ξύν θ' ἱπποκόμοις κορύθεσσιν).

9 telaque trunca: the broken weapons of Mezentius. *trunca* evokes *truncus*, the body/torso of a man and the trunk of the tree upon which the trophy is constructed. **uiri:** = 'soldier' (*OLD* 5), implying a formidable, heroic fighter. Hence more than a replacement for *eius*, a common substitution in V. (see Austin on 2.452, and cf. 12n.).

9–10 bis sex thoraca petitum | perfossumque locis 'the breastplate struck and bored through in twelve spots'. *thoraca* is a Gk acc. form. From the violence done to the breastplate, it appears that A. did not protect Mezentius' body from the fury of his people, as Mezentius' had asked on the battlefield (10.903–6); see Intro. pp. 6–7. *bis sex* is a generic high number, as at 12.899 *uix illum lecti bis sex ceruice subirent.* Serv. ad loc. understands the damaged breastplate as evidence that A. allowed violence against Mezentius, but fancifully contends that the number of blows stands for the twelve cities of Etruria, with a representative from each striking Mezentius' body.

10 perfossumque: *perfodio* is avoided by poets through the Augustan Age (Lyne 1989: 112–13); it occurs later at e.g. Luc. 8.619, Stat. *Theb.* 2.710, and Sil. 1.620 and 10.400 (*multa thorax perfossus cuspide,* in evident imitation of V.). V. uses it to describe graphically the violence done to the breastplate. There is an increase in unpoetic language in the later books of *Aen.*; this is often a consequence of the subject matter (Horsfall 1995: 236). **clipeumque:** a round shield, distinct from the long, rectangular, semi-cylindrical *scutum.* The *clipeus* is more the shield of archaic heroes, whereas the *scutum* was the more familiar Roman object, having been adopted as a regular weapon by the army around the fourth century BCE (cf. Liv. 8.8.3). *clipeus* appears fifty times in *Aen.*, *scutum* thirteen times. **ex aere** 'made of bronze'.

11 ensem . . . eburnum: *ensis* is a poetic word, as opposed to the prosaic *gladius*; it occurs sixty-four times in *Aen.*, *gladius* only four. The sword is attached to a baldric, or sword-belt, which hangs from the tree trunk. It is presumably inlaid or overlaid with ivory (an ivory sword would be a singularly useless piece of weaponry). Others (C–N, Williams ad loc., Ballaira, *EV* II.160) understand a hilt of ivory (also impractically fragile). **collo:** *collum* can be used for the upper part of a tree (and plant); see *TLL* III.1663.18–27. The noun further identifies the trophy with the body of the man.

12 eum: the oblique cases of the pronoun *is* are rare in elevated poetry (Austin on 4.479, Axelson 1945: 70–2) with the exception of acc. *ea*. *eum* appears eight times in V. (six in *Aen.*, twice in *G.*). **tegebat** 'flanked'.

12–13 namque . . . | . . . ducum: V. is fond of parentheses (see Tarrant 1998: 151–7); as elsewhere (2.604, 3.362, 10.19) *namque* introduces the parenthetical remark. The focus on A. in the opening lines gives the impression that he was alone; it is a surprise, therefore, to find him surrounded by his lieutenants. V. isolates A. in his *pietas* before panning out to show the *turba ducum.*

13 ouantis 'rejoicing', with a hint of the *ouatio,* the lesser victory celebration given to a general who had not earned a triumph (cf. Serv. ad 4.543). There is a strong contrast between the rejoicing commanders and A., who displays solemn piety and grieves as a suffering leader (cf. Cairns 1989: 73). Even when he is among his men, A. stands apart because of the painful responsibilities he bears. On A.'s solitude in the poem, including his distance from his men, see Feeney 1990: 182–4.

14–28 A.'s speech to his allied *duces.* It is formally one of command, but up to 21 contains themes of a *cohortatio,* or an address before or during a battle to encourage and rally troops (cf. Tarrant on 12.563–73, Highet 1972: 82–9, Hansen 1993). At 22, A. shifts his focus to the burial of his dead soldiers, particularly Pallas. While still issuing orders and encouragement, he consoles his men and, furthermore, praises the dead. The praise is reminiscent of a *contio,* or a speech after a battle in which the general praises those who have done well. *contiones* were a regular feature of Roman military life (see Oakley on Liv. 7.10.14). V.'s Homeric model is *Il.* 22.378–94, where Achilles addresses his men after the death of Hector and calls for funeral rites for Patroclus. A.'s speech is characteristically brief and restrained (cf. Heinze 1993: 314–18), but there is pathos in that brevity: A. has *curae* pressing upon him that limit his words, much as Achilles did (*Il.* 22.385–8).

14 maxima res effecta: cf. *Il.* 22.393 'we have won us great glory' (ἠράμεθα μέγα κῦδος).

15 quod superest 'as for the rest', 'as for what remains (to be done)', an adverbial phrase also at 5.796 and 9.157 (*quod superest* at 5.691 is a rel. clause). **de rege superbo:** to be taken with *spolia* and with *primitiae* in the next line. *de* indicates the person from whom something is taken, with ellipsis of the verb of taking. *superbus* in *Aen.* is often connected, as here, with the arrogance of kings and tyrants. Cf. 8.481–2 (Evander on the rule of the *rex* Mezentius) *superbo imperio.* The implication is that the Trojan cause is righteous and the enemy evil; for these ideas as motifs in *cohortationes,* see Highet 1972: 85.

16 primitiae 'first fruits' of the war, i.e. the first offerings from it. According to Macrobius (3.5.10–11), *primitiae* alludes to a story told in

Cato's *Origines*, that the tyrannical and impious Mezentius demanded the Rutulians offer him the first fruits they usually gave to the gods. **manibusque meis Mezentius hic est** 'by my hands, *this* is Mezentius'. The instrumental abl. operates in two ways, because A. both killed Mezentius and erected the trophy. Alliteration of *m* conveys strong emotion (seemingly a mix of pride and of loathing for Mezentius).

17 Probably sc. *faciendum est,* with *nobis* dat. of agent: 'now we must march on the king and the Latin walls'. (For *facere iter* of a military march, cf. Caes. *Gal.* 7.68.1.) The passive periphrastic works well with the imperatives that follow. Cf. *Il.* 22.381 'let us go make trial in arms about the city' (εἰ δ' ἄγετ' ἀμφὶ πόλιν σὺν τεύχεσι πειρηθῶμεν).

18 'prepare your weapons, with courage and hope anticipate the battle'. The punctuation follows Mynors and Horsfall rather than Conte. With *arma parate,* A. orders practical preparations in plain language in a soldierly setting (cf. Sal. *Jug.* 43.3 *arma tela equos . . . parare,* Liv. 3.27.4 *dum is arma pararet,* 36.18.1 *arma telaque parant*). For *praesumo* + *animo/animis,* cf. V. Max. 1.5.3 and Sen. *Ep.* 91.8. For *animis* = *animose,* cf. 438 and 7.42. The elision in *parate, animis* does not tell against the punctuation; cf. e.g. 364, 392, 441, and 1.13. Different is 491 below, where *animis* belongs to one clause and *spe* to another. **praesumite:** the verb is not found in extant literature before V. and is quite possibly his coinage.

19 ne qua mora: cf. 12.565 (A. orders an attack on Latinus' city) *ne qua meis esto dictis mora.* Later (446–50), A.'s troops will surprise the Italians with the sort of swift charge envisioned now. **ignaros** 'not knowing what to do', because unprepared; sc. *uos.* **uellere signa:** standard military language, also at *G.* 4.108.

20 adnuerint: the nod of divine permission. For *adnuo* meaning 'grant permission' with an infinitive, see *OLD* 4. The construction goes back to Ennius (*Ann.* 132 Sk.). The indication is that A. will take the auspices, as a Roman general did before battle, and will proceed only when the ritual shows divine approval. 'The assertion of divine support is a frequent motif of the *cohortatio*' (Tarrant on 12.565). It was a bad omen if standards could not be pulled up easily; cf. Liv. 22.3.12–13.

21 impediat . . . tardet: the verbs are strongly emphasised by position. V. commonly frames lines with parallel verb forms; see Norden, Anh. III.A.2, Dainotti 2015: 221–3. **segnisue metu sententia tardet** 'or purpose made sluggish from fear hold (you) back'. *segnis* is better taken as a nom. with *sententia* rather than as an acc. balancing *ignaros.* V. echoes

10.308 *nec Turnum segnis retinet mora,* but instead of having *segnis* modify *mora* at 19, he uses the adj. with the parallel nom. *sententia.* For *segnis* meaning 'sluggish, slow' from fear and, thus, 'cowardly', cf. 10.592 *fuga segnis equorum,* 12.565–6 (A. to his troops) *ne qua meis esto dictis mora . . . | neu quis ob inceptum subitum mihi segnior ito.* Word order makes it difficult not to take *metu* with *segnis.* But the abl. could also be understood with *tardet,* 'hold (you) back through fear'; cf. Ov. *Her.* 17.184 *tardor . . . metu.*

22 socios inhumataque corpora: hendiadys (the expression of a single idea through words linked by a conjunction), 'the unburied bodies of our allies'.

23 qui . . . est: cf. Homeric τὸ γάρ γέρας ἐστὶ θανόντων ('for this is the honour for the dead') at *Il.* 16.457, 16.675, 23.9, *Od.* 24.190, and 24.296; V.'s specific model is probably *Il.* 16.457, where Hera speaks of the burial of Patroclus. The echo implies that A.'s thoughts were especially on Pallas, the Patroclus of *Aen.* V. varies Homer by adding *solus* and *Acheronte sub imo* for emotional force and vividness. **honos:** V. always has this archaic nom. form, with a long second vowel. When intervocalic -s- became -r- in the oblique cases, *honōs* changed by analogy to *honōr,* and subsequently *honŏr.*

24 ite introduces an emphatic command (*OLD* 10). **ait** marks the transition to the conclusion of the speech. *ait* recurrently accompanies an imperative in *Aen.*, especially when placed in the second position in a line (cf. 464, 2.289, 3.103, 3.480, 5.551, 6.318, 8.122). **egregias animas:** an uncommon phrase (*TLL* v.288.27–9).

25 hanc patriam: *hanc* is an example of spatial deixis, referring to physical surroundings. A. has already received definitive signs that Italy is the Trojan homeland and has stated as much (see 7.122 *hic domus, haec patria est*). In this peroration, he praises the dead by stating that they have helped to create that homeland through the role they played in securing victory. This is a way also of encouraging A.'s listeners, as DServ. ad loc. saw: *eleganter hoc et oratorie ad exhortationem audientium sumptum est: nam laus defunctorum uiuentium exhortatio est.* The idea that the Trojan mission leads to the new nation, to be realised by Rome, is essential to V.'s project. **peperere:** in paradoxical juxtaposition with *patriam*; the troops 'bring forth, bring into being' their *patr-ia.* The third-person perfect *-ere* predominates over *-erunt* in V. (231 examples in *Aen.*, against 29 of *-erunt*), as it does in poetry generally, both for metrical reasons and per se; here, as often, it lends an elevated tone. **suo:** in strong contrast with *nobis* in the previous line.

26 maestamque . . . urbem: attention now turns explicitly to Pallas. *maestus*, more common in poetry than in prose, is used in *Aen.* almost exclusively in situations connected to mourning. It is found five more times in connection with Pallas' death up to 92 (35, 38, 52, 76, and 92) (see Anderson 1999: 195–6). The adj. is proleptic, as A. envisions the grief that Pallanteum, and especially Evander, will feel.

27 non uirtutis egentem: Ennian (*Ann.* 605 Sk.). Another possible model is *Il.* 13.785–6 'nor, I think, will we be lacking at all in valour' (οὐδέ τί φημι | ἀλκῆς δευήσεσθαι). Litotes, or deliberate understatement via double negatives, emphasises the courage of Pallas. There is possible etymological play on *Euandri* in the previous line; the name is suggestive of εὐανδρία, 'courage'.

28 = 6.429, of the deaths of infants. **atra dies:** V. always has a feminine form of *dies* in the nom. except with *ille dies*; metre is an obvious consideration. In the oblique cases, singular and plural, he uses the masculine. Romans marked ill-omened days as 'black'; hence *ater* was sometimes used of the day of death (cf. e.g. Prop. 2.11.4, 3.2.4, Stat. *Theb.* 3.636, 8.376, with *TLL* II.1021.47–50). **acerbo** 'premature' (*OLD* 4). The adj. contrasts with *uirtutis*; Pallas was too young when he died, but he fully displayed the traits of manhood. Cf. 9.641 (on Ascanius) *macte noua uirtute, puer.*

29–41 A. returns to his tent, where mourners have gathered around Pallas, and sees the dead, beautiful youth lying on a bier. Putnam 1995: 37–8 argues that several details in the description of the beautiful Pallas imply A.'s sexual attraction to Pallas; cf. Powell 2008: 154–62, with Reed 2007: 35–6. This would correspond to the homoeroticism of Achilles and Patroclus, which was recognised from at least the fifth century BCE (Powell 2008: 155–6). But A.'s homosexual feelings are very difficult to accept given his role as surrogate father to Pallas (see 42–58n.) and given Roman cultural norms regarding homosexuality for those in high military positions: 'The ideal (at higher levels of command), which one can hardly imagine V.'s *Aeneas imperator* not following, was one of prim disapprobation (and exemplary punishment of the older man)' (Horsfall on 36). V. describes Pallas as an ephebic youth, an Antilochus to the Nestor-like Evander (see 139–81n., Quint 2018: 182–3), to vary conventional associations between beauty (especially youthful beauty) and heroism (cf. 6.861, 7.649–50, 9.179–80, and 10.435) and to exploit the pathetic connection between youth, heroism, beauty, and death. His A. keenly feels the pathos of the latter connection (see 39n.); but it is a bridge too far to posit his sexual attraction to Pallas. (The possible feelings of Pallas towards Aeneas are a separate matter; see Quint 2018: 183–4.)

29 recipitque . . . gressum: poetic for *recipit se*, 'withdraw, turn back'.

30 positum: for *compositum*, 'laid out for burial' (*OLD* 4c). The use of a simple verb form for a compound (*simplex pro composito*) belongs to high style and is common in V. The custom at Rome (as in Homer; see *Il.* 19.212–13) was to place a body on a bier and lay it in the vestibule with feet pointing to the door (see C–N, Page ad loc., Flower 1996: 93–4). Pallas' body is similarly situated, with feet pointing to the entrance of A.'s tent. **Pallantis Acoetes:** expressive juxtaposition, emphasising Acoetes' devotion to Pallas. Acoetes was Pallas' attendant, having served as Evander's armour-bearer in the past. Horsfall ad loc. compares Acoetes with ἄκοιτος, 'unresting', and suggests a speaking name based on the Gk word, indicating that Acoetes watched sleeplessly over Pallas' corpse. Paschalis 1997: 371 similarly etymologises the name, but also links it to ἀκοίτης, 'bedfellow, husband'; he proposes that this 'hints at a close relationship between "Acoetes" and Pallas, possibly an erotic one'. Cf. the homosexual lovers Cydon and Clytius at 10.324–6, with Harrison on 10.324–5; Cydon is squire to the warrior Clytius. But it is hard to imagine that V. wished to imply homosexuality, given Acoetes' status as a double for the aged Evander (see 31n.) and, thus, his implied identity as a substitute father to Pallas.

31 senior: the grieving, aged Acoetes stands in for the grieving, aged Evander (cf. 165, 8.508–9, 560–1) while generating pathos in his own right as an old man who outlives his young charge. **Parrhasio Euandro:** *Parrhasio* = 'Arcadian'; Parrhasia was a region in Arcadia. Evander was the grandson of Pallas, king of Arcadia; he was said to have gone into exile after killing his father, Echenus. Having come to Italy, he founded Pallanteum on the site of Rome (cf. 8.333–6, Liv. 1.5.1, Dion. Hal. 1.31). *Parrhasio Euandro* produces a spondaic fifth foot with hiatus (avoidance of elision). On hiatus in V., see Austin on 1.16 and 4.235, Thomas, *VE* II.822, and Trappes-Lomax 2004. Fifth-foot spondees are an Alexandrian mannerism, taken up by Catullus and the neoterics (cf. Cic. *Att.* 7.2.1). V. is more restrained in his use of them than is Catullus, with thirty-three in *Aen.* (about the number that Catullus has in the 408 lines of Catul. 64). Often a line with a fifth-foot spondee in V. contains a Gk proper name. See, further, Norden, Anh. IX.3c. Cf. the spondaic fifth foot with hiatus *Dardanio Anchisae* at 9.647, with the next note.

32 armiger ante fuit: in the same line-position at 9.648. There (9.647–58) Apollo takes the form of Butes, formerly armour-bearer of Anchises and currently guardian of Ascanius, and restrains Ascanius from further fighting after he had killed Numanus Remulus, thus keeping him out of harm's way in battle; this contrasts with Pallas' fate.

32–3 sed . . . | . . . alumno 'but under auspices not so propitious did he then go as an attendant assigned to his dear charge'.

33 Cf. 9.649 (Butes) *tum comitem Ascanio pater addidit. ibat Apollo.* **comes:** predicative; the noun expresses the capacity in which Acoetes went with Pallas to war. Cf. 8.466 *illi comes ibat Achates.*

34 famulum: gen. pl.; see 4n. on *deum.* **Troianaque turba:** the personal adj. *Troiana* is used for a gen. in high poetic style. On adj. for gen., see Austin on 2.543, Harrison on 10.156–7. The *turba* is presumably not the *turba ducum* of 13, since A. appears to have taken leave of them to come to Pallas, but a crowd of other men, to balance the *Iliades,* or Trojan women, of the next line.

35 Cf. 3.65 *et circum Iliades crinem de more solutae,* on the burial of Polydorus. Critics since Servius have tried to explain the appearance of the Trojan women here even though A. left Trojan matrons to settle in Sicily in *Aen.* 5 (5.715, 750), and even though Euryalus' mother states that she is the only *mater* who dared to follow the Trojans (9.217–18). V. does not trouble over these details, and he includes the women because they are appropriate and typical in a scene of mourning. Cf. Achilles' call for women to lament night and day for the fallen Patroclus (*Il.* 18.339–42). **maestum . . . crinem de more solutae:** *maestum* is a transferred epithet (hypallage), from women to their hair, which is let loose in mourning, as was customary in Rome (but not in Homer). On the practice, see Pease on 4.509. *crinem* is a retained acc. after the medio-passive *solutae.* V. likes to use accs. after perfect passive participles; see Harrison, App. D. and Courtney 2004: 425–31 for discussion and classification. *crinis,* like *coma,* is an epic and tragic word for hair; V. has it thirty times and *coma* twenty-five times in *Aen.,* but *capillus* only once (10.832; also at *G.* 1.405). **Iliades** 'women of Troy'. The word with this meaning is found first in V. (also at 1.480, 2.580, 3.65, 5.644, and 7.248) and probably originates with him (Austin on 2.580). **de more** 'in accordance with custom'.

36 foribus . . . altis: indicative of a lofty dwelling. V. is concerned to represent the Trojan camp as a city (Hardie on 9.8), and he depicts A.'s tent as a palace in that *urbs.*

37 ad sidera tollunt: hyperbole in grand epic style; see Hardie 1986: 241–92.

37–8 tunsis . . . | pectoribus 'as their breasts are beaten'; a timeless use of the perfect participle in default of a present (see Eden on 8.636, *NLS*

§103). Cf. 1.481 *tristes et tunsae pectora palmis*; another echo of 1.480–5, where grieving Trojan women supplicate a different Pallas (Athena).

38 immugit 'resounds', with deep-toned lamentation. The onomatopoeic compound verb also occurs at 3.674 (with the meaning 'bellow') *curuisque immugiit Aetna cauernis*; it is found first in extant literature in V. and is rare after him (*TLL* VII.1.499.17–33). **regia** reinforces the impression of a palace in a city.

39 niuei . . . Pallantis: *niueus* has strong connotations of lovely, radiant whiteness. By using the adj., V. aestheticises Pallas' corpse to generate pathos – felt by A. himself, through whom *niueus* is focalised – at the sight of such beauty snatched away prematurely. At the same time, the adj. suggests a loveliness that not even death could mar (so Tib. ad loc.). *niueus* also indicates the partly feminine beauty of the pretty young male (Putnam 1995: 37–8). This sets up the simile at 68–71(n.), and provides the first of several examples in *Aen.* 11 (particularly in the story of Camilla) where gender distinctions and identities are blurred. Feminising descriptions of male bodies killed in war occur in Homer; cf. *Il.* 11.573 and 15.316 χρόα λευκόν, 'white flesh/body', and see Reed 2007: 22–3.

40 leuique patens in pectore uulnus: the separation of *leuique* and *pectore* by *patens* and of *patens* and *uulnus* by *in pectore* reflects how the chest had been split open. **leuique . . . pectore:** absence of hair on the chest is a mark of young beauty. There is also a note of femininity: a smooth chest was commonly a mark of effeminacy in men (*OLD* s.v. leuis 2).

41 cuspidis Ausoniae: the gen. indicates the cause or source of the *uulnus*; cf. 2.436 *uulnere Ulixi.* On *Ausoniae* = 'Italian', see 58n. **lacrimis obortis:** also at 3.492, 4.30, and 6.867. Cf. *Il.* 18.235 (Achilles, seeing Patroclus on a bier) 'shedding hot tears' (δάκρυα θερμὰ χέων).

42–58 A.'s lament over Pallas. The chief model is *Il.* 18.324–42, where Achilles grieves over the death of Patroclus. A section within A.'s speech (49–52), however, derives from *Il.* 22.437–46, where Andromache prepares a bath for Hector, unaware that he had been killed. A.'s grief is mainly social and political in orientation and focused on Evander. His relationship to Pallas is understood in terms of the *contubernium*, in which an aristocratic father sent his son to serve with a commander on active duty. The commander stood *in loco parentis* and played a paternal role for his charge. A. bemoans that he failed in that role, because he was unable to keep his *contubernalis* Pallas safe, and hence that he betrayed the trust placed in him by Evander, thereby falling short of *fides* (see 55) and proving himself an unreliable ally. See, further, Intro. pp. 8–9, 10–11.

42–4 'was it you, wretched boy, that Fortune begrudged me, although she came propitiously, that you not see our kingdom nor be carried in triumph to your father's home?'

42 tene: emphatic by position, with *-ne* stressing the significant word. **miserande puer:** also at 6.882 (Marcellus) and 10.825 (Lausus). Dickey 2002: 192 notes that *puer* is most frequently an address to 'known, named boys unrelated to the speaker' and is often modified by terms of affection, praise, or pity. The noun here indicates not only affectionate pity but also a sense of quasi-parental responsibility, as at 12.942–3 *balteus et notis fulserunt cingula bullis | Pallantis pueri* (see Tarrant ad loc.). **cum laeta ueniret:** probably a concessive *cum*-clause, rather than circumstantial. *laeta* is in strong opposition to *miserande.*

43 inuidit . . . uideres: a verb frame with wordplay. **mihi:** dat. of the person grudged, with *te* at 42 an acc. of the thing grudged; a poetic construction in the Augustan period (*NLS* §59 n. 4). **ne:** best taken as introducing a substantive clause and a second thing grudged A. (a rare but possible construction; see *TLL* VII.2.195.48–55), in apposition to *tene*; *ne* thus operates like *ne* in a clause of prevention. The alternative is that *ne* introduces a purpose clause.

44 neque: the use of *neque* for *neue/neu* is common among Augustan poets and Livy (not in Cicero, Caesar, or Sallust; H–S 536). **uictor uehERERE:** alliteration, as at 45, 46, and, most strikingly, 47, to convey powerful emotion. The language strongly suggests a Roman triumph; cf. 8.714 *Caesar, triplici inuectus . . . triumpho,* Ov. *Fast.* 6.724 *uectus es in niueis postmodo uictor equis,* Liv. 10.7.10, 31.20.2, 38.44.10. **paternas:** emphatic immediately before A. turns his attention to Evander.

45–6: promissa parenti | discedens dederam: cf. Catul. 64.139 (Ariadne laments Theseus' betrayal) *at non haec quondam . . . promissa dedisti.* At 8.536–40, A. assures Evander on the day he departs that he will overwhelm the Latin forces. He does not promise the king anything about Pallas. Perhaps he misremembers here; perhaps he thinks a promise for the boy's safe and triumphant return was implicit in his assurance; or perhaps he gave the promise 'offstage' (see 152–3n.). Cf. *Il.* 18.324–7, where Achilles recalls the assurance he gave Patroclus' father Menoetius that, after he had sacked Troy, he would bring Patroclus home with a share of the spoils. Achilles, however, quickly shifts his attention from Menoetius to Patroclus (whereas A. does the opposite, moving from son to father, his main subject), and he expresses none of the guilt towards Menoetius that A. does towards Evander.

46 complexus: cf. 8.558–9 (Evander clasps Pallas' hand as he departs) *tum pater Euandrus dextram complexus euntis | haeret, inexpletus lacrimans.*

47 mitteret . . . moneret: cf. 6.812 *missus in imperium magnum*, on Numa. *imperium* refers primarily to A.'s command of the army; Evander sent A. to lead a great force and to fight a difficult foe. Yet *magnum* also suggests Rome's *imperium sine fine* (1.278; cf. 6.781–2 *illa incluta Roma | imperium terris . . . aequabit*); A. goes forth to secure a victory that will lead ultimately to the great Roman empire. Evander's warning implies affectionnate case for A., although the safety of Pallas would have been foremost on his mind; that affection and his implied advice to him (i.e. join battle carefully, and prepare for a difficult fight) give his reported farewell qualities of a *propemptikon*, or speech of farewell to a departing traveller (see Cairns 1972: 8–10).

48 acris: an unelided spondaic word in the first foot is rare in *Aen.*, appearing in roughly 2 per cent of lines (see Austin on 1.30, Norden, Anh. VIII). The spondee can emphasise a word, as it does here. **dura:** V. tends to avoid spondaic disyllables comprising the fourth foot, which produce coincidence of ictus and word accent (he much prefers clash of ictus and accent in that foot, to avoid, with the fifth and sixth feet, coincidence throughout the second half of a line). When such disyllables do appear, emphasis is a common aim (Austin on 1.1). *dura* joins with *acris* to underline the strength of the men whom A. and Pallas had been sent to face (see further 518n.). *durus*, indicating hardiness, is used to describe the Italians at 5.730, 7.504, and 9.603; the Trojans are *duri* in this sense at 9.468.

49–52 Evander vainly makes vows and piles up offerings to the gods for Pallas' safe return, not knowing that his son is dead. A moment of deep pathos, as A. imagines Evander's desperate piety and contrasts the father's hopes with the stark reality of the son's death. The focus on religion is missing from V.'s model, *Il.* 22.437–46.

49 nunc marks a pointed contrast, from Evander's warning to his current ignorance of how his warnings have been proved justified. **ille quidem:** *quidem* underlines *ille*; the phrase is in contrast with *nos* at 51. *quidem* signals that the statement at 49–50 needs a second statement (starting at 51) to make its meaning complete (Kroon 2011: 185–6) and marks the contrast between them. Cf. 12.234–6 *ille quidem . . . | . . . | nos.* **spe multum captus inani:** *captus* = 'deluded' (*OLD* 20). Virgil develops *Il.* 22.445, where Andromache is called νηπίη ('foolish', 'unwitting'). Cf. 10.627 (Jupiter to Juno) *spes pascis inanis.*

50–1 Adversative asyndeton (omission of a conjunction), emphasising the sharp difference between Evander's hopes and reality.

50 fors et 'perhaps too'. *fors* is adverbial; on this use, see Austin on 2.139. **cumulatque** 'and piles high'.

51 iuuenem exanimum et: the double elision reflects the emotional distress of the speaker (Dainotti 2015: 172).

51–2 nil iam caelestibus ullis | debentem 'not now owing any debt to the gods above'; because he is now dead, Pallas has no more obligations to fulfil. Cf. Sil. 15.370–2 (on the death of Marcellus) *circumdata postquam | nil restare uidet uirtus, quod debeat ultra | iam superis.*

52 uano . . . honore: the honour of a funeral is empty because Pallas will be unaware of it; presumably, too, because it does nothing for the boy and cannot change what happened to him. Cf. 6.885–6 (funeral rites for Marcellus) *inani | munere.* A.'s pessimism contrasts with 23 above.

53 The spondaic rhythm produces a weighty, sombre effect, as does the number of words; V. recurrently uses five-word lines in that manner (see Winbolt 1903: 226–7). The preceding and following lines are also predominantly spondaic and of five words. **infelix:** often associated with death in *Aen.* (see Hardie on 9.390), and used to describe the dead or dying and those who mourn the dead. The latter use of the adj. occurs at 85, of Acoetes, and at 175, again of Evander. *infelix* also has a sense here of 'unfruitful', because Evander outlives his child and, thus, no longer has an heir. **funus crudele:** cf. 8.849, where Evander asks the gods to end his *crudelem uitam* (*crudelis* proleptic) if Pallas was going to be killed. **uidebis:** cf. 6.873–4 *uel quae, Tiberine, uidebis | funera,* on Marcellus' funeral.

54–5 hi . . . | . . . fides? bitterly rueful rhetorical questions, full of self-recrimination. Anaphoric *hi* and *haec* sharpen the emotion.

54 nostri reditus: *nostri* is a true plural, referring to A. and Pallas returning together to Pallanteum in triumph. *reditus* suggests the grand ceremonial of the return of great figures from battle; on the *reditus,* see Sumi 2005: 35–41. Cf. 10.435–6 *sed quis* [Pallas and Lausus] *Fortuna negarat | in patriam reditus.* **triumphi:** cf. *Il.* 18.326–7 (Achilles on Menoetius) 'I said to him that I would bring back his glorious son to Opoeis when I had sacked Troy, with the share of the spoil that would come to him' (φῆν δέ οἱ εἰς Ὀπόεντα περικλυτὸν υἱὸν ἀπάξειν | Ἴλιον ἐκπέρσαντα, λαχόντα τε ληΐδος αἶσαν).

55 haec mea magna fides? *fides* is a deeply resonant word in Roman culture (see Intro. pp. 8–9). A. ultimately shows *fides* to the king by killing Turnus to avenge the death of Pallas, as Evander enjoins him to do (cf. 178–9, with Intro. pp. 12–14, Gladhill 2016: 143–4). But here, before that duty is laid on A., he bitterly laments his inability to meet his obligations as a reliable ally to Evander. Cf. 6.346 (A. to Palinurus, on Apollo) *en haec promissa fides est?* **Euandre:** the pause at the trochaic caesura in the fifth foot is relatively rare in V. (Austin on 4.28); the effect is to emphasise the name. V. has *Euandrus* rather than *Euander* everywhere (here, 8.100, 8.185, 8.313, 8.545, 8.558) but at 10.515.

55–6 pudendis | uulneribus: the 'shameful wounds' would be those in the back, showing that Pallas had fled the enemy.

56 pulsum 'routed'.

56–7 dirum | . . . funus: surely Pallas' death (contra C–N, Page, Williams, and Fratantuono ad loc., who think the reference is to Evander's); if Pallas had survived through cowardice, Evander would wish him dead, which would be a dreadful thing for a father to want.

57 pater. ei mihi: a bucolic diaeresis, or the coincidence, with a grammatical pause, of the end of the fourth foot with the end of a word. There are sixty-one such diaereses in *Aen.*; the tendency from V. onward is for the word that ends the fourth foot to be a pyrrhic (see Gransden on 8.198). The diaeresis emphasises both *pater* (also emphatic as the last word in its sentence) and *ei mihi,* with its anguished emotion.

57–8 ei . . . | . . . Iule: for the thought, cf. A.R. 2.774–5 (Lycus on Heracles) 'O my friends, what a man whose help you have been deprived of as you undertake such a long voyage to Aeetes' (ὦ φίλοι, οἵου φωτὸς ἀποπλαγχθέντες ἀρωγῆς | πείρετ' ἐς Αἰήτην τόσσον πλόον).

58 praesidium, Ausonia, et: emotional elision, as at 51. *praesidium* is largely avoided in poetry (only here in V., never in Catullus, Tibullus, Propertius, Lucan, Valerius Flaccus, Silius Italicus), but does occur at Hor. *Carm.* 1.1.2 (Maecenas) *et praesidium et dulce decus meum.* **Ausonia:** I take the word as a voc., like Mynors and Horsfall; Conte understands a nom. and hence does not have the comma after *praesidium. Ausones* (Lat. Aurunci) was originally the Gk name for an Oscan-speaking Italian tribe. V. follows Greek practice, including that of Hellenistic poets (Call. fr. 238.28 Pf., A.R. 4.660), in using *Ausonia/Ausonius* for Italy and Italians; there are forty examples in V., with *G.* 2.385 the first extant occurrence in Latin. See Fordyce on 7.39, Horsfall on 7.623. Cf. *cuspidis Ausoniae* at

41. An Italian weapon killed a boy who would have been a great protector of Italy; this suggests the waste of civil war. **quantum:** emotional repetition. **Iule:** the name Iulus is found in *Aen.* almost as often as Ascanius (thirty-five for Iulus to forty-one for Ascanius), and always in the final position except at 12.185. See Rogerson 2017: 10–11, 37–56. Having lamented a father's loss of his son, A. thinks now of his own boy; to A., Pallas would have been an older protector for Ascanius, which means that his death is not only a present pain but also a blow to the future. A. also thinks of Ascanius and Pallas together because he is the father of the former and, in the *contubernium*, the quasi-father of the latter. On fathers and sons in *Aen.*, see Lee 1979.

59–99 FUNERAL PROCESSION OF PALLAS

His lament complete, A. orders a procession to bring Pallas' body back to Pallanteum and Evander. The cortège reflects A.'s deep care for Pallas and his deep respect for Evander; it also compensates, however inadequately, for his guilt. A. has grieved that he will not send Pallas back to his father in triumph (44, 54). The procession he orders, however, is a magnificent military spectacle that incorporates triumphal elements; see Intro. p. 11. A. thus sends Pallas back home to Evander as a *decus magnum* (cf. 10.507 (an apostrophe to Pallas) *o dolor atque decus magnum rediture parenti*). The Homeric model is the armed procession, on foot and in chariots, arranged by Achilles for the dead Patroclus at *Il.* 23.128–37. There are historical parallels, too, in the absorption of military processions and triumphal elements into funerals in Rome, on which see Flower 1996: 100–2, 123–4, and 244 and Beard 2007: 285–6.

59 haec ubi defleuit: the verb *deflere* is nearly a technical term for lament (Kenney on Lucr. 3.907). Cf. 6.220 (the funeral of Misenus) *tum membra toro defleta reponunt.* The prefix *de-* signifies the completion of the action, 'wept his fill'. **miserabile corpus:** cf. *Ecl.* 5.22 (Daphnis) *corpus miserabile.*

60 toto lectos ex agmine 'men chosen from the entire army', i.e. representatives from the Arcadians, Etruscans, and Trojans alike. An honour guard; see Flower 1996: 100–1 on such *lecti* at the funerals of Sulla in 78 BCE and of Marcellus in 23 BCE.

61 mille: cf. μυρίοι ('countless') at *Il.* 23.134, quoted at 93n. **qui supremum comitentur honorem** 'so that they might attend the last rites'; a rel. clause of purpose. The language is close to that at 52 and 76. There is an unusually extensive amount of self-repetition in lines 61–99. Here, V. appears to echo 52 deliberately, to pick up on the content of the earlier line and to create a sense of slow solemnity.

62 intersintque 'share in', with the dative *lacrimis.* **solacia:** acc. in apposition to the preceding part of the sentence, possibly a syntactical Grecism (Harrison on 10.310–11, Adams 2013: 237–9).

62–3 solacia luctus | exigua ingentis: interlocking word order with juxtaposition of two terms of significant contrast, underscoring how unequal to the pain the attempted consolation will be. The fourth-century Ausonius imitates at *Parent.* 16.11 *parua ingentis luctus solacia.*

63 sed: the particle is postponed to second position in its clause. Postposition of particles was a neoteric mannerism, in imitation of Hellenistic practice. It was often for metrical convenience, but could be used to particular effect; in this case it allows the important word *misero* to stand first in its clause. For further examples of the postposition of *sed,* see 631 and 816. See Austin on 4.33, Norden, Anh. III.B.3, Thomas on Hor. *Carm.* 4.4.33.

64 haud segnes: litotes, emphasising the great speed at which the act is done. By the first century BCE and Augustan era, the archaic *haud* is primarily poetic (Livy and, later, Tacitus are exceptional among prose authors in their recurrent use of it, with over twenty examples in each) and belongs particularly to epic. See Axelson 1945: 91–2, Tränkle 1960: 45–6. **cratis et molle feretrum** 'the pliant bier of wicker-work'; hendiadys. The *cratis* is comprised of the *arbuteae uirgae* ('arbutus shoots') and *uimen quernum* ('oak switch') at 65. There is a contrast drawn between pastoral innocence (also suggested by the flower-simile at 68–71) and the violence of war, which implies innocence lost; see Wofford 1992: 188.

65 arbuteis: the adj. in *-eus* denotes material, 'of arbutus'. The word occurs first in extant Latin at *G.* 1.166 *arbuteae crates.* It probably originates with V.; he appears to have coined *-eus* adjs. freely. It has poetic colour, as often with such adjs., while also being metrically convenient; it is rare after V. (cf. Ov. *Met.* 1.104, 13.820, *Fast.* 6.155, Stat. *Theb.* 1.584; *TLL* II.1.430.79–83). On adjs. in *-eus,* see Ross 1969: 60–3. **uimine querno:** cf. Stat. *Theb.* 1.583–4 *uimine querno | texta domus.* Statius contrasts the high birth of Crotopus' grandson and the rustic setting in which he lives: *non tibi digna, puer, generis cunabula tanti | gramineos dedit herba toros* (*Theb.* 1.582–3). This suggests imitation of V. that picks up on his contrast between Pallas and his bier (see 67n.).

66 exstructosque describes the action of making by fitting things together (*OLD* 2). **obtentu:** a word that scans as a molossus (three long syllables) is placed after the principal caesura in the third foot also at 67 (*sublimem*) and 68 (*demessum*). The repetition recalls Catullus, for whom this rhythm was a mannerism; of the first twenty-one lines of Catul. 64, twelve have it, and it appears in three consecutive lines at 64.38–40. V.'s repeated pattern sets the stage for his imitation of a Catullan simile (see 68–71n.). **obtentu . . . inumbrant:** the foliage creates a canopy effect, with a hint of pastoral *umbra*; perhaps, too, V. evokes the wreath customarily placed on the head of the deceased (Toynbee 1971: 44).

67 agresti sublimem: *sublimem* = 'aloft', but also 'noble'. With the second meaning, there is sharp juxtaposition with *agresti*: a noble youth lies on a rustic bier. **stramine:** straw or some kind of rustic foliage upon which the corpse lies when set on the bier. Cf. Stat. *Theb.* 6.56 (a bier) *ima uirent agresti stramina cultu*, in clear imitation of V. *stramen* is not found before V. and may be coined by him from the older *stramentum*. **ponunt:** probably *simplex* for *reponunt*; cf. 6.220, quoted at 59n.

68–71 The simile renders Pallas a 'flower' upon the vegetation of the bier; the suggestion is of the 'flower of youth', ἥβης ἄνθος/*flos* (*aetatis, iuuentutis*, or sim.; *OLD* s.v. flos 8, 8b) (Heuzé 1985: 290–5). Cf. *Il.* 8.306–8, where Gorgythion, killed in battle by Hector, bows his head to one side like a poppy laden with fruit and spring rain. But the more operative comparison is with the simile at *Aen.* 9.435–7, on the death of Euryalus: *purpureus ueluti cum flos succisus aratro | languescit moriens, lassoue papauera collo | demisere caput pluuia cum forte grauantur.* The principal model there and here is Catul. 62.43–7 (though cf. Catul. 11.22–4), which compares a girl who has lost her virginity to a cut flower that has lost its bloom. Through imitation of Catullus, the killing of the young warriors is associated with sexual defloration, implicitly on the wedding night (Catullus' poem is a wedding hymn). This activates a link between battle and sex that goes back to Homer (e.g. *Il.* 13.291 and 17.228); the connection between death in war and the loss of virginity is equally old (see Fowler 1987: 185–98). The imagery points to the violation of Pallas' feminised beauty (see 39n., 40n.) while also underscoring the untimely quality of the youth's premature death upon first entering the adult world of battle (cf. 10.508 (on Pallas) *haec te prima dies bello dedit, haec eadem aufert*); he will not live to marry and, it is understood from the allusion to sex, have children. Gender binaries are blurred; while Pallas showed *uirtus* in the fight (cf. 27), he has been penetrated and deflowered like Catullus' maiden. 'The shadow of a feminine persona figuratively registers the loss of [Pallas' and Euryalus'] adult male potential; the erotic light that falls on them in a sense confirms their now permanent status as boys' (Reed 2007: 23). For further discussion, see Mitchell 1992: 224–30, Putnam 1995: 38, Petrini 1997: 66–7, and Nelis 2001: 321. There is a contrast between the deflowered Pallas and the virgin Pallas Athena (cf. Henderson ad loc.); the goddess' power in war also contrasts with Pallas' death.

68 qualem . . . florem: for *qualis* . . . *flos*; the words are attracted into the acc. by *iuuenem* . . . *sublimem* in the previous line. *qualis* (with and without correlative *talis*) commonly introduces similes in V. The framing pattern, with agreeing noun and adj., was a marked feature of Catullus' neoteric style (see Norden, Anh. III.A) and may represent further imitation of him. **uirgineo . . . pollice:** cf. Catul. 62.43 *tenui* [*carptus*] . . . *ungui*. With *uirgineus* (before V. at Catul. 66.14 and 67.28 and Lucr. 1.87), V. refers to a virgin in a simile comparing Pallas to a virgin; there is a contrast between the idyllic innocence of the girl who plucks the flower and the 'deflowered' Pallas. **demessum:** the verb is found only here in V. There is a possible debt to *demetit* at Catul. 64.354 *flauentia demetit arua*; Catullus' line occurs in a simile comparing an act of military violence (Achilles' killing of Trojans) to reaping.

69 V. moves from the general (*florem*) to the specific, a typical sequence (see Hardie on 9.679–82). **mollis uiolae** 'the tender violet'; cf. *Ecl.* 5.38 *molli uiola*. The flower (not our violet) was used to deck graves and other memorials to the dead (*OLD* 1b). **languentis hyacinthi:** possibly a lily of some kind (a purple martagon?) or an iris; see *OLD* 1, Edgeworth 1992: 28. The flower recalls the mythological Hyacinthus, a youth whom Apollo accidentally killed (cf. Ov. *Met.* 10.162–219). V. has quadrisyllabic endings only when using a Gk word, as here and at 217 (*hymenaeos*) and 255 (*hymenaeis*), or for some special effect (see e.g. 4.215, 4.667). Often the ending is accompanied by a metrical irregularity. Here the short final vowel in *languentis* is lengthened in arsis (the stressed syllable of the foot), reproducing a Gk rhythm found in Catullus (62.4, 64.20, 66.11). Cf. 7.398, 10.720, *Ecl.* 6.53, and *G.* 4.137. See also 111n.

70 'whose brilliance and beauty have still not yet departed'.

71 There is an unstated adversative, to create a contrast with the previous line. A comma at the end of the previous line (so Mynors and Horsfall) is appropriate, rather than a semi-colon (so Conte).

72–7 A. brings out two *uestes*, or cloaks, given to him by Dido (cf. 4.263–4, quoted at 72n.) in which to wrap Pallas' body. Cf. 6.221 (purple *uestes* that enwrap Misenus' corpse) *purpureasque super uestes, uelamina nota*. With them, A. honours Pallas; he bestows on the boy precious objects from a great queen, which stand out against the rustic bier. The cloaks link Dido and Pallas, who follows Dido as a casualty of A.'s fated journey. This connects two deaths that produce in A. a similar mix of sorrow, regret, and guilt (cf. 6.455–68). In addition, the cloaks are erotic objects, given their ties to Dido. The point is very likely not that A. was sexually attracted to A. as he was to the queen (see 29–41n.). Instead, the erotic undercurrent after 68–71 equates Pallas and Dido as (feminised and feminine) figures in whom death and sexuality are joined; in Pallas' case, his metaphorical initial sexual experience is itself the agent of death. Fratantuono 2007: 325 intriguingly suggests that Dido had woven the two cloaks for A. and Ascanius; might, therefore, A. wrap a dead surrogate son in a robe woven for his son? On the funeral robe, see also Gross 2003–4: 142–4. Gifts from Dido appear as well at 5.571–2 (a horse that the queen had given Ascanius) and 9.266 (a bowl that Ascanius promises to Nisus). Pallas had departed for war *chlamyde . . . conspectus* (8.588); he now returns from it, a casualty of the conflict, wrapped in striking *uestes.*

72 auroque ostroque rigentis 'stiff with their gold and purple', i.e. with the gold woven into the purple cloth. *ostrum* indicates a valuable purple dye whose best-known seat of production was Tyre, Dido's original home (see Pease on 4.134). A. anticipates the Roman practice of wrapping the dead in purple (see Austin on 6.221); yet the purple cloak for the dead is also Homeric (*Il.* 24.796). Cf. 1.648 (a gift from A. to Dido) *pallam signis auroque rigentem* (with possible intratextual wordplay between *pallam* and Pallas), 4.263–4 *quae munera Dido | fecerat, et tenui telas discreuerat auro.* For Dido's gift of a *uestis* to A., cf. A.R. 3.1204–6, where Jason dons a dark cloak given to him by Hypsipyle as a memento of their lovemaking (cf. A.R. 4.427–8).

73 laeta laborum 'joyful in her labours'. *laborum* is gen. of the 'sphere within which', also known as gen. of respect; *laetus* with the gen. is a rare construction (*TLL* VII.2.886.31–9), lending a Grecising patina (Görler, *EV* II.266). Cf. Sil. 15.569 *laeta laboris* and Claud. *IV Cons. Hon.* 394 *laetusque laborum.* Poignant irony, since the reader is aware of the fleetingness of Dido's joy. *laeta* is in strong contrast to repeated *maestus.*

74 quondam: another pathetic detail, indicating a past happy time now gone. **Sidonia Dido:** a virtual formula (cf. 1.446, 1.613, 9.266). But the adj. also alludes to Sidonian purple dye after *ostro* at 72; Sidon was famous for its purple-dyeing industry, and Sidonian purple was a luxury item (see Pease on 4.134).

75 '(which Sidonian Dido) had made, interweaving [lit. separating] the cloth with fine threads of gold'. The line is repeated from 4.264 (quoted at 72n.). We are by all appearance to imagine that the cloak described at 4.262–4 is one of the *geminae uestes* here. **et:** epexegetic (*OLD* 11, K–S II.13); the clause that follows details how Dido made the *uestes.*

76 supremum . . . honorem: in apposition to *unam,* 'as a last honour'. *supremum* is in significant juxtaposition with *iuueni,* to contrast Pallas' youth and his obsequies.

76–7 A. wraps Pallas' body in one of the two *uestes* mentioned at 72. What of the other *uestis*? In all likelihood, V. elliptically describes at 77 the veiling of Pallas' head with the second cloak. It would be entirely in character for V. to link the two actions through parataxis and to ask his reader to supply 'and with the other' (so Henry ad loc.). The alternative is that A. uses one *uestis* for Pallas and keeps the other, so that he might continue to remember Dido by it (Paratore ad loc., Lyne 1989: 187–9). But it weakens the sombre sense of lost happiness at 73 and 74 if A. tries to hold on to a token of his past with the queen. The question of how many *uestes* A. used with Pallas recalls a Homeric problem that was recognised in antiquity (Schol. T, *Il.* 24.580, Schol. A, *Il.* 24.588): at *Il.* 24.580 there are two cloaks (δύο φάρεα) and a tunic (χιτῶν) for Achilles to wrap Hector's body, but at 24.588 only one of each. Perhaps V. omitted a connective like 'and with the other' as a nod towards that ambiguity. On V.'s possible familiarity with debates in ancient Homeric scholarship, see Schlunk 1974.

77 arsurasque comas: pathetic prolepsis, or 'flash-forward' to a later event. **obnubit** 'veils'. The rare verb (*TLL* IX.130.48–74) occurs only here in V., its first appearance in extant Latin verse. It has an archaic tint; cf. the old legal formula *caput obnubito* (for the veiling of criminals before punishment; see Cic. *Rab. Perd.* 13, Liv. 1.26.6). Putnam 1995: 40 sees a connection to the veiling of a bride and suggests that Pallas' funeral is 'in some sense his marriage'. This would vary the imagery of 68–71; defloration suggests the loss of virginity on a wedding night. It would also implicitly contrast with Pallas' tragic fate to die young and unwedded (cf. Nelis 2001: 321); Pallas 'marries' death and consequently will marry no other.

78–80 A. includes enemy spoils in the funeral procession. This assimilates the cortège to a triumph; see 59–99n.

78 Laurentis: used of Latinus' forces generally, against whom the *pugna* was waged. Cf. 909, 6.891, 8.537, and 12.137. At 7.63, Latinus is said to have given his settlers the name Laurentes. **praemia:** synonymous with *praedam* in the following line. O'Hara 2017: 229 suggests that V. alludes to the etymological connection between the words, drawn by Varro (*praemium a praeda, L.* 5.178).

79 aggerat 'piles up in heaps'; also at 342, 4.197, *G.* 3.556. The verb is first found in V. and is quite possibly his coinage; see *TLL* 1.1311.70–84.

80 equos et tela: the horses and arms were to be burned on the funeral pyre. Cf. *Il.* 23.171–2, where Achilles sacrifices four horses on Patroclus' pyre. **quibus:** abl. with *spoliauerat,* a kind of abl. of separation. Cf. 5.224, 6.353, 12.935. **spoliauerat:** it is preferable to understand an abrupt shift of subject, from A. to Pallas, so that the three-line description of the arms accompanying the cortège closes with those that reflect Pallas' own *uirtus* and 'triumphal' military prowess. We must imagine Pallas winning the arms during his *aristeia* (see 664–724n.) in the previous day's battle (10.380–425), although V. does not show this and only has Pallas vowing a trophy to Father Tiber (10.423).

81–2 In his rage at the killing of Pallas, A. had taken eight prisoners at 10.517–20 to sacrifice them as funeral offerings to Pallas' shade. Here they are led out to join the procession and, ultimately, to die. Cf. Achilles, who captures twelve young Trojans and kills them as blood price for Patroclus' death (*Il.* 21.26–32, 23.175–83). Human sacrifice stood apart from forms of sanctioned violence in late-republican and early-imperial Rome, including the killing of prisoners of war and of vanquished leaders after a triumph, and was repeatedly viewed as un-Roman. See e.g. Cic. *Font.* 31, Liv. 22.57.6, Str. 4.1.13, with Lintott 1968: 39–40, Schultz 2010. (Earlier Roman attitudes had evidently been different; see DServ. ad 3.67 and Plin. *Nat.* 30.3.12, who notes that a senatorial decree forbidding human sacrifice was passed in 97 BCE. See also Beard, North, and Price 1998: 1.81. For evidence of an unusual human sacrifice later, in Pliny the Elder's time, see Plin. *Nat.* 28.3.12.) Therefore V. must have intended A.'s actions to unsettle (as they did his late-antique reader Lactantius (*Inst.* 5.10.3–9)). Cf. *Il.* 23.176, where Achilles' sacrifice is described as a 'grim task' (κακὰ . . . ἔργα). For further discussion, see Intro. pp. 7–9.

81 uinxerat et post terga manus: modelled on *Il.* 21.30 'and [Achilles] tied their hands behind them with well-cut thongs' (δῆσε δ' ὀπίσσω χεῖρας ἐυτμήτοισιν ἱμᾶσι). Cf. 2.57 (Sinon) *manus iuuenem interea post terga reuinctum.* Sinon claims to have escaped from being sacrificed (2.116–36); by contrast, the captives here will not escape their fate. **quos:** the antecedent (*eorum*) must be supplied. **mitteret:** rel. clause of purpose, revealing A.'s continued intention to sacrifice the prisoners. For *mitto* used of sending funeral offerings, see *OLD* 9d.

81–2 umbris | inferias: cf. 10.519 *inferias quos immolet umbris. umbris* is poetic plural (as at 10.519), referring to the shade of Pallas.

82 inferias 'as offerings'. **caeso . . . sanguine:** the participle is transferred from the victims to the blood (*caeso* = *caesorum*). **sparsurus:** while A. does not directly sacrifice the prisoners, V. uses the active participle to lay the deed at his feet: he is the one killing the men, because he is the commander who orders it.

83 indutosque . . . truncos: trophies, made from the arms of those whom Pallas had killed (see 80n., 172). *indutosque* links the trophies to A.'s own offering to Mars (cf. *induit* at 6 above).

84 inimicaque nomina figi: labels with names are affixed to the trophies to show the fighters whom Pallas had killed. These resemble *tituli* in triumphs; cf. Prop. 3.4.16, Ov. *Tr.* 4.2.20, Tac. *Ann.* 2.18.

85–7 Focus shifts to Pallas' aged squire Acoetes. V. alternates perspectives on the procession, moving from its martial, triumphal elements (78–84, 88, 91–3) to the grief of those close to Pallas (both human and animal) (85–7, 89–90, 94–9).

85 infelix: the adj. links Acoetes to Evander (see 53n.). **aeuo confectus** 'worn out by age'. Acoetes must be helped along (*ducitur*) in the procession because he is old; it is clear, however, that grief exacerbates the effects of age.

86 pectora . . . ora: cf. 4.673 and 12.871 *unguibus ora soror foedans et pectora pugnis*. *nunc* is repeated for emotional effect; assonance in *pectora . . . ora* adds further emotional colour. Scratching the face in grief was associated with women (cf. Cic. *Tusc.* 3.62, DServ. ad 3.67; see, further, Pease on 4.673). Perhaps V. assigned woman-like behaviour to Acoetes to anticipate Evander, who takes on a maternal role when lamenting Pallas (see 139–81n.).

87 'and he throws himself down headlong, full-length to the ground'. Cf. 8.584, where Evander collapses after bidding Pallas farewell: *famuli conlapsum in tecta ferebant.* Ribbeck posits a lacuna after this line, unnecessarily. **sternitur:** middle voice (*OLD* 5); cf. 3.509 *sternimur optatae gremio telluris.*

88 Rutulo perfusos sanguine currus: surely Pallas' chariot (with *currus* thus a poetic plural), unmentioned in *Aen.* 10, and not the two-horse chariot of Rhoeteus, whom Pallas kills at 10.399–404 as Rhoeteus speeds by on the vehicle. The narrative moves from Pallas' squire to Pallas' chariot to Pallas' horse (89–90) to Pallas' arms (91). The blood-strewn chariot is Homeric (*Il.* 11.534–7, 20.499–502). Cf., too, the chariots (not blood-strewn) in the procession for Patroclus at *Il.* 23.130–2.

89 post: adv., 'after that'. **bellator equus** 'war horse'; also at 10.891 and *G.* 2.145, and not found before V. The agent noun *bellator* is used adjectivally; cf. *Ecl.* 8.13 *uictrices lauros*. Perhaps V. had in mind Theoc. *Id.* 15.51 πολεμισταὶ ἵπποι (cf. Str. 15.1.29 πολεμιστής ἵππος) or Call. *H.* 6.109 πολεμήιος ἵππος. **positis insignibus** 'with its trappings taken off', on the occasion of mourning. *Pace* Serv. and Williams ad loc., the trappings need not be confined to *phalerae*, figured bosses worn on the heads or breasts of horses (cf. 5.310, 9.359, 9.458); cf. 7.277–9. **Aethon:** Gk Αἴθων, the name of one of Hector's horses (*Il.* 8.185; also the name assumed by Odysseus at *Od.* 19.183). It means 'hot', 'fiery' (as well as 'tawny'); V. presumably uses it to imply the creature's energy and fighting spirit.

90 The mourning horse derives from *Il.* 17.426–55, where Patroclus' horses weep for him and Zeus consoles them. Cf. Mezentius' horse Rhoebus at 10.860, which grieves (*maerentem*) with and for him. Pliny the Elder attests to horses that mourn and sometimes shed tears for their masters at *Nat.* 8.157, and Suetonius (*Jul.* 81.2) records the story that Julius Caesar's horses wept for him. Cf. *Ecl.* 5.25–8, where animals, including moaning lions, grieve over the death of Daphnis, a possible allusion to Caesar's horses (Clausen on *Ecl.* 5.26). **guttis . . . grandibus** 'big teardrops'. The language recalls Homeric θαλερὸν δάκρυ, 'big tears' (e.g. *Il.* 6.496, 24.9, and 24.794). Cf. *G.* 2.245 *grandes ibunt per uimina guttae*. **umectat . . . ora:** cf. Lucr. 1.920 *lacrimis salsis umectent ora*.

91–2 nam cetera Turnus | uictor habet: emotional force via economical understatement; the enjambment also contributes to the emotion. At 10.495–500, V. describes Turnus stripping Pallas only of his baldric, but here he indicates that he took everything from the boy except his spear and helmet.

92 phalanx: the noun also appears at 2.254, 6.489, 12.277, 12.544, 12.551, and 12.662; it occurs first in extant poetry in V., who likes it for different kinds of military array (Austin on 2.254). **Teucrique:** the name for the Trojans from Teucer, king of Teucria in the Troad, father-in-law of Dardanus, and called by Anchises the earliest ancestor of the Trojans (3.107–9 *maximus unde pater . . . | Teucrus Rhoeteas primum est aduectus ad oras | optauitque locum regno*). Cf. DServ. ad 1.38, Apollod. 3.12.1, D.S. 4.75. **sequuntur:** probably *simplex* for either *exsequuntur* or *prosequuntur*.

93 omnes: to be taken with both *Tyrrhenique* and *Arcades*, and probably with *Teucrique*. The variant *duces* seems designed to eliminate the echo of *omnis* in the following line; the influence of 171 *Tyrrhenique duces, Tyrrhenum exercitus omnis* and 835 *Tyrrhenique duces* is evident. The group of soldiers is probably to be identified with the *toto lectos ex agmine* | *mille uiros* at 60–1, thus creating a frame for the description of the cortège; all the men who comprise the honour guard advance. Cf. *Il.* 23.133–4 'in front were the charioteers, and after them a cloud of infantry followed, countless' (πρόσθε μὲν ἱππῆες, μετὰ δὲ νέφος εἵπετο πεζῶν, | μυρίοι). **uersis . . . armis:** probably weapons turned upside down in mourning (Alessio 1993: 56), as fasces were at *Cons. Liu.* 141–2 *quos primum uidi fasces, in funere uidi,* | *et uidi euersos*, Tac. *Ann.* 3.2.2 *uersi fasces*, rather than shields turned back to front. Cf. Stat. *Theb.* 6.214 (rites at a pyre) *uersis ducunt insignibus ipsi.* **Arcades:** the final syllable is short in this Gk loanword (also at 142 and 835).

94 'after the entire line of his companions had advanced a long way ahead'. **praecesserat:** the cortège advances far ahead of A., who, it appears, was at its rear and escorted it for a time.

95 substitit Aeneas 'Aeneas came to a halt'. *subsisto* is prosy; frequent in Caesar and Livy, it may have a military feel (Tarrant on 12.491).

96–8 A final farewell to Pallas, poignant and powerful in its brevity. The Homeric models are *Il.* 23.19–23 and 23.179–83, which V. strikingly adapts: whereas Achilles is full of rageful sorrow as he addresses Patroclus, A. speaks in sombre strains about the pain of war he must yet endure.

96–7 nos . . . | . . . uocant: cf. 3.493–4 (A.'s farewell to Helenus and Andromache) *uiuite felices, quibus est fortuna peracta* | *iam sua; nos alia ex aliis in fata uocamur.*

96 nos: emphatic by position, contrasting with *Palla* at the end of the following line.

97–8 salue . . . | . . . uale: cf. *Il.* 23.19 = 23.179 'hail, I bid you, o Patroclus, even in the house of Hades' (χαῖρέ μοι, ὦ Πάτροκλε, καὶ εἰν Ἀΐδαο δόμοισι) and Catul. 101.10 *atque in perpetuum, frater, aue atque uale.* **aeternum . . . | aeternumque:** advs.; adverbial *aeternum* is first attested in V.

97 mihi: ethic dat., indicating the person who regards the action with interest (*NLS* §66).

98 uale: A.'s speech ends mid-line, which gives added emphasis to the final words for dramatic and pathetic effect (see Tarrant on 12.45). **nec**

plura effatus: also at 8.443 and 12.896. *effari* is a poetic and augural word; V. uses the perfect participle repeatedly in speech-end formulas (741, 3.463, 6.197, 6.547, 7.135, 7.274, 8.443, 9.22, 9.644, 10.256, 10.299, 10.877, 12.896, *G.* 4.450).

98–9 ad altos | . . . ferebat: theme and variation, in which V. restates a first phrase in different language, thus describing the same action in different ways. A very common feature of Virgilian style.

99 The spondaic rhythm reflects A.'s slowness as he returns to camp in sadness. **tendebat . . . ferebat:** a verb-frame for closural effect, as elsewhere in V. (cf. e.g. 915). The imperfects are inceptive: 'he began to make his way . . .' **muros:** the camp is presented as a city; see 36n. Cf. 9.805 *Teucrorum moenibus altis.* **gressumque:** a framing echo of *gressum* at 29.

100–21 AENEAS AND THE LATIN EMBASSY

An embassy arrives from the Latins to seek a twelve-day truce so that they might bury the dead. V. takes his cue from *Il.* 7.381–411, where the Trojan Idaeus goes to the Greeks, offers them terms of peace, and seeks a burial truce (cf. 7.331–43, 7.365–78); Agamemnon (in agreement with Diomedes (7.400–2)) rejects the terms but grants the truce (7.406–11). A.'s humanity and magnanimity are on display as he accedes to the embassy's request. But he also aims to win his listeners over and to separate them from their leadership by showing sympathy with the Latin people, casting the Trojans as innocent, unwilling combatants, and blaming Latinus and Turnus for the conflict. See, further, Intro. pp. 9–10.

100 Iamque: a temporal transition word, common in V. It is used with different tenses to relate the time of the action to what precedes; here *aderant* shows that the *oratores* approach while A. was returning to his camp. **oratores** 'envoys', as at 331, 7.155, 8.153, and 8.505. A use of the noun from early Latin; see Skutsch on Enn. *Ann.* 202, and cf. Pl. *St.* 290, Cato *Orat.* 130.3, *Orig.* 22. **ex urbe Latina:** V. nowhere names Latinus' city, for unknown reasons; it is not to be identified as Laurentum (see Horsfall on 7.162).

101 uelati ramis oleae 'decked with olive branches'. The envoys carry *uelamenta*, or boughs of olive branches (symbols of peace and peace-seeking; cf. *G.* 2.425 *placitam Paci nutritor oliuam*) decked with fillets of wool; *uelamenta* were symbols of supplication. Cf. 7.153–4, 7.237, 8.116, 8.128, Pl. *Am.* 257 *uelatis manibus orant ignoscamus peccatum suom*, Liv. 30.36.4 *uelata infulis ramisque oleae Carthaginiensium occurrit nauis*, Ov. *Met.* 11.279

uelamenta manu praetendens supplice. **ueniamque** 'indulgence', as at 1.519 *orantes ueniam.*

102 fusa 'laid low, slain' (*OLD* 13b), although the sense 'scattered, strewn' is also felt with *per campos* and *iacebant.* **quae . . . iacebant:** the clause is explanatory and presents an assertable fact independent of the indirect command.

103 redderet: subjunctive in indirect command after *rogantes,* with *ut* omitted, and with sequence of tenses determined by *aderant.* (The same is true for *parceret* at 105.) **tumulo sineret succedere terrae** 'allow them to enter under a mound of earth'. *succedo* implies moving to a place of shelter (*OLD* 1); bodies that now lie exposed on the battlefield are to be given the shelter of a *tumulus.*

104 nullum: emphasised as an initial unelided spondaic word (see 48n.). **aethere cassis** 'bereft of the upper air'. For the periphrasis, cf. 2.85 (on the dead Palamedes) *cassum lumine.* That phrase derives from Lucretius (4.368 (on a shadow), 5.719 (on the moon), and 5.757 (on a solar eclipse; cf. also Lucr. 3.562 (a dead body) *cassum anima corpus*). *aether* = the upper air as distinct from the realm of the dead. The noun is poetic and philosophical–scientific.

105 quondam: creates a pathetic contrast between happy, hopeful past and painful present (cf. 74n.). In reality, only a few days have passed since the Trojans and Latins first met and Latinus pledged to make the Trojans allies and A. his son-in-law (7.259–73); see Della Corte, *EV* II.237–8. **hospitibus . . . socerisque uocatis:** cf. 7.264 (Latinus on A.) *si iungi hospitio properat sociusque uocari,* 7.202 (Latinus to the Trojan embassy) *ne fugite hospitium.* With the plural *soceris,* there is the suggestion that other Latins would have followed Latinus' example and married their daughters to Trojans.

106 bonus Aeneas: the epithet for A. appears only here and at 5.770 *quos bonus Aeneas dictis solatur amicis.* It indicates that A. will grant the envoys' request and points to his outstanding character and ethics in doing so (similarly, Gildenhard ad loc.); *bonus* thus functions as an editorial comment on A.'s behaviour. Within the dramatic world of the poem, A. is also trying to score diplomatic and rhetorical points; the sincerity of his wish that things could have been different is not to be doubted, but it belongs to someone who wants to impress on the Latins his inclination to mercy and peace, the excellence of his leadership, and the rightness of his cause. **haud aspernanda:** litotes; see 64n.

107 prosequitur 'responds to' (*OLD* 7). **uenia:** the noun answers *ueniamque* in 101: the embassy receives what it came to get. **haec insuper addit:** the formula also occurs at 12.358; cf. 2.593 *haec insuper addidit ore*, as well as 95 above. *insuper* = 'besides, in addition'.

108 quaenam: another initial unelided spondee, which stresses the emphatic interrogative. **fortuna indigna:** 'unmerited ill-fortune'.

109 implicuit 'entangled'. The form is metrically necessary instead of the alternative *implicauit.* **qui nos fugiatis amicos:** rel. clause of result.

110 pacem: emphatic; see 104n. and 108n. **Martis sorte peremptis** 'killed by the hazard of war'. Theme and variation with *exanimis*, with Mars a metonymy (the substitution of one word by another closely associated with it) for war.

111 oratis: possible wordplay with *oratores* at 100. The verb takes a double acc., the 'outer' object *pacem* and the 'inner' object *me* in the previous line (G–L §339). The short final syllable is lengthened in arsis before a marked pause. This metrical practice is common in Homer and is found in early Latin poets; V. continues it, but infrequently (fifty-four times, according to Austin on 1.308, and only here with a second-person verb) and, like Callimachus, just in syllables ending in a consonant (see Williams 1968: 687 n. 1). For further discussion, see Fordyce on 7.174, Tarrant on 12.13. Cf. 69n. **equidem** stresses the preceding *ego*; 'I for my part'. **uellem:** imperfect potential subjunctive, conveying that the opportunity for the event to take place has gone by (*NLS* §121, G–L § 258); it also implies A.'s regret at the non-fulfilment.

112 ueni substitutes for *uenissem* in the apodosis of a past contrary to fact conditional. The substituted mood is not a problem, but the tense is irregular, and the pluperfect is expected (*NLS* §200.iii, K–S II.401–5). The indicative seems due to rhetorical exaggeration, in which what might have happened is presented as a fact (*NLS* §200.III). **nisi . . . dedissent:** it is of course a key theme of the *Aen.* that the Trojans come to Italy on a fated mission to found their new homeland. A. refers to fate now to justify the Trojan presence in Italy and to imply that Latin resistance to their arrival contravenes higher dictates.

113–14 nostra . . . | hospitia could equally refer to the alliance offered by Latinus to the Trojans and to the alliance offered by the Trojans to the Latins (cf. 7.231–48); cf. 1.671–2 *Iunonia . . . hospitia* (a 'subjective' adj., 'Juno's hospitality') and 10.494–5 *Aeneia . . . hospitia* (an 'objective' adj., 'hospitality towards Aeneas'). On *hospitium*, see 165n.

114 et . . . armis: A. is correct that Latinus entrusted his fortunes to Turnus to lead the Italian forces. The king does so reluctantly and passively, however: he resists and rails against fighting the Trojans (7.585–99), fecklessly shuts himself up in his palace when confronted with his people's desire to fight (7.599–600), and refuses to open the gates of war (7.618–19). A. says nothing about Latinus' reluctance to abandon an alliance with the Trojans and his resistance to war. This is presumably out of ignorance: the Trojans had left Latinus before the spread of war fever and his response to it, and V. offers no sign that A. had somehow received intelligence about the king's opposition to the conflict. A. portrays the king's actions as a betrayal; he is critical of him and hostile towards him while displaying sympathy towards Latinus' forces in his effort to win them over.

115–18 A. proposes that single combat between Turnus and him would have been the best way to determine the outcome of the war. Cf. 218–21, 370, 374–5, and 442, and see Intro. p. 5.

115 aequius . . . fuerat 'it would have been more just'. The indicative is normal (G–L § 254). The construction with the pluperfect is less common than with the perfect (H–S 327–8). Cf. *Il. Lat.* 267–8 (Hector to Paris) *aequius aduersis tecum concurrat in armis | impiger Atrides.* **huic:** as if pointing to the carnage on the battlefield and the dead who, during the truce, are to be buried. **se opponere morti** 'to place himself in the path of [this] death'. Cf. 2.127 *opponere morti*; the phrase first occurs in V. (*TLL* IX.764.40–1).

116 manu 'by force of arms' (*OLD* 9f). **pellere:** *simplex* for *expellere.* **Teucros:** the collective noun stands in sharp contrast with *mecum* in the next line.

117 apparat 'plans to'. **his . . . telis** 'he ought to have fought me with these weapons'. Deictic *his* seems to refer to the weapons with which Turnus plans to end the war and drive out the Trojans. Other commentators understand the weapons to be those of A. (Page), of A. and Turnus together (Williams), or of the dead on the battlefield (Horsfall; Turnus of course would not literally use the weapons of the slaughtered, and *his . . . telis* would be a way of saying that he should have fought in their stead).

118 Cf. *Il.* 7.396–7 'thus we will fight again until a god judges between us and gives victory to one side or the other' (ὕστερον αὖτε μαχησόμεθ', εἰς ὅ κε δαίμων | ἄμμε διακρίνῃ, δώῃ δ' ἑτέροισί γε νίκην). **uixet** = *uixisset.* The syncopated form (only here in extant Latin literature) creates another (see

104, 108, and 110) initial unelided spondaic word for emphasis. *uixet* is best understood as a subjunctive in the apodosis of a past unreal conditional; the protasis is understood from what precedes (i.e. '[if Turnus had met me in single combat], that man would have lived'). *dedisset* is then subjunctive by attraction. **deus aut sua dextra:** 'independent though concurrent agencies, so that [A.] comes to speak as if the result might be due to either' (C–N). Epic convention allows for natural and supernatural causation (see Hardie on 9.184–5); cf. the double motivation at 901, with the note.

119 miseris . . . ciuibus: *et bene commendatur dicentis bonitas, quasi et ipse misereatur* (DServ. ad loc.).

120 dixerat Aeneas 'Aeneas had finished speaking'. *dixerat* is conventional in epic to mark the end of speeches; V. so uses it twenty-four times in *Aen.*, including at 132. **obstipuere:** the verb implies a blocking of the faculties; it also describes astounded reactions to a speech at 2.120, 8.121, 9.195, and 12.665. The response can signal positive wonder and awe (so at 8.121 and 9.195), and here the envoys are dumbstruck in admiration for the generosity and humanity that *bonus Aeneas* displays. Their reaction at 132 to the speech of Drances supports this interpretation: the *oratores* applaud his comments, which indicates that they are in agreement with his exaltation of A. (124–6). For a different view, see Quinn 1968: 235, who wonders if the embassy was struck by a mournful wish for peace rather than overwhelmed by A.'s magnanimity.

121 'they kept their eyes and faces turned towards one another'. *oculos* and *ora* are retained accs. after *conuersi* (used in a middle sense) as well as objects of *tenebant.* Statius simplifies the syntax when he imitates at *Theb.* 2.173–4 *fixosque oculos per mutua paulum | ora tenent*; cf. 2.1 *intentique ora tenebant.*

122–31 The introduction of Drances, an invented Virgilian character, and one who figures prominently in the Latin council later in the book. His hostility towards Turnus is a defining trait, as V. makes clear by immediately identifying it in him (122–3). That hostility colours Drances' response to A.; he operates on the principle that the enemy of my enemy is my friend, and he understands that a peace treaty with the Trojans runs counter to Turnus' wishes and interests (as becomes clearer in Drances' speech in the Latin council later in the book (343–75)). Drances appears as a smooth-talking opportunist who, whatever his actual feelings towards A., the Trojans, and the war, cosies up to A. and advocates for peace terms with the Trojans to pursue his anti-Turnus agenda. This leads him to near-treasonous excess, as he places the

Latins in a markedly subordinate position to the Trojans (130–1); this is not something that Latinus would endorse (cf. 321–3). Drances' praise for A., however, is consistent with authoritative attitudes in the poem (see 126n.), and the policy of peace that he advances is sound, despite his excess and impure motives. With his verbosity and vitriol towards Turnus, Drances is akin to Thersites, the rabble-rouser of *Il.* 2.212–69 who speaks against the Greek leaders; V. confirms the connection via echoes of Homer (see 122n., 123n.). On Drances, see, further, 336–75n.

122 senior contrasts with *iuueni Turno* in the next line; Drances is a foil to Turnus the young warrior, with an implication of generational conflict. *senior* also indicates why Drances speaks: he is the elder head of the delegation. There is a concentration of older men in the first half of *Aen.* 11 (Drances, Acoetes, Evander, Latinus). **semperque odiis et crimine:** *crimine* works best as a singular for plural, 'charges' levelled by Drances against Turnus (so Thomas, *EV* 1.932). *odiis* is then probably a true plural ('acts of hatred'; cf. 1.668, 4.623, 5.786, 7.298), balancing *crimine.* Cf. *Il.* 2.221–2 (Thersites) 'he was wont to reproach the two [Achilles and Odysseus]' (τὼ γὰρ νεικείεσκε). The characterisation of Drances suggests the *criminosus* figure of the late Republic, using criminal trials to pursue personal feuds (Horsfall ad loc.).

123 infensus iuueni Turno recasts *Il.* 2.220 'hateful was [Thersites] especially to Achilles and to Odysseus' (ἔχθιστος δ' Ἀχιλῆϊ μάλιστ' ἦν ἠδ' Ὀδυσῆϊ).

123–4 sic ore uicissim | orsa refert 'begins to speak aloud thus in response'. Cf. 7.435–6 *sic orsa uicissim | ore refert.* For *orsa* used as a substantive in the sense of 'speech', cf. 7.435. V. likes redundant *ore* with verbs of speaking; the expression goes back to early Latin (see Austin on 1.614). For other examples in this book, see 251 and 535, and cf. 132 and 190.

124 o: the particle makes the voc. more emphatic and emotional. It was especially at home in high-register poetry since Ennius, who 'made *o* sound elevated and poetic as well as Greek and emotional' (Dickey 2002: 227). V. has *o* with 16 per cent of his vocs., including, in this book, at 152, 158, 243, 252, 344, 361, 459, 508, 536, and 732. **fama ingens, ingentior armis:** cf. 291–2, 1.378–9 *sum pius Aeneas . . . | . . . fama super aethera notus.* The combination of positive and intensifying comparative adjs. is a characteristic Latin idiom; see Oakley on Liv. 6.11.1. For a Virgilian example, see *Ecl.* 5.44 (Daphnis) *formosi pecoris custos, formosior ipse*; for other instances in poetry, see Wills 1996: 233–6. The chiasmus, or more accurately antimetabole (a reversal of word order with a repeated word), is in high rhetorical style. This is the only appearance of the comparative *ingentior* before the third century CE.

125 uir Troiane: *uir* = 'hero'; an honorific address, as with *uir Troiane* at 10.598 (the suppliant Lucagus to A.). With *armis* at the end of the previous line, there is an echo of *Aen.* 1.1 *arma uirumque* at this moment when Drances praises the poem's great hero. See 696n. **quibus . . . aequem** 'with what words of praise am I to raise you up to the sky?' An instance of rhetorical *dubitatio*, or feigned hesitation over what to say next; *aequem* is a deliberative subjunctive. This is a version of the common encomiastic hyperbole, particularly in epic and rhetoric, of raising someone to the sky or stars (see Oakley on 7.36.5). V. has in mind *Ecl.* 5.51–2 *Daphninque tuum tollemus ad astra;* | *Daphnin ad astra feremus*, after the variation in the previous line on *Ecl.* 5.44; cf., too, *Ecl.* 5.43 *Daphnis ego . . . usque ad sidera notus.*

126 iustitiaene . . . laborum: gens. of cause after *mirer*, a Gk construction (Mayer 1999: 169–70). The Grecism is perhaps a way of associating Drances with Greek *adulatio*; his speech is Greek both in its syntax and in its lavish praise. Cf. the adulatory half-Greek Persius at Hor. *S.* 1.7.23–5 *laudat Brutum laudatque cohortem;* | *solem Asiae Brutum appellat, stellasque salubris* | *appellat comites.* The contrast between Drances' praise of A. and his hostility towards Turnus is pointed. **iustitiaene . . . belline:** the double particles *-ne* . . . *-ne* introduce a disjunctive question; see H–S II.465–6. Cf. 291–2 below, 1.544–5 (Ilioneus) *rex erat Aeneas nobis, quo iustior alter* | *nec pietate fuit, nec bello maior et armis*, 6.403 (the Sibyl to Charon) *Troius Aeneas, pietate insignis et armis.* Drances has his rhetorical reasons to flatter; yet his panegyrical words, however overheated, compare with others' praise of A. and match up with normative views elsewhere in *Aen.* of the hero (see Hardie 2012: 138–9, 144).

128 si qua uiam dederit Fortuna: V. several times describes Fortune providing or leading a way (2.387–8, 4.653, 12.405, 12.677); the metaphor might derive from Stoic language (Harrison on 10.49 *quacumque uiam dederit Fortuna*). *si qua* = 'if in any way' (*OLD* s.v. qua 9; cf. 1.18 *si qua fata sinant*); it expresses 'hope against hope'. Hence the future perfect of *dederit* principally indicates that the action of the protasis must be completed before that of the apodosis begins, but also has a hint of indefinite remoteness. Drances indicates that he sorely wants to reconcile Latinus and the Trojans and will work against long odds to try to make it happen; his subsequent reference to Turnus makes it evident that he sees the Rutulian as the main obstacle to peace, and that he wants to leave him out in the cold.

129 quaerat . . . Turnus: the bitter jussive drips with personal animosity.

130 quin et 'yes, and even'. An emphatic transition, introducing material that amplifies what precedes, rather than simply adding a new point. *quin et* begins with Horace and V. **fatalis** responds to *nisi fata locum sedemque dedissent* at 112. Cf. 232, 4.355 *quem regno Hesperiae fraudo et fatalibus aruis,* 5.82 *non licuit finis Italos fataliaque arua.* **moles** implies huge size and designates the stone blocks used to construct the walls of a city, whose greatness is understood from the size of its walls. Cf. 9.711 *magnis . . . molibus* (great stone blocks used to build piers).

131 saxaque subuectare: alliteration for solemn effect, as with *murorum . . . moles* in the previous line. The verb suggests laborious effort. Cf. 1.424 *subuoluere saxa,* describing the building of Dido's Carthage. **umeris** signals not just eagerness of effort, but subservient devotion. So Tib. ad loc.: *tantum exhibebimus deuotionis obsequium, cum muros uel quid aliud uolueris struere, collo nostro saxa iam Troiana libentissime perferamus nec erit onerosum nobis quicquid censueris esse faciendum.* The idea that the Latins will be subordinate to the Trojans and will build a Trojan city (*Troiana* implies a reborn Troy) runs counter not only to Latinus' thinking (see 122–31n.) but also to Jupiter and Juno's agreement (12.822–40) that Troy is to disappear forever, and that the Trojans are to be assimilated to the Italians. With his proposal, Drances flirts dangerously with treason and also stands in conflict with the will of the gods and the movement of history.

132 unoque omnes eadem ore: *unoque . . . ore* = 'unanimously'. The positioning of *omnes* between *unoque* and *eadem* is suggestive of complete agreement. **fremebant** describes a noisy din of approval; cf. 1.559, 5.385, 5.555, 8.717, 9.637. Although Drances' offer of aid is extravagant and extends far beyond securing the truce for which the embassy was sent, the *oratores* unanimously commend his position.

133 bis senos pepigere dies 'they settled on twelve days', i.e. on a twelve-day truce. Cf. *Il.* 24.664–70 (with 24.779–81), where Priam secures from Achilles a truce of eleven days for the burial of Hector, with the fighting to recommence on the twelfth day. For truces of similar length in Roman historiography, see the several ten-day truces in Livy (24.27.4, 36.27.3, 36.28.7, 40.25.4); he also mentions a fifteen-day truce (33.12.1). **pace sequestra** 'with peace as the mediator'. *sequestra* is a metaphor from the technical term for 'an intermediary or trustee' (*OLD* 1c). Cf. Luc. 10.472 *pacisque sequester,* Stat. *Theb.* 2.425 *nec sceptra fide nec pace sequestra* [*poscitis*], Sil. 6.347 *pacis sequestrem.*

134–8 The Trojans and Latins seek out and cut down timber to burn for the funerals. The passage echoes 6.179–82, on the burial of Misenus. A model from earlier epic is Enn. *Ann.* 175–9 Sk. *incedunt arbusta per alta, securibus caedunt, | percellunt magnas quercus, exiditur ilex, | fraxinus frangitur atque abies consternitur alta, | pinus proceras peruortunt: omne sonabat | arbustum fremitu siluai frondosai.* In all probability, Ennius' passage describes Pyrrhus' preparations for the cremation of both the Greek and the Roman dead after the battle of Heraclea. A second source, also used by Ennius, is *Il.* 23.117–21: 'but when they proceeded to the spurs of many-fountained Ida, at once they eagerly set upon cutting the high-crested oaks with the sharp bronze; the trees kept falling with a mighty crash. The Achaeans then split the trunks and bound them on the mules' (ἀλλ' ὅτε δὴ κνημοὺς προσέβαν πολυπίδακος Ἴδης, | αὐτίκ' ἄρα δρῦς ὑψικόμους ταναήκεϊ χαλκῷ | τάμνον ἐπειγόμενοι· ταὶ δὲ μεγάλα κτυπέουσαι | πῖπτον. τὰς μὲν ἔπειτα διαπλήσσοντες Ἀχαιοὶ | ἔκδεον ἡμιόνων). Cf., too, *Il.* 7.420 for the gathering of wood for pyres; relevant, given other correspondences with that book (see 100–21n., 182–212n.). The felling of trees for funeral pyres was a lasting topos in Latin poetry (for examples, see Currie 1985: 30, 60–1).

135 iugis 'along the hilltops', a locatival abl. **sonat:** also at 6.180 *sonat icta securibus ilex.* Cf. Enn. *Ann.* 178–9 Sk. *omne sonabat | arbustum, Il.* 23.119 μεγάλα κτυπέουσαι. **bipenni:** an adj., as at Varro *Men.* 389 *ferens ferream umero bipennem securem.* Silius Italicus has the noun *bipennis* when he imitates V. at 10.529–30 *sonat acta bipenni | frondosis silua alta iugis.*

135–6 alta . . . | fraxinus: Ennius has *fraxinus* in the same line-position: *fraxinus frangitur atque abies consternitur alta* (*Ann.* 177 Sk.). V. takes the adj. *alta* from Ennius' description of the fir (*abies*) and combines it with the other tree in Ennius' line. The ash is a very tall tree (Sargeaunt 1920: 48).

136 euertunt . . . pinus 'they fell pines that grew to the stars'. Cf. Enn. *Ann.* 178 Sk. *pinus proceras peruortunt.* V. shifts from having a tree as a subject to having trees as objects; there are precedents in both the Ennian passage and *Il.* 23.117–21, in which trees move from objects to subjects and back to objects. Changes from subject to object are fairly common in V.; they are particularly characteristic of epic style in similes (see Austin on 2.628, 4.445). For *ago* = 'grow', see *OLD* 10.

137 Cf. 6.181–2 *fraxineae trabes cuneis et fissile robur | scinditur.* **robora:** oak trees, as at 6.181 *fissile robur.* Variation on Ennius' *quercus* at *Ann.* 176 Sk. *percellunt magnas quercus. robora* and *cedrum* are both objects of *scindere.* **cuneis** 'wedges', a splitting tool. Cf. *Il.* 23.120 διαπλήσσοντες.

V. moves from cutting down trees (135–6) to splitting them (137) to loading them on wagons (138; cf. Homer's mules at *Il.* 23.121). All the trees mentioned in the passage are felled, split, and carted off. **olentem . . . cedrum:** possibly the cedar, possibly the juniper. 'Both cedar and juniper are resinous woods, which would burn (noisily and) fragrantly' (Horsfall on 7.13).

138 plaustris . . . gementibus: the wagons groan from the weight of the timber (cf. 6.413 *gemuit sub pondere cumba*); much wood is needed for the large number of the dead. **ornos:** the manna-ash, common on the hillsides of southern Europe (Mynors on *G.* 2.71).

139–81 ARRIVAL IN PALLANTEUM AND THE LAMENT OF EVANDER

The funeral procession arrives in Pallanteum, and Evander learns that his greatest fear (cf. 8.577–83) has become a reality. While his anguish is immense, and while this comes out in his language and in the substance of his speech, he nevertheless gives basically orderly expression to his pain, dividing his lament into five parts (152–8, 158–63, 164–6, 166–75, 175–81); the fourth, however, jumps around in a manner indicating emotional turbulence. The quasi-father A. had mourned Pallas; now the boy's *pater* himself gives voice to his raw sorrow. A probable model is Nestor, whose mourning for Antilochus was a *locus classicus* for paternal grief over the untimely death of a son (Quint 2018: 183); V. might have known of Nestor from the *Aethiopis* (whether directly or indirectly, or through an epitome (see Intro. pp. 20–1)). Alessio 1993: 63–4 proposes male θρῆνοι in Greek tragedy as another possible influence. Evander's lament links him not only to A. but also to Mezentius in book 10 and to Euryalus' mother in book 9; he is both a mourning father and, in the absence of his dead wife, a mourning mother. See Intro. p. 12.

139 Fama uolans: cf. 9.473–4 *uolitans pinnata* . . . | . . . *Fama*, where the news of Euryalus' death reaches his mother. Rumour is very likely personified here, as in those earlier lines. *Fama* in *Aen.* is often associated with extreme emotion, particularly as felt by women (Hardie on 9.473–5). On *Fama/fama* in V., see Hardie 2012: 78–149. **praenuntia:** *Fama*, swift-moving, as conventionally (Hardie 2012: 82), arrives ahead of the cortège. Cf. 9.474 *nuntia Fama.*

140 Euandrum Euandrique: variation on the Homeric formula Πρίαμος Πριάμοιό τε παῖδες (*Il.* 1.255, 4.31; cf. 4.35 Πρίαμον Πριάμοιό τε παῖδας); the echo associates Evander and Priam as bereaved regal fathers. See, further, Wills 1996: 37–8. The repetition and elision reflect the movement of *Fama* in rapid succession from Evander through his household (Dainotti 2015: 100 n. 324). **replet:** cf. 4.189 (*Fama*) *haec tum multiplici populos sermone replebat.*

141 modo 'just now'. The adv. signals a sudden, cruel reversal and sharpens the pathos; recent joy gives way to devastation as good news turns to bad. **Latio** 'in Latium'; a locatival abl., with the place standing for the people over whom, according to previous report, Pallas had triumphed. The juxtaposition of *Latio* and *Pallanta* highlights the conflicting sides.

142 ad portas: cf. *Il.* 24.709 'and near the gates they met him [Priam] bearing the dead [Hector]' (ἀγχοῦ δὲ ξύμβληντο πυλάων νεκρὸν ἄγοντι). **ruere:** 'historic' or 'descriptive' infinitive in excited, animated narration. Such infs. normally come in pairs or multiples (Austin on 4.422, *NLS* §21). **de more uetusto** 'in accordance with ancient custom'. Cf. 35.

143 funereas . . . faces: torches were carried at Roman funerals whether they took place by night or by day. But funerals for children were held at night (Toynbee 1971: 46, Flower 1996: 97); the apparent night-time return of Evander's dead child (see on *lucet uia longo* below) recalls the Roman practice. **lucet uia longo:** the line ends with three disyllables; this produces a clash of ictus and accent in the fifth foot. The pattern is rare in *Aen.* and concentrated in later books, especially *Aen.* 10 (302, 400, 442, 772). See Harrison on 10.301–2 and Norden, Anh. IX.4a. The description of the lit *uia* makes best sense if the setting is nocturnal; the brightness bears notice as a contrast to the understood darkness.

144 late discriminat agros 'divides the fields a long way'. For *discrimino* of a road cutting through and, thus, dividing land, cf. Cic. *Phil.* 12.9.23 *Etruriam discriminat Cassia uia.*

145 turba Phrygum: *Phryx/Phrygius,* referring to the Trojans, can be neutral in force (see 170, 677, 1.468, 5.785, 10.255), as here, or contemptuous, with the suggestion of eastern softness and effeminacy (see 403, 484, 769). While A. sent a procession of Trojans, Etruscans, and Arcadians, the *turba* is identified by its principal party.

146 matres: the mothers match the mourning Trojan women at 35; they also balance the mothers who fearfully watch Pallas leave Pallanteum with A. at 8.592–3 *stant pauidae in muris matres oculisque sequuntur | pulueream nubem et fulgentis aere cateruas.* Cf. *Il.* 24.722 (the return of Hector's corpse to Troy) 'the women wailed in chorus' (ἐπὶ δὲ στενάχοντο γυναῖκες).

147 The spondaic rhythm conveys heavy gloom. Repetition of the *m*-sound contributes to the mood. **maestam . . . urbem** echoes *maestamque . . . ad urbem* at 26. The narrative now catches up to the prolepsis of that earlier line. **incendunt clamoribus urbem** 'they inflame the [sad] city with their cries'. *incendo* commonly refers to inflammatory speech (see Feeney 1990: 175–6); V. has it thus at 4.197, 4.360, and 9.500. In all three cases, the verb is used of female speech. At 9.500, the speech is the lament of Euryalus' mother; this is close to the situation here, where the cries of female mourning inflame the city. Cf. *femineum clamorem* at 878 below. V. describes a metaphorical fire that comes to destroy the city figuratively, by expressing and spreading unendurable grief at this blow to its future. Because the image of fire is so present in the metaphor, *incendunt clamoribus* is synaesthetic, since it mixes bright light, heat, and loud sound. The fire imagery also picks up on the long line of torchlight at 144–5. Cf. 4.667–71 for the combination of overwhelming grief and figurative fire. On synaesthesia in V. and other poetry, see Harrison on 10.895, N–H on Hor. *Carm.* 1.14.6 and 2.13.24, and Catrein 2003.

148 Euandrum . . . tenere: the model is *Il.* 22.412, 'the people with difficulty restrain the old man [Priam] in his frenzy' (λαοὶ μέν ῥα γέροντα μόγις ἔχον ἀσχαλόωντα); Priam seeks to leave Troy to ransom the body of the slain Hector. **potis est:** for *potest*; it has archaic colour (see Hardie on 9.796, Fordyce on Catul. 45.5, *TLL* x.2.335.35–44). **tenere:** *simplex* for *retinere.*

149 Pallanta: the acc. is preferable to the abl. *Pallante,* despite the greater manuscript support for the latter. *Pallante* misunderstands *reposto,* which refers to the setting down of the bier, not to the placing of Pallas on it (Gransden ad loc.); *Pallanta* also avoids an awkward string of ablatives. *feretro . . . reposto* is thus an abl. abs., 'when the bier was set down'. The preposition *super* in the following line governs the acc. *Pallanta* in anastrophe (inversion of usual word order). Cf. 9.444 (Nisus flings himself on top of the dead Euryalus) *super exanimum sese proiecit amicum.*

150 Statius imitates at *Theb.* 6.35–6 [*orba parens*] *lacerasque super procumbere nati* | *reliquias ardet.* **haeret lacrimansque gemensque:** cf. 8.559 (Evander clinging to the departing Pallas) *haeret, inexpletus lacrimans.* V. creates pathos by having Evander receive the dead Pallas from the war similarly to how he had sent him away to the war. Double *-que* is a poetic mannerism and feature of epic style; it goes back to Ennius, who was influenced by Homeric τε . . . τε (although Ennius might have also known double *-que* as an obsolescent Latin idiom; see Skutsch on *Ann.* 170). The enclitics usually connect words that are parallel in sense or form; only the second *-que* is a true connective. Cf. 72 *auroque ostroque.*

151 The spondaic rhythm after the initial dactyl and after the dactyls in the previous line reflects the long effort on Evander's part to compose himself and gather his strength to speak. For a similar effect, cf. 3.308–9 (Andromache prepares to speak) *deriguit uisu in medio, calor ossa reliquit,* | *labitur et longo uix tandem tempore fatur.* **uia uix . . . uoci:** Page ad loc. suggests that the alliteration reflects Evander's convulsive sobbing. **uix tandem:** a 'forceful idiom of ordinary speech' (Fordyce on Catul. 62.2), also at 2.128, 3.309, and 5.178. It suggests an action taking very long and nearly not happening at all. **laxata dolore:** *dolore* is a kind of abl. of separation; Evander's grief abates enough to allow him to speak. Claudian imitates at *VI Cons. Hon.* 265–6 *ergo ubi praeclusae uoci laxata remisit* | *frena dolor.*

152–3 The lines point to a touching moment of intimacy between father and son, unseen by the reader. 'Evander had asked Pallas to do what he surely knew Pallas could not possibly do (namely "fight warily"), and Pallas had agreed knowing that he could not and would not. That is the comforting, self-deluding kind of conspiracy that happens between parents and sons on the eve of every war' (Lyne 1987: 160). V. recurrently has his reader find out at a later point in *Aen.* about earlier actions that go unmentioned in the narrative (Heinze 1993: 309). Cf. Patroclus' failure to heed Achilles' call to cease fighting once he saved the Greek ships (*Il.* 16.87–96, 16.685–7).

152 The echo of 45–6 contrasts the grief of A. and Evander. The king does not follow A. (as the reader, not Evander, knows) and fault him for his inability to honour his promises (cf. 164–5), but rather mourns his son's inability to keep his promise to fight with due caution.

153 'that you would be willing to entrust yourself to cruel Mars with some caution'. **ut:** the *ut*-clause is in apposition to *promissa* in the previous line and explains its content. This use of a noun clause is normal Latin; what is bold is *dederas promissa,* a poetic alternative to *promiseras.* Cf. Petr. 93.3 *hoc est . . . quod promiseras, ne quem hodie uersum faceres.* An alternative proposed by older commentators (e.g. Heyne; see C–N's discussion) is to place a full stop after *parenti* in the previous line and to treat *ut uelles* as an unfulfilled wish. This simplifies unnecessarily, and it creates excessively harsh abruptness (even for someone in Evander's state). No need, too, to normalise by supplying an implied *precanti* with *parenti* (Bell 1923: 284) or by reading *petenti* for *parenti* (as Henry does, after the *alii* in DServ.).

154–5 'I was not at all unaware of how powerful new fame in arms and too-sweet glory in first battle could be'.

155 **praedulce**: adjs. with the intensive prefix *prae*- are a distinctive feature of Virgilian style; cf. e.g. 213 *praediues,* 3.245 *praecelsus,* 3.698 *praepinguis,*

G. 2.190 *praeualidus*, *G.* 2.531 and *A.* 10.748 *praedurus*. *praedulcis* is first attested here.

156 primitiae signifies Pallas' first experiences of war (*OLD* 2). **propinqui:** probably to be taken as 'near' in location, rather than as 'recent', particularly in light of Evander's emphasis on the proximity of his enemies at 8.473–80 and 8.569–70. 'The lesson [Pallas] learned was cruel and he had not to go far to learn it' (Page ad loc.).

157 rudimenta 'first lessons' in war. For this military sense of *rudimentum*, see Liv. 21.3.4, Vell. 2.129.2. The noun occurs only here in V. and is very rare in other poetry (e.g. twice in Ovid and Statius, once in Valerius Flaccus and Silius Italicus, never in Catullus, Lucretius, and Lucan). It conjures the *contubernium* of Pallas (see 42–58n.). **exaudita** 'heeded'.

158 sanctissima coniunx: the adj. is an honorific term for the dead (*OLD* 3c). Cf. 5.80 *sancte parens*. At 8.510, Evander refers to his wife as Pallas' 'Sabine mother' (*matre Sabella*); all that V. relates about her is that she is Sabine and that she is dead.

159 felix morte tua: pointed juxtaposition. Cf. Ov. *Met.* 13.521 *felix morte sua est*; Hecuba speaks of Priam, who died before he could see their daughter Polyxena dead. For other examples of *felix* paradoxically paired with something undesirable, see *TLL* VI.445.53–9, to which add Tac. *Agr.* 45.3 *felix opportunitate mortis*.

160 uiuendo uici: *uici* = 'outlasted' (*OLD* 10b). The expression *uiuendo uincere* had a long history (DServ. ad loc. *ueteres enim 'uiuendo uincere' dicebant superuiuere*) and was probably familiar in spoken Latin (Wigodsky 1972: 12). Cf. Lucr. 1.202 *multaque uiuendo uitalia uincere saecla*. V. might have had the Lucretian passage in mind, as he does at *G.* 2.295 *multa uirum uoluens durando saecula uincit*; cf. also Lucr. 3.948 *omnia si pergas uiuendo uincere saecla*. **fata:** the allotted span of life that Evander has exceeded. At 8.573–83, Evander had prayed to Jupiter that he might die before his son suffered any dread disaster.

160–1 superstes | restarem ut genitor: the phrase is set off by the unusual pause at the fifth-foot trochaic caesura (see 55n.); it is stressed by that metrical effect and by the enjambment. Postposition of *ut* adds emphasis to the preceding first word in the line; word order also accents *genitor* for emotional effect. *restarem* = 'remain when all else is lost'.

161 Troum socia arma: cf. 8.119–20 (A.) *Euandrum petimus; ferte haec et dicite lectos | Dardaniae uenisse duces socia arma rogantis*. **secutum:** sc. *me*.

When bidding Pallas and A. farewell, Evander laments, Nestor-like, that his fighting days were behind him (8.560–71); he now wishes that this were not the case.

162–3 obruerent . . . dedissem | . . . referret: optative subjs., expressing wishes that have not been fulfilled. *obruerent* and *dedissem* are past unfulfilled wishes. The imperfect and pluperfect can both be used for such wishes; the imperfect is mainly archaic and poetic (*NLS* §116). Metrical convenience explains the use of the imperfect *obruerent. referret* is a present unfulfilled wish, i.e. 'would now be bringing me back'. Cf. 10.854 (Mezentius) *animam sontem ipse dedissem*; the echo links the two grieving fathers who wished they had died instead of their sons. The wish is a topos of lament (Harrison on 10.854). Cf., too, the wish of Euryalus' mother to die at 9.493–7.

163 me: the diaeresis at the end of the third foot is unusual in V., though more common in the later books of *Aen.* (Winbolt 1903: 37–9). The word before it is almost always a disyllable. The diaeresis emphasises the contrast between *me* and *Pallanta.*

164 arguerim: potential subjunctive. There is often, as here, no observable distinction in sense between the perfect and present tense (*NLS* §119). **foedera:** a *foedus* is fundamentally religious as a divinely authorised agreement, based on *fides*, in either international or interpersonal relations (Samuels, *VE* II.481, Gladhill 2016: 1–31). **nec quas:** double final monosyllables (see 3n.); another example follows at 170.

165 iunximus hospitio dextras: Evander recalls the alliance and good faith pledged in Pallanteum and described at 8.169 (Evander to Aeneas) *ergo et quam petitis iuncta est mihi foedere dextra*, 10.517 *dextraeque datae. hospitium* marks a solemn pledge of mutual hospitality and aid between the Trojans and Pallanteum (the *foedus* of 8.169), which the parties are bound to respect (Horsfall on 3.264, Barchiesi 2015: 46). For the joining of right hands to establish a *foedus*, see Hellegouarc'h 1963: 27, Burton 2011: 40. **senectae:** V. has the archaic *senecta* ten times, always at line-end and only in oblique cases, where forms of *senectus* are metrically intractable. (He has nom. *senectus* eight times.) With the exception of Livy, who has *senecta* six times, prose authors largely avoid the word until the elder Pliny, Tacitus, and Suetonius (see Oakley on 6.8.2).

166 debita refers to the ordinance of fate; all that has happened is Evander's fated lot in old age. **si:** one of eleven instances in V. (seven in *Aen.*) where *si* is elided. Elided monosyllables occur infrequently in

V. and are all but avoided in first-century CE epic (Harrison on 10.19, Norden, Anh. XI.2, Soubiran 1966: 387–433); they are colloquial and, thus, belong especially to informal verse, as demonstrated by their relative frequency in Lucilius and Horace's *Satires* (but never in his *Odes*). The elision here conveys strong emotion.

167 mors gnatum: significant juxtaposition and enjambment increase force and pathos. *gnatus* is archaic and poetic, conveying loftiness and emotion. The form appears eight times in *Aen.* (two other times (178, 181) in this speech), never in *Ecl.* or *G.* **caesis Volscorum milibus:** epic hyperbole, as at 10.508 (an apostrophe to Pallas) *cum tamen ingentis Rutulorum linquis aceruos.* The sense is of a *pulchra mors*, a noble and glorious death in battle (see 647n.). The Volscians are not mentioned in *Aen.* 10; V. presumably includes them now to anticipate the appearance of the Volscian Camilla later in this book.

168 ducentem in Latium Teucros: juxtaposition of *Latium/ Teucros* highlights not opposition, but rather the fact that Latium is the land destined for the Trojans; Evander is proud of the part Pallas played in realising that destiny. Cf. 8.133 (Evander on A.) *fatis egere* [*te*] *uolentem*, 8.477 (Evander to A.) *fatis huc te poscentibus adfers.* **cecidisse iuuabit:** pointed juxtaposition. Evander has heard that Pallas fought well (see 141), and, accepting that to be true, he foresees a time when he can take some comfort from the manner in which his son died. Cf. 55–6. For *iuuabit* in a different consolatory context, see 1.203 *forsan et haec olim meminisse iuuabit.*

169 non . . . digner 'I would not deem you worthy'. The subjunctive is potential.

170–1 'than [the one with which] pious Aeneas and the mighty Phrygians and the Etruscan leaders and the entire Etruscan army [honour you]'. As the cortège demonstrates, Pallas' death helps to bind three different peoples; it is a force for unification, and not only between A. and Evander (see Intro. pp. 28–9, Gladhill 2016: 144).

170 quam . . . quam . . . quam: the triple anaphora (repetition of a word at the beginning of successive sentences or clauses) in a single line is very rare in V. (also at 3.490 and 9.427) and relatively infrequent in Latin poetry (Wills 1996: 369). It emphasises Evander's gratitude (with the final monosyllable heightening still more the emphasis) for the honour that A. and the Trojans have shown his son. **pius:** the distinctive epithet for A. appears nineteen times in *Aen.* (only here in book 11). Its presence is always significant; here it underscores Evander's belief that A. met his obligation to Pallas by attending to his funeral. Cf. 6.176 and 6.232 (*pius* A. mourns Misenus and sees to his funeral). *pius* also anticipates the sacred obligation that Evander will soon lay upon A. (179–80; see Clausen 2002: 208). For a good summary of V.'s use of *pius*, see Austin on 4.393. **Phryges:** the final syllable is short in this Gk loan-word; cf. *Arcades* at 93, 142, and 835.

171 Tyrrhenique . . . Tyrrhenum: *-que* connects the two phrases; the repetition of the proper name then takes the place of a balancing second *-que*. The construction occurs only in the second half of *Aen.*; cf. 641, 7.75–6, and 10.313–14. **exercitus omnis:** presumably an exaggeration, referring to the many Etruscans in the honour guard; see 93n.

172 quos: the antecedent is an understood *eorum*. Cf. 81. **dat . . . leto:** *letum* is archaic and poetic, and the periphrasis belongs to high style. *dare leto* was originally sacral language and was taken up in poetry by e.g. Enn. *trag.* 283 Jocelyn and Lucr. 5.1007; V. also has it at 5.806 and 12.328. The present tense of *dat* for a past action (cf. 9.266) registers a past event that is in some sense still active (as demonstrated here by the presence of the trophies). On this idiomatic use of the present, see Horsfall on 7.363, Görler, *EV* II.272. The tense seems to be used also for vividness, which assimilates it to the historical present.

173 Cf. Pallas' prayer for Turnus at 10.462 *cernat semineci sibi me rapere arma cruenta.* **stares . . . in armis:** *armis* is preferable to the conjecture *aruis*, which eliminates the repetition with *armis* at 175. This is an unnecessary intervention, given V.'s openness to repeating words in close proximity that are not thematic and do not form a rhetorical device (see Housman 1926: xxxiii). With *stares . . . in armis*, cf. 9.581 *stabat in egregiis Arcentis filius armis*, 12.938–9 *stetit acer in armis | Aeneas.* **immanis:** the adj. corresponds to Homeric πελώριος and describes great size, often, as here, of a terrifying or forbidding kind (Fordyce on 7.305). Hence appropriate to the larger-than-life world of epic; of the fifty-three appearances of the adj. in V., forty-nine are in *Aen.* **truncus:** the tree trunk that supports a trophy, but with play on 'torso' to suggest the equivalence of trophy and man (see 9n.).

174 Understand *tibi Palladique.* Cf. 10.459, where Pallas engages Turnus 'with unequal strength' (*uiribus imparibus*). **robur ab annis** 'strength that comes from years'. For this use of *ab* to designate origin, see *OLD* 15a. *robur* seems to play on the meaning 'oak tree', upon which spoils were hung. Cf. 326–7n.

175 Turne: the name is heavily emphasised, implying Evander's intense anger and hatred, through the enjambment, the full stop after the initial trochee (an unusual pattern), and the placement of the name at the end of the sentence in hyperbaton (a separation of words belonging together by other words placed in between, especially for emphasis) with *tu.* **sed . . . quid:** a common turn of speech with first-person verbs, marking a resolution to cease from vain speech, thought, or action. Conversational in comedy (cf. Pl. *Mer.* 218, *Truc.* 766), but used in elevated style from Ennius (*Ann.* 314 Sk.). **armis:** 'from arms'.

176 uadite: the verb is poetic and particularly at home in epic (see Oakley on Liv. 6.8.2); it occurs nine times in *Aen.* Sometimes just a substitute for *ire,* but here it implies rapid, purposeful movement (*OLD* 1).

177–81 The model is *Il.* 18.90–3 (Achilles): 'since neither does my heart bid me to live on and to abide among men, unless first Hector, struck by my sword, will lose his life and pay for making the spoiling of Patroclus, son of Menoetius' (ἐπεὶ οὐδ' ἐμὲ θυμὸς ἄνωγε | ζώειν οὐδ' ἄνδρεσσι μετέμμεναι, αἴ κε μὴ Ἕκτωρ | πρῶτος ἐμῷ ὑπὸ δουρὶ τυπεὶς ἀπὸ θυμὸν ὀλέσσῃ, | Πατρόκλοιο δ' ἕλωρα Μενοιτιάδεω ἀποτίσῃ). Achilles lives to exact vengeance himself; the elderly Evander must call on A. to act as his proxy.

177–9 quod . . . | . . . | . . . uides 'the fact that I drag on a hateful life now that Pallas has been killed is because of your right hand, which you see owes Turnus to both son and father'.

178 dextera refers to A.'s strong right hand in battle with which he is to kill Turnus, but also recalls the pledge of *hospitium* referred to at 165, which A. is to honour by avenging Pallas' death. **gnatoque patrique:** a high-style and solemn line-end (see 150n., 167n. on *gnatus*), also at 10.525; cf. 6.116 *gnatique patrisque.*

179 debere marks an obligation of *fides* that Evander places on A. The verb answers *debetur* at 10.442–3 *soli mihi Pallas | debetur,* where Turnus states that Pallas is owed to him in single combat; now Turnus is owed to Pallas and Evander to pay for that encounter, and via A.'s single combat with him.

179–80 meritis . . . locus 'this is the only spot left open to you for your valour and fortune'; *tibi* is dat. with *uacat,* while *meritis* and *fortunae* are dats. with *locus* (= 'field for displaying merit').

180 non uitae gaudia quaero: *uitae* is dat. rather than gen.; translate 'it is not for [my] life that I seek the joy [of knowing Turnus killed]'. The meaning 'joys of life' for *uitae gaudia* would ill fit the context: a person who has just described his life as *inuisus* (177) will of course seek no such joys, and for him to state as much would be flat and redundant. *gaudia* must therefore refer to a different pleasure, which must be related to the thing that Evander has been discussing: the killing of Turnus to avenge the death of Pallas. *gaudia uitae,* with *uitae* in the gen., is a common line-end in late and Christian Latin but not in extant Augustan poetry (only at Tib. (Lygd.) 3.3.7).

181 perferre: of bringing news or word (*OLD* 2b).

182–212 FUNERALS FOR THE DEAD

With the coming of a new day, the Trojans and Italians, their truce in place, attend to the funerals of the fallen. A primary model is the burial truce at *Il.* 7.421–33, where both Trojans and Greeks cremate those killed in battle; but V. also looks to the mourning and funeral for Patroclus in *Il.* 23 (see 182–3n., 188–91n., 201–2n.) and to the burial of Hector, under a truce, at *Il.* 24.776–802 (see 201–2n.). Details correspond as well to passages in Apollonius Rhodius and to Roman funerary practices (see 188–91n., 188n.). While it is clear that the Trojan dead are significant in number, the Italian casualties are greater (see 207–9n., 208n.). The defeat in *Aen.* 10 was a real disaster for the Italian side; hence the resistance to the war among the Latins, about which we begin to hear immediately after 212.

182–3 Cf. *Il.* 7.421–3 'the sun was now just striking the fields, rising up into the heavens from soft-gliding, deep-flowing Ocean' (Ἠέλιος μὲν ἔπειτα νέον προσέβαλλεν ἀρούρας, | ἐξ ἀκαλαρρείταο βαθυρρόου Ὠκεανοῖο | οὐρανὸν εἰσανιών), 23.108–9 'and rosy-fingered Dawn shone forth to them as they mourned around the pitiful corpse' (μυρομένοισι δὲ τοῖσι φάνη ῥοδοδάκτυλος Ἠώς | ἀμφὶ νέκυν ἐλεεινόν). In V., cf. 5.64–5 *si nona diem mortalibus almum | Aurora extulerit.*

182 Aurora interea: the dawn setting supports the idea that Pallas' cortège arrived in Pallanteum at night; V. moves from night in one scene to morning in the next. The flow of the narrative suggests that it is the following morning, as does the echo of the opening line of the book; V. moves from one day to the next using a similar temporal marker to introduce each. This would presumably mean that the troops who accompanied the procession were absent for the funeral rites because still in Pallanteum or en route, if V. was being strictly realistic about time. But he is silent on the matter, and we are free to suspend disbelief on how the troops were able to return so quickly, and we can assume their presence. **miseris mortalibus:** the phrase (also at *G.* 3.66) renders Homer's δειλοῖσι βροτοῖσιν ('wretched mortals', *Il.* 22.31, 76), already Latinised at

Lucr. 5.944 *pabula dura tulit, miseris mortalibus ampla.* Alliteration for emotional effect. **almam:** often used of daylight as a 'kindly natural force' (Conway on 1.306); cf. 5.64, *Ecl.* 8.17, Hor. *Carm.* 4.7.7. The adj. is pointedly contrasted with *miseris.*

183 opera atque labores: the coupling of *opus* and *labor* is regular in literature; cf. the well-known instance 6.129 *hoc opus, hic labor est,* and see Oakley on Liv. 6.1.6 *in opera ac labore assiduo reficiendae urbis.* The idea that dawn brings toil back to men is a literary topos that goes back to Hes. *Op.* 578–81; cf. e.g. *Hym. Herm.* 98, Ov. *Am.* 1.13.13, *Met.* 4.664–5, Sen. *Her. F.* 125–58, ps.-V. *Mor.* 1–7. Unelided *atque* before a consonant is unusual in V., accounting for only 12 per cent of instances of it. Of the thirty-five cases of unelided *atque* in *Aen.*, twenty-seven are in books 7–12 (Austin on 1.147). In all Augustan poetry with the exception of Horace, elided *atque* is very common. For discussion, see Axelson 1945: 82–5, Ross 1969: 33–9. Here as elsewhere in V., the unelided form seems to add solemnity, perhaps with a note of archaism (Tarrant on 12.239).

184 pater Aeneas: the epithet, long an honorary title in Rome, marks A. as a responsible, statesmanlike leader, full of care for his men. On V.'s use of *pater* for A., see Austin on 2.2, Moskalew 1982: 82, Stahl 2015: 438–9. **Tarchon:** in V., the chief king of the Etruscans. An oracle had told the Etruscans to seek a foreign leader to fight Mezentius; after offering the position to the Arcadian Evander, who refused it due to his age, they joined with the Trojan forces (8.494–513, 10.148–56). Tarchon is traditionally the brother (or son) of Tyrrhenus, who brought the Etruscans from Lydia (see Hdt. 1.94.5–7, Str. 5.2.2); according to Strabo (5.2.2), Tyrrhenus appointed Tarchon to govern the twelve cities of Etruria, and Tarquinia was named after him. See further Harrison on 10.153–4, Bremmer and Horsfall 1987: 93 and 98, Cristofani, *EV* v*.39–40. In making Tarchon A.'s ally, V. adapts a tradition in which Tarchon and Tyrrhenus, with Odysseus, strike an alliance with A.; cf. Lyc. *Alex.* 1242–9, and see Heinze 1993: 146, Muse 2007: 588. Tarchon's position here alongside A. anticipates the leading role that the Etruscans will play in the cavalry battle later in the book and Tarchon's importance in that battle (727–59).

185 corpora . . . suorum: *suorum* is gen. with *corpora*; it is not to be taken with *patrum* in the next line. The periphrasis of *corpora* + gen. is old (see Skutsch on Enn. *Ann.* 88–9 *corpora sancta | auium*) and standard in epic. *corpora* stresses the blunt physical reality of the corpses.

186 more . . . patrum varies *more parentum* at 6.223, on the funeral rites for Misenus. Cf. Catul. 101.7–8 *haec, prisco quae more parentum | tradita sunt tristi munere ad inferias.* **subiectisque ignibus atris** 'and once murky fire was applied below'. *ater* refers to black smoke, as the following line makes clear, but also contains the meaning 'funereal' (*OLD* 7); this gives the adj. strong emotional content, which it often possessed (Fordyce on 7.525; see also Edgeworth 1992: 74–85). Cf. 28 above.

187 'the high sky was buried in darkness from the thick smoke'. Cf. 6.271 (Jupiter) *caelum condidit umbra*, Hor. *Carm.* 2.16.3 *atra nubes condidit lunam.* **caligine:** like *ater* in the previous line, *caligo* operates on two levels: it describes the murkiness of thick smoke (*OLD* 3) and conjures the darkness of death (*OLD* 5a).

188–91 V. reworks *Il.* 23.13–16 (the Greeks mourn Patroclus): 'weeping, they drove their horses with flowing manes around the corpse three times; with them Thetis stirred their desire for wailing. The sands were made wet, and the arms of the warriors were made wet with tears' (οἱ δὲ τρὶς περὶ νεκρὸν ἐΰτριχας ἤλασαν ἵππους | μυρόμενοι μετὰ δέ σφι Θέτις γόου ἵμερον ὦρσε. | δεύοντο ψάμαθοι, δεύοντο δὲ τεύχεα φωτῶν | δάκρυσι). Other plausible models are A.R. 1.1059–60 (funeral rites for Cyzicus) 'marching three times in their bronze around the body' (τρὶς περὶ χαλκείοις σὺν τεύχεσι δινηθέντες | τύμβῳ ἐνεκτερέιξαν) and 4.1535–6 (funeral rites for Mopsus) 'marching three times in arms around the body as it received full honours' (τρὶς δ' ἀμφὶ σὺν ἔντεσι δινηθέντες | εὖ κτερέων ἴσχοντα). The movement around the pyres conjures the Roman *decursio* (see *decurrere* at 189), a ritual march or horseback procession around a general's pyre or tomb (cf. Liv. 25.17.5, Stat. *Theb.* 6.213–16, V. Fl. 3.347–50, Tac. *Ann.* 2.7.3, Suet. *Cl.* 1.3, Dio 56.42).

188 ter: a ritual number, and echoing τρίς at *Il.* 23.13 and at A.R. 1.1059 and 4.1535. *ter* is repeated in anaphora in the following line to introduce the second element in theme and variation; V. describes a single ritual action, circumlustration on horseback, in two ways. **fulgentibus armis:** cf. χαλκείοις σὺν τεύχεσι δινηθέντες at A.R. 1.1059, and σὺν ἔντεσι δινηθέντες at A.R. 4.1535. Cf., too, *Il.* 23.128–30 (the funeral of Patroclus) 'and at once Achilles ordered the war-loving Myrmidons to gird themselves with bronze' (αὐτὰρ Ἀχιλλεὺς | αὐτίκα Μυρμιδόνεσσι φιλοπτολέμοισι κέλευσε | χαλκὸν ζώννυσθαι). The bright arms, polished out of respect for the dead, contrast with the murk of the smoke from the pyres described in the previous lines. *fulgentibus armis* also suggests ready vigour, as elsewhere in V. (see Austin on 2.749); a sharp contrast with the dead.

189 maestum: V. returns to a significant thematic adj. (see 26n.).

190 lustrauere in equis 'circled around on their horses', but with the added sense of ritual purification (*lustratio*), to purify the mourners from the pollution of death. Cf. 6.229 (Corynaeus performs a lustration at the end of Misenus' funeral) *idem ter socios pura circumtulit unda. lustrauere in equis* also occurs at 5.578, on the *lusus Troiae* at the funeral games of Anchises. For *lustro* describing a *decursio,* cf. Stat. *Theb.* 6.215–16 *lustrantque ex more sinistro | orbe rogum.* **ululatusque ore dedere:** *do* = 'utter, produce (sounds)' (*OLD* 26); *ululatus dare* occurs only here in V. and is unique to him. V. likes periphrases with *do* as a feature of high style (Fratantuono and Smith on 5.435, Harrison on 10.870; cf. 172n.).

191 Modelled on δεύοντο ψάμαθοι, δεύοντο δὲ τεύχεα φωτῶν | δάκρυσι at *Il.* 23.15–16 (quoted at 188–91n.). As in Homer, the anaphora (*spargitur . . . sparguntur*) has strong emotional force.

192 it caelo clamorque: V. is partial to the use of *it* with *clamor* and similar nouns (cf. 4.443, 4.665, 8.595, 9.499, 9.664, 12.409). *caelo* produces a standard epic hyperbole; cf. 454–5, 745, 878, 2.338, 2.488, 5.140, 5.451, 9.504, 12.409, 12.462. The hyperbole goes back to Homer; cf. *Il.* 2.153 etc. 'the shouting went up to heaven' (ἀϋτὴ δ' οὐρανὸν ἷκεν). *caelo* is dat. of place to or towards which with a verb of motion. On this use of the dat., frequent in V., see Austin on 2.186 and Görler, *EV* II.266, with G–L §358. **clamorque uirum clangorque tubarum** = 2.313; perhaps Ennian (*Ann.* II.XI Sk.). Double *-que* (see 150n.) here joins related two-word units rather than two related words; cf. 34 *famulumque manus Troianaque turba,* 1.87 *clamorque uirum stridorque rudentum. clamor* signifies a cry of mourning, as at 147. The *tubae* are those of a funeral (in contrast to 2.313, where they are war-trumpets); cf. Hor. *S.* 1.6.44, Prop. 2.7.12, 2.13.20, Pers. 3.103–4. The alliteration of *c* is expressive of the cacophonous noise.

193–5 alii . . . | . . . | . . . pars: the distributive pair is rare (e.g. Sal. *Jug.* 38.5, Prop. 2.29.5–6, Stat. *Theb.* 10.225–6; see *TLL* X.454.48–55, K–S II.72–3) and appears only here in V.

193 hic: temporal, 'at this point', marking a new stage in the funeral. **occisis** 'slaughtered'. The colourful *occido* is generally avoided in poetry (Weber 1969: 47–9, Lyne 1989: 107). V. has it two other times (811 and 10.312).

194 coniciunt igni: *igni* is dat. of the goal of motion, equivalent to *in ignem*; with compound verbs describing motion, poets use the dat. and the preposition + acc. interchangeably (*NLS* §62 n. 1).

194–5 ensesque . . . | rotas: repeated *-que* (polysyndeton, or repetition of conjunctions in close succession) emphasises the large number of objects piled on the pyres.

195 feruentisque rotas: the adj. implies speed; ancient wheels, which had iron rims, must have got very hot when moving fast (N–H on Hor. *Carm.* 1.1.4–5). The burning *rotae* are a synecdoche for well-made chariots. Yet *feruentis* in this context also suggests that the wheels will imminently grow hot on the pyre. This creates a contrast between how the wheels burned with speed and how they now come to burn, and thus between past vigour and present annihilation (Lyne 1989: 23). **munera nota:** the adj. distinguishes these offerings from the enemy spoils just described; the *munera* are familiar because they are the arms that belonged to the dead. *nota* is affective, generating pathos from the sight of these familiar and, it is implied, cherished arms burning on the pyres of those who were not saved by them. On affective *notus* in V., see Austin on 2.256 and Fordyce on 7.491. Cf. 6.221 *uelamina nota,* describing the clothing placed on the dead Misenus (Serv. ad loc. *ipsi cara*).

196 non felicia tela: litotes. The arms are unlucky because they did not bring success in battle. Contrast 7.745 (Ufens) *insignem fama et felicibus armis.*

197 The sacrifice of oxen and sheep at a funeral is Homeric (*Il.* 23.166–7). In Roman practice, only when a pig was sacrificed was a grave legally a grave (Cic. *Leg.* 2.22.57, Toynbee 1971: 50). The sacrifice of the animals also evokes the *suouetaurilia,* a very sacred rite of Roman religion. At this solemn moment, the Trojans and Etruscan allies engage in a proto-Roman religious act. **circa:** V. uses this form of the adv. rather than *circum* to avoid a repeated *-um* after *boum;* for similar uses of *circa,* see 6.865, 7.535, and 12.757. **mactantur:** an ancient term for a ritual offering of sacrifice to a god (see Fordyce on 7.92 for lengthy discussion). **Morti:** the personification seems called for given the verb *mactantur;* Death is the personified deity to whom the sacrifices are made. Cf. Liv. 9.40.10 *eos se Orco mactare dictitans.* This is the sole instance in V. where *Mors* is personified. Heinsius, Mackail, and Fratantuono ad loc. argue against personification. Heinsius and Mackail understand *morti* as an archaic abl. form, 'in death' (tentatively endorsed by Paratore ad loc.;); but the dat. is natural with *mactare* meaning 'sacrifice/offer sacrificially'. Cf. 3.118–20 *meritos aris mactauit honores, | taurum Neptuno, taurum tibi, pulcher Apollo, | nigram Hiemi pecudem, Zephyris felicibus albam.*

198 saetigerosque sues: cf. 7.17 *saetigeri sues,* 12.170 *saetigeri fetum suis.* The adj. belongs to high style; it is found before V. only at Lucr. 6.974. V. likes poetic epithets in *-ger* and *-fer;* see Harrison on 10.169–70, Tränkle 1960: 58–9. *sus* recurrently appears in poetry as an alternative to *porca;* cf. Homeric σῦς (over thirty-five examples). V. has it fourteen times and *porca* once (at 8.641). For *saetiger sus* in poetry after V., see Ov. *Met.* 10.549, *Fast.* 1.352, and Stat. *Theb.* 1.397.

199 in flammam iugulant pecudes 'they slaughter the sheep onto the fire'; also at 12.214. The animals are sacrificed above the pyres, and their blood pours down onto the flames. *flamma* denotes the funeral pyre but indicates, too, a sacrificial fire (*OLD* 2c). **litore toto** 'along the entire shore'.

200 There is a marked alliteration of *s*, perhaps designed to be expressive of hissing flames. **ardentis:** like *feruentis* at 195, the adj. has two meanings: the men who had 'blazed' in a metaphorical sense and been ardent for battle are now ablaze on their pyres.

201 busta: the pyres, now charred. Cf. Serv. ad 11.185 *'bustum' uero iam exustum uocatur*, Paulus-Festus 29.8 *bustum, quasi bene ustum*; O'Hara 2017: 230 suggests that *semusta* is an etymologising gloss on *busta.*

201–2 neque auelli possunt . . . | . . . aptum: a detail of tremendous pathos. Cf. *Il.* 23.154 (Greeks mourning at Patroclus' pyre) 'and now the light of the sun would have gone down on their weeping' (καί νύ κ' ὀδυρομένοισιν ἔδυ φάος ἠελίοιο), 24.713–14 'and now the whole day until sunset they would have mourned Hector before the gates, shedding tears' (καὶ νύ κε δὴ πρόπαν ἦμαρ ἐς ἠέλιον καταδύντα | Ἕκτορα δάκρυ χέοντες ὀδύροντο πρὸ πυλάων). Achilles mourns over Patroclus' pyre all night (*Il.* 23.218–25).

202 'turns the sky fitted with blazing stars'. **inuertit:** the sky is thought to consist of two hemispheres, one bright and the other dark but decked with stars; the hemispheres revolve, so that day and night alternate (Williams ad loc.). Cf. 2.250 *uertitur interea caelum et ruit Oceano nox.* The darkness of night replaces the darkness caused by the smoke from the pyres (187). **stellis ardentibus aptum:** cf. 4.482 = 6.797 *axem umero torquet stellis ardentibus aptum.* There is no need to read *fulgentibus* because of the proximity of *ardentibus* to *ardentis* at 200. The repetition seems deliberate as V. moves from 'blazing corpses to the blazing stars, from man-made fires to the fires of heaven' (Gransden ad loc.). Cf. Enn. *Ann.* 348 Sk. *hinc nox processit stellis ardentibus apta* (though Ennius also has *stellis fulgentibus aptum* at *Ann.* 27 Sk. *qui caelum uersat stellis fulgentibus aptum*).

203 Nec minus et: a transition formula; cf. *nec minus* at *Aen.* 3.482, 8.465, *G.* 1.393, and *nec minus interea* at *Aen.* 1.633, 6.212, 7.572, *G.* 2.429, 3.311. The formula 'gives the impression that what follows is at least as important as what has gone before' (Mynors on *G.* 2.429–30). **miseri:** cf. 119 *miseris . . . ciuibus* and 182 *miseris mortalibus,* with 881n.

204–5 The Latins cremate and bury the dead. Both rites were practised in early Rome; from about 400 BCE into the first century CE and the time of V., cremation was the normal practice. **corpora . . . | multa uirum:** the epic periphrasis also occurs at 7.535, 10.662, and 12.328. As at 185, *corpora* places emphasis on the physicality of the corpses.

206 urbique: it is unclear whether *urbi* refers to Latinus' city or to the different cities of the dead, in which case sc. *unicuique.*

207–9 The bulk of the dead Latin soldiers are cremated en masse. This implies that the Latin casualties were more numerous than those of the Trojans and their allies; there were too many Latin dead to attend to them all individually.

207 confusaeque ingentem caedis aceruum: cf. 10.244–5 *crastina lux . . . | ingentis Rutulae spectabit caedis aceruos.* For *aceruus* of the piled dead before V., see Catul. 64.359 *caesis . . . corporum aceruis.* The interlocking word order reflects the confused mass of bodies. *-que* is epexegetic, explaining *cetera.*

208 nec numero nec honore cremant: *nec numero* joins with *innumeras* at 204 and *confusaeque . . . aceruum* at 207 to emphasise the great number of casualties; *numero* does not mean that the dead were 'held of no account' (so Page ad loc., citing, via C–N, Caes. *Gal.* 6.13.1 *aliquo sunt numero atque honore*), but indicates that they were burned in huge quantities and, hence, were unnumbered. *nec honore* implies that the dead did not receive the honour of an individual funeral and, perhaps, an individual funeral mound or monument (cf. 7.3 (an apostrophe to the dead Caieta) *seruat honos sedem tuus*). C–N suggest that V. may have thought of the 'common tomb' (τύμβον . . . ἄκριτον) at *Il.* 7.336–7 or of the captives and horses burnt on the edges of Patroclus' pyre 'mixed together/in a confused mass' (ἐπιμίξ) at *Il.* 23.242. With the language, cf. 12.630 (Metiscus to Turnus) *nec numero inferior pugnae neque honore recedes.*

208–9 uasti | . . . agri: the adj. implies the great size of the fields in which the huge number of fires burn, but also includes the idea of emptiness and desolation (*OLD* 1; cf. Fordyce on 7.302, DServ. ad 1.52 *uasto, pro uastato*). The landscape devastated by war forms an evocative setting for the mass cremation. Cf. 8.8 *et latos uastant cultoribus agros.*

209 The five-word arrangement, spondaic rhythm, and alliteration combine to create a weighty, solemn line. **certatim crebris conlucent:** the threefold alliteration across the first four feet of the line is exceptional in V. Cf. the alliteration of *c* at 207 (with *cremant* at 208). The alliteration increases the emotional force of the lines; there is also perhaps an evocation of the crackle of the fires (Fratantuono ad loc.). *certatim* captures the intensity of the many fires; each seems to strive to outdo the others. For *certatim* with inanimate subjects, cf. Lep. *Fam.* 10.34a.3, Stat. *Theb.* 5.448.

210 Cf. 3.589 = 4.7 *umentemque Aurora polo dimouerat umbram.* **tertia lux:** it is uncertain if V. means the third day in the book – i.e. one day in the opening line, one day at 182, and a third day here – or the third dawn after the rising of *Aurora* at 182 (counting inclusively). If the latter, the burning of the pyres of the Latin dead can be understood to last two days, assuming that they and the Trojans both held funeral rites on the first day (the coming of night at 201–2 does not imply that the action beginning at 203 occurs on the next day), and that the Latins alone continued their rites on the second, as the transition from the passage on them at 203–9 to *tertia lux* at 210 suggests. Carstairs-McCarthy 2015: 706 argues that the gathering of the wood for the pyres takes place over nine days, as at *Il.* 24.784, and that this is the third dawn (again, inclusive) after the ninth day of preparation. But it is difficult to believe that V. would be quite that elliptical about the passage of time, with the only key an intertextual reference to Homer.

211–12 Cf. 6.226–8 (the funeral of Misenus) *postquam conlapsi cineres et flamma quieuit, | reliquias uino et bibulam lauere fauillam, | ossaque lecta cado texit Corynaeus aeno.* The ritual action described there, consistent with both Homer (*Il.* 23.250–4, 24.791–6) and with Roman custom (Toynbee 1971: 50), is now abbreviated. The bones, however, are not gathered individually in urns, as in the custom, but buried en masse.

211 ruebant 'levelled'; the verb similarly at *G.* 1.105 *cumulosque ruit male pinguis harenae.* The Latins rake the huge piles of burnt remains and level them in order to extract the bones.

212 focis 'from the pyres'. *focus* is used of different places where fires are lit (*OLD* 4b, O'Hara 2017: 282–3), but the meaning 'pyre' is uncommon and first found in V. (*TLL* VI.990.70–4). **tepidoque . . . aggere:** the soil remains warm from the intense heat of the long-burning pyres; not even night's *gelida umbra* could cool it. **onerabant** refers to the topos of remains being weighed down by what covers them; cf. 10.558 *patrioque onerabit membra sepulchro* and the conventional prayer *sit tibi terra leuis,* 'a formula which was worked to death both in literature and in actual use' (Kenney on Lucr. 3.893).

213 iam uero marks a transition here and at 12.704; the new scene is climactic. **praediuitis:** on the prefix *prae-*, see 155n. The epithet creates a contrast between the previous, normal state of prosperity and the current misfortune and suffering; the echo of its prefix in *praecipuus* in the following line contributes to that contrast.

214 Like the Trojans in the *Iliad*, the Latins fight near and for their city; like Homer, V. shows the effects of war on that *urbs* and its civilian population. The grief is intense, and from it arise anger and civil discord, stoked by the opportunistic, demagogic Drances. **praecipuus fragor** 'extraordinary uproar', i.e. of lamentation. *fragor* describes lamentation only here in V.; this use of the word is rare in Latin literature and is poetic (*TLL* VI.1235.39–64). **longi pars maxima luctus:** for this use of *longus* in a temporal sense, cf. 2.26 *longo soluit se Teucria luctu.* The framing alliterative hyperbaton reflects the sense of protracted wailing, itself a sign of inconsolable grief.

215 matres miseraeque nurus: *miserae* modifies both nouns. The pairing of mothers and daughters-in-law in lament is Homeric (*Il.* 24.166). Cf. 2.501 (also Homeric in origin) *uidi Hecubam centumque nurus.*

215–16 cara sororum | pectora maerentum: an epic periphrasis for *carae sorores,* although *pectora* is also appropriate as the seat of emotion and evokes the beating of the chest in lamentation (cf. 37–8). *cara* is here used of the person who feels affection, not the object of affection: 'loving' rather than 'beloved'. Cf. 1.646 *cari . . . parentis,* 9.84 *tua cara parens.* The adj. in V. commonly refers to familial affection (Pinotti, *EV* I.683).

217 dirum exsecrantur bellum 'they curse the dreadful war'. The women and children view the war as ill-omened and impious; this is consistent with its characterisation at 7.58–80 and 595–7. See also 233 below. **Turnique hymenaeos:** on the quadrisyllabic line-end, see 69n. Cf. 7.344 *Turnique hymenaeis,* 7.398 *Turnique . . . hymenaeos.* A segment of the public has soured on Turnus; he takes on a role similar to that of Paris in the *Iliad,* and he is resented because of how, in the mourners' eyes, his private, selfish desire for marriage and, through it, power and standing has led to war and the people's suffering. Turnus had not yet been betrothed to Latinus' daughter Lavinia (contra Liv. 1.2.1 *Turnus, rex Rutulorum, cui pacta Lavinia ante adventum Aeneae fuerat*), but he had been her leading suitor (see 7.53–8), and he expected to marry her (see 440, 7.421–34 (where Juno, disguised as Calybe, plays on Turnus' belief), 9.138, 10.79).

218 ipsum . . . ipsumque: emphatic repetition, reflecting the angry intensity with which the women and children repeat their demand. **decernere**

ferro 'to decide things with the sword', an Ennian phrase (*Ann.* 132 Sk.). V. uses it again at 12.695, where, in a significant echo of this line, Turnus tells the Rutulians that he will settle the war in single combat. For other examples, see 7.525 and 12.282.

219 qui . . . poscat: causal, 'since he demands'. **regnum Italiae et:** hyperbolic: in their hostility to Turnus, his opponents exaggerate Turnus' imperial ambitions, which, they maintain, he seeks to further through marriage to Lavinia. Cf. 8.147, where A. exaggerates the aggressive aims of Turnus' Rutulians: *quin omnem Hesperiam penitus sua sub iuga mittant.* Still, their accusation is not wholly without foundation: Turnus has conquered many towns (cf. 12.22–3) and has campaigned against the Etruscans (cf. 7.426), thereby demonstrating the energy and desire to expand his kingdom and to become a more significant player at least in central Italy (Adler 2003: 172). The initial syllable in *Italiae,* naturally short, is lengthened to fit the hexameter. The elision in *regnum Italiae et* reflects heated emotion.

220 ingrauat 'aggravates'. The verb appears for the first time in extant literature here; it is otherwise predominantly late and Christian (*TLL* VII.1565.79–1566.81). This is its one occurrence in V. **saeuus Drances:** the adj. reflects Drances' violent enmity towards Turnus, already emphasised at 122–3. **uocari:** it is tempting to understand the infinitive as *simplex* for *prouocari*; *prouoco* is regular for challenging to single combat (*OLD* 3). Plain *uoco,* however, is possible (*OLD* 5).

220–1 solumque . . . | . . . Turnum: a distortion of A.'s counterfactual comments at 116–18; see Intro. p. 5. Repeated *solus* echoes 10.442–3 *solus ego in Pallanta feror, soli mihi Pallas | debetur,* where Turnus seeks to fight Pallas by himself, and 12.466–7 *solum densa in caligine Turnum | uestigat lustrans, solum in certamina poscit,* where A. pursues Turnus on the battlefield. The instances of repeated *solus* follow Turnus' progression as a single fighter: he first defeats the overwhelmed Pallas, then is pushed by Drances to take on A. singly, and then finds himself chased by A. in a battle that ends ultimately in their one-on-one fight and Turnus' death in revenge for Pallas. Non-repeated *solus* occurs in connection with the single combat between A. and Turnus at 434, 442, and 12.16.

221 posci in certamina: *posci* pointedly echoes *poscat* at 219. Cf. 434, 12.467 *solum in certamina poscit,* 8.613–14 (Venus) *ne . . . | . . . dubites in proelia poscere Turnum,* and 10.661 *illum autem Aeneas absentem in proelia poscit.* **Turnum:** emphatically positioned at the end of the line and the sentence.

222–3 multa ... | pro Turno: 'but at the same time there was an abundance of sentiment in varied language for Turnus'. *uariis . . . dictis* is probably a modal abl. conveying that Turnus' supporters defended him in different ways. Perhaps, however, *uariis dictis* = 'in conflicting terms'; the abl. would distinguish the opinions of Turnus' supporters from those of his detractors described at 217–21.

223 magnum reginae nomen obumbrat: the queen is Amata, wife of Latinus; Turnus' mother Venilia was her relation (identified as her sister at D.H. *Ant. Rom.* 1.64.2 and Serv. ad 7.366), and she burns to have him marry Lavinia (cf. 7.344–5). Cf. 7.581 *neque enim leue nomen Amatae. obumbrat* = 'shelters'; Serv. ad loc. glosses with *tuetur, defendit.* The verb appears first in V., and occurs only here and at 12.578. Cf. Claud. *Carm. min.* 31.46 *texit pauperiem nominis umbra tui.* Lucan perhaps has V. in mind at 1.135 (Pompey) *stat magni nominis umbra.*

224 multa . . . fama 'great fame'. Turnus' *fama* contrasts with Amata's *nomen* in the previous line, with an implied opposition between the shading cover that Amata's name provides and the visibility that Turnus possesses from the fame that his military prowess has earned him. **uirum:** equivalent to '(fighting) hero'; cf. 9 and 125. **meritis . . . tropaeis** 'with well-earned trophies', an abl. of means.

225–42 At 8.9–17, Venulus (by all appearances an invented minor character; see Horsfall 1991: 73) had been sent to Diomedes, who was settled in Italy (see 243–95n.), to seek an alliance with him in the fight against A. and the Trojans, so that he might join the war as a Latin ally. As now becomes clear, Venulus was part of a larger diplomatic cohort. He and his fellow legates return from their mission with devastating news: Diomedes has refused the Latin proposal.

225 motus refers to the civil disturbance caused by the heated debates over Turnus. **medio in flagrante tumultu** 'in the midst of the burning tumult'. *flagro* describes a city seething with unrest. The *flagrans tumultus* recalls the flaming pyres of the Latin dead and, via wordplay, suggests their *tumuli*; the implication is that the heavy casualties have brought fiery upheaval to the city (Paschalis 1997: 361–2). If this is the same day as the *tertia lux* at 210, it is difficult to understand how the Trojans renew the fight after the twelve-day truce has ended (see 210n., 445–67n.), since the battle takes place on the same day as the one here. The implication is instead that there were several days of tumult, and hence that V. has now jumped ahead in time, and that this is the first day after the completion of the truce.

226 ecce: the deictic signpost marks a change of focus and a sudden disconcerting development, as commonly (Austin on 2.57, 2.203, Dionisotti 2007: 82, 88–90). There are forty-four examples of *ecce* in V. (thirty-seven in *Aen.*, with the greatest number, eight, in *Aen.* 2). **super** 'to top things off'; the adv. in the sense of *insuper*. The news from the embassy arrives to inflame the city on top of all the dissension already blazing there. **maesti** modifies *legati* in the next line; the gloom of the legates foretells the failure of their mission. The adj. is strongly alliterative with *magna*; V. is drawn to alliterative combinations with *maestus* (Traina on 12.514). Cf. *muneribus, maestamque* at 26 and the prominent *m*-sounds in *maestoque immugit* at 38 and *maesti comitamur* at 52. **magna Diomedis ab urbe:** the city is Argyripa or Arpi (see 250n.) in Apulia.

227–30 There was some reason for Latin optimism that Diomedes would accept the embassy's request beyond the fact that he had already fought the Trojans. Diomedes had grown up and ruled in Argos (Apollod. 1.8.4–6, 3.6.1), and V. gives Turnus Argive ancestry (see 7.371–2 *et Turno . . . | Inachus Acrisiusque patres mediaeque Mycenae*). In addition, Venulus apparently comes from Tibur (see 757n.), which had Argive roots via its legendary founder Catillus or Tiburnus, each identified as a son of the Argive king Amphiaraus; cf. 7.672, Plin. *Nat.* 16.237, with Serv. ad 8.9. Yet this bleak summary of the mission in *oratio obliqua*, which reflects the legates' brief initial report, quickly snuffs out all hopes. Diomedes is also said to have helped the Apulian king Daunus defeat the Messapians (see 247 and Malkin 1998: 243); in some accounts, he becomes Daunus' son-in-law (Myers on Ov. *Met.* 14.458–60). V. gives Turnus' father the name Daunus (10.616, 10.688, 12.22, 12.90, 12.723, 12.785, 12.934); he is the first, as far as we know, to do so. There is no evidence in V. that this is the same Daunus as the Apulian king. See, further, Fletcher 2006: 240–1.

227 legati responsa ferunt: *responsum* is common for a reply given by a ruler to envoys (*OLD* 1b); *ferunt* is probably *simplex* for *referunt* (cf. *referte* at 176, *referant* at 240). Cf. Enn. *Ann.* 202 Sk. *orator sine pace redit regique refert rem.* The language has historiographical flavour; cf. Liv. 4.45.4 *legati missi cum responsa retulissent dubia*, 37.28.3 *hoc tam triste responsum cum rettulissent legati*, as well as 2.39.10–11 *oratores atrox responsum rettulerunt*, 37.6.7 *consul idem illud responsum rettulit.* **nihil . . . actum** 'nothing had been achieved'. *nihil agere* is colloquial; the embassy lays out a stark truth in blunt speech.

227–8 nihil . . . | . . . nil: the anaphora emphasises the futility of the mission as well as the deflation of the legates. **omnibus . . . | tantorum impensis operum** 'by all the outlay of so many efforts'. *impensis* (abl. of means) contains a suggestion of wasted energy (*OLD* 3b).

228 dona . . . aurum 'gifts of gold'. The phrase is a special case of hendiadys, in which the second noun gives the material of which the first is composed (see Mynors on *G.* 2.192 *pateris . . . et auro*). Cf. 7.155 *donaque ferre uiro pacemque exposcere Teucris.*

229 arma 'armed forces', as at 10.150–1 *Mezentius arma | quae sibi conciliet.*

230 pacem . . . petendum 'peace must be sought'. *petendum* is preferable to *petendam* as the *lectio difficilior*, despite the evidence of the capital MSS, and despite *quaerenda* earlier in the line. The gerund with direct object is archaic (*NLS* §206 n. ii, H–S 372–3, Penney 1999: 260). Commentators cite as a parallel Lucr. 1.111 *aeternas quoniam poenas in morte timendum*; there are, however, fourteen other Lucretian examples of the construction (Leonard and Smith, Intro. p. 139 n. 142). Cf. Sil. 11.559 *nunc pacem orandum.*

231 deficit ingenti luctu 'falters from deep sadness'. At the beginning of the war with the Trojans (7.594–600), Latinus grieves for his people's folly and sacrilege, which, he knows, will lead to their defeat. Yet he does not have the strength to counter effectively the battle fever. As a result, he neglects his duties as a leader (cf. 7.600 *saepsit se tectis rerumque reliquit habenas*) and only resists passively, shutting himself in darkness rather than opening the gates of war (7.616–19; cf. 114n.). In this first appearance of the king since those lines, he is once more grieving, because the news confirms what he has always known: the Latin forces are destined for defeat. Latinus' initial response to the news about Diomedes indicates frailty similar to that demonstrated in *Aen.* 7. Yet, as will soon become clear, he retains the regal authority to call and preside at a council of leading Latins (even if his power there is far less than absolute; see 302–35n., 312n., 314n.). Cf. 62–3 *luctus* | . . . *ingentis*; the war has taken a toll on the elderly kings Latinus and Evander and, in different ways, burdened them with tremendous sadness. **rex ipse Latinus:** the phrase is formulaic, appearing in the same line-position at 7.432, 7.556, and 12.657; cf., too, 9.274 *rex habet ipse Latinus. ipse* is attached to the name of a person invested with authority, as often (see Rampioni, *EV* IV.313).

232 fatalem: the personal use of the adj. is rare (*OLD* 2b, *TLL* VI.332.48–60) and occurs only here in V. Latinus recognises again what he had understood when he first encountered the Trojans: A. is sent by Fate (cf. 7.255 *hunc illum fatis externa ab sede profectum*, 7.272–3 *hunc illum poscere fata* | *et reor et . . . opto*). **manifesto numine** 'by clear/unmistakable divine will'.

233 ira deum: to Latinus, events have confirmed what he predicted at 7.595: *ipsi has sacrilego pendetis sanguine poenas.* The king views the war with A. and the Trojans as sacrilegious and, thus, of a kind to excite divine wrath.

234 ergo: the particle is common in high poetry. V. prefers it to *igitur* by a wide margin (fifty-four examples of *ergo*, three of *igitur*); even so, *igitur* does not have as strong a prose character as *itaque* (Axelson 1945: 93, Tränkle 1960: 145 n. 1; *itaque* does not occur in V.). **concilium magnum primosque suorum** 'a mighty council of his chief men'; hendiadys. This is the sole example in *Aen.* of an extended wartime assembly (which I distinguish from the *concilium deorum* at 10.1–117, although see 376–444n.). An assembly is the setting in which Nisus and Euryalus volunteer for their sortie (9.226–30), but V. does not show the deliberations; there is also an assembly called at 5.42–71, but the setting is not wartime, and only A. speaks. Assembly scenes are a topos of epic; on models for this one, see 302–35n., 336–75n., and 376–444n. This example comprises both Venulus' report on the embassy to Diomedes and a war-council proper, in which Latinus, Drances, and Turnus speak about what course of action to pursue in the war. The scene combines epic convention with evocations of Roman senatorial meetings (see 235n., 314n.). The meeting is modelled on the Homeric βουλή, or select council.

235 alta intra limina: the palace described at 7.170–91, which also served as the curia (7.174 *hoc illis curia templum*); the sense is of a proto-meeting of the Roman senate in that space. The senate was to meet in *templa per augures constituta* (Gel. 14.7.7). **cogit** 'convenes', also at 304 and 460; the verb for convening a meeting of the Roman senate (*OLD* 4).

236 The line has a weak principal caesura in the third foot. Such caesurae are rare in V., occurring about 1 per cent of the time. Norden, Anh. VII.2d.1 suspects the influence of Ennius; but third-foot weak principal caesurae are rare in his extant poetry, as they are in Lucretius and Catullus. They are common in Homer. The caesura represents excitement, as elsewhere (476, 2.48, 4.164, 4.417, 4.604, 9.732); it can also represent calm or be used simply for metrical variety (see Winbolt 1903: 33–5). **olli:** the archaic form for *illi*, already a deliberate archaism in Ennius (see Sk., pp. 64–5). V. has *olli* twenty-one times (dat. sing. and nom, plural), eighteen times in emphatic line-initial position. (He has the plural *ollis* twice.) Quintilian (8.3.24) remarks that some archaisms, including *olli*, confer dignity, venerability, and distinction. In this case, *olli* is appropriate for the august men and solemn setting and lends a patina of archaic, epic grandeur. Sound, however, might have been another consideration, as V. tends to use *olli* near other words having *o*-sounds (Fordyce on 7.458). *olli* is part of a cluster of archaisms (see 242n. and

248n.), which heightens the sense of antiquity, formality, solemnity, and grandeur. **fluuntque:** the *lectio difficilior* over *ruuntque.* V. is the first attested author to use *fluo* of 'streaming' to a place (*TLL* VI.974.13–21); another example comes at 12.444.

236–7 plenis | . . . uiis 'along the packed streets'. An abl. of route (A–G §429.4a).

237 sedet in mediis: cf. 7.169 (Latinus) *solio medius consedit auito.* **maximus aeuo:** old age is a defining characteristic of Latinus (as it is for Evander and Acoetes in this book); V. introduces him with the words *iam senior* (7.46). Here age confers authority and is one of the things that gives Latinus precedence in the council; kingship was no doubt sufficient to ensure his status, but V. adds seniority to the mix.

238 primus sceptris 'first in power'. *sceptris* is a poetic plural and a metonymy for regal authority (cf. 7.173). It recalls the sceptre held by Homeric heroes in council (cf. e.g. *Il.* 1.234–9, 2.101–8, with Combellack 1948, Unruh 2011); cf., too, Homeric 'sceptred king/kings' (σκηπτοῦχοι βασιλῆες, *Il.* 1.279, 2.86, *Od.* 2.231, 4.63–4, 5.9, 8.41). At 12.206–11, Latinus has an actual sceptre in hand, in imitation of Achilles at *Il.* 1.234–9. **haud laeta fronte:** litotes, for emphasis. The rhythm of the spondaic line reflects the dark mood of the king.

239 Aetola ex urbe: the city is Aetolian because Diomedes was Aetolian through his father Tydeus and grandfather Oeneus (king of Calydon in Aetolia); Tydeus later fled to Argos (see 227–30n.). Cf. 10.28 *Aetolis . . . ab Arpis.*

240–1 responsa . . . | . . . suo: Latinus heard the embassy's report in the summarised fashion recorded at 227–30; hence his response at 231. The king now demands from Venulus an account in detailed order of what Diomedes had said.

242 Venulus: a plausibly Italian name (cf. Turnus' mother Venilia (see 223n., 10.76), an Italian deity). But Venulus also calls to mind Venus, whom Diomedes wounded at Troy when she rescued A. from him. Diomedes considers that act of violence a crime (277) for which he paid the penalty in his suffering after the war (see Intro. pp. 14–15). Hence the name Venulus, assuming it recalled Venus to Diomedes, would presumably have had a chilling effect on his response to the embassy: the name would have made Diomedes remember the suffering that attended his earlier fight with A., and this would have discouraged him from battling with A. again. See Paschalis 1997: 362. **farier infit:** *farier* is an archaic passive form of the infinitive; such infs. appears five other times in V. (4.493 *accingier*, 7.70 *dominarier*, 8.493 *defendier*, 9.231 *admittier*, *G.* 1.454 *immiscerier*). While metrically convenient in the fifth foot, it is joined to another archaism with epic resonance, *infit* (see Lyne 1989: 16), to lend archaising solemnity. That verb with an inf. of speaking occurs several times in Plautus but is otherwise high-poetic and archaising (so Skutsch on Enn. *Ann.* 385).

243–95 THE REPORT OF VENULUS

Venulus gives an extended account of the embassy to Diomedes. For the bulk of his report, he relates in direct speech Diomedes' response to the legates, in which Diomedes refuses the Latins' appeal and presses them to make peace with the Trojans. On the speech, see Intro. pp. 14–15. Stories placing Diomedes in Italy go back perhaps to the seventh century (cf. Mimnermus fr. 22 West, with Malkin 1998: 237); he was said to have settled in Apulia and to have founded a number of cities in the region (Timaeus *FGrH* 566 F 53, Malkin 1998: 234–57; on Diomedes in the west, see also Hornblower on Lyc. *Alex.* 592–632).

As a hero who has become a peaceable leader and who is alive to the value of *pietas* (see 292), Diomedes is an exemplum for A.: the former enemy 'curves back to serve as a model for the peaceful and benevolent [ruler] that Aeneas ... [is] finally meant to be' (Wiltshire 1989: 105).

243 Vidimus: the first word of Venulus' speech conveys that he and the embassy have carried out their orders. With *contigimusque manum* at 245, *uidimus* is a way, too, of claiming accuracy for the report, on the grounds that sight and physical contact demonstrate direct experience of events and establish conditions for a faithful account (see Hardie 2012: 140–1). With 245, the verb suggests Venulus' awe at encountering Diomedes; there is an overtone of wonder at having been in the presence of such a hero. **Diomedem:** *Diomeden*, found in many MSS (including capital ones), is metrically impossible. '"Diomedem" is really supported by "Diomeden," the forms being constantly confused in MSS' (C–N). **Argiuaque:** see 227–30n.

245 contigimusque manum: hands would have been joined in welcome (cf. 8.124 *excepitque manu dextramque amplexus inhaesit*). **qua concidit Ilia tellus:** Venulus exaggerates when he attributes the destruction of Troy to Diomedes, even though the Greek was understood to have played a leading role in it (cf. 2.163–8). This is a sign of his awe; it also underlines the weight of the mission, directed as it was to this significant, heroic enemy of Troy in the Trojan War.

246 patriae cognomine gentis: an allusion to Argos Hippion (Ἄργος Ἵππιον), of which Argyripa was understood to be a corruption (see O'Hara 2017: 230). Ἵππιον = 'of a horse or horses'; the plain of Argos, the home of Diomedes, was associated with horses. Cf. Ἄργος ἱππόβοτον ('Argos, grazed by horses') at *Il.* 2.287, 3.75, 3.258, 6.152, 9.246, 15.30, 19.329, *Od.* 3.263, 4.99, 4.562, 15.239, and 15.274. Apulia was also known for its horses; cf. 678n. on *Iapyge.*

247 uictor: an apparent reference to the story that Diomedes joined with King Daunus to defeat the Messapians (see 227–30n.). **Gargani condebat Iapygis agris:** *Garganus* refers to a mountainous promontory in Apulia (cf. Hor. *Carm.* 2.9.7, Luc. 9.183–4); V. is somewhat loose with the geography, because Arpi lies just outside the promontory. 'Iapygian' is a 'learned anachronism, in that V.'s use of the adj., used in the poet's time for Messapia or Calabria, had once been applied to all of the E. coast up to Gargano' (Horsfall ad loc.). The imperfect *condebat* reveals that Diomedes was still in the process of building the city. Ovid changes tense when he imitates V. at *Met.* 14.458–9 *ille quidem sub Iapyge maxima Dauno | moenia condiderat.*

248 = 1.520. **introgressi:** the verb is first found in V.; it is either an archaism (for which evidence is now lost) or an archaising neologism.

249 munera: the gifts of gold mentioned at 228.

250 The indirect questions depend on *docemus* in the previous line. Venulus performs the task given him at 8.10–13 *Latio consistere Teucros, | aduectum Aenean classi uictosque Penates | inferre et fatis regem se dicere posci | edoceat.* **qui bellum intulerint:** *bellum inferre* = 'make war (on)', a standard, prosaic phrase (cf. e.g. Cic. *Catil.* 1.23, Liv. 26.20.5, Tac. *Hist.* 2.15, Eutrop. *Brev.* 1.11). **Arpos:** the alternative and later name for Argyripa. Once a large, significant city (see Str. 6.3.9), and an ally of Rome (see Liv. 8.25.3, 9.13.6–12); after the Battle of Cannae, it went over to Hannibal, who had his winter quarters near the city in 215 BCE (Liv. 24.3.16–17). Arpi never regained its importance after the consul Quintus Fabius Maximus recovered it in 213 BCE; cf. Str. 6.3.9 (on Arpi) 'but now it is diminished' (ἀλλὰ νῦν ἐλάττων ἐστίν).

251 placido sic reddidit ore: the introductory speech formula anticipates the peaceable Diomedes who follows. *placidus* = 'calm', but also 'calming' (cf. Ov. *Met.* 15.657–8 *placido tales emittere pectore uoces, | 'pone metus'*). Cf. 1.521 (Ilioneus) *placido sic pectore coepit*; after repeating 1.520 at 248, V. here echoes the following line.

252 o fortunatae gentes: a *makarismos*, or declaration of blessedness. Cf. *G.* 2.458–9 *o fortunatos nimium, sua si bona norint, | agricolas*; that passage continues by describing a potential (but unrealised) Golden Age for farmers, far removed from civil war. **Saturnia regna:** Saturn (the great-grandfather of Latinus) was said to have brought the Golden Age to Latium; for the myth, see 8.319–25 and *G.* 2.538–40. The Saturnian period was one of peace; hence *Saturnia regna* implies that the Latins are by origin and inherently a peaceful people. This is a way of rebuking and squelching their desire to fight the Trojans. In V.'s telling, the Golden Age later gave way to times of warfare in Italy (8.326–32), and war was woven into Latin history and its material culture (7.181–6, 7.611–17). When the Trojans arrive, the Latins live in a second age of peace (7.45–6 *rex arua Latinus et urbes | iam senior longa placidas in pace regebat*), although it is a challenge to reconcile this with 8.55 (the Pallanteans) *hi bellum adsidue ducunt cum gente Latina*; for discussion, see Adler 2003: 168–71. There is also a portent (Lavinia's burning hair and headgear) that the age of peace is ending (7.80 *sed populo magnum portendere bellum*). On V.'s treatment of the Golden Age in Latium, see Thomas 1982: 93–103. V. has *Saturnia regna* at *Ecl.* 4.6 and 6.41; the epithet goes back to Ennius (*Ann.* 21 Sk.). Cf. 6.792–4 *Augustus Caesar, diui genus, aurea condet | saecula qui rursus Latio regnata per arua | Saturno quondam.*

253 fortuna 'ill-fortune', in marked contrast to *fortunatae* in the previous line.

253–4 quietos | sollicitat: a sharp juxtaposition, emphasised by the enjambment. V. has the same contrast at 4.379–80 *ea cura quietos | sollicitat.*

254 suadetque . . . lacessere: *suadere* with acc. (*uos* from the previous line) + inf. is found mainly in poetry and post-Augustan prose (Tarrant on 12.814, *NLS* §143). *lacesso* = 'provoke, stir up'. Cf. 10.10 *ferrumque lacessere suasit.* **ignota . . . bella:** after *Saturnia regna*, Diomedes again indicates that the Latins are a Golden Age people that do not know war. This is consistent with 7.45–6, but is a rhetorical exaggeration when read against 8.55 or in relation to the Latins' history (see 252n.).

255 Iliacos: the adj. is Hellenistic in origin (Ἰλιακός, Call. fr. 114.25 Pf.); it is first found in Latin at Catul. 68.86. Cf. *Iliacis campis* at 1.97 and 10.335. **ferro uiolauimus:** in pointed contrast with the Golden Age imagery of the previous lines. A keen expression of Diomedes' guilt, which, along with revealing his thoughts on the Trojan War, does two things: it dissuades the Latins from joining battle with the Trojans by representing war with them in a very negative light, as an act of impiety rather than a glorious, heroic struggle; and it implies that Diomedes is no longer inclined to view the Trojans as enemies and, thus, that he will not join an alliance against them.

256 mitto 'I say nothing of' (*OLD* 5). *ea* follows *mitto* in MSS, including the capital M, P, and R, and in all modern editions. I follow Kraggerud 2012–13 = 2017: 333–4 in deleting *ea* as an interpolated scholastic gloss, on two grounds: preparatory *ea* appears nowhere else in V.; and *quae . . . altis* must be an indirect interrogative (with an understood *sint*), like *quos . . . uiros* in the following line, whereas *ea* makes it a rel. clause. Conte 2016: ix accepts Kraggerud's reading. For *mitto* with indirect interrogatives, see *TLL* VIII.1177.80–1178.4. *mitto* begins a *praeteritio*, in which Diomedes brings up a topic by claiming to bypass it; this calls attention to the topic, thereby suggesting to the Latins the severe difficulty of war with the Trojans. **exhausta** 'drained to the dregs'. This metaphorical use of *exhaustus* to describe the total experience of terrible things is first attested in V.; cf. 4.14 *quae bella exhausta canebat*, with Austin's note, and 10.57 *totque maris uastaeque exhausta pericula terrae.*

257 quos . . . uiros: cf. 1.100–1 *ubi tot Simois correpta sub undis | scuta uirum galeasque et fortia corpora uoluit* (recasting *Il.* 12.22–3). The Simois was a river on the Trojan plain. Cf. *Il.* 21.218–20, where, memorably, the Scamander River complains that Achilles chokes it with dead bodies. **premat** 'submerges' (*OLD* 16). **ille:** probably with negative colour, 'infamous', given that Diomedes is describing the horrors of war. **infanda:** a very strong, emotional word (Austin on 2.3, Pease on 4.85). **per orbem:** Hardie 2012: 142 suggests a pun on the Epic Cycle, κύκλος (*orbis*), which included narratives on what happened to Greek heroes after the Trojan War and as they sought their *nostoi*, or homecomings. Barchiesi 1999: 334 identifies the same pun at 1.457 *bellaque iam fama totum uulgata per orbem.*

258 Ovid will repudiate Diomedes' assertion that all the Greeks paid for their collective guilt when, in imitation of this line, he ascribes guilt to the lesser Ajax (son of Oileus) alone (*Met.* 14.469): *quam meruit poenam solus digessit in omnes.* **omnes:** nom., enclosing 255–8 with the appositive *quicumque* at 255, rather than acc. with *poenas.*

259 uel . . . manus: Serv. ad loc. compares Pacuvius (*trag.* 294 Schierl) *Priamus, si adesset, ipse eius commiseresceret.* Ovid recasts V. at *Met.* 14.474 *Graecia tum potuit Priamo quoque flenda uideri.* Cf. 2.6–8 *quis talia fando | Myrmidonum Dolopumue aut duri miles Vlixi | temperet a lacrimis.*

259–60 triste Mineruae | sidus: the reference is to a storm sent by Minerva to punish Oilean Ajax for violating Cassandra at or on the altar of Minerva; see Hyg. *Fab.* 116 and [Apollod.] *Epit.* 5.22 and 6.6. V. has Juno tell the story of Ajax's death at 1.39–45; cf. *Od.* 4.499–511. *sidus* appears to designate a constellation that controls the weather (*OLD* 5c). Serv. ad loc. suspects that the subject is the stormy spring equinox (Athena watches over Aries).

260 ultorque Caphereus gives more precise geographical information than *Euboicae cautes*; Cape Caphereus was a promontory at the SE end of Euboea (mod. Kavo Doro). For Caphereus as the site of Ajax's wreck, see Hyg. *Fab.* 116 *ad saxa Capharea naufragium fecerunt.* In Homer, Ajax wrecked and died on the great cliffs of the island Gyrae (*Od.* 4.500–10); this was perhaps near, or understood to be near, Caphereus. V. personifies the place as an *ultor* because it is where Minerva gets her vengeance on Ajax. But *ultor Caphereus* might also refer secondarily to Nauplius, the father of Palamedes. To avenge the death of his son, Nauplius lit false beacons for the Greeks off Caphereus; many ships headed for the fires, thinking it was a harbour, and were wrecked (Hyg. *Fab.* 116 and [Apollod.] *Epit.* 6.6–11).

262 Protei . . . columnas: the island of Pharos in Egypt, here balancing the Pillars of Hercules at the western end of the Mediterranean. This supports a reference to Nauplius at 260; V. moves from his false beacons to Pharos, home of the famous lighthouse. For Menelaus' journey to Pharos and encounter with Proteus, see *Od.* 4.351–586; cf. Str. 1.2.30–1. *Protei* scans as two syllables by synizesis (the contraction of two syllables into one). In V., the gen. singular *-ei* of Gk proper names in *-eus* is always a monosyllable (cf. *Idomenei* at 265 below, 1.41 *Oilei,* 1.120 *Ilionei,* 8.383 *Nerei*).

263 Aetnaeos uidit Cyclopas Vlixes: for the famous story of Ulysses and the Cyclops, see *Od.* 9.105–542. V.'s version of it occurs at 3.618–638 (part of the Achaemenides episode (3.588–691)). *Cyclopas* is a Gk acc. form with a short final syllable. Cf. ps.-V. *Cul.* 332 *Aetnaeusque Cyclops.*

264 regna Neoptolemi: Neoptolemus (= Pyrrhus), the son of Achilles and king of Epirus. At 3.330–2, Andromache recounts how Orestes, the son of Agamemnon, killed Neoptolemus (for thorough discussion, see Horsfall on 3.332); after his death, his kingdom was portioned out, partly to the Trojan seer Helenus (cf. 3.333–4). **uersosque:** perhaps 'subverted' (*OLD* 5b), or perhaps *simplex* for *euersos* = 'overthrown' (*OLD* 4).

265 Idomenei: from Crete, a main Greek chieftain in the Trojan War (cf. *Il.* 2.645–52, 13.210–518). With *uersosque penates* in the previous line, the apparent reference is to the story that Idomeneus' wife Meda, at Nauplius' plotting, had got involved with the Cretan Leucus. This man then killed the queen and her daughter and took over the rule of Crete, while driving out Idomeneus when he returned from the Trojan War (Lyc. *Alex.* 1214–25, [Apollod.] *Epit.* 6.10–11). The more famous version of the myth is that Idomeneus was caught in a storm and vowed to Poseidon that, if he escaped and got home, he would sacrifice to the god the first thing he saw; this turned out to be his son. When Idomeneus fulfilled his vow, the gods sent a plague, and as a result, the Cretans drove him into exile (see Serv. ad 264 and 3.121). On Idomeneus, see also 3.121–3 and 3.400–1. **Libycone . . . Locros:** the lesser Ajax was king of the Locrians. At 3.399, Helenus reports that the Narycian Locri (another name for the Opuntian Locri; Naryx was a town in Opuntian Locris and birthplace of Ajax) had settled in southern Italy and built a city (Locri Epizephyrii in Bruttium). V. now has Locri settling in Africa; on the inconsistency, see Horsfall 2016: 82.

266 A stately five-word line (see 53n.) to introduce Agamemnon, the climactic figure in the list of Greek warriors. **ductor:** a more poetic and sonorous word than *dux*; see Austin on 2.14.

267 coniugis infandae: the very strong adj. (see 257n.) paints Clytemnestra in the darkest hue. **prima inter limina:** the detail that Agamemnon was murdered when he first entered his palace is striking; Homer at *Od.* 4.519–37 describes his death at a feast (as does Seneca at *Ag.* 867–907), while in Aeschylus (*A.* 1107–11, 1125–9, 1538–40), he is killed while being bathed. V.'s detail heightens the outrageousness of the deed (so Macr. 4.3.12).

268 oppetiit: the intransitive use of the verb appears to be a Virgilian innovation, varying *mortem oppetere.* Intransitive *oppetere* as an elevated synonym for *mori* also occurs at 9.654, 12.543, and 12.640. Cf. V. Fl. 1.553–4 *quae robora cernes | oppetere et magnis Asiam concedere fatis*; intransitive *oppetere* and *Asiam* strongly indicate imitation of V. **deuictam Asiam subsedit adulter** 'the adulterer lay in wait for the conquest of Asia'. *deuictam* is part of an AUC (*ab urbe condita*) construction, in which the noun and the predicative participle create a noun-phrase; in sense, the construction is equivalent to an abstract noun with a dependent gen. (*NLS* §95, G–L §325.3, 664.2). *deuictam Asiam* = Agamemnon, referred to by the land he has conquered; a concentrated, elliptical phrase that suggests the profound and abrupt reversal of Agamemnon's fortunes and a contrast between the conqueror and his underhanded, adulterous assassin (cf. Quinn 1968: 389–90). Transitive *subsidere*, a hunting metaphor, is first found in V. and is rare and poetic after him (cf. Sil. 13.221 *subsidere saepe leonem*). The rarity of the construction explains the variant *deuicta Asia*, which yields intransitive *subsidere*, as well as the variant *possedit*. Hunting imagery is prevalent in Aeschylus' *Agamemnon* (and in the *Oresteia* as a whole). Cf. *A.* 1223–30, where Cassandra describes Aegisthus as a 'feeble/impotent lion' (λέοντ' ἄναλκιν, 1224) – i.e. a predator after prey – who stays at home plotting retribution and waiting for the return of Agamemnon, the 'commander of the ships and destroyer of Troy' (νεῶν τ' ἄπαρχος Ἰλίου τ' ἀναστάτης, 1227).

269 inuidisse deos: best taken as an acc. + inf. with *referam* at 264. This creates some challenges for the reader/listener, but not enough to suppose a lacuna (Courtney 1981: 20) or to indicate that either 264–5 or 266–8 are out of place, as older editors proposed (for further discussion, see C–N, Williams, and Horsfall ad loc.); it is also preferable to an infinitive of exclamation ('to think that the gods have begrudged', accepted by C–N, Gransden, Fratantuono), which is irruptive and contrary to the tone of the passage. **ut** introduces an object clause after *inuidisse* of the thing grudged, an extremely rare construction, not found again until Christian late antiquity (*TLL* VII.2.195.55–63). Cf. *inuidit . . . ne* at 43(n.).

270 coniugium optatum: *coniugium* = *coniugem*, as at 2.579 (*OLD* 3a). V. departs from most other accounts of the Diomedes myth in not having him make it home to his wife Aigialeia. In other versions, Aigialeia commits adultery at the instigation either of Aphrodite, in revenge for the wound she suffered from Diomedes (Lyc. *Alex.* 610–13, Antoninus Liberalis 37), or of Nauplius himself ([Apollod]. *Epit.* 6.9); she then drives the returned Diomedes from Argos. (Lycophron (*Alex.* 614) also has the adulterous Aigialeia plot to kill Diomedes upon his return to Argos.) Plausibly, V. anticipated knowledge of the bad Aigialeia among at least some of his readers and supposed that they would register the dramatic irony in *coniugium optatum*. For Diomedes, however, his excellent wife stands in pointed contrast with the *coniunx infanda* Clytemnestra. **pulchram Calydona:** *Calydona* is a Gk acc. form. Cf. Καλυδῶνος ἐραννῆς ('lovely Calydon') at *Il.* 9.531 and 9.577.

271–4 The transformation of Diomedes' comrades into birds. The story is attested in different forms from the fourth century BCE (e.g. Lyc. *Alex.* 594–609, Antoninus Liberalis 37, Plin. *Nat.* 10.126–7; see Forbes Irving 1990: 230–2, Malkin 1998: 238–9). V. does not identify the birds; Servius (ad 271) calls them *aues Diomedeae*, and other sources ancient and modern identify them as a kind of seabird or heron (see Capponi, *EV* v*.349, André 1967: 30–40). The birds were said to inhabit the Adriatic Islands of Diomedeia off Apulia (Serv. ad 271, Str. 6.3.9) and to have been friendly to Greek sailors alone (Serv. ad 271, Lyc. *Alex.* 605–11, Antoninus Liberalis 37.6). About these things, too, V. is silent. Ovid expands upon V.'s tale of metamorphosis at *Met.* 14.483–509.

271 horribili uisu 'of dreadful appearance'. An abl. of description with *portenta,* and a variation on supine constructions with *uisu/dictu.* Cf. 7.78 *id uero horrendum ac uisu mirabile ferri,* 9.521 *horrendus uisu.* **sequuntur** 'pursue' or 'chase' in hostile fashion; perhaps *simplex* for *insequuntur.* Sc. *me.*

272 et: epexegetic; what follows explains what the *portenta* are.

273 fluminibusque: V. writes of rivers despite the localisation of the story on the islands off Apulia; this suggests that his imagination is divided between the islands and mainland Apulia (so Horsfall ad loc.), and that he wished to indicate extensive wandering beyond those *insulae.* **aues** 'as birds'. **meorum:** the gen. plural concludes a line ten times in *Aen.*; this is its fixed and exclusive position, due to obvious metrical convenience. *meorum* never appears at line-end in *Ecl.* or *G.* or before V. in extant hexameters. Conte 2016: 86 suggests that V. considered concluding *meorum* to be a feature 'of a sublime or almost grandiloquent stylistic register'; the same can be said of other gen. plural possessive adjs. (e.g. *suorum* at 185 and 234, *tuorum* at 439, *mearum* at 586). *meorum* at line-end occurs twelve times in Ovid's *Metamorphoses,* but only twice in Lucan, four times total in Statius' *Thebaid* and *Achilleid,* twice in Valerius Flaccus, and three times in Silius Italicus.

274 scopulos: rocky sea crags; a reference to the islands where the birds were traditionally located. **lacrimosis uocibus:** suggestive of a bird's mournful call. It is tempting to see, too, an indirect reference to a version of the myth that V. bypasses, viz. the story that Diomedes' men were metamorphosed into birds in grief upon his death (see Serv. ad 271, Forbes Irving 1990: 231). Adjs. with suffix *-osus* in V. can be poetic, as *lacrimosus* is (*TLL* VII.846.70–1), or colloquial; see Ross 1969: 53–60, Adams 2013: 571–8.

275 haec adeo 'these very things'. *adeo* usually emphasises the word it follows – often a monosyllabic pronoun, as here – and comes second in the line (see Clausen on *Ecl.* 4.11, Austin on 4.96). **mihi iam speranda fuerunt** 'I had now to expect/anticipate'. For this meaning of *sperare,* see *OLD* 5, and cf. 1.543, 4.292, and 4.419.

276–7 Diomedes refers to his wounding of Venus as she rescued A. from him, described at *Il.* 5.330–51. He lays the blame for the metamorphoses of his men squarely at his own feet. At *Il.* 5.406–15, the goddess Dione consoles Aphrodite by stating that Diomedes should beware lest he be punished with death for fighting an immortal; Diomedes here recognises a different punishment for his transgression. In contrast to V., the Ovidian Diomedes assigns blame for the metamorphoses to one of his comrades, Acmon, who blasphemously scorns Venus, thereby firing her anger and leading her to transform the men (*Met.* 14.486–93).

276 caelestia corpora: plural for singular, as often in epic with *corpora.* **demens** corresponds to Homer's νήπιος, 'foolish', used of Diomedes at *Il.* 5.406, where Dione criticises him for his rash witlessness in attacking a goddess.

277 Veneris uiolaui uulnere: the heavy alliteration joins with that in *caelestia corpora* in the previous line to suggest strong emotion. For the combination *uiolaui uulnere,* cf. 591 *uiolarit uulnere,* 848 *uiolauit uulnere,* 12.797 *uiolari uulnere.* V. recurrently has alliteration with *uulnus* (cf. 669, 2.561–2, 10.842, 12.5, 12.640); it has a Lucretian feel (5.1321 *uulnere uictos,* 6.420 *uiolento uulnere*). *uiolare* indicates profanation; by echoing *uiolamus* at 255, it extends the theme of Greek sacrilege. With Venus, the verb also has a sexual note: although the wound to her was slight, an attempt was made on the body of the goddess of love.

278 Diomedes vehemently resists a return to hostilities with the Trojans. The inversion of Homer is strong: Diomedes, a leader of the Greek force in the Trojan War, and a fierce warrior who could surpass Achilles (*Il.* 6.96–101) and who got the better of A. and nearly killed him (*Il.* 5.297–317), wants nothing more to do with fighting the Trojans, especially owing to his regard for A.'s strength and skill in war. See Intro. p. 15. **ne . . . ne . . . impellite:** *ne* with the imperative belongs to early Latin as a part of everyday speech. It is found in high poetry first in Catullus (61.193, 62.59, 67.18) and is frequent in V. It is very rare in prose (Liv. 3.2.9, with Ogilvie's note). See Austin on 2.48, Harrison on 10.11. *ne* + imperative can in V. be inhibitive ('stop doing'; cf. 3.316, 6.544), as in early Latin, or, as here, it can function as a prohibitive with future reference (Penney 1999: 253). The repetition of *ne* lends urgency to Diomedes' plea; cf. 8.532 *ne uero, hospes, ne quaere profecto,* and repeated *ne* followed by *neu/neue* with imperatives at 6.832–3 and 12.72–3. **me ad:** *me, te, se,* and *iam* are the most frequently elided monosyllables in V. (Norden, Anh. XI.2); see 166n.

279 mihi cum Teucris: emphatic juxtaposition.

279–80 post eruta . . . | Pergama 'after the destruction of Troy'. *eruta* is an AUC participle (see 268n.).

280 ueterum . . . malorum: not just the wartime suffering of 256–7, but also the impious acts of 255, 258, and 277. **memini laetorue** '[nor] do I remember with pleasure'. The expression is hendiadys-like, with *-ue* linking related words that express one idea (*OLD* 2). The enclosing gens. *ueterum . . . malorum* are straightforward with *memini*; the construction extends to *laetor* (the only example of the verb + gen. in extant literature), although V. perhaps had in mind the gen. with *laetus* at 73.

282 uertite ad Aenean 'transfer to Aeneas'.

283 contulimusque manus 'engaged/came to blows *contulimus* is poetic plural, like *stetimus* in the previous line. *confero manum/ manus* is relatively rare in prose and other verse, and it appears more often in *Aen.* (seven times) than in any other extant text (see Tarrant on 12.345, Oakley on Liv. 9.5.10).

283–4 quantus | in clipeum adsurgat 'how mightily he rises up to his shield'. The meaning seems to be that A. towers on the battlefield with his shield raised high, which he uses as an offensive weapon, as at 12.712 and 12.724. With the phrase, cf. 9.749 *sublatum alte consurgit in ensem* and 12.728–9 *et corpore toto | alte sublatum consurgit Turnus in ensem.* Emphatic *quantus* at line-end indicates both size and power; cf. 1.752 *quantus Achilles.* The description of A. recalls *Il.* 5.297, where he enters the fray with Diomedes by leaping down with his shield and long spear (Αἰνείας δ' ἀπόρουσε σὺν ἀσπίδι δουρί τε μακρῷ), and 5.299, where he, striding like a lion, holds his spear and well-balanced shield before him (πρόσθε δέ οἱ δόρυ τ' ἔσχε καὶ ἀσπίδα πάντοσ' ἐΐσην).

284 quo turbine torqueat hastam 'with what spinning force he hurls the spear'. *torquere* of spears first occurs in V. and Horace. It indicates casting a spear with a thong (*amentum*); this was wound usually several times around the shaft, and it 'spun' the weapon (Tarrant on 12.490, Hollis on *Met.* 8.28–9). While *turbine* is a word for that motion, it also suggests the great power with which A. hurls his weapon.

285–7 The apparent model is *Il.* 2.371–4, where Agamemnon tells Nestor that if he had ten counsellors like him, Troy would be taken and destroyed. To Diomedes, A. and just two warriors like him were needed to defeat the Greeks and even to launch a successful attack on Greece.

285 praeterea 'in addition to him'. **Idaea:** Phrygian Mt Ida; hence = 'Trojan'.

286 ultro: the adv. is used of taking the offensive, as at 2.193–4 *ultro Asiam magno Pelopea ad moenia bello | uenturam.* It indicates action that moves beyond the expected; the Trojans would have not only defended their city but would have even mounted an invasion of Greece. **Inachias:** Inachus was the first king of Argos; cf. 7.372 *Inachus Acrisiusque patres mediae Mycenae.*

287 Dardanus 'Trojan'; a collective substantive adj. Dardanus was the eponymous founder of a city in the Troad and a foundational ancestor of the Trojans; cf. 8.134 *Dardanus, Iliacae primus pater urbis et auctor,* 3.167. See, further, 353n. **lugeret:** note the change in tense: the Greeks would now be mourning if the Trojans had invaded their land.

288–90 'to the extent there was a delay at the walls of enduring Troy, it was by the hand of Hector and Aeneas that Greek victory was impeded and withdrew until the tenth year'. According to Seneca the Elder (*Suas.* 2.20), V. improves upon the phrase *belli mora concidit Hector* of the Augustan poet Abronius Silo, which Silo derived from his teacher in rhetoric, M. Porcius Latro.

288 durae: the adj. points to the *constantia* and *fortitudo* of Troy as it held out for so long against the Greek forces. Cf. *Dardanidae duri* at 3.98. Seneca the Elder (*Suas.* 2.20) quotes the variant *ad aduersae* for *apud durae*; this is of interest as a glimpse into the early corruption of V.'s text.

289–90 Hectoris . . . | haesit: the reference to Hector and A. departs from the traditional idea that Hector, whose name means 'prop, stay', was alone the chief obstacle to Greek victory (cf. *Il.* 6.402–3, and see Tarrant on Sen. *Ag.* 211, Hardie 2012: 138–40). Cf. 9.155 *decimum quos distulit Hector in annum,* 2.291–2 *si Pergama dextra | defendi possent, etiam hac* [Hector's hand] *defensa fuissent.*

289 Graium: V. never uses *Graecus*; *Graius* is the normal form in epic and other elevated poetry from Ennius onward (*Ann.* 165, 357 Sk.). See, further, Austin on 2.148.

291 Anaphora, elision, and assonance emphasise the parallels between Hector and A. Cf. 6.166–70, where Hector's comrade Misenus is said to have become a *socius* to A. after Hector's death, thereby following no lesser standard (*non inferiora secutus,* 6.170). Cf., in the *Iliad,* 6.77–9, where Helenus states that the war-toil rests upon Hector and A. more than upon any other Trojan, and that they are the best in war and counsel, 5.466–7 'low lies a man whom we honour similarly to godly Hector, Aeneas' (κεῖται ἀνὴρ ὃν ἶσον ἐτίομεν Ἕκτορι δίῳ, | Αἰνείας), and 17.513 'Hector and Aeneas, who are the best of the Trojans' (Ἕκτωρ Αἰνείας θ', οἳ Τρώων εἰσὶν ἄριστοι). In Homer, however, Hector is on the whole the clear superior of the two. *arma* and *animus* comprise an old doublet (see Oakley and Kraus on Liv. 6.24.10 *eunt insignes armis animisque*); cf. 12.788 *armis animisque refecti, G.* 3.182 *animos atque arma.* There is very probable imitation of V. at *Il. Lat.* 201 (Meges) *animisque insignis et armis.*

291–2 insignes . . . | . . . prior: cf. 6.403 *Troius Aeneas, pietate insignis et armis,* 1.10 *insignem pietate uirum,* and 1.544–5 *rex erat Aeneas nobis, quo iustior alter | nec pietate fuit, nec bello maior et armis.* A. is recognised for religious piety at *Il.* 20.298–9 'he always gives acceptable gifts to the gods' (κεχαρισμένα δ' αἰεὶ | δῶρα θεοῖσι δίδωσι). It is Hector, however, who is outstanding in that respect (*Il.* 24.66–70). By placing A. above Hector in piety, V. departs from Homer and elevates A. as the greater Trojan hero. In the process, he has Diomedes invest A. with an essential characteristic and draw a sharp distinction between him and the sacrilegious speaker and other Greeks. For Diomedes, too, this is a way of indicating further to the Latins why they should seek peace: a hero who combines outstanding martial prowess and piety will be a formidable opponent and a valuable ally.

292 coeant in foedera dextrae: an echo of Allecto's sarcastic remark to Juno at 7.546 *in amicitiam coeant et foedera iungant,* now spoken in earnest. Cf., too, 12.190–1 *paribus se legibus ambae | inuictae gentes aeterna in foedera mittant.* See 165n.

293 qua datur 'in view of the fact that it is permitted', i.e. 'since it is permitted'. Diomedes urges the Latins to take the opportunity they have to secure peace; he pushes them towards an alliance while there is still time for it. This reformulates the call for peace at the opening of the speech. **ast:** V. and Horace use archaic *ast* as an alternative to *at*; the word does not appear in Lucretius, Catullus, Propertius, or Tibullus. It normally occurs in poetry before a vowel and before a pronoun/demonstrative adj. (in V., *ego, ille, ipse,* and *alius*) or *ubi* and *ibi.* V. has *ast* eighteen times, seventeen before a vowel (the exception is 10.743 *ast de*), and fifteen before a pronoun or *ubi*; only here and at 10.173 (*ast Ilua*) is it found before a noun. **armis . . . arma:** polyptoton to describe military fighting, common in literature with *arma* (see Wills 1996: 193, 195–6). Cf. 4.629 *arma armis,* 9.462 *Turnus in arma uiros, armis circumdatus ipse.* **concurrant:** subjunctive in a prohibition after *cauete,* with *ne* omitted; on the paratactic construction, see *NLS* §130, A–G §565 n. 1.

294–5 A stiffly formal close to the report, appropriate to the official, weighty setting and occasion. The predominantly spondaic rhythm underscores the heavy formality.

294 rex optime, regis: the polyptoton connects the two characters, although *optime* (cf. 353, 8.127, 12.48) gives courtly precedence to Latinus. It highlights the seriousness of the diplomatic situation: this is a report from a king to a king and, thus, is a matter of utmost importance. Cf. 8.17 *Turno regi aut regi apparere Latino,* which closes the passage on Venulus' departure to Diomedes.

295 audisti forms a neat contrastive frame with *uidimus* at 243. **magno . . . bello:** probably 'for the mighty war', a loose predicative dat. (*NLS* §68, A–G §382). Cf. 7.611 *certa sedet . . . sententia pugnae,* where Horsfall ad loc. takes *pugnae* as a dat. (Fordyce ad loc. leans towards the gen. but considers the dat. possible). Other commentators (C–N, Page, Williams, Gransden) understand *magno . . . bello* as an abl. of attendant circumstance, 'in so great a war'.

296–9 The council responds to the news about Diomedes. V. reworks 10.96–9, describing the gods' response to Juno's speech at a *concilium deorum: talibus orabat Iuno, cunctique fremebant | caelicolae adsensu uario, ceu flamina prima | cum deprensa fremunt siluis et caeca uolutant | murmura uenturos nautis prodentia uentos.* Jupiter quiets the murmuring gods when he begins to speak at 10.100–3; by contrast, Latinus waits until the assembly has calmed down before he speaks. The simile picks up on the water imagery in *fluuntque* at 236. Cf. 7.586–90, a simile comparing Latinus, set upon by those calling for war, to an ocean-cliff standing firm against crashing waves, just before he yields to the warmongers' pressure (7.591–600); now other water imagery is applied to the tumult around the king.

296 Vix ea legati: *sc.* a pluperfect verb of speaking. The omission of the verb lends dramatic speed and stresses how quickly the reaction came. Cf. 12.154 *uix ea, cum lacrimas oculis Iuturna profudit.* **uariusque:** the enclitic *-que* = *cum.*

297 Ausonidum: the patronymic by-form of *Ausonius* first appears in V. The gen. plural is the only form he uses (also at 10.564, 12.121). **ceu:** primarily a high poetic word, first found at Enn. *Ann.* 361 Sk.; it does not occur in prose until Seneca the Younger. It appears twenty-four times in V. (twenty in *Aen.*, four in *G.*). **morantur** 'hold back'. The verb is in strong tension with *rapidos* in the following line.

298 clauso gurgite: abl. of source. It describes a pent-up 'swirling mass of water' (*OLD* 1).

299 fremunt picks up *fremor* at 297, creating an explicit correspondence in linguistic detail between simile and main narrative. A subtler correspondence comes with *murmur* in the previous line; the noun was used of responses to speeches (cf. 12.239, Liv. 3.56.8, Ov. *Met.* 1.206, 12.124, Luc. 1.352, with Harrison on 10.98–9). For *fremo* used of the sound of water, see DServ. ad loc. *antiqui aquae sonitus 'fremitus' dicebant: Ennius* [515–16 Sk.] *ratibusque fremebat imber Neptuni.* **crepitantibus undis** 'with the plashing water'. For *crepito* of water (rare), see *TLL* IV.1170.9–15. Propertius uses it of gentle plashing at 2.32.15 *leuiter nymphis toto crepitantibus orbe*; for louder, more forceful plashing, see Corippus, *Iohannis* 4.396 *aequora pulsa gemunt ruptis crepitantia ripis*, in apparent imitation of V.

300 Cf. 6.102 *ut primum cessit furor et rabida ora quierunt.* **trepida ora:** the phrase varies *turbata . . . ora* at 296–7. *trepida* = 'anxious'. V. uses the word repeatedly to mark fear and anxiety (2.380, 2.735, 3.66, 4.672, 6.290, 7.518, 9.169, 9.756, 12.589) but also has it to mark excitement (453, 8.4, 9.233, *G.* 4.69). Both *trepida ora* and *turbata . . . ora* contrast with *placido . . . ore* at 251; Diomedes' tranquil call for peace causes agitation in the Latin assembly.

301 praefatus diuos: *more antiquo,* according to Serv. ad loc., who states that the ancients began every speech with a prayer, citing Cato and one of the Gracchi. Cf. Plin. *Pan.* 1 *bene ac sapienter maiores nostri instituerunt . . . dicendi initium a precationibus capere.* At 7.259–60, Latinus begins his address to the Trojan embassy with a prayer (*di nostra incepta secundent | auguriumque suum*).

302–35 THE SPEECH OF LATINUS

In the wake of the bad news from Venulus, Latinus aims to stop a war he knows to be disastrous (and impious). To that end, he calls upon the Latin council to recognise that theirs is a lost cause, and that it is time to offer terms to the Trojans. Latinus pursues his task with some rhetorical savvy. This includes omitting details, partly by necessity and partly by choice (see 312n.), that could anger and alienate Turnus, whom the king needs on his side. Latinus is statesmanlike in his concern for the public good and in his focus on what needs to be done to end Italian suffering. Yet he is also weary, distressed, and deflated, an old, weakened king who sees that he is on the losing side but lacks the absolute authority to declare an end to war, without the support especially of Turnus. His deeply pessimistic view of the war effort has the rhetorical purpose of making the assembly choose peace, but also reflects his depressed condition. For more on the speech, see Intro. pp. 16–17. V. perhaps had in mind A.R. 1.653–707; in Apollonius, Hypsipyle gathers the Lemnian women in assembly, and she and the aged Polyxo urge granting a peaceful welcome, with gifts, to the Argonauts.

302 Ante: emphatic and in sharp contrast to *non tempore tali* in the following line. **equidem:** with *uellem* in the following line, to emphasise the first person. **summa de re statuisse** 'to have come to a decision on this crisis'. For *res summa* meaning 'crisis', see *OLD* s.v. summus 6.

303 uellem: see 111n. **fuerat melius:** see 115n. on *aequius . . . fuerat.* The echoes of the earlier lines invite comparison of Latinus and A.: both oppose and regret the war (despite A.'s suggestion at 113–14 that Latinus is responsible for the conflict), and both propose a way to achieve peace.

304 cogere: see 235n. **adsidet** 'besieges'. Latinus exaggerates how dire the current situation is (cf. 17 *nunc iter ad regem nobis murosque Latinos*) out of anxious despair and to impress on the council that the time to resolve the crisis is now.

305 importunum 'ill-omened'; cf. 217 *dirum . . . bellum.* V. uses the adj. elsewhere of ill-omened birds (12.864 (a *Dira* in bird form, probably an owl), *G.* 1.470). **ciues:** the term of address gives the *concilium* a republican flavour. Cf. 243 and 459.

306 inuictisque 'inuincible', for reasons explained at 307. This varies the idea, very common in the late Republic and early Principate, of Rome's invincibility (see Oakley on Liv. 7.10.4). **fatigant** 'weary', probably both in a physical and mental sense. The image of the Trojans contrasts with 9.614–20, where Numanus Remulus impugns them for their eastern decadence: Latinus attributes to the Trojans the tough virtue of the Italians and, by extension, of the ideal Roman. *fatigare* appears twice when Numanus describes the rugged country lives of the Italians, which he sets in opposition to the feminised luxury of the Trojans (9.605 *uenatu inuigilant pueri siluasque fatigant,* 9.610 [*iuuencum*] *terga fatigamus hasta*).

307 nec . . . ferro 'and, when beaten, they cannot bring themselves to cease from the fight'. V. ascribes to the Trojans the resilient endurance that the Romans possess in patriotic visions of their national identity. Cf. Liv. 27.14.1 (Hannibal on the Romans) *seu uictus est, instaurat cum uictoribus certamen,* Hor. *Carm.* 4.4.53–60 (Hannibal again on Roman fortitude in the face of disaster and loss). **possunt:** for the sense 'bring themselves, resign themselves', see *OLD* 3 and Horsfall on 7.309, and cf. 7.295 *num capti potuere capi?*

308 ascitis Aetolum . . . in armis 'in the winning of Aetolian arms'. *ascitis* is an AUC participle (see 268n.). On *Aetolum*, see 239n.

309 The diaereses and caesurae (including an unusual weak principal caesura in the third foot; see 236n.) produce a staccato effect, which gives an impression of agitation. **ponite** 'give up, abandon'. Enjambment lends powerful emphasis and pathos to the imperative. The short final vowel before the double consonant beginning with *s* (*spes*) is an anomaly in V.; shortening before the combination of *s* and another consonant was largely avoided in epic (although see the exceptions with the word *smaragdus* (also spelled *zmaragdus*, but see Prisc. *GLK* II.41–2 for *sm-*) at Ov. *Met.* 2.24 *lucente smaragdus*, Luc. 10.121 *distincta smaragdo*, and Stat. *Theb.* 2.276 *igne smaragdos*), but occurs ten times in Lucretius, five in Propertius, and nine in Horace's *Satires*. The strong pause after *ponite* enables the short syllable, with the major grammatical boundary in essence blocking the effect of *sp-* (Hardie 1920: 38, Allen 1973: 140). See, further, Fordyce on Catul. 64.357 *unda Scamandri* (who also discusses *undā spes* at Catul. 64.186). **spes sibi quisque** 'each is his own hope', although Serv. ad loc. is perhaps correct in supplying *sit.* **haec . . . angusta:** refers to the just-mentioned *spes*, rather than a neuter plural, as Horsfall ad loc. suggests; 308–9 form a unit focused on the theme of hope.

310–11 'in what ruin all else lies struck down, it is all before your eyes and between your hands'. The indirect question at 310 is governed by a construction in which *omnia* agrees with *cetera . . . perculsa*, where the more natural construction would have *est omnino ante oculos* etc. as the main clause. The strained syntax is perhaps further evidence of Latinus' disquiet affecting his speech.

310 cetera: i.e. everything else beyond the thin hope that each is to have in himself. **ruina:** to be taken with the alliterative *rerum.* Cf. Liv. 5.51.9 *in ruina rerum nostrarum*, 26.41.12 *in hac ruina rerum.*

311 ante oculos interque manus: *inter manus* is an everyday expression for lifting or handling bodily (Hardie on 9.502); V. uses it metaphorically to indicate palpable awareness of the disaster that besets the Latins. Sight and touch provide direct and sure evidence of conditions; Latinus asserts that the reality of the situation is irrefutable. Cf. 243n.

312 nec quemquam incuso: Latinus hints at Turnus, who is present. The king treads very carefully around the Rutulian, which indicates his wary concern not to provoke Turnus in the hope of convincing him to agree to peace. There is weakness behind this; Latinus does not have the power to bring Turnus to heel. But there is magnanimity as well; the king rises above relitigating the war and fault-finding. Latinus' unwillingness to criticise Turnus distinguishes him sharply from the speaker who will follow him, Drances.

312–13 potuit . . . | . . . fuit 'the very most that valour could be, it has been'. Sharp juxtaposition of *esse* and *fuit*; the caesurae heighten the effect, and the strong pause after *fuit* stresses that word. Latinus recognises that his side fought with all it had, although there is also an underlying suggestion in *fuit* of 'is no more', 'is a thing of the past', particularly in light of the bleakness of 310–11. Cf. 7.412–13 *nunc magnum manet Ardea nomen, | sed fortuna fuit.*

313 certatum est: the impersonal passive recalls the language of military prose, like *certatur* at 10.355 (see Harrison ad loc.); cf. Horsfall on 8.553 (*pugnatur*).

314 quae sit dubiae sententia menti: Latinus' posture of uncertainty is rhetorical; he has settled on a plan, which only in appearance contains different possibilities (see 325n.). The king, however, is not operating with absolute monarchical authority; he must convince the council, and especially Turnus, to accept his position, and he must take a circumspect approach when presenting his point of view in an effort not to alienate them and to make them disposed to what he advises. *sententia* evokes the technical language of the Roman senate, where the word was used for a senator's response to a question put forth (Hellegouarc'h 1963: 117).

315 paucis (animos adhibete) docebo: cf. 4.116 and 8.50 *paucis (aduerte) docebo. paucis* meaning 'in a few words' might have already developed into a high-register linguistic item by Terence's time (Karakasis 2005: 95). For other examples of *paucis* so used in V., see 6.672, 10.16, and 12.71. Cf. Ov. *Met.* 15.238 *quasque uices peragant (animos adhibete) docebo.*

316–21 V. alludes to the tradition that Latinus offered the Trojans land on which to settle; see Liv. 1.1.9–10 and Serv. ad loc. (citing Livy, Cato, and Sisenna), and cf. 7.261–2. The geography is imprecise, characteristically (see Horsfall 1985: 197–208). The territory is considerable (Latinus has large land holdings; cf. 9.387–8) but distant; Latinus no doubt sees the latter fact as a selling point.

316 est . . . mihi: an introduction to a short topographical ecphrasis; such descriptions are a piece of epic technique (see Fordyce on

7.563ff.). The land is presumably a royal domain, like a Homeric τέμενος (cf. e.g. *Il.* 6.194, 18.550). **Tusco . . . amni:** the Tiber, called Etruscan because it flows south from Etruria; cf. 2.781, 7.663, 8.473, 10.199, *G* 1.499.

317 'stretching far to the west, all the way beyond the Sicanian territory'. **finis . . . Sicanos:** the Sicani are mentioned at 7.795 along with the Aurunci and Rutulians; at 8.328, they are very early settlers of Latium. Cf. Dionysius of Halicarnassus (1.9.1), who relates that the Sicani were the first inhabitants of Rome.

318 Aurunci: an *Urvolk* of central Italy (so Horsfall on 7.795; see also Serv. ad 7.206 *Aurunci uero Italiae populi antiquissimi fuerunt*). Like the Siculi, they are mentioned for their archaic patina; there is no apparent identification with the Aurunci who inhabited northern Campania and whom, according to Livy (7.28.1–3), the Romans conquered in 345 BCE. **Rutulique:** V. does not explain how Turnus' Rutulians had come to till Latinus' land, or how and why Latinus feels free to offer that land to the Trojans without any concern for Turnus. This matter was of interest to ancient commentators; see Serv. ad loc. *agrum . . . aut quem tamquam stipendiarium habebant Rutuli et Aurunci, aut ad quem colendum quasi regi operas dabant: unde superfluum est quod ait Donatus, non potuisse fieri ut praesente Turno ager Rutulorum a Latino donaretur Aeneae.*

318–19 uomere duros | exercent collis: Latinus conjures native Italian hardiness: tough Italians are able to work the tough land. Latinus also indicates that he is not giving good, fruitful territory to the Trojans and, thus, aims to make his proposal more palatable; there is a tacit question over whether the Trojans possess the toughness to work the land successfully as the Italians do. When offering the Trojans land at 7.261–2, Latinus conversely states that he will provide them with rich soil: *non uobis rege Latino | diuitis uber agri Troiaeue opulentia deerit.* Cf. 7.798 *Rutulosque exercent uomere collis.*

319 pascunt 'they use as pasturage' (*OLD* 8).

320 haec: V. commonly uses *hic/haec/hoc* or advs. such as *hic, huc,* and *illic* to pick up the narrative after an ecphrasis. **pinea:** also at 786, 2.258, and 9.85. See 786–7n.

321–3 The lines recall Latinus' words at 7.256–7 (on A.) *paribusque in regna uocari | auspiciis* and 7.264–5 *si iungi hospitio properat sociusque uocari, | adueniat*; they also anticipate A.'s proposed terms of alliance at 12.189–94.

In the second half of the poem, peace is recurrently at hand and yet out of reach.

321 cedat amicitiae Teucrorum 'be given over to the friendship of the Trojans'. **aequas:** the treaty will give equal rights to both parties, who will remain independent (*OLD* 4c). Latinus proposes a settlement that is good for the Latins, in that, though defeated, they will not be a subject people to the Trojans. *aequus* is a key term in treaties; see Badian 1958: 25–8.

322 dicamus 'let us state/declare'. **sociosque . . . uocemus:** cf. 7.256 and 7.264, quoted at 321–3n.

323 considant . . . condant: an emphatic frame, with the verbs linked by alliteration and homoioteleuton. **si tantus amor:** also at 2.110 and 6.133. The final syllable of *amor* is lengthened in arsis before a dominant caesura; see 111n. Cf. 12.668 *et furiis agitatus amor et conscius uirtus*, as well as *Ecl.* 10.69 *omnia uincit Amor et nos cedamus Amori.* The original ending of *amor* was *-ōs*; this became *-ōr*, then *-ŏr* by iambic shortening; V. in a sense restores the earlier quantity, but does so under the particular prosodic conditions. See, further, Winbolt 1903: 204. Cf. 7.263 *nostri si tanta cupido est*, after the echo of 7.264 in the previous line. *cupido* there refers to A.'s desire to join in alliance with Latinus, and the king dictates the conditions for that to happen. In the changed circumstances now, the Trojans have the upper hand, and Latinus proposes to yield to their wishes. **moenia condant** activates a crucial subject of the poem, viz. the founding of a new Italian home for the Trojans and, ultimately, of Rome (cf. 1.5, 1.33). Cf. 7.144–5 *diditur hic subito Troiana per agmina rumor | aduenisse diem quo debita moenia condant.* Unlike Drances (130–1), Latinus envisions the Trojans building their own city.

324 capessere 'to go towards, make for'. The infinitive is prolative after a noun expressing desire (*animus* at 325). The strong suggestion with repeated *alius* is that the Trojans will sail to a land other than Italy, not to another part of Italy.

325 possuntque 'and it lies within their power'. An oblique reference to the fated quality of the Trojan arrival in Italy. Latinus was aware that the Trojans were fated to settle there (cf. 7.96, 7.239, 7.254–7, and 7.270–3), and therefore he presumably knows that fate prohibits what he proposes. (Presumably, too, he understands that the Trojans, having arrived at their fated land, will not want to seek other shores.) From this it follows that he is making a show of presenting different options; he is cognizant of the fact that settlement in Italy is the only real alternative, but he worries that this might be too bitter a pill for the council and especially Turnus to swallow, and he softens the prospect of surrender with what he knows to be a fantasy of Trojan departure. *possuntque*, like *est animus*, also gives Latinus an out should the council press for offering the Trojans assistance to leave; the outcome depends on the Trojans – which recognises that they hold the upper hand – and Latinus will not be able to insist on a course of action that they reject and that contravenes fate.

326 Italo . . . robore: abl. of material, presumably oak though perhaps any hard timber. Suggestive of the strength of Italian trees and, thus, implying the stoutness of the ships and conjuring once more (cf. 318–19) Italian hardiness. **texamus:** 'the Indo-European root of *texere* meant "to build, construct (of wood)" as well as "to weave" . . . although this use of the verb [viz. "build, construct"] must have seemed a poetical metaphor when *texere* came to be applied specifically to weaving' (Skutsch on Enn. *Ann.* 504). V. probably responds to *texta* at Catul. 64.10 (quoted at 320n.); cf. *pinea* at 320 and *carinis* at 328.

326–7 robore . . . | . . . ualent: V. likes to use *robur* meaning 'oak tree/hard timber' near words indicating 'strength, vigour, might', as he does here with *ualent* (although the meaning 'be strong/robust' is latent in this case; see the following note). This is to play on the metaphorical meaning of *robur*, 'physical strength, robustness' (Paschalis 1997: 7).

327 complere: of manning a ship (*TLL* III.2092.57–69); cf. Gk πληρόω. **ualent** 'have the ability/power' (*OLD* 6). **iacet** 'lies ready' (*TLL* VII.1.30.80–31.1).

328 materies: wood for shipbuilding (*TLL* VIII.451.3–19). **numerumque modumque** 'number and size'. Cf. Caes. *Gal.* 5.1.1 (built and repaired ships) *quarum modum formamque demonstrat.*

329 aera: a reference to the bronze-sheathed *rostra* or 'beaks' of ships. This is an anachronism; no Homeric ship was equipped with a *rostrum* (see Harrison on 10.156–7), and V. projects Roman warships, which had *rostra*, back into the heroic past. **manus** 'workmen'. **naualia** 'shipyards'. Latinus refers in quick, asyndetic succession to the material to build the ships, the manpower to build them, and the place to build them.

330 At 7.268–73, Latinus offers his daughter Lavinia in marriage to A. as part of his agreement with the Trojans; he hears from the oracle of Faunus that Lavinia is to marry a foreigner (7.96–8), and he concludes that A. must be the destined groom (7.253–8). He is now silent on the topic, to avoid angering and alienating Turnus. **ferant et foedera firment:** statements with forms of *foedus* lend themselves to emphatic alliteration (so Tarrant on 12.200 *foedera fulmine*). Cf. 12.212 *firmabant foedera* and 12.316–17 *foedera faxo | firma.* The alliteration gives *foedera firment* an archaic and formulaic feel. Cf. the formula *foedus ferire* and Enn. *Ann.* 32 Sk. *foedusque feri bene firmum.* On *foedera,* see 164n.

331 centum oratores: at 7.153, A. sends the same number of *oratores,* 'envoys', to Latinus to seek an alliance. In both instances, the large number lends heroic colour but is also a sign of the importance of the mission. At 7.153, the Latins had received a Trojan embassy seeking peace; they now send a peace-seeking embassy to the Trojans. For a historical parallel for the number of envoys, cf. the delegation of a hundred citizens sent from Alexandria in the early 50s BCE to protest against Ptolemy Auletes. **prima de gente** 'of the best stock'. Cf. 7.152–3 *delectos ordine ab omni | centum oratores.* The Trojans, as a small band of exiles, did not have the high-born men to comprise a hundred-person embassy (Horsfall on 7.152).

332 placet: used of a decision made by an authority (*OLD* 5b). **pacisque . . . ramos:** the ambassadors are to carry olive branches decked with woollen fillets as suppliants seeking peace (cf. 101n.). Cf. 7.153–4 (the Trojan ambassadors to Latinus) *ramis uelatos Palladis omnis.*

333 munera 'as gifts'; in apposition to *talenta, sellam,* and *trabeam* in 334. For other gifts sent by Latinus to A., see 7.274–85. At 3.464, Helenus brings the Trojans gifts of gold and carved ivory.

334 The gifts are marks of honour; they are also a symbolic recognition of the sovereignty of the Trojans and of their equality in Latinus' realm, should they settle there (as the king must have anticipated they would). Cf. Liv. 27.4.8 and 27.4.10, where the senate sends representatives to Syphax, the Numidian king, and to Ptolemy with gifts of a purple toga and tunic, an ivory chair, and, for Syphax, a golden *patera* weighing five pounds. **sellam:** a regal throne, but also conjuring the *sella curulis,* or curule seat upon which magistrates with *imperium* and the Flamen Dialis could sit. The seat implies more ivory: the *sella curulis* was made of or veneered with that material. *sella* appears only here in V. For ivory chairs as gifts for kings, see Liv. 27.4.8, 27.4.10, 30.15.11, 31.11.12, and 42.14.10. **regni . . . insignia nostri** 'emblems of my kingdom'. *insignia* is in apposition to *sellam* and *trabeam.* **trabeamque:** the *trabea* was a short ceremonial garment worn by the king in the regal period (cf. Liv. 1.41.6, Ov. *Fast.* 1.37, 2.503–4, 6.375, Juv. 8.259). The Flamines Dialis and Martialis and the Salii also wore the *trabea*, as did consuls on solemn occasions (cf. 7.612–13). V. activates its regal associations, while also continuing, after *sella*, the proto-Roman imagery.

335 consulite in medium 'take counsel for the common good'. *in medium consulere* occurs Frequently in prose (e.g. sixteen times in Cicero; see *OLD* 4b). **rebus succurrite fessis** 'relieve our exhausted state'. Tacitus imitates at *Ann.* 15.50.1 *deligendumque qui fessis rebus succurreret*; cf., too, Ov. *Met.* 15.632 *miseris succurrere rebus*. *fessus* is preferred to *lassus* in high poetry; V. has *fessus* forty times (including at 913), *lassus* twice (9.436, *G.* 4.449 (*lassis . . . rebus*)). Cf. 3.145 *quam fessis finem rebus ferat.*

336–75 THE SPEECH OF DRANCES

Drances follows Latinus with a speech also urging the council to come to terms with the Trojans. His main concern, however, is to oppose Turnus and to stir up opposition in the council against him. To introduce the scene (336–7), V. echoes 122–3 and establishes enmity towards Turnus as a motivating force behind Drances' speech. But V. then goes further and portrays Drances as a demagogic type – a man skilled in speech and in stirring up discord (see La Penna 1979, Hardie 2012: 129). The politician is also no fighter. This makes him a foil to Turnus, whose *gloria* won through battle Drances envies.

While the characterisation of Drances is negative, the narrator notes grudgingly (see 339) that Drances is considered capable of providing useful counsel. This is precisely what happens now: Drances is no less right to advocate for peace than he was at 124–31, however ugly his motives. See, further, Intro. p. 18. Drances is a considerably less admirable version of two Homeric models, the Trojan advisers Antenor and Polydamas; see 338–9n. He is also a version of Thersites, as in his earlier appearance in the book; see 336–41n., 344n., 348n., 369n.

Readers since at least the Renaissance have understood Drances to represent Cicero (see La Penna 1979, McDermott 1980, Alessio 1993: 83–6, Canfora 2006). Like Cicero, Drances was a *nouus homo*, an excellent speaker, not given to military service (despite Cicero's experiences while governor of Cilicia in 51), and a bitter enemy of a military man (in Cicero's case, Antony). See, too, 340–1n. For Cicero as wealthy, seditious, and slanderous, moreover, see Q. Fufius Calenus' invective against him in Dio 46, esp. 2–4. Yet the idea that V. modelled Drances on Cicero looks very much like a kind of wishful historical fiction, arising from a desire to link the two famous Roman authors (much like the anecdote recorded at Serv. ad *Ecl.* 6.11 on Cicero's astounded respect at a performance of

V.'s sixth *Eclogue*; chronology argues against the historical accuracy of the story). The most that can be said is that the parallels between the two are enough to lead readers to think of Cicero when encountering Drances; they are hardly conclusive evidence that V. created Drances in part to resemble Cicero. The same is true, for that matter, of Drances' similarities to M. Licinius Crassus: Drances is like that important figure of the late Republic in his wealth and in his jealousy of another's military glory (Crassus was notoriously jealous of Pompey).

336–41 Heinze 1993: 299–300 observes that V. characteristically provides more information about Drances in this, his main, scene, when that level of detail is appropriate, instead of laying everything out when Drances initially appears at 122–3. This is the most extensive expository account of character, backstory, and motive in V. A model is *Il.* 2.212–23, an ample description of Thersites. Yet V. says nothing about Drances' appearance, whereas Homer devotes *Il.* 2.217–19 to Thersites' ugliness (which reflects his character).

336 idem 'the aforementioned'. **infensus:** repeated from 122; sc., therefore, *Turno.*

337 'riled with the bitter goads of sidelong/hidden envy'. **obliqua inuidia:** an evocative phrase whose meaning is difficult to pin down. V. may activate the link between *inuidia* and the eye (cf. *inuideo*) and use *obliqua* to indicate that Drances looks askance, i.e. with sidelong envy, on Turnus' *gloria* (so Page ad loc). Cf. Gk λοξός 'slanting', used of looking askance (e.g. Anacr. 75.1, Sol. 34, Theoc. 20.13), Ov. *Met.* 2.776 (on personified *Inuidia*) *nusquam recta acies,* 2.787 *obliquo . . . lumine.* The phrase, however, could suggest that Drances expresses his envy indirectly rather than frankly (see *OLD* 6b, *TLL* IX.102.30–61). *inuidia* was connected in the late Republic to political opposition (Hellegouarc'h 1963: 195–6).

338 largus opum 'lavish with his wealth'. The implication is that Drances uses his wealth to achieve influence and standing; more darkly, *largus* suggests *largitio,* bribery. *largus* can take either the gen. or abl.; in this, it is analogous to an adj. denoting fullness (*NLS* §73.3, A–G §§349, 409a). Cf. Sil. 8.248 (the demagogic Varro) *auctus opes largusque rapinae.*

338–9 et . . . | dextera: the contrast between eloquence and arms is conventional (see Horsfall ad loc., Hardie 2012: 131–3) and goes back to Homer (e.g. *Il.* 4.400, 13.726–9, 16.631, 18.106). Cf. *Il.* 18.252, which opposes Polydamas, far the best in speech, and Hector, far the best with the spear (ἀλλ' ὁ μὲν ἄρ μύθοισιν, ὁ δ' ἔγχεϊ πολλὸν ἐνίκα). Cf., too, Ov. *Met.*

9.29 (Hercules to Achelous) *melior mihi dextera lingua*, probably in imitation of V. Heroes in Homer, however, also combine the ability to speak and the ability to fight (e.g. *Il.* 1.258, 9.53–4, 9.443), as Turnus will. **lingua melior** 'superior of tongue'. *lingua* is preferable to the variant *linguae* because of the strong MS support for it, despite V.'s experimentation with gens. (see 73n., with Görler, *EV* II.265–6), including in Drances' speech at 126, and despite how *linguae* would produce a tidy chiasmus (cf. 902). Cf. Sil. 7.619 *melior dextrae Torquatus*, in evident imitation of V.; this suggests that Silius knew the reading *linguae melior*, although adaptation of V. is of course possible. **frigida** indicates that Drances has no spirit for battle (*TLL* V.926.14, VI.1.1329.59). A basis of Drances' *invidia* towards Turnus now comes into focus: 'He envies Turnus' fame, because he himself, although rich and articulate, is militarily unfit' (Heinze 1993: 300). Cf. the Renaissance poet Marco Girolamo Vida (*Christ.* 2.708–9): *non adeo effugit cum sanguine uiuida uirtus* | *pulsa annis, nec dextra mihi tam frigida languet*; this is one of several instances where Vida imitates V.'s material on Drances (*Christ.* 1.62, 2.820, 3.195, 4.348, 4.676, 4.883, 5.103, 5.115, 5.155–6).

339 non futtilis 'not worthless'. The adj. appears elsewhere in V. only at 12.740 (where it has the meaning 'brittle') *glacies ceu futtilis ictu* [*dissiluit*]. It is rare in poetry; although it occurs in Ennius (*trag.* 262 Jocelyn) and then after V. in the Flavian epicists (Stat. *Theb.* 8.297, V. Fl. 8.354, and Sil. 5.297, 9.376, 10.339, 11.557, 13.363, 15.298, 15.794, 16.655), it does not appear in Lucretius, Catullus, Horace, Propertius, Tibullus, Ovid, or Lucan. For the adj. used of persons see *TLL* VI.1663.11–25. The litotes offers reluctant praise.

340 seditione potens indicates that Drances is *seditiosus*, a term of late-republican political polemic (Hellegouarc'h 1963: 531). V. perhaps wished to draw a contrast between Drances, capable of stirring up discord, and the statesman, *pietate grauem ac meritis* (1.151), who quells *seditio* in the famous first simile in *Aen.* (1.148–53); the word *seditio* occurs only in that simile (1.149) and here. Cf. Ov. *Met.* 8.56 (Scylla) *proditione potens*, Tac. *Hist.* 2.86 (Primus Antonius) *discordiis et seditionibus potens*.

340–1 Drances' background is decidedly mixed. *genus* . . . | . . . *incertum* implies bastardy (*OLD* 7b); if V. wished to indicate instead that Drances was low-born (so Fantham 1999: 265 n. 19), he could have used *ignotus* (cf. e.g. Cic. *Flac.* 40, Hor. *S.* 1.6.5–6 and 1.6.36, Vell. 2.128.3). The description of Drances' background suggests an extreme sort of proto-*nouus homo*: the illegitimate Drances would have been unable to claim a pre-Roman equivalent to a senator or consul on his father's side, while his mother fits with the observation of Wiseman 1971: 54 that 'the wives and mothers of *noui* were seldom referred to except for their nobility or notoriety'. Cf. the description of Cicero's parentage at Plu. *Cic.* 1.1: 'It is said of Helvia, the mother of Cicero, that she was well born (Κικέρωνος δὲ τὴν μὲν μητέρα λέγουσιν Ἑλβίαν καὶ γεγονέναι καλῶς) . . . but of his father nothing can be learned that is within measure (μέτριον). For some say that he was born and raised in a fuller's shop, while others trace his family's origin to Tullus Attius, an illustrious king of the Volscians who ably waged war against the Romans.' On Cicero's low-born father, cf., too, Dio 46.4–5.

340 superbum 'distinguished, excellent'; the adj. is used in a positive sense, describing something that is a source of pride (*OLD* 3).

341 incertum: adversative asyndeton underlines the difference between the two sides of Drances' family. **ferebat** 'he derived' (*OLD* 38). *ferebat* is preferable to the reading *ferebant* ('men said'). Either verb changes the subject from *nobilitas* (*pace* Fantham 1999: 265 n. 19), and very probably, V. installs Drances as that subject, as he is of the entire passage outside the parenthesis. *huic* in the previous line also seems to point ahead to Drances as the subject of *ferebat*.

342 aggerat iras 'builds up their anger'. Cf. 4.197 (the effects of *Fama* on Iarbas) *inceditque animum dictis atque aggerat iras.*

343–4 rem . . . | consulis: a conventional announcement of intended brevity (Hardie 2012: 131), but also a way of making matters look clear-cut: Drances begins in deliberative mode, but indicates that what he is about to advise is self-evident to all. Hence an oblique swipe at Latinus, under the guise of convention: Drances suggests that everyone, including Latinus, knows what really needs to be done, but, as will become clear as Drances proceeds, the king avoided the crux of the matter out of timidity.

344 o bone rex: superficially, an expression of ceremonial respect. But hostile irony lies just below the surface, as *optime regum* at 353 confirms (see the note). It is easy to find reasons why Drances is bitter and disdainful towards Latinus beyond his feeling that the king obfuscated about what was to be done: Latinus' personal and familial (via Amata) relations with Turnus, including Turnus' favour as a suitor of Lavinia; his giving Turnus command in the war; and his gentle treatment of Turnus in his preceding speech. Drances is thus opposed to both Turnus and Latinus, though to different degrees; he resembles Thersites in his hostility towards leaders (cf. *Il.* 2.214, 2.220–2).

345 quid fortuna ferat populi 'what the fortune of the nation occasions', i.e. what course needs to be taken in the dire circumstances. For *fero* meaning 'prompt' or 'occasion', see *OLD* 31. **mussant** 'hesitate', with the understanding that fear keeps all from speaking out. For this use of *mussare,* see *TLL* VIII.1709.42–4; V. is probably indebted for it to Ennius (*Ann.* 168, 327, 435 Sk.). The verb also implies that all instead mutter what they know must be done; *musso* meaning 'mutter' is found in late-republican criticism of cowed assemblies (cf. Sal. *Hist.* 1.77.3, 3.48.8, with Horsfall 1995: 190). *musso* is often 'applied to the powerless or the ruled, who lack the ability to complain openly' (Tarrant on 12.657). In this case, Drances insinuates that members of the council cannot voice their complaints because the powerful Turnus, whom they fear, is present. *nulli* at 343 and *cuncti* at 344, therefore, refer to those at the meeting.

346 det: Drances refers to Turnus in the third person without naming him. Although name addresses are less common in high poetry than in other forms (Dickey 2002: 42–3), Drances' resistance to naming Turnus is a mark of his contempt for him. **flatusque** 'blustering pride' (*OLD* 4).

347 ob: V. prefers this preposition to *propter* (he has *ob* seventeen times, *propter* three). This is not because *ob* is the literary and poetic word (so Harrison on 10.681–2); no such distinction can be made between it and *propter* (Axelson 1945: 78–80, H–S 246–7). **auspicium infaustum:** generals took the *auspicia* before campaigns and battles, and the fighting was done under their *auspiciis*/*auspicio.* By extension, *auspicium* came to mean 'leadership, authority, command' of a general. Like Latinus (305), Drances portrays the war as ill-omened, but he ties this directly to Turnus. **moresque sinistros** 'harmful ways'. After *auspicium infaustum,* a secondary reference in *sinistros* to unfavourable augury is impossible to miss.

348 dicam equidem: a self-dramatising (and self-aggrandising) pose of bravery in response to *dicere mussant* at 345, with *equidem* stressing the first person. **arma mihi mortemque minetur:** *arma . . . mortemque* = 'violent death'; hendiadys. The imagined threat recalls Odysseus' beating of Thersites at *Il.* 2.265–8, although Turnus will in fact take no such action against Drances. V. has around a dozen examples of triple alliteration in the second half of a line; the pattern is a continuation of Ennian practice (Fordyce on 7.189) and possibly goes back to the Saturnian metre (Austin on 4.29, Hardie on 9.563), as in Naevius' epitaph (*mortales immortales si foret fas flere . . . obliti sunt Romae loquier Latina lingua*). Cf. *Rhet. Her.* 4.52 *clamore maximo mortem minari.* The alliteration here and in *fandi flatusque* in the previous line are emotional and expressive of disdain. Contemptuous alliteration continues at 350, 351, 353, and 354; the device is a marked feature of Drances' speaking style. Silius Italicus imitates V. at 2.279–81 (Hanno begins his speech to the Carthaginian senate) *cuncta quidem, patres, (neque enim cohibere minantum | irae se ualuere) premunt formidine uocem. | haud tamen abstiterim, mortem licet arma propinquent.*

349 lumina . . . ducum: an epic periphrasis to describe excellent leaders (*TLL* VII.1821.13–51). **uidemus:** a true plural. Drances uses the first person plural at different points in his speech (358, 362, 367, 373) to align himself with his audience and, thus, to try to create solidarity with them and to isolate Turnus. The verb continues the mini-theme of sight as a source of evidentiary certainty (cf. 243, 309, 311); with it, Drances highlights the direct Latin experience of the suffering.

350 temptat 'makes an attempt on, tries to capture (by military force)' (*OLD* 9a).

351 fugae fidens: a charge of cowardice, referring to one of two events, or to both. The first is 9.788–818, where Turnus is forced to retreat from his bold and rash attack on the Trojan camp. The second is 10.633–88, where Juno sends a phantom A. to the battlefield so that Turnus will pursue it all the way to Ardea and escape death at A.'s hand. In neither passage does Turnus actually demonstrate any cowardice. **caelum territat armis:** the hyperbole underlines Turnus' arrogance and folly and 'suggests the impious assault on heaven by Titan or Giant' (Hardie 1986: 149).

352 unum etiam 'one thing still'. **quae plurima** 'which in abundance'.

353 Dardanidis: used for the Trojans twenty-two times in *Aen.* On Dardanus, see 287n. Because he was said to have originated from Hesperia/Italy (cf. 3.167, 7.207, 7.240), the patronymic might have special force here, as it seems to elsewhere (see Harrison on 10.4 and 10.545–6, Tarrant on 12.775), and might stress the Italian roots of the Trojans. Latinus marries his daughter to a stranger (cf. 7.98) but also to someone who in a sense comes from Italy. **dicique** 'promised' (*OLD* 11). **optime regum:** the sneering irony is even more apparent than at 343. Drances calls Latinus out for omitting one crucial gift, with the suggestion in the next line that he did so because he was cowed by Turnus and sought not to anger him; to Drances, of course, this is not the conduct of an excellent king.

354 ullius: Turnus, still unnamed. **uiolentia:** Turnus is the only person to possess the quality of *uiolentia* in *Aen.* (376, 10.151, 12.9, and 12.45);

it indicates angry, even raging aggression (physical and otherwise) and lack of control.

355–6 An apparent model is *Il.* 7.350–1, where Antenor proposes in a war-council the return of Helen to the Greeks. That Turnus refuses Drances' proposal sets him up as another Paris, who refuses to give back Helen (*Il.* 7.357–62).

355 **quin** introduces a subjunctive clause after a negatived verb implying hindering (A–G §558). **egregio . . . hymenaeis:** an insult to Turnus through tacit contrast. While Drances aims to denigrate and provoke Turnus, he also addresses a vital matter for those opposed to the war (see 217).

356 **pater** 'as her father'. Emphatic by position. **aeterno foedere:** Suetonius (*Rel.* Reiff. 276) notes that a *foedus* was struck either in perpetuity or for a certain number of years (*foedus in perpetuum aut in annorum certum numerum feritur*). Cf. 12.190–1 *paribus se legibus ambae* | *inuictae gentes aeterna in foedera mittant,* 12.504 *aeterna gentis in pace futuras.* Drances picks up on Latinus' *foederis aequas* | *dicamus leges* at 321–2, but identifies an essential condition of the treaty that the king had omitted.

357 **tantus habet mentes et pectora terror:** Drances circles back to the terror Turnus inspires among the council (*mentes* and *pectora* are true plurals), including Latinus. Cf. Ov. *Fast.* 3.288 (Numa) *rex pauet et uolgi pectora terror habet.*

358 **obtestemur:** an elevated word, describing a solemn or emotional appeal (Tarrant on 12.820); spoken with cutting mock-deference.

359 **cedat:** the strong pause after the initial spondee expresses indignation (cf. Winbolt 1903: 18). **ius proprium** 'his own right', i.e. Turnus' right to the bride Lavinia. In reality, Turnus has no such right, as Drances knows. This is a way of bringing out Turnus' arrogance and presumption; the suggestion, too, that Turnus wrongfully claims a bride calls Paris to mind after 355–6. Drances must suspect that Turnus will not want to give up the claim to marriage that he assumes is his (see 440). Drances tries to back Turnus into a corner; as he frames matters, Turnus must either do what is intolerable to him or stand in the way of the peace that Latinus and others want. **patriaeque:** pointed, as is *ciues* in the following line; Drances calls upon Turnus to give up the selfish consideration of marriage for the public good.

360 **aperta pericula** 'naked peril'. Cf. 9.663 *animasque in aperta pericula mittunt.* The phrase occurs first in V. (although Dingel on 9.663 thinks that it predates him) and is exceedingly rare otherwise (Amm. Marc. 14.5.7; cf. *discrimina . . . aperta*, 'open dangers', at Amm. Marc. 17.12.8 and Fro. *Ep.* 211.10).

361 proicis: strongly emphatic enjambment. **o . . . malorum:** Drances now addresses Turnus, though still not by name. Strong emotion is conveyed by the use of the particle *o* (see 124n.) and the alliteration in *caput* and *causa.* The latter is also expressive of contempt (see 348n.). Cf. 12.600, where Amata laments her role in bringing about the sorrows of the war: *se causam clamat crimenque caputque malorum.*

362 bello: pacem: significant juxtaposition, which placement at the principal caesura sharpens. **omnes:** Drances tries further to isolate Turnus, by arraying all the members of the council on one side and Turnus on the other.

363 Turne: Drances at last names his adversary. The voc. appears in the same position at 175. In both cases, position lends stress and emotion; like Evander, Drances spits out the name in hatred and contempt. **solum inuiolabile pignus** = Lavinia. *inuiolabilis* appears only here in V.; it is found before him at Lucr. 5.305 and is unattested in other Augustan authors. (Some later prose writers, notably Seneca the Younger, use it with some frequency, although it remains very rare in poetry.) Cf. 2.154 *non uiolabile uestrum* [*numen*], the first occurrence of *uiolabilis* in extant Latin.

364–5 inuisum . . . | nil moror '[I] whom you suppose/imagine to be hostile to you (and I make no objection to being so)'. For this meaning of *fingo,* see *OLD* 8b; 'misrepresent', 'pretend' for *fingo* would not make sense, since in his parenthetical remark Drances admits to the truth that he is hostile to Turnus. For the colloquial *nil moror,* see *OLD* 4c. Context demands that *inuisus* = *inimicus*; the contrast lies between Drances' hostility towards Turnus and the fact that, despite his feelings, he comes to him as a suppliant. The active sense of the adj. is confined to this line in extant literature (Lewis and Short wrongly cite Luc. 1.9 and 1.488 as other examples) and is a poetic licence (*TLL* VII.2.198.78–83). Ovid uses *inuisus* with the customary meaning 'hateful', 'disliked' at *Tr.* 5.2.43 when, probably in imitation of these Virgilian lines, he presents himself as a suppliant to Augustus: *ipse sacram, quamuis inuisus, ad aram | confugiam . . . | alloquor en absens absentia numina supplex* (*Tr.* 5.2.43–5).

365 en supplex uenio: *magna nocendi calliditas, supplicem se efficit inimicus, ut hoc modo desiderata perficiat* (Tib.). *en* strongly suggests an accompanying gesture. **miserere tuorum:** sneering, as the withering next line confirms. The tone is different at 12.653 (Saces) *Turne . . . miserere tuorum.*

366 animos 'proud spirit'. Cf. 4.414 *supplex animos summittere amori* (Dido as a suppliant must bow down her proud spirit to love). **pulsus** 'defeated in battle' (*OLD* 5). **abi:** 'withdraw [from the field of battle]', as at 10.859 *bellis hoc uictor abibat, G.* 3.225 *uictus abit.*

367 uidimus: cf. *uidemus* at 349. **ingentis et desolauimus agros** 'and we have left vast fields desolate'. *desolare* with the meaning 'leave (a place) desolate, deserted' first occurs here in extant literature (*TLL* V.1.734.26–7). Cf. Ov. *Met.* 1.349 *desolatas . . . terras,* Col. 1.3.11 *quos hostis profugiendo desolasset agros.*

368–9 Drances now bitterly appeals to Turnus' interests. There is vicious bathos in the tricolon, which ascends by word count: after two clauses referring to heroism and bravery, Drances sneeringly suggests that Turnus is after a regal dowry.

369 si adeo 'if indeed'. V. elides the monosyllable in an emotional context, as at 166–7(n.). **dotalis regia:** an attempt to fan the kind of resentment found at 217–19; Drances wants the council to recognise that many have died so that Turnus might pursue his private, selfish aims. Cf. 9.737 (the Trojan Pandarus taunts Turnus) *non haec dotalis regia Amatae*, 'Pandarus, like Drances at 11.369, implies that T. is motivated by selfish personal ambition' (Hardie ad loc.). Cf., too, *Il.* 2.226–7 (Thersites, questioning why the Greeks need to fight, to Agamemnon) 'there are many choice women in your huts' (πολλαὶ δὲ γυναῖκες | εἰσὶν ἐνὶ κλισίῃς ἐξαίρετοι), 2.232–3 (Thersites again to Agamemnon) 'or is there some girl for you to know in love, whom you will keep apart for yourself' (ἠέ γυναῖκα νέην, ἵνα μίσγεαι ἐν φιλότητι, | ἥν τ' αὐτὸς ἀπονόσφι κατίσκεαι). **cordi:** predicative dat.; the *dotalis regia* serves as a source of desire. For *cordi* so used in *Aen.*, see 7.326, 9.615, 9.776, and 10.252.

370–5 Drances contends that Turnus should fight A. in single combat (see 375n.). This is to present him with a Hobson's Choice: Drances must have supposed that Turnus faced defeat and probably death if he chose to fight, given his powerful opponent – and Drances venomously goads him into making that choice – or dishonour if he chose not to do so.

370 The spondaic rhythm, elisions, and assonance/alliteration lend gravity to the command. **aduersum:** it seems preferable to take the adj. with *pectus* rather than with *hostem,* despite the fact that it usually refers to a foe, and despite parallels for the adj.–noun pattern *aduersum . . . hostem* at 12.266 *dixit et aduersos telum contorsit in hostis,* 12.456 *talis in aduersos ductor Rhoeteius hostis,* 12.461 *primus in aduersos telum qui* *torserat hostis*; parallels for *aduersum pectus* are less compelling (9.347 *pectore in aduerso* 10.571 *aduersa pectora*, 12.950 *aduerso sub pectore*). *aduersum* with *pectus* allows Drances to hint that Turnus has up to now avoided confronting A. and has instead turned away in flight (thus showing A. his *tergum* instead of his *pectus*); Drances calls on Turnus to change his behaviour and face A. The echo in *fidens* of *fugae fidens* at 351 supports this interpretation.

371–3 scilicet . . . | . . . | . . . campis: I depart from Conte, Mynors, and Horsfall (but follow Gransden) in understanding this sentence as an indignant rhetorical question. Cf. 12.570–1 *scilicet exspectem libeat dum proelia Turno | nostra pati rursusque uelit concurrere uictus?*

371 scilicet expresses sarcastic irony. Of the fifteen instances of *scilicet* in V., five are ironic (here, 387, 2.577, 4.379, 12.570); all of the ironic uses occur in speeches. **regia coniunx:** also of Lavinia at 2.783; there she is A.'s future wife.

372 nos: opposed to *Turno* in the previous line. **animae uiles** 'worthless lives'. For the phrase, cf. Luc. 5.683 *uiles animas*. Cf. the more common *uile caput*, sometimes used to designate people sacrificed for the good of others (Liv. 9.9.19, with Oakley's note, Sen. *Oed.* 521, *Thy.* 996). **inhumata infletaque turba:** emotional apposition, intensifying the force of *animae uiles*; V. often uses apposition in this way (Conte 2007: 97, Dainotti 2015: 46 n. 159). Cf. 6.325 *inops inhumataque turba est. inhumata infletaque* resembles *Il.* 22.386 νέκυς ἄκλαυτος ἄθαπτος ('a dead man unwept, unburied') and *Od.* 11.54 = 11.72 ἄκλαυτον καὶ ἄθαπτον.

373 sternamur 'are strewn/scattered', but with an underlying sense of 'are killed, laid low'. *sterno* is the most common verb in V. for 'kill' (Weber 1969: 46) and is a common substitute for the prosy *occidere* and *interficere* (Lyne 1989: 106–7). **uis:** monosyllabic verse endings are an archaising feature found in less than 1 per cent of lines in V. (but 8 per cent of lines in Ennius' *Annales*; see Harrison on 10.2). The monosyllable creates strong conflict of ictus and accent (cf. 3n.). V. also has terminal *uis* at 4.132 and 10.864 (with *ui* at 9.532 and 12.552). *uis* at line-end is Ennian (*Ann.* 229 Sk. *Marsa manus, Paeligna cohors, Vestina uirum uis*; cf. *ui* at line-end at 151 and *Ann.* 405 Sk.). The metre strengthens the emphasis on the force word *uis* (Hough 1975: 21).

374 si patrii quid Martis habes 'if you have any of your father's martial spirit'; for this metonymic use of Mars, cf. 389. Turnus' father is Daunus (see 227–30n.). **illum aspice contra** 'look him in the face'.

375 There are fifty-eight incomplete lines in *Aen.*; this book contains just two (here and at 391). It is impossible that V. considered the lines to have their final form; there is no precedent for unfinished verses in Greek and Latin hexameter poetry or in the *Ecl.* and *G.*, and it is unimaginable that V. would innovate in his epic in such a manner. The lines instead point to a lack of revision (cf. *Vita Suetoniana-Donatiana* 23–4, 41). See, further, Sparrow 1931, Fordyce on 7.129, Power, *VE* II.585. The conclusion of a speech, as the end to a major section in composition, is an obvious place for a stopgap (Harrison on 10.284); examples of incomplete lines at such points are 5.815, 7.455, 10.284, and 10.876. The incompleteness here is rhetorically satisfying, since it suggests the suddenness with which Turnus broke in to respond to Drances. But this need not mean that V. deliberately left the line unfinished for that effect. **uocat:** cf. *uocari* at 220(n.); the repetition is a clear sign that Drances is calling on Turnus to fight A. singly. As at 220–1, Drances distorts what A. had said at 116–18.

376–444 THE SPEECH OF TURNUS

Turnus responds both to Drances and to Latinus' proposal before the council. The speech is divided into three parts (see 410 and 434, with Heinze 1993: 327), with subdivisions in each. The first and third rebut Drances (377–409, 434–44). Anger and scorn mark especially the first section, although those emotions flare up again at 442–4; Turnus disdains Drances and has been pricked by him, and he counters by attacking his adversary and savaging his claims. The passages form a wrathful *refutatio* of Drances' speech (on the *refutatio*, see Quint. 5.13, Lausberg 1997: §430; see also *Rhet. ad Her.* 1.18, on the *confutatio*). They include the refutation of individual points, which Turnus quotes (392, 399, 442); quoting an opponent's point before refuting it occurs in oratory (cf. Cic. *Planc.* 31–3, *Phil.* 2.28–30) and earlier in *Aen.* at 10.67 and 85. A deliberative assembly to determine what course of action to pursue becomes a site for a kind of forensic speech, in which Turnus defends himself against Drances while also counter-attacking that opponent. The verbal conflict between Turnus and Drances resembles that between Juno and Venus in the *concilium deorum* at 10.17–95; see Fantham 1999: 274–6.

The second section of the speech counters Latinus' proposal to come to terms with the Trojans (410–42). The tone is very different from that of the response to Drances (see 410n.). This section is also tidily arranged and divided into propositions (divisions at 411 and 419). Yet while Turnus shows himself able to deliver a well-composed speech, he remains a passionate young man with a powerful need to fight on.

While refuting Latinus, Turnus exhorts the council to show valour and to continue the war, because all is not lost, and the Latin side still possesses the resources to win. In this, his address resembles a *cohortatio* (see 14–28n., 725–67n.). Turnus is every bit the proud, brave, defiant warrior in this section of his speech that he is in the other two. But he is also completely misguided, and his exhortation distorts the current reality and what it demands. See, further, Intro. pp. 19–20.

A Homeric model for Turnus' speech is *Il.* 18.285–309, where Hector angrily counters Polydamas' call in a war-council to cease from fighting and states that he will fight singly with Achilles. Cf., too, *Il.* 7.357–64, where Paris rejects Antenor's call to return Helen, with 442n.

376 Closely imitated at *Il. Lat.* 58 (Agamemnon) *exarsit subito uiolentia regis.* **talibus exarsit dictis:** cf. 7.445 *talibus Allecto dictis exarsit in iras*; there Allecto blazes in fury in response to Turnus' dismissive words towards her (disguised as Calybe). **uiolentia:** see 354n. Cf. 12.45–6 (Turnus reacts to Latinus' call for peace) *haudquaquam dictis uiolentia Turni | flectitur.*

377 dat gemitum: a poetic, weighty alternative to *gemo*, also at 1.485 and 4.409 to describe a person's groaning, and at 2.53, 9.709, and 12.713 to describe natural phenomena. Presumably archaic in origin, and a long-lived poeticism after V. (cf. e.g. Ov. *Met.* 2.606, 6.565, 8.513, 8.521, 10.509, 10.599, 15.612, Stat. *Theb.* 4.23, 6.107, 6.527, *Ach.* 1.68, Prudent. *Cath.* 10.66, *Psych.* 797). **rumpitque has imo pectore uoces:** cf. 2.129 *rumpit uocem* and 3.246 *rumpitque hanc pectore uocem.* The idiom, in which the words or sounds that break a silence become the object of the verb, is first found in V. It is a variation on *silentium rumpere* (found at 10.63). It conveys angry or excited speech; *imo pectore* also reflects the intense emotion of the speaker (cf. 840, 1.485, 2.288, 6.55). Cf. Gk ῥῆξαι φωνήν (Herod. 1.85.4).

378–9 larga . . . | . . . poscunt: Turnus opposes words and deeds, speaking and fighting (see 338–9n.), and he scorns Drances as a man of all talk and no action, in understood contrast to himself; as this speech reveals, Turnus is a man of talk as well as action, but his self-image focuses on the latter. There are at least two Homeric models. The first is *Il.* 2.246, where Odysseus begins his response to Thersites by addressing him as 'Thersites, reckless of speech, clear-voiced speaker though you are' (Θερσῖτ' ἀκριτόμυθε, λιγύς περ ἐὼν ἀγορητής). The second is *Il.* 2.796–7, where Iris, in the guise of Polites, says to Priam, 'Old sir, endless words are always dear to you, as when in peace; but unceasing war has risen' (ὦ γέρον, αἰεί τοι μῦθοι φίλοι ἄκριτοί εἰσιν, | ὥς ποτ' ἐπ'εἰρήνης· πόλεμος δ'ἀλίαστος ὄρωρεν). V. might have also had in mind the epithet ἀμετροεπής ('of unmeasured speech') for Thersites when he is first introduced at *Il.* 2.212.

378 quidem points forward to a contrast, marked by *sed* at 380; see 49n. **Drance:** Gk voc. form, as at 384; cf. *Alcide* at 10.461. The name is perhaps meant to associate with Greece a character who possesses the stereotypical Gk enthusiasm for and skill in speaking, as opposed to fighting. Drances had waited to address Turnus by name; by contrast, Turnus uses Drances at once, presumably in disdainful response to his adversary's approach. **copia fandi:** also at 1.520, where it means 'the freedom to speak'; here it has the sense 'plentiful supply of speech'. Maybe, too, a play on *copia* = 'band of military men, troop'; when the time calls for fighters, Drances provides a different *copia.*

379 patribusque uocatis: *uocare* is a technical term for convening the Roman senate; cf. *curia* in the next line. *patres* is used of Latin proto-senatorial men at 7.176 (with *curia* at 7.174), 7.611, and 12.211.

381 tuto: dat., agreeing with *tibi,* rather than an adv.; predicative, 'in safety'. **tibi:** best taken as dat. of agent with a passive notion in *uolant*; the words fly once they are issued by Drances. Cf. the dat. *uesano . . . Ligeri* at 10.583–4 *uesano talia late | dicta uolant Ligeri.* The alliteration (continued in *dum distinet*) expresses contempt, as at 379–80, 385, and 386 – a stylistic trait that Turnus shares with Drances (see 348n.). **magna** 'big words', i.e. brash, bold speech (*TLL* VIII.136.1–18). Cf. 10.547 *dixerat ille aliquid magnum.* **uolant:** used of words moving through the air, as at 10.584, Hor. *Ep.* 1.18.71 *semel emissum uolat irreuocabile uerbum.* There is also a contrast with the flight of weapons (cf. e.g. 10.336, 10.476, 10.777, 12.270, 12.923). Cf. V. Fl. 5.599–600 *magna superbo | dicta uolant.*

382 agger moerorum: probably more than a periphrasis for protective walls (*pace* Serv. ad 10.24). Turnus wishes to emphasise the fortified strength of the defence that protects Drances; there is not simply a wall, but an *agger,* or rampart built up at the base inside a wall, which provided soldiers a position from which to fight. Cf. 9.43 *tutos . . . aggere muros.* The archaic spelling *moerus* appears in V. only in the phrase *agger moerorum* here and at the closely parallel 10.24 *aggeribus moerorum et inundant sanguine fossae* and 10.144 *aggere moerorum.* It is plausible that this was a set formula from an older poet such as Ennius (who has *moeros* at *Ann.* 418 Sk.) and that V. retained the archaic spelling, which was normalised to *murorum* in several MSS here and at 10.24 and 10.144. **inundant sanguine fossae:** the verb is intransitive, unusually (see Görler, *EV* II.272). Cf. *Il.* 4.451 = 8.65 ῥέε δ'αἵματι γαῖα ('the earth flows with blood'), 12.430–1 πάντῃ δὴ πύργοι καὶ ἐπάλξιες αἵματι φωτῶν | ἐρράδατ' ('everywhere the walls and battlements were sprinkled with the blood of men'). A *fossa* was a ditch below the *agger.*

383 proinde 'so then'; the adv. heightens the derisive irony of the imperative. It is disyllabic by synizesis, as at 400, its only other appearance in V. **eloquio:** only here in V.; the noun is first found in Augustan poetry (Prop. 3.22.41, Hor. *Ars* 217) as a metrically convenient alternative to *eloquentia* (see *TLL* V.2.412.28–9).

383–4 meque . . . | . . . tu: an emphatic contrast of pronouns; Turnus is galled that Drances of all people should accuse him of cowardice.

384–6 Turnus' sarcasm recalls that of Ajax in a tragic fragment whose authorship is disputed (Warmington assigns it to Accius (115–17), but Dangel does not): *uidi te, Ulixes, saxo sternentem Hectora, | uidi tegentem clipeo classem Doricam; | ego tunc pudendam trepidus hortabar fugam.* See, further, Hardie 2012: 148.

384–5 stragis aceruos | Teucrorum 'the piles of heaped Trojan bodies'. Cf. 207, 6.504 *confusae stragis aceruum.* For *strages* of heaped bodies, see *OLD* 3b.

385 dedit: with *stragis aceruos* in the previous line, a variation on *do stragem* (12.453–4, *G.* 3.247, 3.556, Lucr. 1.288, Liv. 4.33.8, 7.23.10, 8.30.7, 21.32.8), itself a 'rather more choice [expression] than *s. edere* or *facere*' (Oakley on Liv. 7.23.10).

385–6 tropaeis | insignis 'you adorn with trophies'. Silius appears to imitate at 6.108–9 *tuque insignite tropaeis | Sidoniis Trebia*; cf., too, Sil. 14.32 *portus aequoreis sueta insignire tropaeis.*

387 experiare 'make trial of'. Cf. 7.434 *Turnum experiatur in armis.* The verb introduces the indirect question in the previous line.

388 circumstant undique muros: cf. 304 *cum muros adsidet hostis.* Turnus does not actually believe that the Latins and their allies are in the desperate straits that Latinus describes at 304 – and, strictly speaking, he is right – but he echoes the king to exaggerate how close the enemy is and, thus, how very little Drances needs to search to find them.

389 imus in aduersos: *imus* is present of immediate intention, a feature of spoken language (Görler, *EV* II.272); cf. 9.21–2 (Turnus expresses his intention to follow the omens of war) *sequor omina tanta,* 12.13 (Turnus expresses his intention to fight A.) *congredior.* **an** introduces a sardonic question. **Mauors:** Turnus answers Drances' words at 374; the person really without martial spirit, Turnus relates, is Drances, not himself. *Mauors* is the archaic name for Mars and is found in high-style poetry (especially epic) since Ennius (*Ann.* 99 Sk.). V. has the nom. five times in *Aen.* (here, 8.700, 10.755, 12.179, 12.332); he also has the gen. *Mauortis* twice (6.872, 8.630) and the adj. *Mauortius* four times (1.276, 3.13, 6.777, 9.685). (*Mauortius* also occurs once in *G.* (4.462).)

390 uentosa: while *uentosus* belongs to elevated diction in Catullus and Augustan poetry when describing natural phenomena (Ross 1969: 55), it takes on a colloquial hue, like *uerbosus,* when used, as here, to mean language that is 'puffed up, vain' (*OLD* 6). On adjs. in *-osus,* see 274n. **pedibusque fugacibus istis:** Turnus remains stung by Drances' *fugae fidens* at 351, and he counters his adversary by stating that he, Drances, is the true fleeing coward. The phrase is thick with contempt, and we should imagine an accompanying dismissive gesture. Accusations of cowardice in epic battle are as old as Homer (e.g. *Il.* 1.225–8); Turnus' charge against Drances here might owe something to *Il.* 12.244–7, where Hector rebukes Polydamas for his fearful aversion to battle. The influence of first-century BCE Roman political rhetoric is also possible (so Horsfall ad loc., 1995: 248). Close to V. is ps.-Sal. *Rep.* 2.9.2 *lingua uana, manus cruentae, pedes fugaces* and *in Cic.* 3.5 *lingua uana, manus rapacissimae . . . pedes fugaces.*

391 semper erit: the incomplete line has psychological plausibility in a string of excited questions (so Sparrow 1931: 45); Turnus breaks off in an agitated state. Still, there is every reason to think that V. would have completed the line in revision (see 375n.).

392 pulsus ego? echoes Drances' *pulsus abi* at 366; the appearance of *ego* in reply to criticism marks the forceful personal reaction of the speaker to what was said (see Austin on 4.333). Cf. ps.-Cic. *in Sal.* 3.10 *ego fugax?,* against *pedes fugaces* at ps.-Sal. *in Cic.* 3.5. The elision of *ego* reflects the speaker's strong emotion. Cf. 12.882–3 (the deeply emotional Juturna) *immortalis ego? aut quicquam mihi dulce meorum | te sine, frater, erit?* (although see Tarrant on 12.882–4 for doubts about the authenticity of the lines) and 12.637 (the emotional Turnus) *nam quid ago? aut quae iam spondet Fortuna salutem?,* with Tarrant, Intro. p. 42. *pulsus* forms a polyptotonic frame with *pulsum;* this emphasises the words to reflect Turnus' outrage at the charge. **quisquam:** regularly used when a universal negative is expressed or suggested; hence it implies a negative answer. **foedissime:** only here does V. use *foedus* of a person. For the adj. of people, see *TLL* VI.1.1000.34–52. Cicero uses the superlative personally several times (*Phil.* 13.35, *Prov.* 7, *Fam.* 10.6.1), once in direct address (*Pis.* 31 *tune etiam, immanissimum et foedissimum monstrum*); it is tempting to think that V. was adapting a late-republican term of invective, to which Cicero gives expression.

393–8 Turnus' recitation of his achievements in battle recalls Hector's response to Polydamas at *Il.* 18.293–5: the warrior tells the counsellor not to advise retreat to Troy when Cronos has allowed him, Hector, to win glory at the Greek ships and to hem in the Greeks by the sea. The vision of the war that Turnus offers is, of course, selective: 'No one can fail to note here the *omission* of all that happened in the battle *after* the death of Pallas' (Otis 1964: 367), viz. the rampage of A., Turnus' flight in chase of the phantom A., and the Trojan victory. Turnus instead focuses on his successes on the first day of battle described in *Aen.* 9 and on the next day of battle described in *Aen.* 10 up to and including Pallas' death.

393–4 Iliaco . . . | sanguine: cf. 6.87 (the Sibyl prophesies about war in Italy) *Thybrim multo spumantem sanguine cerno.* For other descriptions of the Tiber filled with blood and other remnants of battle, see 6.86–7, 8.537–40, and 12.35–6. A river blood-stained from battle was a gruesome cliché (N–H on Hor. *Carm.* 2.1.33). Cf. 257n.

393 Thybrim: the Greco-Etruscan form (Θύ(μ)βρις, Thebris) of the name of the Tiber, found first in V. and quite possibly his innovation. V. has *Thybris* eighteen times in *Aen.* and the everyday *Tiberis* just once (7.715; also at *G.* 1.499). V. does, however, have the adj. *Tiberinus* nine times (eight in *Aen.*, including 449 below). *Thybris* is overwhelmingly preferred over *Tiberis* in epic poetry after V. For further discussion, see Austin on 2.782, Cairns 2006.

394 cum stirpe: = 'completely', i.e. 'root and all', but *stirpe* also seems to allude to Evander's 'offspring' (*stirps*) Pallas. **uidebit:** the tense makes better sense if the verb is understood to mean 'see with the mind's eye, consider' (*OLD* 7); Turnus does not appeal to direct sensory experience (*pace* Hardie 2012: 141), but rather states that no one who will ponder his achievements will assert that he was *pulsus.* Hence a different use of *uideo* from that at 243, 309, 311, 349, and 367; still, mental reflection provides evidentiary certainty no less than direct sight.

395 procubuisse 'has fallen'. Cf. 150 *procubuit*; the echo, recalling the devastating scene in which Evander mourned over Pallas' corpse, lends credence to the idea that *stirpe* in the previous line refers on one level to Pallas – i.e. V. signposts the reference through the echo. **exutos Arcadas armis** 'Arcadians stripped of arms'. *exuere armis* is a military phrase; cf. Liv. 21.61.9, 22.21.5. Turnus kills no other Arcadian but Pallas in *Aen.*

10. It is more straightforward to suppose that Turnus thinks just of Pallas but pluralises to exaggerate than that he killed and stripped Arcadians in the time between the death of Pallas (10.479–508) and his pursuit of the phantom A. (10.633–88), and that this went unreported in *Aen.* 10. The phrase thus seems to pick up on and vary the allusion to Pallas in *cum stirpe. Arcadas* is a Gk acc. form with a short final syllable (cf. *Cyclopas* at 263 and *Arcades* at 93, 142, and 835).

396 Bitias et Pandarus ingens: brothers and guardians of the Trojan camp, whom Turnus killed at 9.672–755. *Pandarus ingens* also occurs at line-end at 9.735. V. emphasises the giant size of the brothers in *Aen.* 9; see Hardie 1986: 143–54.

397–8 An allusion to Turnus' assault on the Trojan camp at 9.756–815, and echoing 9.783–5 (Mnestheus rallies the Trojans to resist Turnus) *unus homo et uestris, o ciues, undique saeptus | aggeribus tantas strages impune per urbem | ediderit?*

397 mille die: vaunting hyperbole, emphasised by juxtaposition. **sub Tartara misi:** also at line-end at 8.563. Cf. 12.14 *sub Tartara mittam,* 4.243 *sub Tartara tristia mittit,* 6.543 *ad impia Tartara mittit. sub Tartara mitto* resembles Homeric Ἄϊδι προΐαψεν, 'sent to Hades' (*Il.* 1.3, 6.487, 11.55).

398 inclusus . . . saeptus: the line-frame reflects the subject matter: participles describing Turnus enclosed within the Trojan camp enclose the line. Turnus does not mention that he made his escape from the camp by jumping into the Tiber (9.815–19). To do so would be to associate himself with flight and, thus, potentially to lend some credence to Drances' *fugae fidens* (351).

399–400 capiti . . . | Dardanio: *caput* is a synecdoche for the person (*TLL* III.404.4–406.29). The periphrasis expresses loathing. Cf. 4.613 *infandum caput,* 4.640 *Dardaniique rogum capitis*; in both cases, Dido speaks of A. with hatred.

399 cane 'utter'. The suggestion is that Turnus sees *nulla salus bello* as words of ill omen; so DServ. ad loc. *et bene hic male ominantem canere dicit, ut uatem.* **demens:** Homeric νήπιος. The specific model is presumably *Il.* 18.295, where Hector uses νήπιε for Polydamas.

400 tuisque rebus 'and for your affairs'. Turnus suggests that Drances wants and will benefit from Trojan victory (not least, certainly, because he will see his adversary Turnus defeated).

401 ne cessa: caustic sarcasm, heightened by *proinde* in the previous line (cf. 383). On *ne* + imperative, see 278n. **metu:** Augustan poets as a rule avoid elision of iambic words when the elided final syllable is the stressed syllable of a foot; the exception here seems to reflect strong emotion (see Horsfall ad loc. and on 7.464).

402 gentis bis uictae: Turnus probably refers to the sacks of Troy by Hercules and by the Greeks (cf. 2.642, 3.476, 8.291). This makes better sense than a reference to the Greek sack and to Turnus' own initial victory over the Trojans in *Aen.* 9. While Turnus got the better of the Trojans on the first day of battle, his success was short-lived and reversed when A. joined the fighting; he is unlikely to refer to his defeat of the Trojans when it was so partial and so thoroughly answered by Trojan strength, as his audience knew all too well. Cf. 9.599 (Numanus) *bis capti Phryges,* with Hardie's note. **contra** 'and on the other hand' (*OLD* 8). **premere** 'disparage' (*OLD* 23).

403 With scornful irony, Turnus presents what he considers a preposterous impossibility, to match Drances' equally ridiculous estimation of Trojan strength (Fantham 1999: 270). **Myrmidonum:** the Myrmidons, of Thessaly, who follow Achilles to fight in the Trojan War. **Phrygia:** juxtaposed in significant contrast with both *Myrmidonum proceres* and *arma*: *Phrygia* is contemptuous and implies the unmanliness and soft decadence of the east (see 145n.). **tremescunt:** the transitive use of the verb is not found before V.; see Görler, *EV* II.267, with 625n. on transitivising in V. Cf. 3.648 *sonitumque . . . tremesco.*

[404] Probably an interpolation adapted from 2.197 *quos neque Tydides nec Larisaeus Achilles* (with *Myrmidonum* in 403 leading to the line featuring Achilles). The reference to Diomedes would undercut the rhetorical point that Turnus tries to make: his listeners would know that Diomedes has come very close to showing fear of Trojan arms and, therefore, that the emotion is not so very impossible for him. Achilles, meanwhile, is dead; even in a statement of impossibility, this makes him an awkward choice for someone who now (*nunc*) trembles at the Trojans, alongside the still-living Diomedes. **Larisaeus:** = 'Thessalian'; Larissa was (and is) a chief city of central Thessaly, the homeland of Achilles.

405 A backward-flowing river is a stock image of the *adynaton*, in which extreme hyperbole implies total impossibility. For this impossibility topos, cf. e.g. Hor. *Carm.* 1.29.10–12, *Epod.* 16.28, Prop. 2.15.33, 3.19.6, Ov. *Trist.* 1.8–10, *Pont.* 4.5.43, 4.6.45–6. On the *adynaton* generally, see Clausen on *Ecl.* 1.59–62, N–H on Hor. *Carm.* 1.29.10, Frank on Sen. *Phoen.*

85–6. **Hadriacas . . . Aufidus undas:** imitated at Luc. 2.407 *Hadriacas qui uerberat Aufidus undas.* **Aufidus:** the Aufidus (mod. Ofanto) is a river in southern Italy that flows through Campania, Basilicata, and Apulia into the Gulf of Manfredonia in the Adriatic Sea. V. probably selects it because it was known for its violent flow (cf. Hor. *S.* 1.58, *Carm.* 3.30.10, 4.14.27–8); that would make the prospect of its reversal all the more striking. C–N and Horsfall ad loc. suggest that V. chose the Aufidus because it flowed through the territory of Diomedes. This is less likely if 404 is an interpolation. Williams and Gransden ad loc. propose that V. mentions the river because it flowed through Daunia, the homeland of King Daunus, in the northern part of Apulia (cf. Hor. *Carm.* 3.30.11–12, 4.14.25–6); they identify King Daunus as Turnus' father – hence Turnus' reference to the river – but V. himself does not do the same (see 227–30n.).

406 uel cum: a colloquial transition; 'in his excitement and contempt Turnus is talking informally' (Highet 1972: 62 n. 21). The meaning is something like 'or take the case when' or 'or hear him again when'; cf. Hor. *Ep.* 12.12 *uel mea cum saeuis agitat fastidia uerbis.* Quintilian (9.3.14) cites the line (though with *iactat* for *fingit*) for the antiquity of this use of *uel cum*, coupling it with the use of *sed enim* at 1.19, and he notes that phrases of the kind appear in the old tragic and comic poets. Evidence in extant comedy and tragedy is lacking; but the colloquial hue of V.'s transitional *uel cum* would of course be at home on the comic stage. **contra mea iurgia** 'in the face of my abuse'. *iurgium* is an undignified word that appears in *Aen.* only here and at 10.95 *inrita iurgia iactas,* where Juno verbally spars with Venus. (It is also found at *Ecl.* 5.11.) The noun is focalised through Drances; as Turnus tells it, Drances feigns fear at what he, Drances, claims is abuse. **fingit** echoes Drances' *fingis* at 364, although Turnus uses the verb to mean 'pretend' (*OLD* 9e).

407 artificis scelus: also at 2.125, where Ulysses is the 'schemer' (*artifex*); although Turnus cannot know it, the echo connects Ulysses and Drances as skilful but dishonest speakers. *scelus* is probably acc. (as at 2.125) in apposition to the sentence, '[a schemer's] trick'. The alternative is to take *scelus* as a nom. in apposition to the subject of *fingit* (so Page, Mackail, Fratantuono ad loc.). *scelus* as a personal insult is almost entirely confined to comedy and belongs largely to the world of slaves (Dickey 2002: 168); hence the nom. would give Turnus' language further colloquial colour. *artificis scelus* in that case = 'the cunning villain' and varies insults like *scelus uiri* ('scoundrel of a man') (Pl. *Mil.* 1434, *Truc.* 621) and *flagitium hominis* ('infamous villain of a man') (Pl. *As.* 473, *Cas.* 155, *Men.* 489, 709). **et . . . acerbat** 'and worsens the accusation with fear'. *acerbo* first appears here in extant literature; it is rare after V. (e.g. twice in Statius, once in Valerius Flaccus), though a bit more common in late antiquity (*TLL* 1.367.22–46).

408 numquam: emphatic. 'The use of *numquam* as a reinforced *non* is markedly colloquial' (Horsfall ad loc.). **talem:** disdainful; understand 'so worthless/contemptible'. **dextra hac:** Turnus shows or raises his hand, presumably with his sword in it. The gesture recalls *Il.* 2.264–5, where Odysseus strikes Thersites with a staff in response to Thersites' speech against Agamemnon. Turnus opts against violence and for withering contempt. **absiste moueri** 'do not be alarmed'; equivalent to a negative imperative. The parenthetical phrase gives the impression of lively talk, as at 6.399 *nullae hic insidiae tales (absiste moueri).* It can be understood in different ways. Most plausibly, because it flows best from 406–7, Turnus means that Drances should not feign fear of Turnus' raised hand as he had falsely claimed to fear his *iurgia*; hence *absiste moueri* is scornfully sarcastic and implicitly = *noli te pauidum fingere.* Another possibility is that Drances actually displays fear, in contrast to his feigned emotion mentioned in the previous lines, and that Turnus seizes on the opportunity to call attention to how Drances shows his true colours as a coward.

409 habitet: the subject is *anima.* **isto:** sneering and emphatic by position; cf. *istis* at 390.

410 The line marks the start of a new section of Turnus' speech; while there is continuity between his rejection at 399–405 of Drances' claim *nulla salus bello* and his arguments in this section to fight on, the shift in the speech here is clearly articulated, not least by the change in addressee. **magna, pater, consulta:** the change in tone and attitude is striking as Turnus moves from Drances to Latinus, although some sarcasm is detectable in *magna ... consulta.* His language throughout this second part of his speech is more 'measured and mannerly' (Horsfall 1995: 191) than in the first part. *consulta* refers to the king's proposals at 316–34.

411–14 Turnus restates Latinus' words at 308–11. He emphasises the extreme pessimism of the king's view with the aim of showing him and the council that the darkly defeatist stance is unwarranted and even absurd, as well as unworthy of the Italians.

411 ultra 'any longer'.

412 si tam deserti sumus 'if we are so forsaken', i.e. because Diomedes refused to ally himself with them. **semel agmine uerso** 'when our army was put to flight once', i.e. after one defeat. *semel* is in strong contrast with *funditus* in the following line.

413 neque habet Fortuna regressum: probably 'and Fortune cannot return (to us)' rather than 'and Fortune cannot withdraw (from where it now lies)', thus anticipating 426–7, where good Fortune returns after a bout of bad Fortune. Statius imitates V. at *Silv.* 3.3.157, but uses *regressum* to mean 'withdraw': *blanda diu Fortuna regressum* (*maluit*). 'Since warfare was proverbially uncertain, fortune was often held to be responsible for success in it' (Oakley on Liv. 9.17.3 *Fortuna per omnia humana maxime in re<bu>s bellicis potens*).

414 dextras tendamus inertis: a suppliant posture. Cf. 10.595–6 *frater tendebat inertis | infelix palmas,* Ov. *Met.* 5.175–6 *inertia frustra | bracchia tendentem.* The adj. means 'powerless' but also, in anticipation of what follows, has the secondary suggestion of 'unwarlike'.

415 Turnus seeks to shame Latinus and the council into continuing to wage war by appealing to their sense of honour. Appeals to honour, including the idea that death is preferable to dishonour, were standard in *cohortationes* (Highet 1972: 85).

415 quamquam o si: *quamquam* is adversative, 'and yet' (*OLD* 3c), while *o si* introduces a wish (*OLD* s.v. o 3a, *NLS* §113), a poetic construction also at 8.560 *o mihi praeteritos referat si Iuppiter annos.* The line stands alone as an exclamation; it is not the protasis to 416–18, as C–N, Page, and Gransden understand it. **adesset** expresses a wish unfulfilled in present time (thus, with *o si,* closely akin to a present counterfactual condition).

416–18 A *makarismos* (see 252n.); for Turnus, death is a blessing if it means not seeing the Latins without *uirtus* as they accept a cowardly, disgraceful peace. Cf. 1.94–6 *o terque quaterque beati, | quis ante ora patrum Troiae sub moenibus altis | contigit oppetere.*

416 mihi: ethic dat. (see 97n.).

416–17 fortunatusque laborum | egregiusque animi: *laborum* and *animi* are gens. of the sphere within which, or respect. Gens. of the sphere with *animi* are regular (cf. e.g. Plaut. *Trin.* 454, Ter. *Hec.* 121); but *animi* with *egregius* is first found here. (V. has the adj. with the abl. of respect (or specification) at 6.770, 6.861, 7.258, 8.290, 10.435, and 12.275.) Cf. *egregias animas* at 24. This is also the first occurrence of *fortunatusque laborum.* It has a similar Grecising patina to *laeta laborum* at 73 (Serv. ad loc. identifies *fortunatusque laborum* as a Grecism), although the construction must have also been influenced by the following gen. with *animi.* Both phrases are examples of V.'s free use of the gen. with adjs. (see Görler, *EV* II.266). Cf. Stat. *Theb.* 1.638 *fortunate animi.*

417 ne quid tale uideret: for the sentiment, cf. 12.641–2 (Turnus speaks) *occidit infelix ne nostrum dedecus Vfens* | *aspiceret. tale* is disdainful, like *talem* at 408.

418 Cf. *Il.* 2.418 'lying prone in the dust may they bite the ground' (πρηνέες ἐν κονίῃσιν ὀδὰξ λαζοίατο γαῖαν), A.R. 3.1394–5 'they fell, some prone, biting a churned clod of earth with their teeth' (πῖπτον δ', οἱ μὲν ὀδὰξ τετρηχότα βῶλον ὀδοῦσιν | λαζόμενοι πρηνεῖς), and 'they bit the ground/ earth' (ὀδὰξ ἕλον οὖδας / γαῖαν ὀδὰξ εἶλον) at *Il.* 11.749, 19.61, 22.17, 24.738, and *Od.* 22.269. Similar is 10.489 *terram hostilem moriens petit ore cruento.* **semel:** corrupted in some MSS to the banal *simul*; it means here 'once and for all' (*OLD* 3).

419 sin introduces a preferred alternative (i.e. to the idea that all is lost and that the Italian forces should surrender), which, Turnus wants to convince the council, is in fact the right way of looking at things; *sin* at 421 adds a second part to that alternative. Cf. 10.31–5 *si sine pace tua atque inuito numine Troes* | *Italiam petiere, luant peccata neque illos* | *iuueris auxilio; sin tot responsa secuti* | *quae superi manesque dabant, cur nunc tua quisquam* | *uertere iussa potest aut cur noua condere fata?* **opes** 'forces/ troops'. **intacta iuuentus:** *iuuentus* = 'soldiery', i.e. a body of young people of military age; theme and variation with *opes. intacta* signifies that the youths are unharmed; cf. 10.504 *intactum Pallanta.* Turnus seems to be referring to those who have fought and escaped injury; these form one part of the Latin resources, while the allies not yet called to battle in the next line form another. Turnus will return to the soldiers that remain on the Latin side at 429–34.

420 Turnus posits a remaining store of potential allied reserves. His proposition that enough allies are left to swing the war is presumably overoptimistic; to judge by the long catalogue of Italians already involved (7.641–817; cf., too, *tot populi* at 11.430), there must have been few remaining Italian allies upon whom to call. **auxilioque** 'for (our) aid'; a predicative dat. in a double-dat. construction with understood *nobis* from the previous line.

421–2 cum . . . | sanguine: cf. Serv. ad loc. *ac si diceret: non est iudicanda uictoria quae per inmensa detrimenta contingit.* Cf. *Il.* 17.363 'these [the Greeks] fought too not without bloodshed' (οὐδ' οἵ γὰρ ἀναιμωτί γε μάχοντο).

422–3 parque per omnis | tempestas 'the storm is the same for all'. The figurative use of *tempestas* to describe violent disturbances of varied kinds has a long history (*OLD* 4), and the metaphor extends to the disturbance and violent destruction of battle, especially attacks (*OLD* 5; cf. e.g. Liv. 3.7.3, 43.18.7, 44.39.2). Cf. 7.222–3 *quanta per Idaeos saeuis effusa Mycenis | tempestas ierit campos.* While the Trojans and their allies lost many men, Turnus distorts the facts with *par,* given that the Latin side has endured more casualties (see 182–212n.). Turnus suffers from the self-delusion of the proud, passionate warrior who cannot tolerate defeat. He has convinced himself of a different reality and seeks to convince his listeners of the same thing.

423 indecores: Turnus is governed by the heroic ideal of *decus* (Fantham 1999: 273); hence disgrace is unendurable to him. Cf. 12.679–80 (Turnus to Juturna) *neque me indecorem, germana, uidebis | amplius,* 10.681 (Turnus) *ob tantum dedecus amens.* The adj. is relatively rare; it appears before V. in Accius (*trag.* 436 Dangel) and is found again after him in Flavian epic (*TLL* VII.1127.17–31). It occurs four other times in *Aen.* (845, 7.231, 12.25, 12.679), always with *non/nec* in litotes. **in limine primo:** for Turnus, the war has just begun, whereas Latinus and Drances are concerned with how to bring it to an end: a crystallisation of how divergent their positions are.

424 deficimus '(why) do we give out?' The last of three examples of enjambment in consecutive lines; these reflect Turnus' angry exasperation at the lack of Latin resolve. For examples of interrogative sentences with enjambment to express similar emotions, see 4.265–7, 4.600–1, 7.302–3, 9.783–5, and 10.88–90. Cf. 12.1–2 *Turnus ut infractos aduerso Marte Latinos | defecisse uidet.* **ante tubam:** i.e. before the battle is truly joined. For the *tuba* as a battle-signal, cf. 2.313 *clangorque tubarum,* 7.268 *signaque ferre iuuat sonitusque audire tubarum,* 9.503 *at tuba terribilem sonitum procul aere canoro* [*increpuit*]. The war-trumpet appears in Homer only in a simile (*Il.* 18.219–20); it was in use in the Roman legions (cf. e.g. Liv. 30.33.12, 33.9.2; see Horsfall on 7.628, Harrison on 10.310–11). **tremor occupat artus:** also at 7.446, describing Turnus' terror at seeing Allecto. V. adapts the Homeric line-end τρόμος ἔλλαβε γυῖα ('trembling seized the limbs') (*Il.* 24.170, with slight variations at *Il.* 3.34 and 14.506 = *Od.* 18.88). Cf. *G.* 4.190 *sopor suus occupat artus.*

425–7 'A day and the changeable labour of inconstant time have brought many things back to a better state; Fortune, returning alternately, has mocked many men and once more set them on solid ground.' Macr. 6.2.16 quotes Ennius as V.'s source (*Ann.* 258–60 Sk.): *multa dies in bello conficit unus | et rursus multae fortunae forte recumbunt: | haud quaquam quemquam semper fortuna secuta est.* Assuming that Macrobius is correct, V.

reverses his model: whereas in Ennius the idea is that success may be followed by disaster on the same day, Turnus contends that one day could turn defeat to victory. Lucan imitates V. at 8.331–5, where Lentulus (an anti-Drances; see Bruère 1971: 31) tries to rally Pompey after Pharsalus. The uncertainty of war is proverbial (see McKeown on Ov. *Am.* 1.29–30).

425 **multa:** acc. obj. of *rettulit.* **uariique labor mutabilis aeui** builds upon *dies* in theme and variation. *mutabilis* = 'changeable'. Page ad loc. construes it as active, = *qui mutat*; this is not impossible (cf. 10.481 *penetrabilis,* 'penetrating', and see N–H on Hor. *Carm.* 1.3.22), but where the active cannot be proven, it is preferable to understand the passive, given the strong tendency of *-abilis* adjs. formed from first-conjugation verbs to be passive in sense (see Harrison on 10.481). Cf. 4.569–70 *uarium et mutabile semper | femina.*

426 **rettulit in melius:** cf. 1.281 *consilia in melius referet.* **alterna reuisens** 'revisiting in alternating guise'. *alterna* is probably an adj. with *Fortuna* in the next line, rather than a neuter plural internal acc.; cf. 3.318 (A. to Andromache) *quae digna satis Fortuna reuisit.*

427 Turnus' statement refutes *neque habet Fortuna regressum* at 413. **lusit:** i.e. Fortune has fun with people for a time by making them suffer, before changing course. This activates the idea that Fortune plays and sports through its vicissitudes (cf. Hor. *Carm.* 2.1.3 *ludumque Fortunae,* with N–H's note). Cf. Hor. *Carm.* 3.29.49–52 *Fortuna saeuo laeta negotio et | ludum insolentem ludere pertinax | transmutat incertos honores | nunc mihi nunc alii benigna,* Spenser, *Faerie Queene* 3.7.4–5 'that fortune all in equal lance doth sway, | and mortal miseries doth make her play'.

428 **auxilio:** as at 420, a predicative dat. in a double-dat. construction with *nobis.* **Aetolus:** Diomedes; see 239n. **Arpi:** see 250n.

429 **Messapus:** introduced at 7.691–2 as a child of Neptune and invulnerable: *Messapus, equum domitor, Neptunia proles, | quem neque fas igni cuiquam nec sternere ferro*; cf. 9.523, 10.353–4, 12.128, and 12.550. While Messapus is usually associated with Messapia in Apulia, in *Aen.* he leads a force from southern Etruria (7.695–7). See, further, 464n., Horsfall on 7.691–705, Harrison on 10.353–4, Saunders 1940: 548–9, and Bremmer and Horsfall 1987: 8. **felixque Tolumnius:** an augur at 12.258, where, spurred by an omen sent by Juturna, he leads the Latin side to break the treaty with the Trojans; his death comes at 12.460. The epithet *felix* implies success as a warrior and may be taken with both Messapus and Tolumnius.

431 gloria: in his heroic world-view, Turnus sees war as a means of winning glory (cf. 421 and 444, as well as 336) and dedicates himself to its pursuit. **delectos** 'chosen', but with the implication of 'choice'; these are the flower of Latium and Laurentine land. Cf. 2.18 *delecta uirum ... corpora*, 4.130 *delecta iuuentus*, 8.499–500 *o Maeoniae delecta iuuentus, | flos ueterum uirtusque uirum*, 9.226 *ductores Teucrum primi, delecta iuuentus*, *Ecl.* 4.34 *delectos heroas.* Similar is Homeric ἐξαίρετος (*Il.* 2.227, *Od.* 4.643); cf., too, A.R. 4.831 λεκτοὺς ἡρώων. *delectos* also suggests a mustering of troops (*OLD* 3). **Latio et Laurentibus agris:** cf. 12.24 *Latio et Laurentibus aruis.* The first term is general and the second more specific, since the *ager Laurens* was part of Latium.

432 Camilla appears in the narrative for the first time since *Aen.* 7.803–17, where she was the final warrior introduced in the catalogue of Italians. Serv. ad loc. notes that V. separates Camilla from the male fighters, as he does in *Aen.* 7 (*ut in septimo segregem eam a uirorum efficit multitudine*). He does not see, however, that in both cases V. emphasises her as a climactic ally, and that here this foreshadows the significant role she will play later in the book. **egregia de gente Camilla:** cf. 7.803 *Volsca de gente Camilla.* The use of *egregia* attests to Turnus' desire to champion the forces on the Latin side. Servius ad loc. offers sexist drivel: *quoniam a sexu non potest, laudat ex gente.* On the commentators' sexism towards Camilla, see Keith 2000: 27–31.

433 = 7.804. The close echoes of 7.803–4 serve to reintroduce Camilla. **agmen agens:** also at 7.707 and 8.683; cf. *agebat | agmen* at 5.833–4 and *agmen agit* at 12.457. A *figura etymologica* (combination of a verb and a cognate obj.); such *figurae* were archaic in V.'s day and were used for stylistic elevation (see Tarrant on 12.457, Wills 1996: 245–6). **florentis aere cateruas:** cf. 8.593 *fulgentis aere cateruas.* For *florere* meaning 'shine/glow (with colours, metalwork, etc.)', see *OLD* 2. Cf. Acc. *trag.* 79–80 Dangel *aere atque ferro feruere, igni insignibus | florere*, Gel. 5.5.2 *exercitum insignibus argenteis et aureis florentem.* Similar is Gk ἀνθέω (cf. X. *Cyr.* 6.4.1 ἤνθει δὲ φοινικίσι πᾶσα ἡ στρατιά, 'the entire army shone with crimson').

434–44 Turnus concludes by returning to Drances and responding to the end of his speech (367–5), in which Drances calls on Turnus to face A. and fight him singly.

434 solum Teucri in certamina poscunt: cf. *solum posci in certamina Turnum* at 220. It is tempting to suppose that Turnus had heard (directly or indirectly) Drances' public statements that he, Turnus, had been challenged to single combat and now responds to them; but *solum* would also fit if Turnus was simply answering the taunting close to Drances' speech. *solum* is juxtaposed with *Teucri* to suggest grandiosely a brave single fighter up against a whole force.

435 'and if this is your will and I so stand in the way of the common good'. **placet:** see 332n. The authoritative resolution would come from the council, with Latinus at its head. **tantum . . . obsto:** Turnus speaks 'with proud and bitter irony' (Gransden ad loc.).

436 **exosa:** a strong word ('detesting, loathing') found first in V.; other examples are at 5.687, 12.517, and 12.818. Cf. *perosus*, also first attested in *Aen.* (6.435, with Norden's note, and 9.141).

437 **tanta . . . pro spe** 'for so great a hope'. Turnus refers to the hope of saving his people, rather than to his desire for marriage and royal succession (*pace* C–N). Turnus would not want to suggest that he fights for the latter personal reasons (although he surely does in part), since that would be consistent with, and would even give credence to, Drances' contention that the Latins die to satisfy his selfish desires.

438 **ibo animis contra:** Turnus answers Drances' concluding words at 374–5, but also echoes Hector at *Il.* 18.307–8 'I will stand against him [Achilles]' (ἀλλὰ μάλ' ἄντην | στήσομαι). *animis* = *animose.* **magnum praestet Achillem:** *praestet* = 'play the part of', not 'excel, surpass', as Serv. and Tib. ad loc. suppose (followed by Henry, Williams, Paratore, and, more tentatively, Mackail); *praesto* without a reflexive to mean 'play the part of' is unusual and is perhaps a Virgilian innovation (*TLL* x.2.923.2–12). As the next line indicates, Turnus imagines A. as an imitation Achilles, fitted out in divinely crafted armour like the Homeric hero's (*paria . . . arma*), rather than as superior to him. There is no sign that Turnus is aware of A.'s armour, made by Vulcan (*Aen.* 8.370–453, 608–731), and therefore is aware that A. is indeed another Achilles in possessing divinely crafted armour. (Turnus refers to the armour of Achilles, not of A., at 9.148–9 *non armis mihi Volcani . . . | est opus in Teucros.*) Turnus' comment here certainly seems hypothetical, not factual. This lends his words keen dramatic irony: to a degree that Turnus does not understand, A. has, in fact, become a second Achilles. The subjunctive *praestet* (like *induat* in the next line) depends upon *licet* at 440.

439 Turnus has a sword crafted by Vulcan and given to Turnus' father Daunus (12.90–1); Turnus forgets the weapon when joining battle at 12.735–6, and although it is restored to him by Juturna at 12.785, Jupiter ensures that it has no efficacy (cf. 12.798–806).

440 licet: with *uel* at 438, 'even though'. **soceroque Latino:** Turnus treats his claim to marry Lavinia as a fixed matter, despite the fact that she is not yet his *sponsa* (see 217n.). His position is risky, since he would not want to raise the spectre of his selfish motives for fighting. Turnus uses *socer* to affirm both the authority that lies in his relationship to Latinus and his quasi-filial commitment to the king. In addition, *socer* implies Turnus' sense that he is in a position close to that of Menelaus, whose bride has been abducted (cf. 9.136–9, with 7.321–2, 7.361–6); through parallels with Homer, V. will correct this at 442.

441 Turnus ego: Turnus' use of his own name lends solemnity to the vow while at the same time showing defiant pride. Turnus also refers to himself by name at 12.11, 12.74, 12.97, and 12.645. Elided *ego* is emotional. **haud ulli ueterum uirtute secundus:** Turnus demonstrates all the more how important *uirtus* is to him; cf. 386, 415, and 444. Thomas 1998: 285 understands *ueterum* to be on one level focalised from the time of V. and, from that perspective, to recall republican ancestors, including the Decii (see the next note).

442 deuoui: the verb, emphasised by the enjambment, conjures the *deuotio*, in which a leader 'devoted' his life for his people by voluntarily sacrificing himself to save them and deliver victory. The two Decii (Publius Decius Mus father and son) provide famous examples in Roman history of *deuotiones* (in 340 and 295 BCE respectively). On the *deuotio*, see Oakley on Liv. 8.8.19–11.1. Yet while Turnus' gesture resembles a *deuotio*, in that he asserts his willingness to die for the public good, he is not actually vowing such a self-sacrifice, because he does not offer himself up as a victim to bring salvation and victory. Instead, he states that he has committed his life to the Latin cause and is ready to die while fighting for it against A. in single combat; this is a grand, heroic gesture, self-sacrificing in ways akin to that of a *deuotio*, but not an actual vow of death. Turnus also holds out strong hope of victory and *gloria* (see 444). In this, he is close to Hector, who ends his response to Polydamas' counsel not to fight Achilles by stating that he will face the Greek with a chance to win a great victory (μέγα κράτος, *Il.* 18.308). On Turnus and the *deuotio*, see Johnson 1976: 117–19, Pascal 1990, Leigh 1993, Panoussi 2009: 56–77, and Tarrant on 12.234 and 12.694–5. **uocat? et uocet oro** answers Drances' final words at 375. Cf. *Il.* 3.67–75, where Paris, chided by Hector, agrees to fight Menelaus in single combat to decide the outcome of the war. Turnus is thus both Hector and Paris (rather than Menelaus, as Turnus would have it) on the intertextual level. Further development of a crucial plot element in *Aen.* 11 and 12; Drances has successfully manipulated A.'s hypothetical remark at 115–18 to goad Turnus into stating that he would welcome single combat with A. This brings the fight closer to reality.

443–4 'and do not let Drances instead, if this is divine anger, appease it by his death; or if there is victory and glory, do not let him win the prize'. Turnus returns to Drances, thus underlining how much that adversary is on his mind and under his skin. His epiphonema (a striking comment concluding a speech or other discourse) presents an implicitly impossible scenario, given Drances' cowardice. What Turnus imagines is deliberately and derisively absurd: he digs at Drances with a final salvo of disdainful sarcasm while also distinguishing himself from that craven foe.

444 luat: the verb suggests expiation of the gods through a *deuotio*; cf. Liv. 10.28.13 (P. Decius Mus (the Younger)) *datum hoc nostro generi est ut luendis periculis publicis piacula simus,* V. Max. 1.7.3 (P. Decius Mus (the Elder)) *ut is capite suo fata patriae lueret.*

445–67 PREPARATION FOR BATTLE

As the Latin council deliberates, the Trojan forces move to attack; the news of their surprise advance dissolves the council and creates tumult in the city. The Homeric antecedent is *Il.* 2.786–810, where Iris, disguised as Polites, tells a Trojan assembly of the approach of the Greeks and bids the polyglot leaders of the Trojan forces to spread the news; in response, Hector breaks up the assembly, and the Trojans rush to arms. In contrast to Homer's Trojans, the Latins react in panic and chaos to the unexpected news.

The frantic surprise of the Latins does not signal that the Trojans broke the twelve-day truce established at 133 (so Frantantuono on 445–6, Carstairs-McCarthy 2015). V. provides no narrative marker that the twelve days of the truce have now passed (see Della Corte, *EV* II.238). Still, it beggars even perfervid 'pessimistic' belief that V. presented A. and the Trojans as treaty-breakers. Hence we need to assume that the truce is complete; see 225n. By giving no textual sign to that effect, V. produces in the reader something of the sense of surprise felt by the Latins. Dissension and uncertainty over what course of action to pursue has left the Latin side in disarray and unprepared for the renewal of hostilities.

Turnus responds to the news of the Trojan attack by at once stirring to action and taking command, while disparaging the Latins for deliberating as the enemy prepared for battle (459–67). Turnus is on the side of deeds, not words, despite his oratorical abilities, and he burns to join the fray; he now has a chance, too, to vindicate his call to continue the fight.

445–6 For the quick, asyndetic cut from one subject and perspective to another, cf. 10.146–7 *illi inter sese duri certamina belli | contulerant: media Aeneas freta nocte secabat.*

445 Cf. Enn. *Ann.* 569 Sk. (probably on a debate) *olli cernebant magnis de rebus agentes,* Lucr. 5.393 (on the battle of the elements) *magnis inter se de rebus cernere certant.* **agebant** 'were debating' (*OLD* 40).

446 certantes; castra: adversative asyndeton, with the enjambment and strong pause heightening the contrast, and with play on *certo*: the Latins are 'disputing, contending with arguments' (*OLD* 4) instead of getting ready to 'contend in battle' (*OLD* 2), as the Trojans are prepared to do. **castra Aeneas aciemque mouebat:** *castra mouere* usually means 'break camp' (cf. 3.519) or 'move camp', but here it is part of a compressed expression that apparently = 'moves his fighting force from the camp'. Cf. 7.429–30 *armari pubem portisque moueri | laetus in arma para.* At 17–21, A. had told his men of his plan to move quickly and attack Latinus' city; he now sets that plan in motion.

447 nuntius 'message/report', rather than 'messenger'; cf. 4.237, 6.456, 7.437, 8.582, and 9.692. This spreads quickly, through the regal palace and city, and excites terror.

448 ecce: the discourse marker for the sudden, disconcerting development; see 226n. **ruit:** cf. 9.474 *nuntia Fama ruit.* **implet:** used of filling with news; see *OLD* 5b. Cf. 896, 5.340–1 *hic totum caueae consessum ingentis et ora | prima patrum magnis Salius clamoribus implet*; cf., too, *Fama . . . | . . . replet* at 139–40.

449–50 The *oratio obliqua* gives the substance of the news and, at the same time, enlarges upon the narrator's description of the Trojan advance at 446. Cf. *Il.* 2.801 '(the Greeks) march over the plain to fight against the city' (ἔρχονται πεδίοιο μαχησόμενοι προτὶ ἄστυ), with 455n.

449 instructos acie 'in battle array'. This must not be the case literally, since the Trojans are still marching (see 511–14). The phrase is instead a way of saying 'ready for battle'.

450 Tyrrhenamque manum: A.'s Etruscan allies commanded by Tarchon. *Tyrrhenam* is adj. for gen. The phrase is also found at 7.43. **totis . . . campis** 'over all the plain'. **descendere:** for the verb meaning 'descend to lower or open ground for battle', see *OLD* 3. Poetic licence; in reality, the Trojans would have been marching from near the Tiber mouth to higher ground (see Della Corte 1972: 287–8).

451 extemplo turbati animi: also at 8.4; in both cases, the phrase describes excited mobilisation, with a strong undertone of alarmed agitation. *extemplo*, 'immediately', in origin an augural term, occurs in ordinary usage in Plautus, but is elevated in verse after Ennius (*Ann.* 377 Sk., *trag.* 362 Jocelyn). It is common in Lucretius (seventeen times) and missing from lyric and elegiac Augustan poetry; in prose, Livy has it very often (over 300 times). V. uses it fifteen times, all but one in *Aen.* (also at *G.* 1.64). The elision in *turbati animi* is emotionally coloured and expressive of nervous excitement. **concussaque** 'aroused, excited' (*OLD* 5); theme and variation describes Latin mobilisation.

452 et . . . irae 'and rage was stirred by no gentle goads'. **stimulis haud mollibus:** litotes, again at 728. **irae:** battle-rage (Homeric χάρμη).

453 Cf. 7.460 *arma amens fremit, arma toro tectisque requirit.* **arma manu:** the repetition of *ma* underscores the sense of urgency and haste (Dainotti 2015: 78 n. 254); cf. 8.219–20 *hic uero Alcidae furiis exarserat atro | felle dolor: rapit arma manu,* 7.460 *arma amens* (where the reversal of *-ma* in *am-* has the same effect). Such collocations of repeated syllables are not avoided by Latin writers, despite school prescriptions to the contrary (see Austin on 2.27 *Dorica castra*). *manu* suggests gesticulation and, thus, excitement as the men call for weapons. **trepidi:** of the agitated excitement and haste of sudden mobilisation. Cf. 300n., 7.638 *hic galeam tectis trepidus rapit.* **fremit arma** 'roar for arms'. Repeated calls for weapons are common in literature, as they no doubt were in reality when troops readied suddenly for battle (see Serv. ad loc. *hoc fremebant 'arma arma'. et militaris uox est,* Horsfall on 7.460). Cf. 2.668 *arma, uiri, ferte arma,* Hor. *Carm.* 1.35.15, Ov. *Met.* 12.241, Stat. *Theb.* 3.348–50, 6.618, 11.305–6, Sil. 4.09. **iuuentus** 'soldiery', as at 419; cf. 8.5 *saeuitque iuuentus.*

454 maesti mussantque: *mussant* = 'mutter' in anxious discontent; it contrasts sharply with *fremit* in the previous line. *maesti* is paired alliteratively (see 226n.); the alliteration suggests the sound of the murmuring. **patres:** in antithesis with *iuuentus.* V. varies the theme of fathers and sons so prevalent earlier in the book and describes a generational divide in the city: the young soldiers eagerly prepare to fight, while their elders lament the resumption of hostilities, despairing at the prospect that more young men, including their sons, will die.

454–5 clamor | . . . in auras: conventional hyperbole; see 192n.

455 dissensu uario refers to the discordant sounds of excited soldiers and weeping fathers. V. probably adapts *Il.* 2.804 (on the Trojans' polyglot allies) 'one tongue of the widely scattered men differs from another' (ἄλλη δ' ἄλλων γλῶσσα πολυσπερέων ἀνθρώπων); the divergent sounds of varied languages become the dissonant mixture of animated shouts and sorrowing. *dissensus* is first found here in Latin literature (*TLL* v.1455.71–2); this is its only occurrence in V. Statius adapts V. at *Theb.* 10.557–9 *urbem | scindunt dissensu uario Luctusque Furorque | et Pauor et . . . Fuga.*

456–8 A double bird-simile. Cf. 7.699–705, another double simile (or perhaps unrevised alternatives; see Fordyce and Horsfall ad loc.), with which this passage is comparable. Homeric antecedents for the bird-similes are at *Il.* 2.459–65 (part of a quadruple simile) and 3.2–6. Cairns 1989: 103 proposes that V. contradicts the latter Homeric simile and offers up a new, 'corrected', version of it when applying it to the Latins: in Homer, the Trojans were noisy and compared to cranes, while the Greeks were silent, disciplined, and eager to fight. Very possibly, V. also took as a model A.R. 4.1298–1302, a double bird-simile whose second part describes swans that 'raise their song' (κινήσουσιν ἑὸν μέλος) on the banks of the Pactolus River.

456 cateruae: of flocks of birds, as at 12.264. The word suggests as well an army squadron and, thus, establishes a correspondence with those preparing to fight in the main narrative.

457 piscosoue: the adj. also occurs at 4.255 and 12.518. It first appears at Hor. *S.* 1.5.97, as a seemingly colloquial epithet for the fishing town Barium (mod. Bari); cf. Ov. *Met.* 12.10 *piscosa Aulis.* V. uses it as a high-register alternative to the Homeric adj. ἰχθυόεις (e.g. *Il.* 9.4, 9.360, 16.746, 19.378, 20.392); the adj. is thus tonally adaptable to context. **Padusae:** V. locates the bird-simile in Italy; Padusa was a marshy area in the southern part of the Po Delta. Cf. 7.701, where the swans are at the Cayster River in Lydia (following *Il.* 2.461).

458 dant sonitum: a recurrent phrase; see 614, 799, 2.243, 3.238, 3.584, 5.139, 7.567, 9.667, 10.488, 12.267, 12.524, *G.* 2.306, 4.409. The compound expression goes back to Ennius (*Ann.* 411, 450 Sk.). For *sonitus* of a bird-cry, see 10.265–6 (Strymonian cranes) *aethera tranant | cum sonitu.* **loquacia:** transferred epithet (hypallage). Cf. 12.475 *nidisque loquacibus.*

459 immo 'all right, then'. The particle, used ironically, has a corrective force. **arrepto tempore** 'seizing the moment'. For Turnus, this is the right moment (= Gk καιρός) to denigrate deliberation and the Latin peace movement, when Trojan aggression makes clear the immediate need for military action.

460 cogite . . . laudate: derisive imperatives. *cogite concilium* scornfully echoes Latinus at 304 *cogere concilium.* **sedentes:** emphatic, and perhaps responding to Roman prejudices against sitting in assembly (see V. Max. 2.4.2, DServ. ad 9.227).

461 illi . . . ruunt: in strong, asyndetic opposition to the previous line. Cf. 446 and *Il.* 2.796–7 (quoted at 378–9n.). **nec plura locutus:** most speeches in *Aen.* ending before the close of the line pass straight into action. Here the medial break captures the suddenness with which Turnus quits the meeting and moves to preparations for battle and his enthusiasm for the fight. There is a strong contrast with 7.599–600 (the sole other appearance of *nec plura locutus* in V.) *nec plura locutus | saepsit se tectis rerumque reliquit habenas,* where Latinus shuts himself up in his palace and drops the reins of power; Turnus instead bursts forth from the palace to take command.

462 corripuit sese 'he hastily roused himself'. **citus:** adj. for adv.

463 Voluse: not otherwise mentioned in *Aen.* **edice:** the verb is technical for proclamations of magistrates and other authorities (*OLD* 1). The archaic imperative form contrasts with *duc* in the following line. **armari:** infinitive after *edice.* V. uses the subjunctive of indirect command with *edico* at 3.234–5 and 10.258–9, the other two occurrences of the verb in *Aen.*; he has the verb with acc. and inf. at *G.* 3.295–8. **Volscorum** anticipates the arrival of Camilla. **maniplis:** dat. with a verb of commanding. A Roman military term applied to the pre-Roman past; it designates a small infantry unit, in contrast to the cavalry fighters in the following line. For Volscian infantry, see 9.505 *accelerant acta pariter testudine Volsci.*

464 equitem Messapus: V. insistently associates Messapus with horses; his father was Neptune, the god of horses (cf. *G.* 1.13–14, 3.122). See 8.3–6, 9.26–7, 9.124, 9.351–3, 9.365–7, 9.523, 10.354, 10.749–50, 12.128, 12.288–91, 12.294–5, 12.550. *Messapus* is nom. for voc. (at least in part *metri gratia*), unlike *Voluse* at 463. Horsfall ad loc., following C–N, suggests a nom. as if *diffundat* follows; but Messapus is an addressee of *diffundite* at 465 along with Coras and his brother. On nom. for voc., see Eden on 8.77, Löfstedt 1956: 1.92–102. **in armis** 'under arms' (*OLD* 5b).

465 cum fratre Coras: Coras is mentioned at 7.672 with his twin brother Catillus. They come from Tibur, which, according to V., was named after another brother, Tiburtus (519, 7.671). On other accounts of the founding and naming of Tibur, see Fordyce on 7.672 and Horsfall on 7.670–7. **latis . . . campis:** abl. of extension, like *totis . . . campis* at 450.

466 capessant 'take up position in/man' (*OLD* 6).

467 iusso: an archaic form, probably future perfect (see Serv. ad loc., Sen. *Ep.* 58.4), but possibly a future like *faxo* at 9.154 and 12.316. **inferat arma:** military language. Cf. e.g. Liv. 1.30.8, 9.43.24, 10.31.11, 17.27.6, 32.10.6, 40.47.6, 42.30.10.

468–97 PREPARATIONS CONTINUED

V. keeps the focus on the Latin side as it prepares for the coming battle. V. presents the preparations *per partis,* by dividing the account into very brief sketches of varied actions. This was a way of creating *enargeia* or vividness; such division is found in historiography, and especially in scenes of disorder and confusion (Rossi 2004: 143–4), and is prescribed for oratory at Quint. 8.3.66–9.

The passage is bookended by Latinus and Turnus. Their reactions to the return of war are in sharp contrast: Latinus, who wants peace, despairs, and retreats, while Turnus, who wants war, exults, and advances. V. conveys Turnus' heedless excitement through a striking epic simile, on which see 492–7n.

468 ilicet: also at 2.424, 758, 7.583, and 8.223; each line describes a moment of heightened emotion and/or intense action. *ilicet* is an archaism and was originally a ritual word of dismissal; it appears in Roman comedy as a term of despair or resignation (cf. Pl. *Am.* 338, *Cist.* 685, *Epid.* 685, Ter. *Eu.* 54). V. revives archaic *ilicet* and adapts it to mean 'immediately', like *ilico.* See DServ. ad 2.424, Serv. ad 2.758. **tota . . . urbe** 'across the whole city'. **discurritur:** the intransitive verb is used impersonally in the passive, emphasising the action in progress over the agent. This idiom of spoken language was taken up by the poets and was particularly embraced by V. (see Austin on 4.416), although the impersonal form also recalls military prose (Horsfall on 7.553); cf. Liv. 5.36.5 *accensis utrimque animis ad arma discurritur,* 24.39.6 *inde passim discurritur,* 2.45.11 *totis castris undique ad consules curritur.*

469–72 As the council dissolves, Latinus is prey to events that he cannot control, as he was in *Aen.* 7 once war fever had taken hold. Sharp, impotent regret is all that he can muster.

469 pater: the final syllable is lengthened in arsis before the dominant caesura (see 111n., 323n.), as at 5.521 *ostentans artemque pater arcumque sonantem.* The noun links Latinus to the *patres* at 454 who do not want war;

by contrast, Turnus is one of the enthusiastic young (see 496n.). **magna incepta:** the plans for peace that Latinus had sought to set in motion. Cf. *magna . . . consulta* at 410, 7.259 (Latinus offers an alliance with the Trojans) *di nostra incepta secundent.*

470 tristi turbatus tempore 'distraught by the disastrous circumstances'. For *tempus* = 'circumstances', see *OLD* 10. The heavy alliteration, rounded off by the final *t* in *differt* and flanked by two alliterative verbs, is emotional. The contrast with *arrepto tempore* at 459 underscores how differently Turnus and Latinus respond to the news of the Trojan attack. **differt** 'postpones, defers'; understand *magna incepta* as the object.

471 Some ninth-century MSS insert this and the following line after 12.611; see Tarrant on 12.612–13 for discussion. **incusat:** cf. 312, 12.580 *Aeneas magnaque incusat uoce Latinum.* **acceperit:** subjunctive in a causal relative clause, as with *asciuerit* in the following line. **ultro** 'on his own initiative'. Latinus had sent word back to A. through Ilioneus that he had chosen him, A., to be Lavinia's groom (7.268–73); in the face of the fury around him, however, the king had dropped the arrangement. Here, he rebukes himself for not taking the initiative and seeing things through, whatever the resistance to the marriage.

472 Dardanium: for the force of the epithet, see 353n. **asciuerit:** the verb describes Latinus taking A. into his family as his son-in-law (*OLD* 1c), but, with *urbi,* also suggests that A. would be an ally (*OLD* 1). The phrasing points to the public dimension of a royal marriage: the tie with the king's daughter is simultaneously an alliance with his kingdom.

473 praefodiunt 'dig trenches in front of'. The verb first occurs here in extant literature, is a *hapax* in V., and nowhere else is used with this meaning (*TLL* x.649.17–26). **saxa sudesque:** the rocks and pointed stakes are prepared as weapons rather than as barriers. Cf. 894, where Latin women use seared *sudes* as swords, and 7.524; for stones as missiles, cf. 9.569 and 12.896–907. For the alliterative pair, cf. Liv. 23.37.3 (*saxis sudibusque*), 27.28.12 (*saxis sudibus*), 34.15.5 (*saxisque et sudibus*). Statius imitates V. at *Theb.* 5.352–4 *huc saxa sudesque | . . . | subuectant.*

474 subuectant: cf. 131 *saxa subuectare.* A pointed contrast with that earlier line: instead of helping the Trojans to build the walls of their city in peace, the Latins and their allies prepare in their own city for war against the Trojans. **cruentum:** transferred epithet, from *bellum* to *signum.*

475 bucina: a war-trumpet (*TLL* II.2.2232.25–52); V. is the first extant poet to so use the noun (before V. in prose at Cic. *Mur.* 22). There is probably a deliberate echo of 7.519–20 *bucina signum | dira dedit* (the only other appearance of *bucina* in *Aen.*), where the *bucina*, a pastoral object (*TLL* II.2.2231–2232.24), calls Latin country-dwellers to fight the Trojans in the first encounter of the war; now Latin city-dwellers prepare for a decisive battle. In recalling 7.519–20, the *bucina* reminds the reader that the Latins remain new to war while also contrasting their earlier pastoral life, upon which war intrudes, with the now urban experience of warfare.

475–6 uaria cinxere corona | matronae puerique: *uaria corona* = 'a motley ring of defenders'; the women and boys are to take to the walls as a last line of defence. Cf. 891–5. *corona* for a ring of soldiers (either defending or attacking) is a military term, and *cingere corona* a military phrase (*TLL* IV.986.60–3). Cf. 10.122 *rara muros cinxere corona.*

476 puerique: a weak principal caesura, after the trochee in the third foot; see 236n.

477–85 The queen Amata, her daughter Lavinia, and other Latin matrons ascend to the temple of Minerva to pray to the goddess. The Homeric model is *Il.* 6.286–310, where the Trojan queen Hecuba, attended by matrons, goes to Athena's temple to pray to the goddess. In V., the women call upon Athena to break A.'s spear and to have him fall (484–5); in Homer, the women call upon the goddess to break Diomedes' spear and to have him fall (6.306–7). A. thus becomes a double for the Homeric Diomedes soon after Diomedes refused to renew hostilities with the Trojans. See Knauer 1964: 287–9, Gransden 1984: 184–5. The procession of Trojan women was depicted on the temple of Juno in Carthage (1.479–82). As V. notes there (482), Trojan prayers to Athena were to no avail, and the same will of course be true here. Also depicted on the temple was Penthesilea (1.490–3); obliquely, the recollection of the temple ecphrases anticipates the arrival of the Amazonian Camilla at 498.

477 nec non 'and what is more'. An emphatic transition formula first found commonly in poetry in V.; also at 603, 6.183, 6.645, 8.646, 9.169, 9.334, 10.27, 12.23, 12.125, *G.* 2.385, 2.413. **summasque ad Palladis arces:** cf. *Il.* 6.297 'now when they approached the temple of Athena in the citadel' (αἱ δ' ὅτε νηὸν ἵκανον Ἀθήνης ἐν πόλει ἄκρῃ).

478 subuehitur 'is conveyed up to'. V. pictures Amata carried in a carriage, probably conceived as a *pilentum* (so Serv. ad loc.); according to Livy (Liv. 5.25.8–9, see also D.S. 14.116.9), Roman matrons were granted the right to ride in *pilenta* to festivals and games as a reward for their contribution of jewellery to the treasury in 395 BCE. Cf. 8.665–6 *castae ducebant* *sacra per urbem* | *pilentis matres in mollibus*. An imagined *carpentum*, or a two-wheeled carriage that women could use, according to Livy, from 395 BCE on holy days and work days, is also possible. On the origins of the use of *carpenta*, see also Ov. *Fast.* 1.619–28.

479 **dona ferens:** cf. *Il.* 6.293 'Hecabe brought [a robe] as an offering to Athena' (Ἑκάβη φέρε δῶρον Ἀθήνῃ).

480 **causa mali tanti:** cf. 6.93 (the Sibyl prophesies a second Trojan War in Italy) *causa mali tanti coniunx iterum hospita Teucris*. This links Lavinia to Helen; cf. *Il.* 22.116 (on Helen) 'who was the beginning of the strife' (ἥ τ' ἔπλετο νείκεος ἀρχή). The description of Lavinia is consistent with Latin opinion (217) and with Drances' view (355–6, 363, 369, 371) about what lies at the root of the war, despite 7.481–2 (the killing of Silvia's stag) *quae prima laborum* | *causa fuit belloque animos accendit agrestis* and 7.553 *stant belli causae*. **tanti, oculos:** hiatus (see 31n.). Hiatus occurs most frequently in V. before a marked pause, as here. It seems in this case to emphasise the contrast between the halves of the line and, thus, the striking fact that a modest girl could be the cause of so great an evil. The alternative readings *mali tantis* and *malis tantis* look like attempts to eliminate V.'s hiatus. **oculos deiecta decoros:** a lowered gaze was a conventional sign of maidenly modesty. Perhaps Lavinia casts down her eyes both out of modesty and because of her guilt and shame at being the *causa belli* (so Tarrant on 12.64–9); in that case, although she has no culpability and moral responsibility in the war, which distinguishes her from Helen (cf. e.g. *Il.* 3.154–8, 6.344), she nevertheless suffers emotionally due to the role she plays in the conflict. *oculos . . . decoros* are retained accs. after the passive participle.

481–2 The spondaic rhythm reflects the gravity and sorrow of the moment.

481 **succedunt** 'come up to/approach'. The women proceed as far as the threshold of the temple (see *alto . . . de limine* in the following line); as in Roman practice, the Latin women appear to worship in the portico in front of the temple building (the Roman *cella*). Contrast *Il.* 6.298 'fair-cheeked Theano opened the doors [of Athena's temple] to them' (τῇσι θύρας ὤϊξε Θεανὼ καλλιπάρῃος); Theano (probably alone) then enters the temple and lays a robe on the statue of Athena. **ture uaporant** 'fill with the smell of incense'. The verb occurs only here in V.; it appears earlier at Lucr. 5.1131 *inuidia quoniam, ceu fulmine, summa uaporant* (with the meaning 'are burned'). Cf. Stat. *Theb.* 1.556 *ture uaporatis lucent altaribus ignes*, 5.174 *alta etiam superum delubra uaporant*.

482 maestas: cf. 454; both *matres* and *patres* despair as war resumes. This is the last instance of the recurring adj. in *Aen.* 11.

483 The ritual triple address derives from *Il.* 6.305 'Lady Athena, protector of the city, fairest of goddesses' (πότνι' Ἀθηναίη, ἐρυσίπτολι, δῖα θεάων). **armipotens:** a high-sounding compound from early poetry (Acc. *trag.* 260 Dangel, of Minerva). V. has *armipotens* for Minerva at 2.425; he uses the epithet for Deiphobus at 6.500, for Achilles at 6.839, and for Mars at 9.717. Cf. *bellipotens* at 7. **praeses belli** '(tutelary) mistress of war'. **Tritonia:** the cult-title also occurs at 2.171, 2.615, and 5.704. It was believed in antiquity to come either from Lake Triton in Africa, near which the goddess was said to have been born or to have come to earth after her birth (cf. Luc. 9.354), or from a river of that name variously placed in Africa, Boeotia, or Thessaly (cf. Hdt. 4.180, Paus. 9.33.7, Apollod. 1.3.6, 3.12.3, Serv./DServ. ad 2.171, where curious Gk etymologies are also proposed); see Austin on 2.171, Maltby 1991: 623.

484–5 The lines are very close to *Il.* 6.306–7 'break now the spear of Diomedes, and grant that he may fall headlong before the Scaean gates' (ἆξον δὴ ἔγχος Διομήδεος, ἠδὲ καὶ αὐτὸν | πρηνέα δὸς πεσέειν Σκαιῶν προπάροιθε πυλάων).

484 manu: sc. *tua.* The noun is an example of pleonasm for emphasis; it stresses the force and violence with which Minerva is to smash the arms. **Phrygii praedonis:** a double insult. For contemptuous *Phrygius,* see 145n., 403n. *praedo* as an insult is fairly strong (see Dickey 2002: 351); it occurs in comedy and prose (especially Cicero) before V. (see Opelt 1965: 81–3, 133–4, Lyne 1989: 161–2, *TLL* x.584.13–19, 49–72). It obviously ties A. to Paris (cf. e.g. *Il.* 3.444, Hdt. 1.3.1–2). *praedo* is also used of A. at 7.361 (Amata) and 10.774 (Mezentius). Cf. *Il. Lat.* 291–2 (Menelaus attacking Paris) *misso fixisset corpora telo* | *praedonis Phrygii.*

485 effunde: theme and variation with *pronum sterne solo,* and in response to πρηνέα . . . πεσέειν at *Il.* 6.307.

486–91 The passage recalls Homeric arming scenes; the specific model is *Il.* 6.503–5, where Paris arms himself for battle. Cf. 12.87–94 for another description of Turnus' arming.

486 cingitur 'arms himself'; middle voice. **furens:** signals battle-lust. Allecto had fired Turnus with that emotion in *Aen.* 7; cf. 7.460–2 *arma amens fremit, arma toro tectisque requirit;* | *saeuit amor ferri et scelerata insania belli,* | *ira super,* 7.464 *furit. furo* also describes Turnus' battle-rage at 9.691 and 9.760; cf. 12.680 *sine me furere ante furorem;* see also 11.901. Turnus is associated with *furor* beyond that of battle-lust; he embodies the irrational, destructive rage that A. must face and overcome (including, at the end of the poem, homeopathically, by meeting *furor* with *furor*; see Tarrant, Intro. pp. 15–24). Literature on the subject of Turnus and *furor* is vast; a starting point is the bibliography of Traina, *EV* v.334–6.

487 iamque adeo: also at 2.567, 5.268, 5.864, 8.585. It marks a transition either to a new subject or, as here, to the final stage in a narrative. **rutilum:** the first of several colour terms in the passage. Wordplay in connection with the Rutulian Turnus is also possible. Cf. Hardie on 9.65 *haud aliter Rutulo muros et castra tuenti* [*ignescunt irae*]: 'The use of *Rutulus* to refer to Turnus in this fiery context perhaps puns on *rutilus*.' **thoraca indutus:** *induo* contains a strong reflexive element; hence *thoraca* is a retained acc. with a participle acting as a middle. This construction with *indutus* goes back to early Latin; see Courtney 2004: 426.

487–8 aënis | horrebat squamis: the reference is to bronze scale-armour. The topos of soldiers 'bristling' with armour, shields, and weapons is as old as Homer (*Il.* 4.281–2, 7.62). See further 601–2n.

488 surasque incluserat auro: also at 12.430, where A. arms. As at that line, the tense of *incluserat* indicates the speed of Turnus' response; he had already put on his greaves (as he had his breastplate and, as the following line reveals, his sword).

489 tempora nudus: *tempora* is an acc. of respect after an adj., a Gk construction not found until Augustan verse (Courtney 2004: 430). DServ. ad loc. gives a practical explanation of why Turnus keeps his helmet off: *quia mox Camillam adloquitur, et ut hortans et incendens ceteros facilius nosceretur.* While this seems partially correct, the detail also suggests Turnus' brash confidence; see 497n.

490–1 Cf. *Il.* 6.512–14 'thus Paris, son of Priam, came down from high Pergamus, gleaming in his arms like the sun, laughing, and his swift feet bore him on' (ὣς υἱὸς Πριάμοιο Πάρις κατὰ Περγάμου ἄκρης | τεύχεσι παμφαίνων ὥς τ' ἠλέκτωρ ἐβεβήκει | καγχαλόων, ταχέες πόδες φέρον).

490 Cf. 2.41 *Laocoon ardens summa decurrit ab arce.* **alta . . . arce:** Latinus' palace, where the council had been; the palace is described at 7.171 as the highest point in the city (*summa fuit urbe*).

491 exsultatque: the verb indicates unbridled pleasure, but also confident aggression in a martial context, as at 648 and 663 and 2.386, 2.470, 10.550, 10.643, 10.813 (where see Harrison's note), and 12.700. **et spe**

iam praecipit hostem 'and in his hope already anticipates the enemy'. Turnus eagerly and hopefully imagines battle already joined.

492–7 The simile derives from *Il.* 6.506–11 (= 15.263–8) 'as when a stalled horse, having fed at the manger, breaks his halter and runs stomping over the plain – being accustomed to bathe in the fair-flowing river – exultant; he holds his head high, and his mane flows over both shoulders; he revels in his beauty, and his knees swiftly carry him to the haunts and pasture of horses' (ὡς δ' ὅτε τις στατὸς ἵππος, ἀκοστήσας ἐπὶ φάτνῃ, | δεσμὸν ἀπορρήξας θείῃ πεδίοιο κροαίνων, | εἰωθὼς λούεσθαι ἐϋρρεῖος ποταμοῖο, | κυδιόων· ὑψοῦ δὲ κάρη ἔχει, ἀμφὶ δὲ χαῖται | ὤμοις ἀΐσσονται· ὁ δ' ἀγλαΐηφι πεποιθώς, | ῥίμφα ἑ γοῦνα φέρει μετά τ' ἤθεα καὶ νομὸν ἵππων). (The parallels with *Il.* 6.503–5 (486–91n.) and 6.512–14 (490–1n.) show that *Il.* 6.506–11, not 15.263–8, is V.'s Homeric model.) V. might have also had in mind A.R. 3.1259–61, where Jason is compared to a war horse eager for battle (a simile itself indebted to Homer). Ennius adapts the Homeric simile at *Ann.* 535–9 Sk. *et tum, sicut equos qui de praesepibus fartus | uincla suis magnis animis abrumpit et inde | fert sese campi per caerula laetaque prata | celso pectore; saepe iubam quassat simul altam, | spiritus ex anima calida spumas agit albas.* Macrobius (6.3.7–8) cites the passages of Homer, Ennius, and V. to illustrate that V. borrowed from his Latin predecessor rather than from Homer. But while it is at times difficult to know if V. was responding to Ennius or Homer (or both), Macrobius is wrong to exclude Homer as V.'s model (see 494n., 495n., 497n.). In adapting *Il.* 6.506–11, V. implicitly weaves Paris into the narrative; the horse in the simile corresponds to him. Turnus impetuously burns for war, while Paris, notoriously more a lover than a fighter, had to be stirred to battle by Hector and is only then eager to fight. Yet that eagerness still links the two; what is more, the erotic element in their behaviour partially equates them (see 494n.). The correspondences between Turnus and Paris counter the comparison of A. to Paris at 484. The horse-simile anticipates the cavalry engagement to come (although Turnus himself will not take part in it). It implies that Turnus rushes heedlessly, irrationally, and, thus, irresponsibly to war.

492 abruptis . . . uinclis: cf. *Il.* 6.507 δεσμὸν ἀπορρήξας, Enn. *Ann.* 536 Sk. *uincla . . . abrumpit.* **fugit praesepia:** cf. Enn. *Ann.* 535 *de praesepibus fartus,* from ἀκοστήσας ἐπὶ φάτνῃ at *Il.* 6.506. V. omits the detail that the horse was well-fed, probably because that detail did not correspond to Turnus' experience in the council; Schlunk 1974: 26–8, however, suggests that V. was responding to uncertainty in ancient scholarship over how to understand the Homeric phrase.

493 tandem liber indicates the horse's joy at having finally won his freedom. The corresponding implication is that Turnus felt confined in the Latin *concilium* and thrills at having broken free from it. Cf. *G.* 3.194–5 (a horse being trained for war) *per aperta uolans, ceu liber habenis | aequora.*

494 ille: deictic, to emphasise the subject of the simile and enhance vividness, as elsewhere in similes (see Fordyce on 7.380). **pastus armentaque . . . equarum** responds to ἤθεα καὶ νομὸν ἵππων at *Il.* 6.511; Ennius goes in a slightly different direction (*Ann.* 537 Sk. *fert sese campi per caerula laetaque prata*). The picture is of a stallion fired by sexual desire and eager to satisfy it. Since the horse corresponds to Turnus, it indicates that an erotic impulse stirs him on to fight. On the one hand, this implies that Turnus is in a form of heat, eager for the aggressive violence of war that the simile sexualises. On the other hand, Turnus comes to resemble Paris as someone driven by the erotic: he fights for Lavinia, whom he already considers his bride, but is more like Paris than he knows, and he wishes to keep Lavinia from her rightful husband A. Yet V. alters Homer by making the visit to the mares only one of the possible destinations for the stallion. This suggests that the erotic does not define Turnus to the degree that it does Paris. See further Kühn 1957: 31–4, Williams 1968: 732–3. In A.R. 6.1259–61, meanwhile, Jason thrills for the fight after sprinkling himself with a drug from Medea, who is of course in love with the hero. This provides a second erotic subtext for V., although as his simile presents matters, it is love for a princess, rather than the love of a princess, that lay behind Turnus' eagerness for the fight.

495 'accustomed to bathe in the well-known stream of water'. V. adapts *Il.* 6.508 (not in Ennius). Bathing for the horse corresponds to fighting for Turnus; like the river for the stallion, familiar battle represents freedom for Turnus and is a locus of pure physical pleasure. **aquae:** gen. of identity (H–S 63–4) with *flumine.* Cf. Lucr. 2.664 *flumine aquai.* **noto:** builds on *adsuetus* (and on *Il.* 6.508) and underlines the familiarity of the *flumen.*

496 emicat 'darts forward'. The enjambment (cf. enjambed κυδιόων at *Il.* 6.509) conveys a sense of speed; cf. 5.318–19 *longeque ante omnia corpora Nisus | emicat,* 9.735–6 *tum Pandarus ingens | emicat,* 12.326–7 *saltuque superbus | emicat in currum.* The sense 'coruscate, flash with a sudden radiance' is also felt, to correspond with *fulgebat* at 490. **arrectisque . . . ceruicibus alte:** cf. *Il.* 6.509 ὑψοῦ δὲ κάρη ἔχει, Enn. *Ann.* 538 Sk. *celso pectore,* A.R. 6.1261 '[the horse] bearing itself proudly, with ears erect, lifts its neck' (κυδιόων ὀρθοῖσιν ἐπ' οὔασιν αὐχέν' ἀείρει). There is correspondence with *horrebat* in the main narrative (488). *alte* is taken naturally with *arrectis,* but should perhaps be understood also with *luxurians* in the following line, 'deeply, intensely'. **fremit:** cf. *fremit* at 453. Possibly a deliberate echo to link the horse to the young soldiers who clamour for their arms; the horse thus corresponds to a particular youth thrilling to the prospect of battle and to the wider soldiery that feels similarly.

497 luxurians 'gambolling, frisking', also of a horse at *G.* 3.81. The image corresponds to *exsultatque animis* at 491. Cf. *Il.* 6.509 κυδιόων. **luduntque iubae per colla, per armos** 'and the mane dances across its neck and shoulders'. Cf. *Il.* 6.509–10 ἀμφὶ δὲ χαῖται | ὤμοις ἀΐσσονται; Ennius' imagery is different (*Ann.* 538 Sk. *saepe iubam quassat simul altam*). Schlunk 1974: 27–8 notes that Homeric scholiasts took the mane as a symbol of pride and irrational arrogance. V. uses the mane similarly, as an emphatic final image for Turnus' psychological state; he is not vain about his beauty like Paris (cf. *Il.* 6.510 ὁ δ' ἀγλαΐηφι πεποιθώς), but rather is awash in arrogant confidence. This suggests that Turnus' bare head at 489 operates in like fashion: the mane corresponds to it in both image and function. For *ludo* meaning 'dance, flutter' of inanimate things, see *OLD* 1c.

498–521 PREPARATIONS OF CAMILLA AND TURNUS

Camilla, anticipated at 432–3, enters with a plan for battle that she presents to Turnus. The Volscian queen is deferential to him because she is subordinate to him, the general of the allied Italian force to which she belongs. At the same time, she confidently and assertively proposes a plan that threatens to overshadow Turnus by giving her and her cavalry force a vanguard role in the coming battle and him a secondary one. Camilla deeply impresses Turnus (cf. 432–3), and he grants her command over the entire Italian cavalry. But he also feels the need to push back against her and to reassert his authority by devising a plan of his own that gives him an important role in the fight, in command of a force that will ambush A. and his men. Gender might play some part in Turnus' response, i.e. he might wish to establish male authority in the face of female strength and assertiveness in the arena of war; cf. 7.444 (Turnus to the disguised Allecto) *bella uiri pacemque gerent, quis bella gerenda.* There is nothing explicit to that effect, however, and even if Turnus is driven (consciously or unconsciously) to affirm male authority, he is also powerfully moved by the warrior spirit of this *uirgo,* and he not only accepts her presence in battle but also promotes her to a leadership position.

This is Camilla's first experience of war (see 711n., 803–4n.). Even so, she is clearly up to the task, as she has the native qualities to be an excellent fighter and warlord and has been completely integrated into the military culture of the native Italians (so Sharrock 2015: 162). Hence there is no real incompatibility with the end of *Aen.* 7, where Camilla is called a *bellatrix* (7.805) and possesses the hardiness for battle (*proelia uirgo* | *dura pati*, 7.806–7; I follow Page and Horsfall in taking *dura* as a nom. with *uirgo*). That description implies not that she is a veteran of war, but that she is altogether suited to and ready for it; the battle in this book will illustrate the point.

498 A characteristically abrupt return to the main narrative, with *cui* referring back to Turnus, and a sudden transition to a new scene: 'Virgil loves to start the action with a *sudden strong impetus*, rather than slowly and gradually' (Heinze 1993: 251). The abruptness also reflects the action: the decisive, forceful Camilla rushes up suddenly with an aggressive plan. **Volscorum acie:** the cavalry force introduced at 7.804 (Camilla) *agmen agens equitum*; Camilla is in command of it, while Volusus leads the Volscian infantry (see 463). For *acies* of cavalry, cf. Liv. 4.19.5, 8.39.1. V. departs from Homer by including a cavalry battle (Heinze 1993: 157–9); such a battle is appropriate for the Amazonian Camilla, since Amazons had long been depicted fighting on horseback. We need not doubt that the Volscian cavalry was predominantly male (although see 655–63) any more than that the Volscian *manipli* were men (*pace* Horsfall ad loc.). If it had been comprised of women, V. very likely would have stated as much at some point, because a female cavalry force would have been marked rather than unmarked. (Thus V. describes Camilla's female *lectae comites* at 655–63.)

499 regina: according to V., Camilla's father Metabus, a king of Privernum (see 540n.), was driven from his throne and escaped into exile with his daughter (see 539–66). See, further, Bremmer and Horsfall 1987: 9. V. is silent on how she subsequently came to occupy the position of Volscian *regina*.

501 defluxit 'glided down', indicating 'ease and grace in alighting' (C–N). M. Furius Bibaculus (fr. 8 Courtney), quoted at 827–8n., and Liv. 2.20.3 *moribundus Romanus labentibus super corpus armis ad terram defluxit* use *defluo* of a mortally wounded rider slipping from his horse. 'If this association [of *defluo* with a dying horseman] was firmly established, perhaps by similar use in Ennius, Vergil's use of the word at Camilla's first appearance in XI might have ominous overtones' (Wigodsky 1972: 100).

502 Turne: the initial voc. in a speech is unusual in V.; it indicates marked urgency (see Horsfall on 7.421) and reflects Camilla's vigorous, no-nonsense approach. **sui . . . forti** 'if the brave may justly have any confidence in themselves'; *sui* is an objective gen., *forti* a dat. of possession. Camilla's statement is of a kind to resonate with Turnus, who possessed *sui fiducia* in battle (cf. 9.126, 10.276). Cf. Caes. *Civ.* 2.37 (Curio) *tantam habebat suarum rerum fiduciam.*

503 audeo et: V. normally avoids first-person singular present verbs with a cretic pattern (long–short–long), which necessitate an elision; the only other example is *nuntio et* at 1.391. The elisions here and later in the line, with *promitto occurrere,* reflect Camilla's eagerness. The shortening of final *-o* in cretic forms, as an extension of spoken Latin practice, was very limited in V., who applies it only to *nescio* to create a dactyl; see Austin on 1.391. **Aeneadum:** a patronymic of the Trojans, found fifteen times in *Aen.*; it is also used of the Romans at 8.341 and 648. Lucr. 1.1 *Aeneadum genetrix* is the first attested use of the word. **occurrere:** the infinitive in a hostile sense (*OLD* 5) contrasts with *occurrit* at 499; *obuia* in the next line likewise contrasts with *obuia* at 498. The echoes link the actions: Camilla goes to meet her ally Turnus to ask to go against the enemy. **turmae:** the technical term for a Roman cavalry squadron.

504 Tyrrhenos equites: the Etruscans play the leading role on the Trojan side in the cavalry fighting.

505 me: cf. *sola* in the previous line, the first-person *audeo* and *promitto* at 503, and *sui* at 502. Camilla puts herself front and centre, even though this will of course be no solo mission, and even though she respects Turnus' authority (see *sine*). This is a mark of her bravery, but also of her self-regard and egocentrism; while Camilla fights with her forces and for them and the Italian alliance, she conceives of the mission as an expression of her single and singular heroism. **prima manu temptare pericula belli:** Camilla volunteers to lead a front line against the Trojan cavalry before they reach the city; that vanguard effort = the *prima . . . pericula belli. manu* = 'by force', as at 116. With *temptare pericula belli,* cf. Lucr. 5.1299 *biiugo curru belli temptare pericla.*

506 pedes 'foot soldier, infantryman'. **subsiste** 'stay behind'.

507 oculos horrenda in uirgine fixus: *oculos* is a retained acc. Cf. 12.70 *figitque in uirgine uoltus,* where Turnus gazes intently at Lavinia. V. distinguishes between the two gazes, despite the verbal echoes: at 12.70, Turnus is agitated by *amor,* while here the strong adj. *horrenda* implies a feeling in Turnus of almost religious awe (cf. 6.10 *horrendae . . . Sibyllae*). The use of the adj. for a mortal woman is striking and unusual (Morello 2008: 41 n. 12). Turnus considers Camilla a great wonder, μέγα θαῦμα (on Camilla as a θαῦμα in *Aen.* 7, see Boyd 1992: 222–9); he is astonished by this powerful, courageous woman, who does not fit with his sense that warfare is masculine business (see 7.444, quoted at 498–521n.).

508 o decus Italiae uirgo: *decus* denotes a person who confers distinction and is a source of pride (*OLD* 3); *o* gives strong emotional colour (see 124n.). Cf. Ov. *Met.* 8.317 (Atalanta) *nemorisque decus Tegeaea Lycaei. uirgo* is an important thematic term for Camilla (cf. 565, 604, 664, 708, 718, 762, 841, 7.806); virginity is prominent in her characterisation (Boyd 1992: 217). Cf. *Cloelia uirgo* at Liv. 2.13.6. There are suggestive parallels between the early Roman heroine Cloelia in Livy and Camilla: both escape across a river (see 562–6, Liv. 2.13.6); both are brave, female leaders in war (Liv. *dux agminis uirginum inter tela hostium Tiberim tranauit*); and both are linked to *decus* (Cloelia is among the *feminae quoque ad publica decora excitatae* in the Livian passage). Camilla's Italian origins and identity are fundamental to her; yet she is also a mixture of Italian and non-Italian/eastern elements. See 648–63n., 768–93n.

508–9 quas . . . | . . . parem?: rhetorical *dubitatio*, as at 125. The distinction lies between expressing thanks in words and, with (*grates*) *referre*, in deeds (*OLD* 13b). *dicere grates* occurs only here.

509–10 est . . . | . . . supra 'since your courageous spirit surpasses all'.

509 omnia: probably used in a general sense, to convey just how superior Camilla is. The alternative is that *omnia* = 'all I can say or do in thanks' (Serv., C–N, Page ad loc.), thus picking up on the *dubitatio* at 508–9; but split command would seem to constitute adequate thanks. **quando:** causal.

510 supra governs *omnia* in the previous line in anastrophe and hyperbaton; word order stresses the prepositional phrase. **partire:** imperative. Turnus' command answers Camilla's offer to take the vanguard position in the coming engagement while assigning him a secondary role; he proposes that they play equal parts in the fighting. While not confrontational, his words are a corrective to Camilla's bravado. They are also a reflection of his own pride and egotism: Camilla's spirit surpasses all, and therefore she is fit to share command with Turnus.

511 fidem refers both to 'belief' in rumour (*fama*) and 'confirmation' that comes from the scouts.

512 exploratores: to be taken separately from *fama* in the previous line, rather than hendiadys-like with it ('the report of the dispatched scouts'), as Williams ad loc. understands it; *fama* denotes the unattributed rumours that fly around in war (the *nuntius* of 447), while the *exploratores* bring back a specific report. The news is more thorough than at 449–50; Turnus has received a detailed picture of enemy movements, although V. does not say how and when. **equitum leuia . . . arma** = *equites leuiter armatos.* **improbus:** Turnus considers A. shamelessly unjust in planning the surprise attack he does; he acts without regard for doing what is fair and right (*OLD* 4, Austin on 4.386). The adj., recurrent in V. (fourteen times, eleven in *Aen.*), can have a range of other meanings, 'from "rascally" (*cornix . . . improba, G.* 1.388) to "unconscionably cruel" (*improbe Amor, Aen.* 4.412) to "insatiably savage" (the bloody jaws of a lion in a simile describing Mezentius, *Aen.* 10.727)' (Thomas on *G.* 1.145–6). For *improbus* used elsewhere of A., see 4.386 and 12.261.

513 quaterent: the subjunctive depends on the idea of 'command' implied in *praemisit*; it is used without the conjunction *ut*, as often with verbs of commanding (A–G §565a). The imperfect after the perfect definite ('has sent') is unproblematic (*NLS* §140). *quatio* probably = 'make [a place] vibrate with noise', i.e. with the thunder of hooves; cf. 8.596 *quadrupedente putrem sonitu quatit ungula campum* (which derives from Enn. *Ann.* 263 Sk. *summo sonitu quatit ungula terram*). But a combination of that meaning and 'cause [the ground] to shake' from the force of the horses' hooves is plausible; cf. 875. Whether V.'s primary model, Enn. *Ann.* 242 Sk. *explorant Numidae, totam quatit ungula terram*, refers to sound or to shaking, or to both, is uncertain.

513–14 ardua montis | per deserta: it is better to take *ardua* (*montis*) separately from *per deserta*; *ardua* then stands as the direct object of *superans.* Cf. 8.221 *petit ardua montis,* 5.695 *ardua terrarum.* A prepositional phrase with *ardua* and *deserta* in agreement is possible (cf. *G.* 3.291 *deserta per ardua*) but necessitates intransitive *superans* when the transitive form is more common and is easily understood (cf. 903 *exsuperat iugum* and 6.676 *hoc superate iugum*). The landscape does not reflect reality and is the product of poetic licence; '[Turnus] appears to be talking about mountains; the hills round Lavinium reach three hundred feet' (Horsfall on 522–9).

514 iugo 'over the ridge'.

515 furta paro belli: *furta* = 'stratagem', 'secret operation'. Serv. ad loc. compares Sal. *Hist.* 1 frag. 112 *gens ad furta belli peridonea.* Cf. 9.150 (on the Trojan Horse) *inertia furta.* While Turnus' plan for an ambush is sound, it is a surprise from him; given his youthful bellicosity and exuberance at the prospect of joining battle, he might have been expected to commit himself only to immediate, open fighting. Such combat is preferred to stealth in a straightforward version of the heroic ethic; cf. 10.735 (Mezentius) *haud furto melior sed fortibus armis*, *Il.* 7.243–4 (Hector to Ajax) 'I do not want to strike such a man as you by sighting you secretly, but rather openly' (ἀλλ' οὐ γάρ σ' ἐθέλω βαλέειν τοιοῦτον ἐόντα | λάθρῃ ὀπιπεύσας, ἀλλ' ἀμφαδόν). For Roman thinking along the same lines, cf. Liv. 42.47.5–8, Tac. *Ann.* 2.88.1 *non fraude neque occultis, sed palam et armatum populum Romanum hostes suos ulcisci.* But Turnus is responding to A.'s own surprise attack and hidden, flanking movement; in *Aen.*, open pitched battle is only one type of possible engagement, and V. makes the element of surprise a key feature of warfare. This is one of the ways in which he presents a war that is 'complex in military character as well as in political démarches' (Rossi 2004: 103, referring to Alexander 1945). See also Heinze 1993: 256, and cf. 2.390 *dolus an uirtus, quis in hoste requirat?* On ambush and stealth in Homer, see Dué and Ebbott 2010: 31–87. Turnus' plan differs from Camilla's at 506; however non-confrontationally, he further modifies her proposal and gives himself something other than a secondary, defensive role in the coming fight. In narrative terms, both Turnus' ambush and A.'s movements have the purpose of removing them so that Camilla can take centre stage in the ensuing engagement; A. does not appear again in the narrative until 904. **conuexo in tramite:** it is preferable to take *conuexo* to mean 'sunken, hollow' and to refer to a track in a low valley of the wood. This works well with 513–14; Turnus contrasts high and low spaces, and he implies that A. and his troops will come to the valley when making their way through the mountainous terrain. Cf. 1.607–8 *dum montibus umbrae | lustrabunt conuexa* (where *conuexa* seems to mean 'valleys, hollows'), Plin. *Nat.* 5.5.38 *uallis repente conuexa.* Page, Williams, and Fratantuono ad loc., however, propose 'arched path', with the idea that trees grow over the *trames* to make it ideally dark for an ambush.

516 biuias . . . fauces: the phrase describes a narrow passage with openings at two ends. With his forces, Turnus will lie in ambush and seek to trap the Trojan troops in the valley between the defile that leads into it and the defile that leads out of it. The adj. *biuius* is first found here and is very rare after V. (*TLL* II.2025.43–9); V. has the noun *biuium* at 9.238 *biuio portae.* **obsidam** 'blockade'. A military term (*TLL* IX.221.82–222.23). Cf. Liv. 29.32.4 *Masinissam persecutus in ualle arta faucibus utrimque obsessis inclusit*, 31.40.3 *obsessasque fauces.*

517 conlatis . . . signis: *signa conferre* is a standard idiom for joining battle (*OLD* 15b, Lyne 1989: 111). V. has it only here, to lend realism to Turnus' speech. **excipe** 'meet [the attacking cavalry]'. Horsfall ad loc. and *TLL* V.2.1264.68 are mistaken that Turnus calls for Camilla to surprise the enemy. Rather, he tells her to do what she had volunteered to do at 504–5 and to meet the enemy forces openly while he goes off to set his trap.

518 tecum: *ingenti honore 'tecum' dixit, hoc est non tu illi adiuncta eris, sed ille tibi* (DServ. ad loc.). But Turnus also answers Camilla's first-person verbs at 503, *solaque* at 504, and *me* at 505; in another corrective response to her proposal, he counters her go-it-alone attitude and assigns her allied fighters, thus demonstrating his authority to arrange troops and to control the composition of Camilla's forces. **acer:** a common epithet in *Aen.*, applied to fourteen heroes in the poem (Messapus, A., Turnus, Aconteus, Atinas, Coras, Eryx, Licurgus, Lucagus, Mezentius, Mnestheus, Orontes, Romulus, Serestus); it implies energy, intensity, and mettle. A sign of the same defiant optimism that Turnus displays at 429–33.

519 ducis et tu concipe curam 'you, too, assume a leader's command'. There is an element of paradox in *ducis . . . tu*, since Camilla is a woman; cf. 705–6n., 1.364 *dux femina facti.* For *cura* meaning 'command of a military force', see *OLD* 7. At 464–5, Turnus called on Messapus and the brothers Coras and Catillus to take charge of the cavalry; he now places the men under Camilla, although they will continue to command forces as her lieutenants.

520 sic ait: the speech formula, resembling Homeric ὣς φάτο, appears eleven times in *Aen.* on its own and twice with *inlacrimans* (including at 29). **paribus . . . dictis** 'in similar strains'.

521 pergit: the verb substitutes for *it*; *pergo* for *eo* is largely literary (Adams 2013: 800–4).

522–9 An ecphrasis on the place of ambush. Commentators compare the description of the Caudine Forks at Liv. 9.2.7–9 *saltus duo alti angusti siluosique sunt montibus circa perpetuis inter se iuncti; iacet inter eos satis patens clausus in medio campus herbidus aquosusque, per quem medium iter est; sed antequam uenias ad eum, intrandae primae angustiae sunt, et aut eadem qua te insinuaueris retro uia repetenda aut, si ire porro pergas, per alium saltum artiorem impeditioremque euandendum.* Livy relates the famous story of how, in 321 BCE, the Samnites trapped the Roman army in a plain after sealing the two defiles that offered ingress and egress (Liv. 9.2–6). The location here is dangerous to the Trojans as the Caudine Forks were to the Romans (although, ultimately, the situations are contrasting, since the Trojans emerge unscathed). Statius develops V.'s description of the site of ambush at *Theb.* 2.496–526.

522 Est introduces a short topographical description, as at 316. **accommoda:** the adj. is first found in V. Statius imitates at *Theb.* 6.614–15 *fraudique accommoda sensit* | *tempora* and 10.192 *nox fecunda operum pulchraeque accommoda fraudi.* Cf., too, Stat. *Theb.* 7.441–2 (a ridge) *tutisque accommoda castris* | *arua,* which reverses V.'s *accommoda fraudi* while principally imitating 526–7.

523–4 quam densis . . . | . . . latus: a very close echo of 7.565–6 (the Vale of Ampsanctus, where Allecto returns to the Underworld) *densis hunc frondibus atrum* | *urget utrimque latus nemoris.* In both cases, the wood is not simply dark, but is gloomy, sinister, and associated with death; *ater,* a colour term of strongly emotional content (see 186n.), has the implication 'dreadful', 'deadly'.

524–5 tenuis . . . | . . . maligni 'to where a narrow path leads, and tight defiles and narrow entranceways bring you'. *maligni* corresponds to *tenuis* and *angustae* and thus means 'narrow, thin' (*OLD* 2b), but also implies the danger that the narrow entranceways pose to an army.

525 The adjectival frame reflects how narrow and closed-in the path is.

526–7 'above it, on a high vantage point, on the mountaintop, lies an unknown plain, a safe refuge'.

527 ignota: the *planities* is 'unknown' to those unfamiliar with the area, including A. and the Trojans; for Turnus, the situation is different (see 530 *nota . . . regione*). The adj. also indicates that the plain was not visible from the *ualles* and was unfrequented. **receptus:** Turnus' troops withdraw to a safe spot, where they can await the Trojans without fear of attack.

528–9 'whether one would want to go meet in battle from right or left or to take a stand on the heights and roll down huge rocks'.

528 uelis: a generalising and depersonalised second-person potential subjunctive (only here in V.).

529 iugis: the mountain ridges above the valley; they are different from the *iugum* over which A. traverses at 514.

530 huc marks the return to the main narrative after the ecphrasis (see 320n.). **nota . . . regione uiarum** 'by the familiar line of paths'. Cf. 2.737 *nota excedo regione uiarum.* **fertur:** middle voice, of the warrior's swift self-propelled motion; see Zucchelli, *EV* II.495, and cf. 678, 730, 906, 2.337, 12.346, 12.478, 12.855, and *G.* 3.236.

531 arripuitque 'and he occupied [the position]', with a sense of rapid action. This use of the verb is first attested in V. (*TLL*

11.643.24–34). **insedit** 'held, seized', but plausibly also with the meaning 'lay in ambush', activating an etymology that links the verb with *insidiae.* Cf. Serv. ad loc. *'insidere' est dolose aliquem exspectare: unde et insidiae nominatae sunt,* Isid. *Etym.* 10.151. This is the last we see of Turnus until 896; see 515n. **iniquis:** the adj. is common for an unfavourable military position (*OLD* 6b). The position is unfavourable not for those occupying it, but for the Trojans; cf. Liv. 22.28.3 *tumulus erat . . . quem qui occupasset haud dubie iniquiorem erat hosti locum facturus.*

532–96 DIANA TELLS THE STORY OF CAMILLA

The goddess Diana speaks to the nymph Opis about Camilla, who is dear to Diana above all others. To explain why Diana cares so much about the girl, V. gives her a long passage recounting how Camilla came to be her devotee and describing Camilla's youth as a devoted virgin huntress, before she became the warrior seen in this book's cavalry battle and at *Aen.* 7.803–17. A probable model for this inset story is A.R. 4.783–832, where Hera delivers a long speech to her favourite sea nymph Thetis in which she recounts Thetis' backstory. See 537n., 595–6n.

Critics have suggested that Diana's speech was originally written as a piece of direct narrative and then transferred to its current location (e.g. Mackail, Intro. to *Aen.* 11, p. 418, Williams 1983: 285, Heinze 1993: 342 n. 63). A piece of evidence adduced in support of that argument is the use of *Dianae* at 537, *Triuiae* at 566, and *Diana* at 582; the claim is that the names are appropriate for a third-person narrative, and hence that V. wrote the scene for such a narrative, decided to change it into a speech by Diana, but failed to adapt the three moments in question to it. That V. would have been so lax is implausible (and to suppose that he would have revised, but died before getting the chance to do so (cf. *VSD* 35–6), is dubious biographical speculation). But the argument founders anyway because speakers in *Aen.* recurrently refer to themselves using their own name in the third person; cf. 2.79, 4.308, 6.510, 7.261, 7.401, 10.73, 12.11, 12.56, 12.74, 12.97, and 12.645, and see Austin and Norden on 6.510, Horsfall on 7.401. Where else in *Aen.*, moreover, would V. have thought to place the passage? It certainly would not have fit at the end of the catalogue in *Aen.* 7, where Camilla first appears (7.803–17); a lengthy account of her backstory would have created intolerable imbalance with the rest of the catalogue.

The close integration of the speech into its narrative context further supports the idea that V. intended it for precisely this moment in *Aen.* 11. The speech is an instance of epic retardation; it stops the action at an important moment and creates suspense and pathos. V. generates both by having Diana foresee her beloved Camilla's death (535–6, 591–4);

pathos comes, too, because Diana is unable to keep a mortal favourite from dying. In this, she resembles Zeus at *Il.* 16.431–61, who cannot stop Sarpedon's death. On Camilla and Sarpedon, see Quint 2018: 173–4. Diana, however, will be able to avenge Camilla, and she dispatches Opis at the end of the speech to do precisely that, while the goddess vows that she will herself tend to Camilla's corpse.

The story of how Camilla came into Diana's service begins with the exile of her father Metabus. V. tells us that he was driven from power because of the hatred for his tyrannical rule (539); this is all the information that V. provides, and there is no reason to follow Serv. ad 567 and to suspect that Metabus was exiled because he was an Etruscan or a representative of Etruscan rule in Volscian territory (*pace* Alessio 1993: 118). As an exiled tyrant, Metabus does partly resemble the Etruscan Mezentius. Yet Metabus is not sacrilegious as Mezentius is (see 557–60, 565–6); and while Mezentius is an unworthy father of Lausus (7.653–4), Metabus is full of loving care for his infant daughter as he flees with her into exile.

Metabus is to some extent a mothering father to Camilla (544, 571–2; cf. Horsfall on 570–2). This mix of the maternal and paternal connects him to Evander (see 139–81n.); his blurring of gender roles also inverts that of Camilla, the woman in the male role of warrior.

532 The abrupt shift to the new scene displeased Serv. ad loc. (*abruptus est et uituperabilis transitus*) but is characteristic of V. (cf. 498n.). **Velocem:** swiftness is also salient attribute of Camilla (see 718n., 760n., 7.807–11); hunters were associated with speed (Seelentag 2012: 128, on ps.-V. *Cul.* 119). Cf. *G.* 4.344, where Arethusa, a nymph associated with Artemis, is called *uelox*, a 'suitable epithet for one who prefers hunting to spinning' (Mynors ad loc.); At *G.* 4.343, the name Opis appears with Arethusa in a list of nymphs around Aristaeus' mother Cyrene. **Opim:** DServ. ad loc. and Macr. 5.22.1–6, relying on the poet Alexander of Aetolia, observe that Opis was a cult name for Artemis at Ephesus. Cf. Call. *Hym.* 3.204 (Artemis) 'Oupis, queen, fair-faced bringer of light' (Οὖπι ἄνασσ' εὐῶπι φαεσφόρε). It is reasonable that V. knew this and transferred the cult name for Artemis to the goddess' follower. There was also a Hyperborean Oupis who helped to raise Apollo and Diana (Call. *Hym.* 4.292). V. might have had this figure in mind when creating his Opis; at 858, she is identified as Thracian (Hyperborea was the region beyond Thrace). For other ways of identifying Opis, see the lengthy note of DServ. ad loc.

533 'one of the companion virgins of her consecrated band'. **sacraque:** i.e. dedicated to the service of the divinity.

534 Latonia: Diana, daughter of Leto. The matronymic occurs for the first time in extant literature at Catul. 34.5. V. has matronymic *Latonia* for Diana also at 9.405; for adjectival *Latonia*, see 557 as well as *G.* 3.6, where it is applied to Delos.

535 crudele: the war is cruel because Camilla will die in it; hence Diana foreshadows her favourite's fate.

536 uirgo: clearly Opis, picking up on *uirginibus* at 533, and not Camilla in an emotional apostrophe to her (so *quidam* in DServ., Fratantuono ad loc., tentatively). **nostris . . . armis:** i.e. the bow and arrow; cf. 7.816–17 (Camilla) *Lyciam ut gerat ipsa pharetram.* **nequiquam:** further foreshadowing, and a stark description of futile action. **cingitur:** middle voice, as at 486.

537 cara mihi ante alias: cf. A.R. 4.790–2 (Hera to Thetis) 'But come! For ever since your infancy I myself raised you, and I have loved you beyond all others who dwell in the sea' (ἀλλά σε γὰρ δὴ | ἐξέτι νηπυτίης αὐτὴ τρέφον ἠδ' ἀγάπησα | ἔξοχον ἀλλάων, αἵ τ' εἰν ἁλὶ ναιετάουσιν), Ov. *Met.* 2.415–16 (Callisto) *miles erat Phoebes, nec Maenalon attigit ulla | gratior hac Triuiae.* **iste:** better 'that (love) which you know well' than 'that (love) just described'. This works better with *neque . . . nouus*; Opis is very familiar with a long-standing love. **Dianae:** probably dat. with *uenit* in the next line. If gen., subjective rather than objective. *Dĭanae* is usual in V.; he has the name with a short *i* nine times (always at line-end), including at 652, 843, and 857 below, while using *-ī-*, the original quantity, just once (1.499). With Diana's reference to herself in the third person after *mihi,* cf. 2.78–9 *me . . .* | *. . . Sinonem,* 6.510–11 *Deiphobo . . .* | *. . . me,* 7.401–3 *Amatae* | *. . .* | *. . . mecum.* The third-person possesses grandeur because it is spoken by a goddess, while also having a strong emotional note.

538 subitaque . . . dulcedine 'with a sudden tenderness'.

539 pulsus ob inuidiam regno: like Mezentius at 10.852 *pulsus ob inuidiam solio sceptrisque paternis.* **inuidiam . . . uirisque superbas:** hendiadys, 'hatred of his haughty power'. Cf. 8.481–2 *rex deinde superbo | imperio et saeuis tenuit Mezentius armis.*

540 Priuerno: a powerful Volscian town in the early Republic, and, according to Livy (8.19–21), a holdout against Rome until agreeing to terms of peace (which included citizenship without the vote (*ciuitas sine suffragio*)) in 329 BCE. Modern Priverno is about 45 miles SE of Rome in the lower Amaseno valley; the remains of Roman Privernum are located a little less than 2 miles from the modern town, but the site of the Volscian town is unknown (Oakley on Liv. 7.15.11). At 9.576, the Italian warrior Privernus, named after the town, is killed by the Trojan Capys, who gave his name to Capua. Adkin 2010 etymologises the name of the town and warrior from *primus* and *uis*; it is tempting from there to see *uiris* in the previous line as a gloss on the name (Gildenhard ad loc.). **Metabus:** in all likelihood an invented character, like Camilla herself (see Intro. p. 20). A Metabus was known as the founder of Metapontum (on the Gulf of Tarentum); cf. DServ. ad loc, Str. 6.1.15, and see Saunders 1940: 549 n. 44. If V. indeed drew the name from that Metabus, he freed it from its geographical and mythological associations and used it for its ancient Italian patina; see Horsfall ad loc. and 2016: 57.

541 **media inter proelia belli:** *proelia belli* is first attested in V. (*TLL* x.2.1654.64–5); the phrase also occurs at Ov. *Tr.* 2.71.

542 **sustulit** 'took away'. V. perhaps sought to activate the verb's association with fatherhood; *tollo* was used of a father picking up a newborn child from the ground to recognise it as legitimate (*OLD* 2). **exilio comitem:** variation on the gen. with *comes/comites*, which is standard in historical prose (see Liv. 6.3.4 (with the notes of Kraus and Oakley), 34.35.7, Vell. 100.5, Tac. *Ann.* 4.13.3). **matrisque:** V. does not say what happened to Camilla's mother; we can reasonably assume that she is dead.

543 **nomine Casmillae mutata parte Camillam:** an example of metonomasia, or changed or alternative names. Alexandrian precedent for metonomasia is abundant (O'Hara 2017: 89). V. includes it here as a form of etymological wordplay, signposted by *uocauit* | *nomine. Casmilla* is understood to be an older form than *Camilla*, like *Casmena* for *Camena.* Varro (*L.* 7.34) identifies *camilla* as a synonym for *administra*, meaning 'female attendant' in matters of a secret nature; he continues that *camillus* designated an attendant at a wedding, and that Casmilus was a name given in the Samothracian mysteries to a certain divine person who attended on the great gods (cf. Serv. ad 11.558). Varro notes that Casmilus seems to be Greek, since he found it in Callimachus (fr. 723 Pfeiffer). DServ. ad loc. and Macr. 3.8.6–7 (both citing Statius Tullianus on Callimachus) observe that the Etruscans called Mercury Camillus, to signify 'attendant of the gods'. Varro, DServius, and Macrobius also cite Pacuvius for *camilla* meaning 'attendant': *caelitum camilla* (of Medea). *camillus* and *camilla* were also used of child attendants of the *flamines* and their wives (see Macr. 3.8.7). Hence through a number of possible associations, the name Camilla implies that she was an attendant of Diana. See, further, Arrigoni 1982: 77–88. For more on the possible meaning of Camilla's name, see 552n.

544 sinu indicates that Metabus holds his baby to his breast for protection (*OLD* 2), with maternal overtones (*OLD* 2c) to suggest Metabus' role as a mothering father in the absence of Camilla's *mater.* Cf. Ov. *Met.* 6.338 (on Latona) *inque suo portasse sinu, duo numina, natos.*

546 circumfuso . . . milite: *cirumfuso* = 'spread round'; Metabus' pursuers are fanned out and hope to surround him. The participle also suggests overflowing water (*OLD* 1); in this, it anticipates the Amasenus in the next line. The only escape from the *circumfusi milites* is the flooding Amasenus.

547–8 summis . . . | spumabat ripis 'was foaming along the top of its banks'.

547 Amasenus abundans: a small river below Privernum, also mentioned at 7.685 *Amasene pater.* The small river becomes a torrent in flood; cf. *G.* 1.115 *amnis abundans.*

548–9 tantus . . . | ruperat: the enjambment here and in the previous line suggests an overflow.

549 ille: resumptive. **infantis:** objective gen.

550 caroque oneri timet: on *carus* in V., see 215–16n. Metabus' feelings for Camilla, described through characteristic subjective style (the introduction of emotional colour into narrative from a character's perspective), resemble those of Diana (537, 586). Cf. 2.729 (A. fearing for Ascanius and Anchises) *pariter comitique onerique timentem.*

551 subito uix: the juxtaposed combination of adverbs (only here in V.) is striking. Its oxymoronic quality reflects how Metabus is pulled in different directions: because of the emergency, he has to come to a sudden decision, but because of the danger to Camilla, he arrives at the decision reluctantly. **sedit:** for the verb meaning 'is settled/decided on', see *OLD* 11; this use first occurs in V. and is plausibly his innovation. Cf. 7.611 *ubi certa sedet patribus sententia pugnae.* Claudian imitates at *DRP* 1.121 *certa requirenti tandem sententia sedit,* with *tandem* replacing *subito.*

552–63 Plutarch tells a similar story about Pyrrhus of Epirus (*Pyrrh.* 2.3–6). Pyrrhus was taken as a baby from Epirus to escape a faction that had expelled his father, the king Aeacides. The party that included Pyrrhus approached Megara, a safe haven, but could not cross a river swollen by rains to get to the city. Seeing people on the other side of the river, they wrote of their plight on a piece of bark and identified the baby, and they attached the bark either to a stone or a javelin, which they threw across the water. Those on the other side immediately made a bridge from felled trees and rescued the party. V.'s account of Camilla's escape very probably arose independently of this tale (Horsfall 1988: 41). DServ. ad 554 notes that the Roman grammarian Marcus Valerius Probus considered the account of Camilla's escape an 'unconvincing fiction' (ἀπίθανον πλάσμα). While the attribution to Probus is uncertain, the judgement fits with a strand in ancient Virgilian criticism that took issue with moments of free invention in *Aen.*, particularly those deemed incredible (Horsfall 1988: 41, 49–50).

552–4 Anacolouthon (change and discontinuity in syntactical structure): there is no verb in the main clause with the subject *telum*, which creates discontinuity with the new construction introduced by *huic*. One effect is to emphasise the *telum*. The syntax reflects, too, the nervousness and necessary quickness of the decision.

552 telum immane: for the adj., see 173n. An epic-size weapon wielded by the *bellator* Metabus, though now the epic warrior acts as a desperate father. That Camilla is saved by a thrown weapon anticipates her later life as both a hunter and a fighter. Egan 1983: 19–26 and 2012: 32–5 links Camilla's name to -κασμ- and argues that the Gk element is connected to armour and the meaning 'armed' through a series of derivations; hence Camilla's name points to her identity as a warrior, alongside signalling her identity as Diana's attendant (543n.). **forte** marks a coincidence that is essential to the action, as often (Tarrant on 12.270–3).

553 solidum nodis et robore cocto 'solid with knots and seasoned wood'. *cocto* here means 'seasoned' by being dried in smoke. Cf. 9.743 (Turnus' spear) *rudem nodis et cortice crudo*. For the use of *robore* after *ualida* in the previous line, cf. 326–7n.

554 libro et siluestri subere clausam 'wrapped in the bark of the woodland cork oak'. The cork is used for its buoyancy, so that the *telum* would float should it enter the river. Cf. Liv. 5.46.8 (Pontius Cominius, sent to Rome on the matter of Camillus' dictatorship) *incubans cortici secundo Tiberi ad urbem defertur*. The cork oak (*suber*) is also mentioned at 7.742; it grows in Italy and around the western Mediterranean.

555 habilem 'easily fitting' (*OLD* 1b). *habilis* can also mean 'easy to handle or wield' (*OLD* 1), and that idea seems present as well; Camilla is so positioned as to be convenient for throwing. This shades into a transferred epithet with *hastae,* since the spear, with Camilla attached, is the thing easily thrown.

556 dextra ingenti: cf. 5.487 (A.) *ingentique manu malum de naue Seresti* [*erigit*], where *ingenti manu* refers to A.'s heroic mighty hand, rather than, as Serv. ad loc. supposed, to a large throng of helpers (see Fratantuono and Smith ad loc.). **librans** 'poising to throw', a meaning first found in V. (*TLL* VII.1352.11–43; cf. 5.479, 9.417, 10.421, 10.480, 10.773). **ita ad aethera fatur:** also at 10.459 (the only two occurrences of elided *ita* in V.)

557–60 A variation on prayers before discharging a missile, on which see 784n. Cf. 9.404–9, where Nisus prays to Diana (identified with Luna) before casting his spear, killing Sulmo.

557 alma: a recurrent epithet for goddesses in V. and used of Diana at 7.774 and 10.215; for Metabus, it is not only conventional but also wishful. **nemorum cultrix:** *cultrix* = 'inhabitant' (cf. 3.111 *mater cultrix Cybeli*), but has an undertone of *custos.* The huntress Diana was naturally associated with woods and woodland; cf. 9.405 *nemorum Latonia custos,* Catul. 34.9–11, 64.300, Hor. *Carm.* 3.22.1, Stat. *Theb.* 4.425. Cf. the cult of Diana Nemorensis at Lake Nemi and the grove of Aricia in the Alban Hills (Arrigoni 1982: 92–8, Green 2007). Diana was also associated with rivers (cf. 1.498–9 *qualis in Eurotae ripis aut per iuga Cynthi* | *exercet Diana choros,* Catul. 34.12, Hor. *Carm.* 1.21.5).

558 ipse pater emphasises Metabus' authority, inhering in his *patria potestas,* to devote his daughter to Diana. **famulam:** predicative, 'as your servant'. **uoueo:** cf. 10.774–6 (Mezentius) *uoueo praedonis corpore raptis* | *indutum spoliis ipsum te, Lause, tropaeum* | *Aeneae.* These are the only two appearances of *uoueo* in *Aen.* The echo directs attention to the contrast between the vows of Metabus and Mezentius: the latter's is a 'perversion of a religious formula' (Harrison ad loc.), whereas Metabus offers up a vow to Diana that he subsequently meets, to the deep satisfaction of the goddess. **tua:** to be taken with *prima* and, in the next line, *tela* (cf. *nostris . . . armis* at 536); '[holding] your weapons first'. 'The fact that [the spear] is the first weapon the infant "holds" is a symbol of her dedication to the huntress-goddess' (Page ad loc.), but it also foreshadows her future in warfare. With *tuam* at 560, it is difficult not to give *tua* double duty and to join it also to *supplex* at 559, with *tua* and *tuam* a version of sacral repetition. **per auras:** to be taken with *hostem fugit* in the following line.

559 testor 'I entreat (you)/adjure'. The verb also appears at 9.429, in the Nisus and Euryalus episode (on the significance of this, see 563n.).

560 tuam: sc. *famulam.* The juxtaposition with *diua* reflects the close relationship between Diana and Camilla for which Metabus prays. **dubiis committitur auris:** cf. Lucr. 5.782 *incertis . . . committere uentis.* To commit something to the winds was to act recklessly (Harrison on 10.69). Metabus feels that he has no choice, but he shows trepidation over the attendant risks to his infant daughter.

561–2 dixit . . . | immittit: variation on a pattern; cf. 10.776–7 *dixit, stridentemque eminus hastam | iecit,* 10.886 *dixit, telumque intorsit in hostem,* 12.266–7 *dixit, et aduersos telum contorsit in hostis | procurrens.* At 9.52–3, V. alludes to the ritual whereby a fetial priest hurls a spear into enemy territory as a declaration of war (cf. Liv. 1.32.12–14). Perhaps he has that ritual in mind here, but as a contrast to Metabus' actions: the king throws his spear so that he and Camilla might escape war (see 541 *media inter proelia belli*).

561 Cf. 9.402 (Nisus casts his spear) *adducto torquens hastile lacerto.* **adducto . . . lacerto** 'bringing the arm into the body'. V. imagines Metabus bending his arm at the elbow and drawing the arm towards his body to throw the shaft. Cf. Ov. *Met.* 8.28 *adductis . . . lacertis,* describing a similar movement. The phrase also suggests muscular effort (Horsfall on 7.164). *lacertus* is the upper arm between shoulder and elbow, but is common, especially in poetry, as a synecdoche for the entire arm. **contortum:** the intensive prefix *con-* indicates the effort put into the throw. The participle signals a spear discharged with a rotatory movement (*OLD* 3b); an *amentum* can be assumed (cf. 284n.). It is perhaps overliteral to note that this would not have been a pleasant experience for the baby Camilla. **hastile:** originally as a substantive = 'spear-shaft', but from Enn. *Ann.* 392 Sk. a synecdoche for a spear; the figure is predominantly poetic (*TLL* VI.2557.18–43, Lyne 1989: 106).

562 immittit: enjambment to underline the exertion and force of a throw is common in *Aen.* (Dainotti 2015: 70–6). **sonuere:** V. places the verb after *immitit* to describe the immediate effect of the throw (hence *sonuere* is a perfect of instantaneous result; see Tarrant on 12.283, N–H on Hor. *Carm.* 1.34.16); the waters resound with the noise of the spear. For a similar effect, see 2.52 (*hastam*) *contorsit. stetit illa tremens.* **rapidum super amnem:** the sight of Camilla flying above the water recalls 7.810–11: *uel mare per medium fluctu suspensa tumenti | ferret iter celeris nec tingueret aequore plantas.*

563 infelix: probably proleptic, with *infelix* associated with death, as often in V. (cf. 53n.): when recounting Camilla's escape, Diana thinks again of her ultimate unhappy destiny (see 535–6) and of how she is killed by a *iaculum* (cf. 760). The adj. is used of Euryalus at 9.390 and of Nisus at 9.430. Another in a series of echoes of the Nisus and Euryalus episode; on Euryalus and Camilla, see Intro. pp. 27–8. **fugit** echoes *fugit* at 559 (and *fugiens* at 541), though now the verb = 'escapes' (*OLD* 12). **iaculo stridente:** *strido* of the noise of hurled/shot weapons goes back to Ennius (*Ann.* 355, 356 Sk.); cf. 5.502, 7.531, 9.419, 9.632, 9.705, 10.645, 10.776, 12.319, 12.859, 12.926.

564 magna . . . caterua 'as the huge band of troops now pressed closer'. **iam:** an elided monosyllable (see 166n., 278n.). *iam* is elided eighteen times in *Aen.* (four times in *G.*, once in *Ecl.*). Usually the elision occurs in certain patterns: it follows a monosyllable (see 807); precedes a monosyllabic preposition (see 846 and 900); or is part of a word-group (e.g. 6.385 *iam inde ut,* 6.389 *iam istinc et*) (Austin on 2.254). This is a rare case where the elision follows no such pattern; another occurs at 8.557 *Martis iam apparet imago.* It conveys tension as the band of troops approaches ever nearer.

565 cum uirgine uictor: Metabus is *uictor* in the sense that he has triumphed over his enemies by escaping with Camilla and has achieved his aims. The alliteration with *uictor* has epic colour; cf. 6.856 *uictorque uiros supereminet omnis, G.* 3.9 *uictorque uirum uolitare per ora,* and Enn. *Ann.* 181–2, 366, and 513 Sk.; see Cresci Marrone, *EV* v*.546.

566 gramineo 'grassy'; this *-eus* adj. (see 65n.) occurs seven times in V., all in *Aen.*; it appears before V. at Cic. *Ver.* 2.4.125 *gramineas hastas.* Cf. Ov. *Am.* 2.16.10 *gramineus . . . caespes, Tr.* 5.5.9 *gramineo . . . de caespite,* ps.-V. *Cul.* 393 *gramineam uiridi . . . de caespite terram.* **donum Triuiae:** ambiguous. On the one hand, the phrase can be read as 'a gift to Diana'. (*Triuiae* in that interpretation looks at first glance to be dat., but might well be gen., like *Mineruae* at 2.31 *donum exitiale Mineruae* (see Austin and Horsfall ad loc.) and 2.189 *dona Mineruae.*) Having had his prayer at 557–60 answered, Metabus honours his vow and dedicates his daughter and spear to Diana. On the other hand, the phrase could mean 'a gift of Diana'; the success of Metabus' throw, and hence the *hasta* and Camilla on the grassy riverbank, are a gift that the goddess bestows. *Triuia,* 'goddess of the crossroads', derives from an epithet of the chthonic divinity Hecate (Τριοδῖτις), who was identified with Artemis; it then passed to Diana and was the earliest of her epithets (Green 2007: 128). It is presumably used because 'Trivia [was] particularly called on in moments of danger, moments when death could threaten' (Green 2007: 129). *Triuiae* may reflect how Metabus dedicated his spear and daughter – i.e. the vow that he made was to *Diana Triuia*. But in any event, Diana's use of the third person is unproblematic (see 532–96n.).

567 Cf. Liv. 22.39.13 (Q. Fabius Maximus on Hannibal) *nullae eum urbes accipiunt, nulla moenia.*

568 neque . . . dedisset 'nor, in his wildness, would he have yielded', i.e. if anyone had offered him shelter. For *manus do* meaning 'yield, surrender', see *OLD* do 18a, manus 9d. *feritate* is an abl. of cause (lit. 'by reason of his wildness').

569 'and he lived the life of shepherds in the lonely mountains'. **pastorum . . . aeuum:** it is better to take *pastorum* as gen. with *aeuum* than with *solis . . . montibus*; the point of the passage is to describe how Metabus lived, not just where he lived (cf. Serv. ad loc. *et pastorum aeuum exegit in montibus solis, id est pastorali usus est uita*). Cf. the traditional motif of the exposed royal child raised by a shepherd (notably Romulus and Remus); Camilla's childhood with her deposed regal father is a variation on this. **exegit:** the use of *ago* and its compounds with *aeuum* belongs to poetic diction (Harrison on 10.53); *aeuum exigo* is Lucretian (4.1235). Cf. 7.776–7 (Diana, called Trivia, hides away Hippolytus, who becomes Virbius) *solus ubi in siluis Italis ignobilis aeuum | exigeret uersoque ubi nomine Virbius esset.* The echo links Metabus to Hippolytus as a male favourite of Diana/Artemis; at the same time, Hippolytus resembles Camilla as a devotee and favourite of Diana/Artemis and as someone whom the goddess could not save from death – although she does restore Hippolytus as Virbius, in which capacity he was located at Aricia, the cult site of Diana (cf. 7.761–82, Hor. *Carm.* 4.7.25–6, Ov. *Met.* 15.497–526).

570 in dumis interque horrentia lustra 'in the thorny brush and amid the bristling lairs'. With *horrentia lustra,* sc. *ferarum*; cf. 3.646–7 *in siluis inter deserta ferarum | lustra, G.* 2.471 *saltus ac lustra ferarum.*

571 armentalis equae: a wild broodmare; *armentum* can be used of cattle or horses. *armentalis* = 'of a wild group of horses'; the rare word is first found here (*TLL* II.610.25–36). Cf. Symmachus *Ep.* 6.17 *armentali lacte.* There is possible etymological wordplay with *armentum* and arms/arming (cf. Serv. ad 3.540 *armenta dicta sunt quasi apta armis*; see Maltby 1991: 53 and Egan 2012: 46); this would indicate that the early nourishment is appropriate for Camilla, who will soon bear arms (574) and will wield them as huntress and warrior. Appropriate nourishment, too, for a baby who will become an expert cavalry fighter. Cf. Harpalycus, the regal father of Harpalyce mentioned at DServ. ad 1.316–17 and Hyg. *Fab.* 193, 252, and 254; Harpalycus – exiled, according to DServ., *propter ferociam* – is said to have suckled his daughter from animals (the girl's mother was dead). See Intro. p. 21. **mammis et lacte ferino:** 'wild milk from the teats'. *ferino* is a transferred epithet. Philostratus (*Her.* 57.6) claims that Amazons nourished their babies with mare's milk (γάλακτί τε φορβάδων ἵππων) along with honeydew; see further Mayor 2014: 145–6. A presumably deliberate echo of Amazonian practice here, given that Camilla will go on to be an Amazonian warrior. Scythians were drinkers of mare's milk since Homer (*Il.* 13.5–6); the Amazons were from Thrace and, hence, from that region of milk-drinkers.

572 nutribat: for the metrically impossible *nutriebat*. V. has *nutrio* two other times, both describing men in nurturing roles (7.485, Tyrrhus helping to rear the stag; 12.344, Iambrasus raising his sons Glaucus and Lades). **teneris immulgens ubera labris** 'milking/squeezing its teats into her tender lips'; a vivid picture of how Metabus played the part of a mother to Camilla. Cf. Liv. Andron. *trag.* 38 Ribbeck *lacteam immulgens opem. immulgeo* appears elsewhere only in writers after V., including, in imitation of him, Plin. *Nat.* 11.232 (on screech owls) *fabulosum . . . ubera eas infantium labris immulgere.*

573 plantis: cf. *plantas* at 7.811 (Camilla) *celeris nec tingueret aequore plantas*; the echo reminds the reader of the runner that the newly walking Camilla will become.

574 institerat 'had planted', an unusual transitive use of the verb (*TLL* VII.1.1922.51); cf. 7.689–90, *uestigia nuda sinistri* | *instituere pedis.* **palmas:** contrasted with *plantis* in the previous line; once Camilla can walk, Metabus puts arms in her hands, which she no longer needs to crawl.

575 Metabus gives Camilla child-size versions (see 578) of the arms of Diana and, thus, of the hunt. She will later use similar adult arms in battle (see 652–4, 676); the suggestion is that Camilla's life as a huntress, to which she was acculturated from early childhood, is significantly preparatory to her life as a warrior, even though the two are also contrasted (not least by Diana).

576 crinali auro: presumably a hairpin, like the *fibula* that Camilla wears at 7.815–16 *ut fibula crinem* | *auro internectat.* There is a contrast between the wild young Camilla and the adorned Queen Camilla; the appearance of the latter shows the extent to which she has left behind her pastoral life. (For a different interpretation, see Boyd 1992: 220–1). The adult Camilla has a strong taste for gold and fine things (see 768–82). **pallae:** a long outer garment worn by Roman women over the *stola* for outdoor use.

577 tigridis exuuiae: the tiger-skin marks Camilla as a huntress who lies outside civilised norms (which the hairpin and the *palla* represent); cf. the lynx-hide of the huntress (i.e. the disguised Venus) at 1.323 *succinctam pharetra et maculosae tegmine lyncis.* Amazons were recurrently depicted wearing spotted pelts (Mayor 2014: 187); perhaps Camilla's hide is in part an allusion to them. Cassius Dio (54.9.8) states that Romans first saw tigers in 20 BCE, when a delegation from India gave them as gifts to Augustus in Samos; Pliny the Elder (*Nat.* 8.25) reports that Augustus first exhibited a tiger in Rome at the dedication of the Theatre of Marcellus (according to Pliny, in 11 BCE; the theatre was more probably dedicated in 13 BCE). **a uertice:** the tiger-skin covers Camilla's head, as a *palla* could.

578 tela . . . puerilia: children's toy weapons, but used for actual hunting rather than for pretend play, as 580 indicates; Camilla wields her *tela* as she does her slingshot and learns to hunt with them. Cf. V. Fl. 1.269–70 (Peleus to Chiron) *sub te puerilia tela magistro | uenator ferat.* Ahl 2007: 432 sees wordplay with *tela,* 'cloth on a loom/the loom'; whereas Roman girls learned to weave, Camilla learns to hunt. Cf. 7.805–7 (Camilla) *non illa colo calathisue Mineruae | femineas adsueta manus, sed proelia uirgo | dura pati cursuque pedum praeuertere uentos.* **manu . . . tenera:** *manu* emphasises personal exertion and force, while *tenera* creates an element of paradox: these are the forceful throws of a child of tender age. *tela manu* recalls Metabus at 552, while *torsit* echoes *contortum* at 561; like father, like daughter.

579 Cf. 9.586–7 *stridentem fundam positis Mezentius hastis | ipse ter adducta circum caput egit habena*; *funda* ('slingshot') occurs in *Aen.* only in these two places. A further connection between Mezentius and Metabus: the former uses a *funda* in battle (as did Roman troops; see Horsfall on 7.686, Hardie on 9.585–9), while the latter's daughter uses it to hunt, presumably having received it from Metabus. For slingshots used for hunting, cf. *G.* 1.308–9 *tum figere dammas | stuppea torquentem Balearis uerbera fundae.* Cf. the Amazon slinger on the lekythos (oil flask) of the so-called Klugmann Painter, now at the Metropolitan Museum in New York, with Mayor 2014: 223–6. **tereti:** 'smooth', to describe leather, despite *OLD* 1c, which takes the adj. to mean here 'rounded into a bulge'. **circum caput egit** 'she whirled [the sling] around her head'.

580 Strymoniamque gruem: the crane (*grus grus*); see Arnott 2007: 53–4. 'Strymonian' refers to the Thracian river Strymon (mod. Struma), which flows from today's Bulgaria into Greece and the Strymonian Gulf in the Aegean Sea; the river was associated with the crane because it was a stop on the bird's migratory route. The adj. also appears at 10.265 and *G.* 1.120 (where see Mynors' note). More than ornamental here, it conjures Thrace, the home of the Amazons. *grues* is also found at *G.* 1.307; V. clearly has that passage in mind (see the previous note). **deiecit:** also used of bringing down a bird at 5.542 *quamuis solus auem caelo deiecit ab alto.* **olorem:** the native Latin word, mainly poetic in extant literature (*TLL* IX.571.69–572.25) is an alternative to *cycnus*, a loanword from Gk.

581–2 multae . . . | . . . nurum: cf. Catul. 62.42 *multi illum pueri, multae optauere puellae*; verbal echoes and thematic correspondences (Catullus' poem is a marriage hymn, and 62.42 belongs to a passage on a *uirgo*) guarantee imitation. A second model appears to be Call. *Aet.* 3, fr. 67.9–10 Pf.), on Cydippe: 'many mothers sought Cydippe, still a child, as a bride for their sons in exchange for horned oxen' (πολλαὶ Κυδίππην ὀλίγην ἔτι μητέρες υἱοῖς | ἑδνῆστιν κεραῶν ἤτεον ἀντὶ βοῶν). See Tissol 1992: 264. Cydippe and Camilla form a strong contrast: Cydippe inadvertently vows to Artemis that she will marry Acontius, while Camilla rejects all suitors in her total devotion to Diana. Cf. 7.812–13 *illam* [Camilla] *omnis tectis agrisque effusa iuuentus* | *turbaque miratur matrum.*

581 Tyrrhena per oppida: DServ. ad loc. sees the phrase as a sign that the Volscians were under Etruscan authority, which implies Etruscan occupation in southern Latium (see, too, Serv. ad 567). But V. could have imagined that Metabus and Camilla had moved north into Etruria, or that Camilla's appeal had spread north of the Tiber (so Horsfall ad loc.). The reference to Etruria anticipates Camilla's main opposition in the coming cavalry fight; Camilla rejected Etruscan marriages as a huntress and battles Etruscan soldiers as a warrior.

582 sola: in strong opposition to *multae* in the previous line.

583 A striking line. The effect of the framing pattern 'is to emphasise C.'s self-contained and sequestered life' (Gransden ad loc.). The metre is strange; there is a diaeresis at the end of the third foot (see 163n.), and no fourth-foot caesura to balance the one in the second foot. **aeternum** 'life-long' (*OLD* 4).

583–4 uirginitatis amorem | intemerata colit: closely imitated by Auson. *Parent.* 26.3–4 *innuba deuotae uirginitatis amorem* | *parcaque anus coluit.* *intemerata* = 'inviolate, chaste, pure (from sexual intercourse)'; the adj. first appears in V. and is probably his coinage (*TLL* VII.2103.58–9), like other negatived participial adjs. (see 594n., 639n., 651n., 711n.); on V.'s penchant for such adjs., see Horsfall on 7.11, Harrison on 10.430.

584 uellem haud correpta fuisset | militia tali 'I wish that she had not been swept away by warfare such as this'. *uellem* is past potential and *correpta fuisset* a past unfulfilled wish; parataxis with subjunctive after *uolo* is common (H–S 530). *militia tali* refers to fighting in real warfare, as opposed to the 'warfare' of hunting, and also to this particular war against the Trojans, which Diana seems to understand to be wrong, deadly, and doomed for the Italians (see 589n.).

585 conata lacessere Teucros 'in trying to challenge the Trojans'; *lacessere* also suggests provocation and, thus, points to Camilla's rashness (Page ad loc.). The clause explains *tali*; this is the warfare that has swept away Camilla. Cf. 254 *suadetque ignota lacessere bella.*

586 The line does not contradict 537: Diana still considers Camilla a favourite but laments that she is no longer a *comes*, because the maiden has gone to fight the Trojans. The goddess knows that Camilla has made a mistake in doing so, and she is pained by this, rather than angry about it. **comitumque . . . mearum:** cf. Ov. *Met.* 2.426 (Jupiter, disguised as Diana, to Callisto) *o comitum, uirgo, pars una mearum.* **foret:** subjunctive in a present unfulfilled wish.

587 uerum age: an unconventional, seemingly more elevated alternative to *age, ergo age,* or *age* with an immediate imperative, which belong to conversational style (Austin on 2.707, Tarrant on 12.832). **quandoquidem:** rather common in comedy, and probably colloquial in Plautus' and Terence's time. In the late first century BCE, the word seems to have lost its colloquial character and to have become archaic in tone, fit for high poetry, and suitable in pathetic contexts; see Lyne on ps.-V. *Cir.* 323. V. has it two other times in *Aen.* (7.547, 10.105), both also in speeches by divinities and at emotionally charged moments. After Ovid, who has it three times in the *Metamorphoses*, it falls out from first-century CE epic diction (never in Lucan, Statius, Valerius Flaccus, and Silius Italicus). The *o* is shortened for metrical reasons. **acerbis:** of premature death; see 28n.

589 infausto . . . omine 'under an evil omen'. The fight is ill-omened (and *tristis*) to Diana because Camilla will die in it. But the goddess seems to allude as well to the ill-omened character of the Italian war against the Trojans. **committitur . . . pugna:** *pugnam committo* is standard for joining battle.

590 haec: Diana's bow, quiver, and arrows, as is clear from what follows. **ultricem pharetra depromе sagittam:** the use of *depromo* for removing arrows from a quiver (also at 858–9, 5.501) is rare (*TLL* v.1.616.9–10, 22–3). Cf. ps.-V. *Cul.* 160 (Cupid) *aurea fulgenti depromens tela pharetra*; *ad ulciscendum* at *Cul.* 158, which corresponds to V.'s *ultricem*, ensures imitation. Cf., too, Stat. *Silv.* 2.3.27 (Diana) *depromit pharetra telum breue*, Apul. *Met.* 5.23 *depromit . . . de pharetra sagittam.* The theme of vengeance links the stories of Pallas at the start of the book and Camilla here (and at 836–67); A. is to avenge the death of the former and Diana that of the latter.

591 uiolarit uulnere: closely echoed at 848 below; cf. 277 and 12.797 *quicumque tuum uiolauit uulnere corpus.* Because Camilla's body is *sacrum* to Diana, violence against it is a violation. There is also a hint that the mortal wound will violate Camilla sexually; see 803–4n.

592 Tros Italusque: *-que* is disjunctive, 'or' (*OLD* 7); hence a variation on 10.108 *Tros Rutulusne* and on 1.574 *Tros Tyriusque* (where *-que* seems to be copulative).

593–4 The model is *Il.* 16.667–75, where Zeus bids Apollo to cleanse Sarpedon's corpse of its 'dark blood' (κελαινεφὲς αἷμα), prepare it for burial, and then have it conveyed to Sarpedon's home in Lycia. Omitted, however, are the details about the cleansing and preparation of the corpse. This seems to reflect Diana's difficulty in facing the prospect of Camilla's death in all its harsh physical reality; certainly she will aim to minimise the violence done to her corpse (cf. *inspoliata* at 594). According to Schlunk 1974: 12–13, this might be a nod to ancient criticism on Homer that considered it inappropriate for Apollo to tend to the body and, thus, athetised the lines.

593 nube caua: the hollow cloud will conceal the body; cf. 1.516 (A. and Achates) *dissimulant et nube caua speculantur amicti*, 5.809–10 (A. saved from Achilles) *nec dis nec uiribus aequis | nube caua rapui. nubes caua* (also at 10.636) is Lucretian (6.176, 6.272), although Lucretius uses it in a meteorological sense, of round, massed clouds.

594 inspoliata: in contrast to Sarpedon, whose arms are stripped (*Il.* 16.663–5) from his defiled body (*Il.* 16.638–44). Another negatived participial adj. that quite possibly originates with V.; it occurs only here in V. and is otherwise rare (*TLL* vii.1963.4–11). **tumulo:** dat. of direction after a verb containing the idea of motion. Cf. *Il.* 16.674–5 'there shall his [Sarpedon's] brothers and kin bury him with a tomb and sepulchral pillar' (ἔνθα ἑ ταρχύσουσι κασίγνητοί τε ἔται τε | τύμβῳ τε στήλῃ). Against speculation that V. offers an aetiology for an actual tomb of Camilla,

Horsfall 1988: 42–3 convincingly argues that the *tumulus* is fictional like Camilla herself. **patriaeque reponam** 'and I will restore (them) to her native land'. V. adapts *Il.* 16.672–3 '(Sleep and Death) who will quickly set (Sarpedon) in the rich land of wide Lycia' (οἵ ῥά μιν ὦκα | θήσουσ' ἐν Λυκίης εὐρείης πίονι δήμῳ).

595–6 caeli delapsa per auras | insonuit: *delapsa* is an acceptable reading as a deliberate echo of *labere* at 588. The author of the *Ilias Latina* apparently knew it (*Il. Lat.* 96 *at illa leues caeli delapsa per auras*). *insonuit* refers to the sound of the arrows that Opis carries. V. probably imitates Apollo's clanging arrows at *Il.* 1.46 ('the arrows rattled on the shoulders of the angry one' (ἔκλαγξαν δ' ἄρ' ὀϊστοὶ ἐπ' ὤμων χωομένοιο)); see also V.'s *nigro circumdata turbine corpus* in 596 and *Il.* 1.47 '(Apollo) came like the night' (ὁ δ' ἤϊε νυκτὶ ἐοικώς, *Il.* 1.47). Cf., too, A.R. 4.842–3 (Thetis after her encounter with Hera) 'leaping down from the sky she plunged into the swirls of the dark sea' (ἀναΐξασα κατ' αἰθέρος ἔμπεσε δίναις | κυανέου πόντοιο).

596 nigro . . . turbine 'in a black whirlwind'. *turbo* is also used for the motion of arrows and other projectile weapons (cf. 284, Tarrant on 12. 855), and thus it anticipates the vengeance that Opis is to take on Camilla's killer. **corpus:** retained acc. after a passive participle with middle force.

597–647 THE CAVALRY ENGAGEMENT IS JOINED

Tension builds as the two sides face each other in formation (597–608) and is then released when they join battle with great force and ferocity. The encounter at this initial stage is an even fight; Camilla will soon change that. Serv. ad 608 states that the whole scene is Ennian, but this very likely exaggerates, as ancient criticism could do when dealing with imitation (Horsfall ad loc.); cf. Macr. 5.2.4, 5.17.4. There is some resemblance between 597 and Enn. *Ann.* 550 Sk. *atque atque accedit muros Romana iuuentus,* and see 601–2n.

598–9 Etruscique . . . | . . . turmas defines the composition of the *manus Troiana*; it is an allied force with Etruscan leadership and, it is understood, mainly Etruscan troops (cf. 504).

598 Cf. 171. **equitumque exercitus:** an extremely rare collocation (see *TLL* v.2.711.40, 1396.64–5).

599 compositi numero in turmas 'organised by number into squadrons'. For *compono* of organising troops, see *OLD* 6. *compositi* is plural with the collective noun *exercitus*. *numero* refers to the number of men per cavalry unit, in contrast to 5.560, where it refers to the number of cavalry units (*tres equitum numero turmae*). **fremit** describes loud neighing and suggests the animal's keen readiness for the fight, as at 12.82 (Turnus looking at his steeds) *gaudetque tuens ante ora frementis*; cf. 496 above, Hor. *Carm.* 4.14.23–4 *frementem | mittere equum medios per ignes.* **aequore toto** 'over all the plain'. Several passages suggest an etymologising association of *equus* with *aequor* (understood as a derivative of *aequus*, from which *equus* was etymologised) even when, as here, V. uses a synonym for *equus* (see 706–7 5.817–21, 7.781–2, 7.804–11, 10.569–71, 12.333, and 12.614–16, with Paschalis 1997: 20).

600 insultans 'prancing'. **sonipes:** collective singular. The word is poetic and has an archaic air. It is attested since Acc. *trag.* 400 Dangel *quadrupedantum sonipedum* and Lucil. 15, 16 M.; cf. Catul. 63.41 *uegetis sonipedibus.* See also Gk καναχήπους, 'with sounding feet' (of horses). The aural element in *sonipes* is clearly active in this example. V. is our first evidence for the noun in epic (see also 638 and 4.135), although we might reasonably suspect that Ennius had it in the *Annales.* After V., Lucan, Flavian epicists, and Claudian are partial to it (it does not appear in Ovid). **pressis pugnat habenis** 'fights the tightly drawn reins'; the horses are straining against their reins. *pressis* is dat. after *pugnat,* a Grecism (μάχεσθαί τινι); cf. 4.38 *pugnabis amori,* with Pease's note, and see Mayer 1999: 167–8. *pressis* is emphatic as a disyllabic spondaic word in the fourth foot (see 48n.); this amplifies the alliteration in *pressis pugnat.*

601–2 ferreus hastis | horret ager: a variation on the recurrent motif in V. of a (frequently bristling) 'harvest/crop of weapons'; cf. 3.45–6 *ferrea texit | telorum seges,* 7.525–6 *atraque late | horrescit strictis seges ensibus,* 12.663–4 *strictisque seges mucronibus horret | ferrea, G.* 2.142 *nec galeis densisque uirum seges horruit hastis.* Cf. Enn. *Varia* 14 *sparsis hastis longis campus splendet et horret* and A.R. 3.1355, where the field from which the sown men spring bristles (φρῖξεν) with shields, spears, and shining helmets. V.'s description also varies the images of bristling arms (see 10.178 *mille rapit densos acie atque horrentibus armis,* Enn. *Ann.* 267 Sk. *densantur campis horrentia tela uirorum*) and of soldiers bristling with armour and weapons (see 487–8n., and cf. Enn. *Ann.* 384 Sk. *horrescit telis exercitus*). See Tarrant on 12.663–4, Lyne 1989: 142–3, Nelis 2001: 298–302.

602 campique armis sublimibus ardent: C–N compare E. *Ph.* 110–11 'the entire plain gleams brass' (κατάχαλκον ἅπαν | πεδίον ἀστράπτει).

603–4 Messapus . . . | . . . Coras: cf. 464–5, and see 519n.

604 ala: a Roman military term. *alae* were cavalry wings of an army, comprised of *turmae.*

605–6 hastasque reductis | protendunt longe dextris 'with hands drawn back, they extend their spears far before them'. The soldiers' hands are behind them, because they are in ready position to throw their weapons, while the spears are long enough to project far in front of them. With *reductis* | . . . *dextris,* cf. 5.478–9 (Entellus preparing to punch a sacrificial bull) *reducta* | . . . *dextra.*

606 spicula uibrant 'they brandish javelins'. Cf. Homeric σείειν ἐγχείην/ἔγχος/μελίην 'brandish/shake a spear' (*Il.* 3.345, 5.563, 13.134–5, 13.557–8, 22.133).

607 'The onset of men and the neighing of horses burn more intense.' A weighty five-word line, to cap the description beginning at 597. V. contrasts the sight of advancing soldiers, appearing brightly on the plain with spears brandished, and the sound of horses; but the noise of the *aduentus* is also understood.

608 progressus: in the military sense of proceeding *ad pugnandum,* not found in poetry before V. and predominantly found in prose after him (*TLL* v.1768.40–54, 1770.41–1771.2).

609–11 Meteorological imagery builds in the lines and then is made explicit in the snowstorm simile: *erumpo, furo,* and *fundo* can all be used of wind and rain. See also 613–14n., 615–17n.

609 substiterat 'had come to a halt'. On the verb, see 95n. The enjambment emphasises the halt of the armies, while *subito* immediately after the verb highlights the sudden rush into action. **subito erumpunt:** *erumpo* is used in the military sense of troops springing forth in attack (*TLL* v.2.837.71–838.2). The elision conveys speed, while the shift to the present tense lends sharp immediacy. **furentisque:** the enclitic *-que* creates a hypermetric verse; the final syllable is elided with *exhortantur* in the following line. V. has twenty-one hypermetric lines, all but three with *-que* or *-ue*; see Soubiran 1966: 466–8, Harrison on 10.895. Hypermetre is very rare in extant Latin hexameters before V. (Austin on 4.558); its only occurrence in Gk dactylic poetry is at Call. *Ep.* 41.1–2. Here it reflects the forward charge of the excited riders and horses.

610 exhortantur equos: the verb is first found in V. (also at 7.472, 8.510, and 12.159). **simul undique:** the collocation of advs. captures the intensity of the moment when the battle is joined. It occurs only here in V. and is rare elsewhere (cf. Luc. 7.54, Stat. *Theb.* 5.161, V. Fl. 1.121, Liv. 9.14.9, 30.3.3, 36.10.7; cf. also Catul. 68.101, although the text is uncertain).

611 niuis ritu: the simile is Homeric; cf. *Il.* 12.156–8, where volleys of missiles and stones are compared to a snowstorm, and 12.278–86, where volleys of stones are so compared. Cf. Pac. *trag.* 258 Schierl (in apparent imitation of Homer) *sagittis niuit.* **caelumque obtexitur umbra:** cf. 12.578 *obumbrant aethera telis.* Commentators compare Hdt. 7.226: at Thermopylae, the Spartan Dieneces, having heard that the Persian arrows hide the sun, responds that, if this indeed happened, the fight would take place in the shade rather than in the sun. Cf. Cicero's version of the anecdote at *Tusc.* 1.101: *cum Perses hostis in conloquio dixisset glorians: 'solem prae iaculorum multitudine et sagittarum non uidebitis', 'in umbra igitur' inquit 'pugnabimus'. obtexo,* a *hapax* in V., first occurs here in extant literature. Cf. Stat. *Ach.* 1.790 *omne fretum longa uelorum obtexitur umbra,* Corippus, *In laudem Iustini minoris* 2.157 *mens non cedit tenebris, non fusca obtexitur umbra.*

612 continuo aduersis: the first of three consecutive lines with elision in the same position; the effect is to heighten the sense of energy, exertion, and force (Dainotti 2015: 166). V. has *continuo* sixteen times in *Aen.* (twelve in *G.*); his affinity for the word probably reflects the influence of Lucretius, who has it fifteen times. Otherwise before V., the adv. does not belong to high poetry (*TLL* IV.728.19–729.11). Most first-century CE epic successors to V. use it rarely (once in Ovid's *Metamorphoses,* once in Lucan, twice in Statius' *Thebaid* and none in *Achilleid,* three times in Silius Italicus; Valerius Flaccus, however, has it eight times). **Tyrrhenus et acer Aconteus:** cf. 12.661 *Messapus et acer Atinas. -eus* in *Aconteus* scans as one syllable by synizesis. The trochaic caesura in both fourth and fifth foot, which produces a 'false ending' in the middle of the fifth foot, is unusual in V. Most examples of the rhythm contain *-que* (e.g. 637); see Austin on 2.380, Norden on 6.140, Fordyce on 7.27. V. has Tyrrhenus only here as a name for an individual fighter on the Etruscan side; he is presumably to be identified as the brother/son of Tarchon. The name Aconteus looks to be significant and to play on Gk ἄκων, 'javelin', or ἀκοντίζω, 'hurl the javelin'; see O'Hara 2017: 231. *acer* in that case is presumably on one level a pun; it is a conventional epithet (see 518n.) but also suggests the sharpness of a javelin.

613–14 ruinam | dant sonitu ingenti 'they rush onward with a huge sound'. For *do ruinam* = 'rush onward', see *OLD* 1 and 1b. This is probably the meaning rather than 'fall headlong': V. varies the preceding description of Tyrrhenus' and Aconteus' charge and only at 615–17 describes the result of that charge, where just Aconteus is described as falling headlong. *ruinam* also continues the storm imagery: the word was used for floods, landslides, avalanches, and approaching storms (in the phrase *ruina caeli*, *OLD* 3b). These lines, 615, and 618 are all of five words, lending weight and grandeur to the onset of the battle.

614–15 perfractaque quadrupedantum | pectora pectoribus rumpunt 'they shatter and burst open their chargers' breast against breast'. *quadrupedans* (also at 8.596) is old (cf. Acc. *trag.* 400 Dangel, quoted at 600n., Enn. *trag.* 169 Jocelyn) and belongs to high poetry; Plautus uses it at *Capt.* 814 *qui aduehuntur quadrupedanti crucianti cantherio* and *As.* 708 *calcari quadrupedo agitabo aduorsum cliuum* in parodies of high, tragic style. The five-syllable word at line-end is very unusual in V.; all other examples include enclitic *-que*, and three involve Greek names (6.483 = 12.363 *Thersilochumque* (in imitation of *Il.* 17.216), 10.413 *Demodocumque*; the other instance is at 5.589 *ancipitemque*). *pectora pectoribus* is an instance of 'battle polyptoton' (Wills 1996: 194–201; cf. 293n.). Alliteration underscores the violence of the collision.

615–17 Further meteorological language, active on a secondary, metaphorical level, to further the 'latent storm-comparison' in the passage (Hardie 1986: 178–9 n. 61): *rumpo* is used of the production of lightning from clashing clouds at Lucr. 6.432, and *excutio* of the same subject at Lucr. 6.161, while *praecipito* can describe precipitation, as at 10.803–4 *effusa si quando grandine nimbi* | *praecipitant.*

615 excussus Aconteus: although the horses of both Tyrrhenus and Aconteus collide violently and are presumably killed, V. focuses only on what happens to Aconteus. The inference is that Tyrrhenus gets the better of his adversary and is not thrown headlong and far to his death as Aconteus is, but rather somehow escapes triumphant: 'If Tyrrhenus is overthrown . . . the special mention of Aconteus is remarkable and the terror of the Latins unaccountable' (Page ad loc.). *excutio* was colloquial and largely avoided in high poetry before V.; he, however, has it twenty-two times (all in *Aen.*), and his recurrent use of the verb sets a precedent for his epic successors (Lyne 1987: 58–9; to his statistics on usage add Statius, who has *excutio* twenty-five times in the *Thebaid*).

616 'in the manner of a lightning-bolt or a weight flung by an engine'. Perhaps further play on the name Aconteus: 'ἀκοντίζομαι is used of a "flash" at Arist. *Mund.* 392b 3, ἀκοντιάδες of "meteors" at Plin. *HN* 2.89, ἀκοντισμοί of "shooting stars" at Ptol. *Tetr.* 102, and ἀκοντιστήριον of a "siege-engine" at Agathias 3.5 (admittedly very late)' (Hardie 1986: 178–9 n. 61). For the association of *fulmen* and *tormentum*, cf. 12.921–3 *murali concita numquam | tormento sic saxa fremunt, nec fulmine tanti | dissultant crepitus.* The connection might derive from Lucr. 6.328–9, which compares a thunderbolt to a missile thrown from a siege engine: *uolat impete miro | ut ualidis quae de tormentis missa feruntur.*

617 uitam dispergit in auras: cf. 4.705 (Dido) *in uentos uita recessit* (with Pease's note), 10.819–20 (Lausus) *tum uita per auras | concessit.*

618 turbatae acies: for *turbo* used of troops thrown into disorder, cf. 12.269. The use of *turbo* in descriptions of fleeing forces is familiar from historiography; cf. e.g. Liv. 4.31.3 *castra propinqua turbatos ac terga dantes accepere*, 33.18.18 *turbati extemplo tumultum primo inter se fecerunt, terga deinde uertunt, postremo abiectis armis in praecipitem fugam effunduntur.* **uersique** 'put to flight' (*OLD* 9b).

619 No tactical retreat (*pace* Serv. ad loc.), although the Latins will soon regroup and counter-attack, but rather disordered flight in response to the death of Aconteus. **reiciunt parmas:** V. apparently has in mind the *parma equestris*, or small round shield of the cavalry in the Roman period. The retreating Latins sling their shields over their shoulders to protect their backs. (If they threw them away, as Frantantuono ad loc. tentatively proposes, they would have been in no position to mount the counter-attack that they subsequently do.) The dactylic scansion of *rēĭcĭo* is normal in hexameters and occurs at 10.473 and *G.* 3.389, in contrast to *Ecl.* 3.96 *Tityre, pascentis a flumine reice capellas.* **uertunt** 'direct backwards in flight' (*OLD* 9a). The verb is rather awkward after *uersique* in the previous line.

620 Troes: the final syllable of the Gk loanword is short (cf. *Arcades* at 93, 142, and 835). **agunt** 'give chase/pursue'. **Asilas:** a recurrent name in *Aen.* At 9.571, an Asilas appears to be a Rutulian, paired with Liger (an enemy of A. at 10.576) and killer of Corynaeus (a Trojan at 6.228; a different Trojan Corynaeus appears at 12.298). At 10.175, another Asilas appears in the catalogue of A.'s Etruscan allies, a seer skilled in haruspicy, astrology, ornithomancy, and divination by lightning; this is presumably the same captain Asilas found at 12.127 and 12.550 (see Tarrant on 12.127). Asilas here is to be identified as that Etruscan. This creates a nice balance with *Troes*: the frame reinforces that the Trojan cavalry contains both Trojans and Etruscans and that the latter play the leading role (*princeps*) in that blended force.

621 rursusque 'when once again'. *-que* = *cum*; the enclitic connects a verb of motion with the main action (*OLD* 5a).

622 clamorem tollunt: a war-cry for joining battle, as at 9.566–7 *undique clamor | tollitur.* Cf. Liv. 10.40.3 *priusquam clamor tolleretur concurrereturque,* 25.39.3 *signa canunt et tollitur clamor.* **mollia colla:** sc. *equorum.* The necks are *mollia* because the horses are well trained and obedient; hence the cavalry forces are able to turn suddenly and counter-attack. Cf. *G.* 3.204 *molli . . . collo.* Corippus closely imitates V. at *Iohannis* 1.556–7 *sed colla reflectunt | mollia quadrupedum uersi.*

623 The dactyls reflect the movement of rapid retreat. **penitusque** 'and to a distance far away'; with *referuntur.* **datis . . . habenis:** abl. abs. *datis* is the opposite of *pressis* at 600; the Trojans and Etruscans give rein to their horses to ride with all speed. Cf. 1.63 *et laxas sciret dare iussus habenas, G.* 3.107 *proni dant lora.* **referuntur:** middle force.

624–8 A simile for the ebb and flow of battle. Cf. *G.* 3.236–41, a simile comparing a bull advancing on a foe to huge waves that strike the shore; its Homeric precedent is *Il.* 4.422–6. Cf., too, 7.528–30, a simile derived from *Il.* 7.63–5 and comparing Trojan and rustic Italian forces before a battle to swelling seas that lift their waves ever higher. Wave imagery in the context of war is recurrent in ancient literature (cf. e.g. *Il.* 11.307–8, Tyrt. 12.22 κῦμα μάχης, A. *Th.* 64 κῦμα . . . στρατοῦ, Lucr. 5.1289–90 *belli | . . . fluctus,* 5.1435 *belli magnos . . . aestus,* Hor. *Ep.* 2.2.47 *ciuilisque rudem belli tulit aestus in arma, Carm.* 2.7.15–16 (quoted at 627n.)).

624 alterno . . . gurgite refers to the breaking of waves upon a rocky beach and the subsequent flow of the water back to the sea. **pontus:** Latinised πόντος; except in the name *Pontus Euxinus,* the word belongs almost exclusively to poetry (see Skutsch on *Ann.* 217, where *pontus* first appears). V. (like other hexameter poets) frequently has it in the sixth foot (twenty-seven times, twelve times in other positions); metrical need is clearly the crucial factor for its use in that position as an alternative to the more common *măre.* For the occurrences of *pontus* and *mare* in V. and other poets, see the numbers gathered at *TLL* x.2686.42–61.

625 superiacit 'dashes over'. The verb is a *hapax* in V.; it fits with his penchant for compounds with *super-* (see Harrison on 10.384, Tarrant on 12.306) and for compounds to avoid prepositions (see Serv. ad loc. *super scopulos undam iacit: nam more suo dedit uerbo detractam nomini praepositionem*). V. 'transitivises' the compound with an acc. object; on 'transitivising' in V., a marked feature of his style, see Görler, *EV* II.267. The alliteration of *s*, which continues with *spumeus* and *sinu* in the following line, seems designed to reflect the hissing of the waves. With V.'s use of the verb, cf. Hor. *Carm.* 1.2.10–11 *superiecto pauidae natarunt | aequore dammae*, Sil. 15.155 (Corus) *Isthmon curuata sublime superiacit unda* (although the text is uncertain).

626 spumeus: first found in V. (five times) and probably coined by him, like several other adjectives in *-eus* (see 65n.). **extremamque sinu perfundit harenam** 'and drenches the topmost edge of the beach with its curve'. *sinu* seems to refer to the curve of the water that extends, fan-like, upon the sand all the way up to where the beach ends. An unparalleled use of the noun.

627 rapidus: adverbial. **retro . . . resorbens:** the repetition of the prefix *re-* emphasises the intensity of the backwash. Cf. 9.261–2 *reuocate . . . | reddite . . . recepto*, 2.750–1 *renouare . . . reuerti | . . . rursus* [< *re-uorsus*]. With *resorbens*, cf. Hor. *Carm.* 2.7.15–16 (to Pompeius) *te rursus in bellum resorbens | unda fretis tulit aestuosis*, Lucr. 6.695 *aestumque resorbet.*

628 uado labente: *uadus* is the water remaining on a beach after a huge wave has broken, which then flows back into the sea. *labente* is *simplex* for *relabente*; cf. 10.307 *unda relabens.*

629 Tusci Rutulos: significant juxtaposition of the warring forces. **egere ad moenia uersos** echoes *uersique, ad moenia*, and *agunt* at 618–20, emphasising the repetition of the action.

630 reiecti 'beaten back'. Cf. *reiciunt* at 619. The changed use of the verb reflects the changed circumstances: the Etruscans are now driven into retreat, not the Latins. **armis:** it is natural to take the abl. of means with *reiecti*, given the word order. *armis*, however, is to be understood also with *terga tegentes*, 'covering backs with shields', to describe the same action as at 619, though now taken by the Trojans. For *arma* used of shields, see 10.411, 12.491, *OLD* 2a and b.

632–5 Cf. *Il.* 4.448–51 (= 8.62–5) 'and the bossed shields closed with one another . . . then there rose alike the groaning and triumphant shouting of men killing and being killed, and the earth flowed with blood' (ἀτὰρ ἀσπίδες ὀμφαλόεσσαι | ἔπληντ' ἀλλήλῃσι . . . | ἔνθα δ' ἅμ' οἰμωγή τε καὶ εὐχωλὴ πέλεν ἀνδρῶν | ὀλλύντων τε καὶ ὀλλυμένων, ῥέε δ' αἵματι γαῖα). V. omits the shouts of triumph and focuses grimly on the carnage. Valerius Flaccus closely imitates V. at 6.182–8.

632 implicuere 'interlocked'; elision with *inter* reinforces the sense. **legitque uirum uir** 'and man marked man'. A form of battle polyptoton (see 614–15n.). Cf. 10.361 *haeret pede pes densusque uiro uir*, with Harrison's note, and 10.734–5 *obuius aduersoque occurrit seque uiro uir | contulit.* The final monosyllable is archaising (see 373n.), and the polyptoton with *uir* in that position almost certainly Ennian; line-position sharpens the antithesis between *uirum* and *uir* (Hough 1975: 21). V. gives new meaning to the formula *uir uirum legit*, which described a kind of conscription in which individuals selected others to fill up an army; cf. Liv. 9.39.5 *cum uir uirum legisset*, 10.38.12 *ut uir uirum legerent donec sedecim milium numerum confecissent*, Tac. *Hist.* 1.18.2 *more diui Augusti et exemplo militari quo uir uirum legeret.* Now men pick opponents rather than comrades, and they thin forces rather than add to them (Wills 1996: 195). V. adapts the formula under the influence of Homeric ἀνὴρ ἕλεν ἄνδρα, 'man killed man' (*Il.* 15.328, 16.306).

633 tum uero: a frequent connective (twenty-four times, twenty-two in *Aen.*), often, as here, marking a heightened, climactic moment of drama (see Harrison on 10.647–8, Tarrant on 12.494). The phrase is largely confined in poetry to the higher genres (Myers on Ov. *Met.* 14.485).

633–4 et . . . et . . . | -que . . . -que et: polysyndeton, to convey the varied horror of the battle scene.

634 armaque corporaque et: a strange rhythm, created by the epic double *-que* (see 150n.) uncommonly placed at the front of the line; the purpose is perhaps to underscore the sense of disorder. Cf. Stat. *Theb.* 10.275 *tergaque pectoraque et*, also in a scene of carnage, and probably reflecting the chaos of the action (cf. *Theb.* 10.274 *subit ordine nullo*). **permixti:** the intensifying prefix *per-* emphasises close physical mingling. Cf. Lucr. 5.1313–14 (on lions in battle) *permixta caede calentes | turbabant saeui nullo discrimine turmas.*

635 semianimes 'dying', as at 4.686, 10.396, 10.404, and 12.356. Scanned as a four-syllable word; the first *i* is consonantal. The adj. goes back to Ennius (*Ann.* 484 Sk.). **uoluuntur** 'rolled on the ground'; middle voice, like *uoluitur* at 640. **pugna aspera surgit:** in the same position at 9.667; cf., too, 12.124–5 *aspera Martis | pugna*, where Traina compares Homeric δριμεῖα μάχη ('bitter battle', *Il.* 15.696). The verb is often used of winds and waves. It and *sanguine in alto* at 633, which suggests swimming in blood, both correspond to the imagery in the simile at 624–8; 'the bodies rolling in deep blood and the rough battle rising are both the metaphorical application of the world of the simile to the world of the narrative' (West 1990: 442).

636 Orsilochus Remuli: once more, significant juxtaposition of adversaries, as at 629 and 640. Orsilochus is a Trojan; see 690 and 694. There are several mythological Orsilochi, and different figures with that name appear in Homer. At *Il.* 8.274, a Trojan Orsilochus is slain in an *aristeia* of Teucer. For Greek Orsilochi, see *Il.* 5.542, 5.546, 5.547, 5.549, *Od.* 3.489, 13.260, and 15.187. The name Remulus is used of other Italians at 9.360 (the dead Tiburtine Remulus) and 9.590–633 (Numanus Remulus).

637 reliquit: used of leaving a weapon fixed in its target, as at 4.71 *pastor agens telis liquitque uolatile ferrum.* The sense is of a forceful throw that sticks in the animal. Cf. Stat. *Theb.* 11. 565–7 *erigit occulte ferrum . . . | . . . et ensem | iam laetus fati fraterno in corde reliquit.*

638–40 Cf. 10.892–4 (Mezentius' horse, hit between the temples by A.'s spear) *tollit se arrectum quadripes et calcibus auras | uerberat, effusumque equitem super ipse secutus | implicat eiectoque incumbit cernuus armo.*

638 furit arduus 'rears high in fury'. **arduus altaque iactat:** each of the last three feet consists a single word and shows coincidence of ictus and accent. An unusual pattern in V., although he has it again at 746, 756, and 810. The dactylic rhythm seems to reflect the rapid kicking of the reared front legs.

639 impatiens: only here in V., and for the first time in extant literature; probably a coined negatived adj. Imitated at Stat. *Theb.* 9.872 (Parthenopaeus) *uulneris impatiens.* **arrecto pectore:** cf. 10.892 *tollit se arrectum.* The repetition of *-ect-* lends force.

640 excussus: see 615n. **Catillus Iollan:** Catillus is the brother of Coras (see 465 and 604); he is mentioned with Coras at 7.672. Iollas appears only here in *Aen.*, but the name is found at *Ecl.* 2.57, 3.76, and 3.79. The Iollas here has no pastoral filiation; the following lines show him to be in the mould of an epic warrior.

641 ingentemque animis: cf. Homeric μεγάθυμος ('great-hearted'), an epithet for heroes (*Il.* 2.518, 2.706, 4.479, 5.25, etc.). **ingentem corpore et armis:** for the omission of the second *-que* after *ingentemque,* see 171n. Repeated *ingens* emphasises the heroic quality of Herminius. Cf. 124 and Homeric μέγας μεγαλωστί ('mighty in his mightiness') at *Il.* 16.776, 18.26, *Od.* 24.40. *armis* is an abl. of *arma,* as at 124, not of *armus,* 'shoulder'; the description moves from spirit to body to weapons. Cf. 12.642 *Teucri potiuntur corpore et armis.* At 644, V. has both *arma* and *armos*; this seems almost to allude teasingly to the potential for ambiguity in *armis.* Cf. 4.11 (Aeneas) *quam forti pectore et armis,* another moment of ambiguity with *armis.*

642 deicit 'brings down', for felling a warrior (cf. Gk καταβάλλειν), but also 'unhorses' (cf. 12.509 *equo deiectum Amycum*). **Herminium:** the name recalls Titus Herminius, who, with Horatius Cocles and Spurius Lartius, defended the Sublician Bridge against the forces of Lars Porsenna (Liv. 2.10.6–7, 2.11.7–9), and killed the Latin commander at the Battle of Lake Regillus, but suffered a fatal wound in the process (Liv. 2.20.8–9). A name associated with hardy Italian heroism, then; but this Herminius believes too much in his bodily strength, since he wears no armour. It is tempting to think that V. contrasts Herminius' lack of armour with the death of Titus Herminius, killed while taking spoils from the Latin Aebutius. Herminius is to be identified as an Etruscan (cf. *Tusci* at 629); quite possibly V. understood the Herminii to have an Etruscan origin (cf. the Herminius who was consul in 448, and who might have had the Etruscan praenomen Lars, although the evidence about his name is conflicting). **fulua:** cf. Homeric ξανθός ('fair-haired'), particularly applied to Menelaus (*Il.* 3.284, 3.434, 4.183, 4.210, etc.). Like other colour terms, *fuluus* is difficult to identify precisely, but the colour lies somewhere between red and yellow (Fordyce on 7.76, Edgeworth 1992: 130–2). 'Striking chromatic contrast . . . with the *ater cruor* (646) that will soon flow' (Fratantuono ad loc.).

643 nudique 'uncovered' (*OLD* 1c), as with *nudo* in the previous line, because he lacks armour (*OLD* 4); cf. Homeric γυμνός ('without armour, unarmed', *Il.* 16.815, 17.122, 17.693, 17.711, 18.21, 21.50, 22.124). **nec uulnera terrent:** sc. *quem.*

644 tantus in arma patet 'so great in size he stands exposed to arms'. **latos huic hasta per armos:** cf. Stat. *Theb.* 7.634 (Tydeus' spear runs through the warrior Pterelas' horse) *uenit hasta per armos.* For epic broad shoulders, see 679, 2.721, and 5.376 *latos umeros,* 9.725 *latis umeris,* and cf. Homeric εὐρέας ὤμους (*Il.* 3.210, 3.227).

645 tremit: cf. 2.52 (Laocoon's spear thrown at the Trojan horse) *stetit illa tremens.* **duplicatque** 'and doubles [him] over'. Cf. *Il.* 13.618 'he doubled over and fell' (ἰδνώθη δὲ πεσών). **transfixa:** used of the weapon, but more naturally of the person wounded/killed. For the construction and *tranfigere* with the rare meaning 'driven through' (rather than 'pierced'), cf. Luc. 9.138 *ora ducis quae transfixo sublimia pilo.*

646 funditur ater ubique cruor: the rhythm is anomalous, with coincidence of ictus and accent across the first three words, feminine caesurae in the second and third feet (very rare; cf. 7.724, with Fordyce's note), and no principal caesura until the fourth foot. Perhaps expressive of the unchecked, abundant flow of blood. For *ater* of the darkness of blood, see 3.626, 9.472, and 9.700. *cruor* is used of fresh-spilled blood (Harrison on 10.349, *OLD* 1). **dant funera:** also at 8.570–1, 12.383, and *G.* 3.246–7. *do* = 'cause, produce'. **ferro:** the abl. is instrumental with *do,* as at 8.570–1 *ferro saeua dedisset* | *funera,* and probably also with *certantes* in the next line.

647 pulchramque petunt per uulnera mortem: taken from *G.* 4.218, on bees that willingly die for their king (*sic*); the clause is varied at 9.401 (Nisus) *pulchram properet per uulnera mortem.* Cf. also 2.317 *pulchrumque mori succurrit in armis. pulchra* is a moral rather than aesthetic term; the idea of seeking an honourable, glorious death is very common in antiquity and fundamental to the military ideal (see Serra Zanetti, *EV* III.590). Cf. *Il.* 15.496–7 'not unseemly is it for him to die while fighting for his country' (οὔ οἱ ἀεικὲς ἀμυνομένῳ περὶ πάτρης | τεθνάμεν), Hor. *Carm.* 3.2.13 *dulce et decorum est pro patria mori,* with N–R's note.

648–63 CAMILLA ENTERS THE FRAY

Focus now turns back to Camilla, who confidently exults in the fight. In this, she has shades of Turnus (see 648n.). But the explicit comparison in this passage is between Camilla and the Amazons, including the Amazon queens Hippolyte and Penthesilea (648, 651, 659–63). This heightens the Otherness of Camilla: she is not only an anomalous female warrior but is also assimilated to the Amazons from Thrace, the legendary female Other in the masculine world of war. In addition, Camilla resembles the Parthians (see 649n.), who shared cavalry tactics with the Amazons (see 654n.). At the same time, V. is concerned with preserving and underscoring Camilla's Italian identity; he does this here by giving her a circle of comrades whose names have a decidedly Italian timbre (Sharrock 2015: 164). While partly strange and foreign, Camilla is firmly of Italy, and her hard ferocity in battle is expressive of both her Amazonian and her native Italian character. In her, binaries (foreign/native, east/west, male/female) coexist, creating a complex character comprising conflicting and sometimes competing elements.

The Amazons were associated with Artemis (La Penna 1988: 228–9, Mayor 2014: 151–3); in this, they further resemble Camilla, given her ties to Diana.

648 exsultat: used of Turnus at 491(n.); Camilla and Turnus are alike in their enjoyment of battle and confidence in it. The verb is juxtaposed with *caedes*; Camilla delights to find herself amid widespread slaughter. Claudian imitates at *DRP* 2.62–3 *Amazonidum . . . exultat . . .* | *pulchra cohors.*

649 unum exserta latus: Camilla makes an Amazonian entrance: Amazons traditionally kept one of their breasts uncovered in battle, often their right but sometimes their left, to leave the arm free. Cf. Prop. 3.14.15 *qualis Amazonidum nudatis bellica mammis* (*turba*) and 4.3.43 (Hippolyte) *nuda tulit arma papilla,* with Hutchinson's note. (Other accounts had them cutting or searing off a breast so that it would not interfere with the use of the javelin or bow and arrow; cf. e.g. Serv. ad 1.492, Apollod. 2.5.9, Justin 2.4.9. Full discussion at Mayor 2014: 84–94; see also Man 2018: 43–9.) Cf. 803 and 1.492 (Penthesilea) *aurea subnectens exsertae cingula mammae.* At the same time, the *latus* is the part of the body particularly vulnerable in battle (cf. 10.314). A suggestion, then, of the danger that the exposed Camilla faces. *latus* is a retained acc. after the medio-passive participle. **pugnae** 'for the fight'. **pharetrata:** also at *G.* 4.290 *pharetratae . . . Persidis,* where it refers to Parthian bowmen; the adj. first occurs in V. and is rare and almost entirely poetic after him (*TLL* X.2011.5–28). The *pharetra* is associated with Diana (see 590, 1.500; cf. e.g. Grat. 124, Ov. *Am.* 1.1.10, *Met.* 3.252, Claud. *Stil.* 3.242) and with the Amazons (5.311). Camilla also has a *pharetra* at 7.816.

650 lenta: 'light enough to be whippy' (Horsfall on 7.164). **manu:** added pleonastically to emphasise personal exertion and force, an inheritance from Ennius (Ann. 398 Sk.); cf. Homeric χερί. This use of *manu* occurs often in *Aen.*, especially in its second half (Fordyce on 7.621, Harrison on 10.264); see 676, 799, and 893. **spargens** 'showering'. For the verb used of hurling numerous weapons, see 8.694–5 *telisque uolatile ferrum | spargitur,* 12.50–1 *ferrumque haud debile dextra | spargimus,* Enn. *Ann.* 266 Sk. *hastati spargunt hastas, fit ferreus imber.* **denset** 'causes [them] to come thick and fast' (*OLD* 2c). MSS vary between *densere* and *densare* and their compounds (see 7.794, 10.432, 12.264, *G.* 1.248, 1.419). *denseo* is preferable as the apparently more poetic form. Servius and DServius declare for *denseo* here and at 7.794 and 10.432.

651 ualidam . . . bipennem: the adj. used of a heroic weapon, as at 696, 10.401, 10.815, 12.93; cf. Homeric ἄλκιμος, 'strong, stout' (e.g. *Il.* 3.338, 10.135, 11.43, 14.12, 15.482, 16.139). The battle-axe (often double-edged) is traditionally a weapon of the Amazons (in Gk, typically identified as a σάγαρις); cf. e.g. Hor. *Carm.* 4.4.20, Ov. *Met.* 12.611, Claud. *DRP* 2.66, Str. 11.5.1, Plin. *Nat.* 7.201, and see Mayor 2014: 219–22. **rapit:** the unusual third-foot diaeresis (see 163n.) is used here, as elsewhere (e.g. 2.528, 9.330, 10.545), to express excitement and haste. **indefessa:** a negative participial adj. probably coined by V.; it occurs only here in his poetry.

652 aureus: to be understood with both *arcus* and *arma*. Cf. 1.492 (Penthesilea) *aurea subnectens exsertae cingula mammae.* Camilla's taste for gold will prove to be her undoing (see 779–82). **ex umero sonat arcus:** cf. 4.149 (the shafts of Apollo) *tela sonant umeris,* 9.660 (the quiver of Apollo) *Dardanidae pharetramque fuga sensere sonantem.* Ovid imitates V. at *Met.* 8.320–1 (Atalanta) *ex umero pendens resonabat eburnea laeuo | telorum custos, arcum quoque laeua tenebat.* **arma Dianae:** a periphrasis for arrows, i.e. weapons characteristic of the archer-goddess; Camilla's golden arrows resemble divine arms, which were customarily golden. As at 536 *nostris . . . armis,* Camilla fights with weapons of the hunt, which are equally suitable to the cavalry fight; see Intro. p. 25. *arma Dianae* occurs at line-end elsewhere only at Grat. 497, one of several parallels in Grattius with Virgil's Camilla episode (Kayachev 2018: 101–3). Cf. Ov. *Her.* 4.91 *arma tuae tibi sunt imitanda Dianae,* in probable imitation of V. (see *arcus* earlier in *Her.* 4.91 and *fessaque* at *Her.* 4.90, with V.'s *indefessa* at 651); hence *imitanda* looks like a meta-poetic signpost.

653 si quando 'whenever'.

654 The primary model are the Amazons, who were often depicted firing weapons in this manner (Arrigoni 1982: 38). But Camilla's tactic also recalls the Parthian shot, named after Parthian cavalry who pretended flight and shot arrows behind them; cf. *G.* 3.31 *fidentemque fuga Parthum uersisque sagittis,* Hor. *Carm.* 1.19.10–12, 2.13.17–18. This identifies the Amazonian Camilla with that eastern enemy and, thus, adds a second layer of Otherness to her (see, further, Hardie 2007: 138). **fugientia:** transferred epithet, for *fugiens.*

655 lectae comites: Camilla is surrounded by female comrades, like the Amazons, to whom she and her *comites* are subsequently compared, but also like Diana (see 533 above). **Larinaque:** the name suggests Larinum, a town located in SE Italy (mod. Larino in Molise, province of Campobasso), which became a Roman *municipium* in the first century BCE. Alessio 1993: 129 sees a reference to Acca Larentia or Larentina, the obscure Roman goddess with a festival (the Larentalia) on 23 December; for the different traditions surrounding her, see e.g. Liv. 1.4.7, Plut. *Rom.* 4.3–5.5, and Macr. 1.10.11–17. Larina is not close enough to Larentia and Larentina to make the case on its own; but see Acca at 820(n.).

656 Tullaque suggests Tullus Hostilius, the third Roman king (see 6.814, 8.644). **Tarpeia** recalls the famous Tarpeia who sought to betray Rome to the Sabines in exchange for their gold bracelets; instead, the Sabines crushed her with their shields (Liv. 1.11.6–9, Ov. *Met.* 14.776–7, with Myers' note, *F.* 1.259–66).

657 Italides: first attested here; a *hapax* in V. and rare and poetic after him (cf. e.g. Ov. *Fast.* 2.441, Stat. *Silv.* 1.2.274, Sil. 7.429, Mart. 11.53.4). The initial *i* is lengthened *metri gratia*; cf. *Italiae* at 219 and 508. **decus:** the noun is predicative, like *ministras* in the next line. Cf. 508 *o decus Italiae uirgo.* **dia:** the adj. only here in V.; its rarity led to the variants *diua* and *dura.* An archaism (cf. Enn. *Ann.* 60, 106 Sk.), in keeping with the archaic tenor of the Italian names of Camilla's allies, and mainly poetic. Cf. Homeric δῖα, used of goddesses, 'bright, glorious' (*Il.* 2.820, 3.389, 3.413, 5.370, etc.), and of women, 'noble, queenly' (*Il.* 5.70, 6.160, etc.); both senses seem operative here. Varro (*L.* 7.34) uses the adj. when discussing the Samothracian *casmilus*: *casmilus nominatur dius quidam administer Dis Magnis.*

659 Threiciae: agreeing with *Amazones* at 660 in hyperbaton. The high-sounding adj. also occurs at 6.120 and 10.350; cf. Homeric Θρηΐκιοι (*Il.* 10.559). Silius has it at 2.73 *quales Threiciae Rhodopen Pangaeaque lustrant* [*saxosis nemora alta iugis*] (which also imitates *G.* 4.461–2), in a simile comparing Asbyte, a devotee of Diana, to the Amazons. V.'s Camilla is a heavy influence on Silius' Asbyte (2.56–269). **Thermodontis:** the four-syllable Greek name produces a spondee in the fifth foot; see 31n. The Thermodon is a river in what was said to be the Amazon homeland. It is the modern Terme River, which flows into the Black Sea in today's central northern Turkey. For its association with the Amazons, see e.g. A. *Pr.* 724–5, A.R. 2.369–74, Apollod. 2.5.9, Prop. 3.14.16, 4.4.71, Ov. *Met.* 9.189, 12.611, *Pont.* 4.10.51, Sen. *Med.* 215, *Her. O.* 21, Sil. 2.80 and 8.430, Claud. *DRP* 2.66.

660 pulsant: the verb is emphatic as an initial unelided spondee (see 48n.) and captures the heavy pounding of the horses' hooves. The suggestion is that the Amazons make the river echo with the sound of their horses when they ride along its banks or in very close proximity to it (or perhaps in its shallows). Cf. Sil. 8.428–30 *ubi mille per agmina uirgo | lunatis acies imitatur Martia peltis; | perstrepit et tellus et Amazonius Thermodon.* **pictis . . . armis:** presumably of emblazoned arms, as at 8.588 and 12.281, where the same phrase occurs, rather than of painted shields, as at 7.796 (*picti scuta Labici*). **bellantur:** the deponent occurs only here in V. and is rare elsewhere (*TLL* II.2.1816.82–1817.1). Cf. Sil. 2.349 (Libyan squadrons) *nudis bellantur equis.* **Amazones:** a Gk loan-word with a short final syllable.

661 Hippolyten: the Amazon queen killed by Hercules in battle when he sought her belt as one of his twelve labours. The name is also assigned to another Amazon queen, who married Theseus after he abducted her.

Subsequently, she gave birth to Hippolytus, was abandoned by Theseus for Phaedra, and was finally killed by Theseus or Penthesilea ([Apollod.] *Epit.* 1.16–17, 5.1, 5.2; cf. Quintus of Smyrna 1.25–7). This latter figure, however, is more commonly identified as Antiope, the sister of Hippolyte. **Martia:** Penthesilea was the daughter of Ares ([Apollod.] *Epit.* 5.1, Hyg. *Fab.* 112). The epithet also alludes to her bellicosity. **curru:** references to Amazonian chariots are relatively rare (Mayor 2014: 123, 177–8); but cf. Sil. 2.81–2, where the Amazonian Asbyte rides a chariot and has charioteers among her warriors.

662 Penthesilea: the Amazon queen and Trojan ally in the Trojan War; after much success in battle, she was killed by Achilles, who fell in love with her corpse and slew Thersites for jeering it ([Apollod.] *Epit.* 5.1). **ululante:** of a victory cry; cf. Caes. *Gal.* 5.37.3 *tum uero suo more uictoriam conclamant atque ululatum tollunt,* Luc. 6.261 *laetis ululare triumphis.* The verb is also appropriate because it is characteristic of women (see Austin on 4.667, with Plin. *Ep.* 6.20.14 *audires ululatus feminarum, infantium quiritatus, clamores uirorum*). V. uses *ululo* of Hecate (4.609 *nocturnis Hecate triuiis ululata per urbes*); a link here to the Hecate aspect of Diana, however, is unlikely (*pace* Alessio 1993: 128).

663 feminea: the *-eus* adj. (see 65n.) occurs ten times in V., including (*plangoribus*) *femineis ululant* at 2.488 and *femineo ululatu* at 4.667; it is perhaps found at Cic. *Tusc.* 2.20 *carm.* 18 (translating Sophocles) *feminae uir feminea interimor manu,* although the text is uncertain. **exsultant:** echoes *exsultat* at 648, thus framing the scene and further linking Camilla and the Amazons. **lunatis . . . peltis:** also at 1.490 *Amazonidum lunatis agmina peltis.* The *pelta* (Gk πέλτη) was a light shield associated with Thrace (see Hdt. 7.75.1, E. *Alc.* 498, Paus. 1.41.7, Sen. *Phaed.* 402–3, Sil. 2.76); for the tradition of Amazonian *peltae,* see Rocca, *EV* I.128, Mayor 2014: 217. The shields were *lunatae* because they were in the shape of a crescent moon. V. seems to have introduced both adj. and noun into Latin poetry (Austin on 1.490).

664–724 THE *ARISTEIA* OF CAMILLA

Camilla now embarks on an *aristeia,* i.e. a period in battle when a hero has his or her finest moments and overwhelms the enemy. The hero in an *aristeia* is in a fighting frenzy and seems invincible, although this frenzy can lead to rashness that places the hero in mortal danger; Camilla will experience a version of this at 779–82. The *aristeia* is an epic convention; examples in V. occur at 9.525–89, 9.756–77 (Turnus), 10.380–425 (Pallas), 10.510–605 (A.), 10.689–746 (Mezentius), 12.324–82 (Turnus), and 12.500–53 (Turnus and A., a double *aristeia*).

Camilla's *aristeia* begins with a rapid succession of killings (666–77) but slows to describe in greater detail the deaths of her victims – a recurrent pattern in V.'s *aristeiae.* The passage on the first of these, Ornytus (677–88), prominently features the theme of hunting; see Intro. pp. 24, 25. Wolf-imagery, moreover, is significant in the passage on Ornytus (680–1n.); this belongs to a wolf-leitmotif to which Virgil returns later in Camilla's battle scenes. See 768–93n. and 794–835n., with Stephens 1990: 125.

Some of Camilla's victims have names associated with Thrace, the land of the Amazons. V. probably gives the fighters Thracian names to indicate that they were Trojan allies who had journeyed with A.; Thrace was confederate with Troy. But he presumably also wished to suggest Amazonian combat with men in their homeland; the Amazonian Camilla fights Thracian men in Italy as the Amazons fought men in Thrace.

In her *aristeia,* Camilla is every bit the equal of a male hero, and she reacts with rage to taunts against her as a woman. This is the Amazonian Camilla at home and formidable in the masculine world of battle, who confronts, with deadly force, the prejudices she faces as a female warrior.

664–5 The Homeric model is the apostrophe/question at *Il.* 16.692–3 'Then whom first, whom last did you kill, Patroclus, when the gods called you to death?' (ἔνθα τίνα πρῶτον, τίνα ὕστατον ἐξενάριξας, | Πατρόκλεις, ὅτε δή σε θεοὶ θάνατόνδε κάλεσσαν;); tacitly, via allusion to Patroclus, who dies after his *aristeia* (*Il.* 16.855–7), V. foreshadows Camilla's doom. For similar questions before *aristeiae,* but without apostrophes, see *Il.* 5.703–4, 8.273, and 11.299–300, and in V., 12.500–4.

664 aspera uirgo: an oxymoron.

665 deicis: see 642n. The enjambment isolates *deicio* for emphasis, as at 10.753 and *G.* 1.333 and 3.422; it also belongs to a common pattern in interrogative sentences in which the first question ends with the verb in enjambment and the second ends at line-end (as at 424). For that pattern, see Dainotti 2015: 119–20. **aut** introduces a second question that is not an alternative to the first, a lively colloquialism found in high poetry since Ennius (*trag.* 71 Jocelyn; see Harrison on 10.675–6, *TLL* II.1565.38–67). **humi morientia corpora fundis:** cf. 1.192–3 (A. hunting deer) *septem ingentia uictor* | *corpora fundat humi.*

666 Eunaeum: otherwise unknown in *Aen.* V. probably adapts the name from Homer's Εὔνηος (*Il.* 7.468 and 23.747), the son of Jason. Evidently a Trojan, like other figures with Argonautic associations (see Horsfall on

670). Manuscript evidence is very strong for the spelling Eunaeus. Statius has Euneos (with a short antepenult) at *Theb.* 6.343, 433, and 464, but Eunaeus at 7.649. The acc. is governed by the verbs in the previous line. **Clytio . . . patre:** Clytius is a heroic name from κλυτός, 'renowned'; several mythological figures have it, including one of Priam's advisers at *Il.* 3.147 (apparently Priam's brother) and an Argonaut (A.R. 1.86, 1.1044, 2.117, 2.1043, Hyg. *Fab.* 14.8). The name also occurs at 9.774 (a Trojan son of Aeolus, killed by Turnus), 10.129 (the father of Acmon, from the allied Trojan city Lyrnesus), and 10.325 (the beloved squire of the Italian warrior Cydon). The abl. is probably an abl. abs. to describe paternity; cf. 10.205 *patre Benaco,* 10.704 *genitore Amyco,* with Harrison's note. **apertum** 'exposed, unprotected'.

667 transuerberat 'transfixes/impales'. A vivid verb to capture the violence of Eunaeus' death; also at 10.336 and 10.484. Its placement between the hyperbaton *apertum* | . . . *pectus* is iconic, reflecting how the exposed breast is split apart by the blow; cf. 40 above. A brief (and often gory) description of the manner of death is standard in an *aristeia.* **abiete:** metonymy; 'pine-wood' = 'spear made of pine-wood'. *abiete* is scanned as a dactyl, with *i* having consonantal value; cf. 8.599 *abiete cingunt,* with Eden's note.

668 sanguinis ille uomens riuos: cf. 9.414 *ille uomens calidum de pectore flumen,* itself derived from Lucr. 2.354 *sanguinis exspirans calidum de pectore flumen.* **atque:** on the unelided form, see 183n. **cruentam:** frames the line with *sanguinis*; the semantically related words emphasise the gory violence.

669 mandit humum: see 418n. **moriensque suo se in uulnere uersat** 'and, dying, he writhes upon his wound'.

670 Lirim Pagasumque: the same acc. construction as *Eunaeum* at 666. Both names occur only here in *Aen.* Liris evokes the river Liris (mod. Liri), a river in central Italy flowing from the Apennines to the Tyrrhenian Sea. The Liris is, for much of its course, a Volscian river; this makes the name a somewhat odd one for an opponent of Camilla. Saunders 1940: 545 suggests that Liris is Etruscan, and that the name is meant to evoke Etruscan rule to the south, but this is very uncertain (cf. 532–96n.). The name Pagasus perhaps derives from Pagasae, from which the Argonauts departed (A.R. 1.238, 1.318, 1.411, 1.524, 4.1781). **super** 'besides'.

671 suffosso 'hamstrung/stabbed underneath'. Cf. Caes. *Gal.* 4.12.2 *suffossis equis compluribus nostris deiectis,* Liv. 42.59.3 *equorum . . . nunc ilia* *suffodere*, Tac. *Ann.* 1.65.6 *suffosso equo.* Preferable to *suffuso*, which would presumably have the unusual meaning 'sprawled out beneath' (*OLD* 4). The gathering of the reins in the next line indicates a staggering horse, not one lying on the ground; and *labenti* at 672 implies that Liris has not yet fallen from his horse, which means that the creature cannot yet be 'sprawled out'. Instead, Liris slips from a gravely injured creature as it staggers from being hamstrung, and he clutches the reins to try to steady it and to keep himself from falling. **reuolutus:** Liris rolls backwards or to the side on the horse (hence *suffosso . . . equo* is an abl. of place where with *reuolutus*); cf. 4.691 (Dido) *reuoluta toro est.* While thus slipping from his mount, he tries to regain control of the reins.

672 subit 'comes up to help'. Cf. 10.338 *huic frater subit Alcanor fratremque ruentem | sustentat dextra*; similar to Pagasus, Alcanor is then struck by a spear. **inermem:** Pagasus throws aside his weapon to aid his friend.

673 praecipites pariterque ruunt 'headlong and together they tumble down'. Alliteration is expressive of the violence of their fall. **Amastrum:** only here in V. Amastris was a city in Paphlagonia mentioned at Catul. 4.13; another name for it was Sesamos, which occurs at *Il.* 2.853 and A.R. 2.941. V. uses the name to indicate a Trojan ally (cf. *Il.* 2.851–5, where Paphlagonia, including Sesamos, appears in a catalogue of Trojan allies). Amastris was also the name of an Amazon, according to the sixth-century Stephanus of Byzantium, who, citing Demosthenes, claims her as the eponym for the city (*Ethn.* s.v. Ἄμαστρις). But this is an obscure variant (Amastris, the niece of Darius III, is commonly believed to be the founder of the city).

674 Hippotaden: the patronymic is applied to Aeolus at *Od.* 10.2 and 10.36 and at A.R. 4.778. Why V. uses it for Amastrus is unclear; perhaps its connection to ἵππος, 'horse', was reason enough to have it for a cavalry fighter. **sequiturque** indicates pursuing/chasing in a hostile manner; it combines the senses of military pursuit and of a hunt for animals. *sequitur* as a *simplex* form for *persequitur* would bring that out more forcefully, but *sequitur* itself is sufficient. **incumbens** 'pressing the attack/bearing down on' rather than 'bending forward (to throw her spear)'. The former meaning creates an oxymoron with *eminus* that effectively captures the great danger Camilla poses: even at a distance, she presses the attack, because of the deadly threat of her spear-cast. **eminus:** in a military sense, of fighting at a distance (*TLL* v.2.496.55–497.3). It occurs nine times in V. and is found in poetry before him only at Lucr. 6.904, 'but may well have occurred in Ennius' (Harrison on 10.345–6).

675 A 'name-line', as at 6.483, 9.344, 9.767, 10.123, 10.413, 12.341, and 12.363. Such lines are conventional in epic since Homer, and they are convenient in an *aristeia* for listing several victims in a row; thus 9.767, 10.413, 12.341, and 12.363 all occur in *aristeiae*. Multiple *-que* reflects Homeric multiple τε in name-lines (e.g. *Il.* 5.678 Ἄλκανδρόν θ' Ἅλιόν τε Νοήμονά τε Πρύτανίν τε, 17.216 Μέσθλην τε Γλαῦκόν τε Μέδοντά τε Θερσίλοχόν τε). There is no principal caesura; this is unique in Virgilian name-lines, although they often have metrical irregularities. The absence of a caesura gives the impression of victims that run together in rapid succession. **Tereaque Harpalycumque:** Tereus shares a name with a Thracian king, infamously the husband of Procne and brother-in-law of Philomela (although V. reverses or conflates those roles at *Ecl.* 6.78–81). Harpalycus ('rapacious wolf' in Gk; the name thus anticipates the wolf-imagery in the passage on Ornytus) calls to mind the Thracian Harpalyce, the counterpart to Camilla (cf. 1.316–17). It is unclear if V. conceived of this Harpalycus as Harpalyce's father. Still, it is somewhat disorienting to find Camilla killing a man who could be the father of a girl whom Camilla resembles. **Demophoonta Chromimque:** the name Demophoon is perhaps another way of conjuring Thrace: Demophon/Demophoon, the son of Theseus, stopped in Thrace and married Phyllis, the daughter of a Thracian king, on his way back from Troy (ps.-V. *Cul.* 131–3, Ov. *Her.* 2, *Ars* 3.459–60, *Rem.* 591–608, [Apollod.] *Epit.* 6.15.16–17, Hyg. *Fab.* 59). One tradition made Theseus and the Amazon Antiope the parents of Demophon; see Martina, *EV* II.23. Chromis is probably taken from Χρόμις at *Il.* 2.858, a Trojan ally as a leader of the Mysians. Chromis is also the name of one of the boys who tie up Silenus at *Ecl.* 6.13; V. takes that Chromis from Theoc. 1.24. V. perhaps wished on a secondary level to conjure the bucolic world leading into his treatment of Ornytus, still a sylvan figure though now a soldier.

676 contorsit: cf. *contortum* at 561(n.).

677 uiri: in strong contrast with *uirgo* in the previous line. **Ornytus:** an Etruscan, as Camilla reveals at 686; V. moves from Trojan casualties to an Etruscan one. The name occurs in Apollonius Rhodius (1.207, 2.65); V. perhaps chooses it for its etymology from ὄρνυμι, which is used of rousing animals for the hunt. Cf. Hor. *Carm.* 3.9.14 *Thurini Calais filius Ornyti,* also apparently indebted to Apollonius (N–R ad loc.). An Ornytus later appears in Statius' *Thebaid* (12.141–66).

677–8 armis | ignotis 'with unfamiliar arms'.

678 uenator: as a hunter, Ornytus is a foil for Camilla: she has assimilated to battle and, in her *aristeia,* thrives in it, whereas Ornytus has not sufficiently moved from hunter to fighter and is unprepared for combat. In response to V., Calpurnius Siculus has the name Ornytus for a pastoral character and treats him as a liminal figure between bucolic and epic (see Hubbard 1998: 154). **Iapyge:** Iapygia was known for its good horses (like Kentucky in the United States). Cf. Liv. 24.20.16, Var. *R.* 2.7.6, Sil. 4.555–6. **fertur:** probably middle voice, as at 530, and like *uertitur* at 683, 'moves/rides (on his horse)'. For the middle with *equo/equis*, cf. 730, 5.574, and 12.478. The passive is tempting, however (cf. 1.476, *G.* 1.514), as a way of showing that Ornytus, new to war, is not in control of his horse.

679 pellis . . . erepta iuuenco: cf. the tiger-skin of the huntress Camilla (577) as well as the lynx-hide of the huntress at 1.323. Ornytus' animal skin reveals that he remains a hunter and, thus, that he is now displaced in the arena of war. **latos umeros:** cf. *latos . . . armos* at 644(n.). Ornytus has the bulk of an epic hero, but he will win no hero's victory in battle because he is no warrior.

680 pugnatori: to be taken with *cui* in the previous line, in effective contrast with *uenator* at 678; Ornytus the hunter has become Ornytus the fighter 'but has not made the necessary adjustments to his equipment in order to go to war' (Williams ad loc.). To take *pugnatori* with *iuuenco,* as Page ad loc. does, is to miss the essential contrast. Bullocks are also not usually aggressive.

680–1 ingens . . . | . . . albis 'a huge gaping mouth and the jaws of a wolf, with white teeth in them, covered his head'. For *cum* = 'having within, containing', see *OLD* 8. Cf. 7.667–8 (the lion-skin of Aventinus, son of Hercules) *cum dentibus albis | indutus capiti.* The wolf's head worn by Ornytus is a spoil and trophy of the hunt. The head develops the wolf-motif hinted at by the name Harpalycus at 675. Ornytus is a wolf-hunter, but with his wolf's head and bullock-skin is also a kind of animal prey for Camilla. Although she has made the transition from hunting to fighting and distinguishes warfare from the hunt (686–9), V. muddies the distinction by having her kill a man who is animal in appearance. A wolf-helmet could be a symbol of primitive toughness and ferocity; cf. Romulus' helmet at Prop. 4.10.20 *galea hirsuta compta lupina iuba* (the wolf is also a totemic animal, of course, for Romulus). Cf., too, the wolf pelts on the helmets of Roman *velites,* or light infantrymen (Plb. 6.22). But in the case of Ornytus, the wolf-helmet is a strange, exotic object symbolising his outsider status in battle; the helmet is fearsome and epic in size (*ingens*), but is anomalous battle-gear. Bronze coins from Amisus in Pontus, dating to 85–65 BCE, show Amazons wearing wolf-head helmets (see Mayor 2014: 351–3). Cf. Str. 11.5.1, on how Amazons used skins of wild animals for helmets. Could

V. have known the iconography, if not the coins? From there, one might speculate that V. significantly has an Amazonian fighter kill a male wearing an Amazonian helmet to reclaim that object for women and to assert her Amazonian identity. On other links between the Amazons and wolves, see Mayor 2014: 353. Connections to the wolf-symbol of Rome are easy to propose but hard to prove (*pace* Trundle 2003: 176); it is also fanciful to see in Ornytus both the wolf, the symbol of Rome, and the bull, the symbol of Italy in the Social War of 91–88 BC (not least because Ornytus wears a bullock's hide, not a bull's), as Trundle 2003: 176–7 does.

682 sparus: a hunting javelin or spear. The *sparus* is distinguished from proper military weapons at Sal. *Cat.* 56.3. *sparus* is found only here in V. *ignota arma* indeed, and a further marker that Ornytus is a stranger in this martial setting. A bucolic diaeresis occurs after *sparus*; there is perhaps a deliberate correspondence between the rhythm and rustic object. Silius Italicus has *sparus* before a bucolic diaeresis at 3.388–90, in imitation of V.: *Rhyndacus his ductor, telum sparus; ore ferarum | et rictu horrificant galeas; uenatibus aeuum | transigitur.*

683 Ornytus has not only the broad shoulders of an epic warrior but also the height; cf. 7.784 (Turnus) *uertitur arma tenens et toto uertice supra est*, *Il.* 3.227 (Ajax) 'towering above the Argives in his head and broad shoulders' (ἔξοχος Ἀργείων κεφαλήν τε καὶ εὐρέας ὤμους). **uertitur** 'moves to and fro' (*OLD* 3); Ornytus, unaccustomed to battle, moves confusedly among the ranks.

684 exceptum indicates that Camilla intercepts Ornytus unawares. *excipio* also implies catching or trapping an unsuspecting animal (cf. *Ecl.* 3.17–18 *caprum | excipere insidiis*, Hor. *Carm.* 3.12.12, Prop. 2.19.23–4) and thus contributes to the hunting theme. **neque enim labor agmine uerso** 'and it is not hard when the army is in retreat'. Mackail and Gransden ad loc. place *agmine uerso* outside the parenthesis, but the point is that Camilla finds it easy to catch Ornytus amid the general confusion of the rout.

685 super . . . fatur: also at 10.556 as a taunt-formula. *super* is an adv.

686–9 Cf. V. Fl. 6.536–9, where Aron taunts Armes, a livestock-thief, who fights while clothed in shaggy hide and wearing stags' horns: *'pauidos te' inquit 'nunc rere magistros | et stolidum petiisse pecus? non pascua nec seps | hic tibi; nocturnis mitte haec simulacra rapinis, | neue deum mihi finge; deus quoque consere dextram'.*

686 Tyrrhene: the ethnic address is used by a speaker who does not share the addressee's nationality, as customarily (Dickey 2002: 207). Scornful in tone, the voc. reflects Camilla's anger at the Etruscan taunts directed at her (see 687–8). Perhaps, too, it expresses a deeper antipathy towards the Etruscans; cf. Camilla's rejection of the Etruscan mothers' plans for marriage at 581–4 (and see 581n.). Cf. 12.359, where Turnus disdainfully addresses Eumedes with *Troiane* after killing him in battle. **agitare** 'hunt'; cf. 7.478 *feras agitabat, G.* 3.372 *agitant pauidos* (*ceruos*), 3.409 *timidos agitabis onagros.* **putasti:** syncopated perfect forms are archaic and colloquial (G–L §181b n. 2). V. likes them in speeches and in emotional contexts (see Austin on 1.201, Harrison on 10.244).

687–8 qui . . . | . . . redargueret: a rel. clause of purpose.

687 dies: the antecedent of *qui*, absorbed into the rel. clause. **muliebribus armis:** a strong indication that Camilla responds to sexist insults about her abilities as a female fighter. Cf. Ov. *Met.* 8.392 (Ancaeus to Atalanta) *discite, femineis quid tela uirilia praestent.* Camilla seems to respond to Etruscan taunts generally, with Ornytus representing his people, and with *uestra . . . | uerba* meaning 'the words of you Etruscans'. It is unclear when she heard those insults.

688 uerba: juxtaposed with *armis* in the previous line; words have been met by a woman's forceful action. **redargueret** 'refute'. The imperfect after the perfect definite ('has come') is unproblematic (see 513n., and cf. *Ecl.* 9.47–9).

688–9 nomen . . . | . . . Camillae: this type of consolation is an epic topos; see Bömer on Ov. *Met.* 5.191, 12.80–1. Camilla's use of it is a further sign that she is fully assimilated to, and very accomplished and confident in, the world of martial epic, even though this is her first experience of war (711n., 803–4n.). Cf. 10.829–30 (A. to Lausus) *hoc tamen infelix miseram solabere mortem: | Aeneae magni dextra cadis.* Camilla, however, is not sympathetic towards Ornytus as A. is towards Lausus. Her governing emotion is instead bitter pride, which is coupled with a strong undercurrent of disdain. **patrum | manibus:** cf. 10.827–8 *teque parentum | manibus . . . remitto.*

690 Orsilochum et Buten: the accs. are governed by the verbs at 665. For Orsilochus, see 636n. Butes is the name of a champion Bebrycian boxer who had fought Dares at Hector's tomb in Troy (5.372–4) and of an aged Trojan squire of Ascanius (and former armour-bearer of Anchises) at 9.647. The powerful Butes here is not the old man in *Aen.* 9, and he is not to be identified with the boxer in *Aen.* 5, despite that figure's large size

(5.372 *immani corpore*). The fighter seems to have been killed in his bout with Dares at Troy (5.374 (*Buten*) *moribundum*); at any rate, he is evidently not with the Trojans during the funeral games in *Aen.* 5, where Dares squares off against Entellus (5.362–484). A warrior Butes from Athens appears at A.R. 1.95.

690–1 maxima Teucrum | corpora: the epic periphrasis (see 185n.) stresses the physicality of the men and the size of their bodies.

692 loricam galeamque inter: a vulnerable spot; cf. 12.380–2 *Turnus secutus | imam inter galeam summi thoracis et oras | abstulit ense caput, Il.* 22.321–7 (Achilles fatally strikes Hector in his exposed throat at the collar-bone). **sedentis:** sc. *equo.*

693 lucent 'was visible', with the sense that the neck was clear and conspicuous to Camilla as a place to strike. Cf. Stat. *Theb.* 8.524–5 *qua . . . | . . . iuguli uitalia lucent.*

694 agitata: the huntress-warrior has momentarily become the hunted (see 686n.).

695 Camilla was in tactical flight as Orsilochus pursued her, but she pulls inside the circle in which Orsilochus rode; by tightening her circuit (and, implicitly, checking her speed), she is able to come upon him from behind after he passes by her. **eludit** 'eludes' by means of a stratagem. **gyro:** cf. Sil. 2.171 (the warrior maiden Asbyte, pursued on horseback by Theron) *fallaci gyro campum secat.*

696–8 Cf. *Il.* 20.397–400 (Achilles) 'he pierced (Demoleon) in the temple through his helmet with cheek-pieces of bronze. And the bronze helm did not check the spear, but the bronze point broke through the bone and all his brains were splattered within' (νύξε κατὰ κρόταφον, κυνέης διὰ χαλκοπαρῄου. | οὐδ' ἄρα χαλκείη κόρυς ἔσχεθεν, ἀλλὰ δι' αὐτῆς | αἰχμὴ ἱεμένη ῥῆξ' ὀστέον, ἐγκέφαλος δὲ | ἔνδον ἅπας πεπάλακτο). Imitation is extremply probable and comparison instructive: V.'s repeated prepositions (cf. κατὰ and διὰ) are more forceful than Homer's, representing as they do repeated blows and their penetration, and the victim's prayers generate emotion not in Homer. Very close to *Il.* 20.397–400 is *Il.* 12.183–6, although κατὰ and διὰ do not appear together at 183 to correspond to 20.397.

696 perque . . . perque: cf. 7.499 *perque uterum sonitu perque ilia uenit harundo.* **arma uiro:** one of the eleven instances in *Aen.*, including at 747, where V. echoes the opening words of the epic; see Hardie on 9.57. A variation of the epic *incipit* at a moment of vivid epic fighting and, thus, of martial and heroic content (cf. Oliensis 2004: 31). *uiro* gives heroic colouring to Orsilochus. There is a contrast between the *uir* and the (superior) female warrior who kills him.

697 altior exsurgens: Camilla rises on her horse to deliver the axe blows. Cf. 755 *arduus insurgens,* 12.902 *altior insurgens.* **oranti et multa precanti:** pleas in battle to be spared death are unsuccessful in *Aen.* (most notably Turnus' at the end of the poem; see, too, the three examples at 10.521–601 and Intro. p. 7), as conventionally in epic. *multa,* an internal acc., is to be understood with both participles.

698 congeminat: the verb in enjambment savagely breaks off Orsilochus' prayers; 'prayer follows prayer, but she only "redoubles (the blows of) her axe"' (Page ad loc.). Cf. V. Fl. 6.378–9 (Euryale) *regina grauem nodis auroque securem | congeminans.* The verb is alliterative with *calido* and *cerebro,* underlining the force and violence of Camilla's actions. **uulnus calido rigat ora cerebro** 'the gash soaks his face with hot brains'. Cf. 12.308 *sparso late rigat arma cruore.*

699–724 It is characteristic of V. to give fuller treatment to the final encounter in an *aristeia*; in this, he departs from Homer (see Tarrant on 12.371–82).

699 incidit huic 'happened to come upon her'. **aspectu territus haesit:** cf. 3.597 (Achaemenides when seeing the Trojans) *aspectu conterritus haesit.* For *haereo* meaning 'stop dead, freeze', see *OLD* 10.

700 Four-word lines are rare in V. (twenty-two in *Aen.*, six in *G.*); see Winbolt 1903: 227–8, von Albrecht 2006: 167, Dainotti 2015: 79 n. 261. For other examples with long, elevated adjs., see 3.328, 7.410, and *G.* 4.111. **Appenninicolae:** apparently a coinage, of archaising colour. The adj. occurs later in Silius Italicus (5.626, 6.167) and Prudentius (*Symm.* 2.521); cf. Ov. *Met.* 15.432 *Appenninigena.* **bellator:** an adj., like the preceding *Appenninicolae*; V. organises the line in a chiastic pattern (Adj. (1) Adj. (2) Noun (2) Noun (1)). V. includes the Ligurians among the vigorous men of Italy (*G.* 2.168); Livy testifies to their hardiness in battle (27.48.10 *Ligures durum in armis genus*). Cf. 10.185 (Cinyras) *Ligurum ductor fortissime bello.* The Ligurians' toughness was displayed in wars against Rome and in later service in the Roman army (Harrison on 10.185–6). *bellator* here at first seems consistent with this; but rather than displaying battle hardiness, this Ligurian is terrified at the sight of Camilla and plots his escape from engaging her. His conduct in the scene makes *bellator* look contemptuously ironic; V. plays on the expectation of courage, but has the Ligurian demonstrate anything but the traits of a *bellator*. One might imagine that the Ligurian is no *bellator* here only because of Camilla's fearsomeness; but see *fugax* at 713(n.). **filius Auni:** Serv. ad loc. asserts that the son had the same name as the father, but this is uncertain.

701 haud Ligurum extremus 'not the least among the Ligurians'. With the rest of the line, the suggestion is that this figure was not worst among his race in craftiness. The Ligurians were known not only as hardy and fierce but also as duplicitous; see DServ. ad 715 (quoting Nigidius Figulus and Cato the Elder), Cic. *Clu.* 26.72, *Sest.* 32.69, *Agr.* 2.95, Str. 4.6.2, Bertinelli, *EV* III.221–2. **dum fallere fata sinebant:** cf. 4.651 *dum fata deusque sinebant. fallere* appears instead of the expected *uiuere*, 'as if with him to live was to deceive' (C–N ad loc.).

702 euadere pugnae: *euadere* is intransitive; Gransden ad loc. is mistaken to consider *se* its object. The dat. construction with *euadere* is first found here, and probably only here in V.; at 9.99 *euaserit undis, undis* is likely to be an abl. of separation, as at 11.905 *siluaque euadit opaca.* It is an example of V.'s common use of the dat. with compound verbs that express separation (see Görler, *EV* II.266).

703 auertere 'to turn aside', in the military sense of repelling an enemy attack (*OLD* 5).

704 'having set about weaving a trick with scheming guile'. **consilio . . . astu:** a frame of synonymic terms, linked in hendiadys. *astus* is an archaism (see Tränkle 1960: 38–9) found in V. here and at 10.522. **uersare dolos:** cf. 2.61–2 (Sinon) *in utrumque paratus, | seu uersare dolos seu certae occumbere morti*, 4.563 (Dido) *dolos dirumque nefas in pectore uersat.*

705 tam: one of only two examples of elided *tam* in V.; the other is at 1.568. On elided monosyllables, see 166n.

705–6 si femina forti | fidis equo 'if, as a woman, you trust in a strong horse'. Cf. 4.94–5 *magnum et memorabile nomen, | una dolo diuum si femina uicta duorum est.* The alliteration (which continues with *fugam*) expresses scorn; this is part of the Ligurian's strategy of baiting Camilla. For other examples of alliteration of *f* for scoruful effect, cf. 4.218, 4.603, and 12.573, with Basson 1986: 67–8 n. 35. According to Cicero (*Orat.* 163) and Quintilian (12.10.28–9), the letter had an ugly sound; this would make it suitable for expressing contempt. The use of alliteration of *f* here of course differs from 1.364 *femina facti.* The adj. *fortis* means both 'strong' and 'brave/heroic in battle'. The Ligurian pointedly applies the epithet to the animal instead of to Camilla; in a calculated jab at her warrior pride, emphasised by the juxtaposition of *femina* and *forti*, he insults her by suggesting that, instead of fighting like a man in hand-to-hand combat, she is a cowardly woman on a good horse. Cf. Quintus of Smyrna 1.575–6 (Achilles to Penthesilea) 'o woman, how you have come against us, exulting in vain vaunts, eager to battle' (ὦ γύναι, ὡς ἁλίοισιν ἀγαλλομένη ἐπέεσσιν | ἡμέων ἤλυθες ἄντα λιλαιομένη πολεμίζειν). *femina* is marked in this epic context, in contrast to unmarked *uir*, 'subject and norm of the epic genre in general and the *Aeneid* in particular' (Keith 2000: 23). With the word, the Ligurian implies her abnormality and inadequacy in the male arena of battle.

706 comminus: opposite of *eminus* (see 674n.), and used here of close fighting on foot, as distinguished from a cavalry engagement.

706–7 aequo | . . . solo: cf. 9.56 *non aequo dare se campo. aequo* refers to ground that, being level, offers no advantage to either side (*OLD* 1b). The etymologising association of *equus* with *aequus* (see 599n.) seems operative. Cf. 710 *equum . . . paribusque . . . in armis*, with *par* a synonym for *aequus.*

707 pugnaeque . . . pedestri: cf. Liv. 3.61.9 *hostem pedestri iam turbatum pugna*, 10.28.6 *lentior uidebatur pedestris pugna*, 21.55.8 *pedestris pugna par animis magis quam uiribus erat*; the phrase does not occur in Caesar or Sallust.

708 'you will now learn to whom hollow vainglory brings harm'. The Ligurian taunts Camilla that her pride in her fighting skill is really puffed up, unfounded vanity (cf. Gk κενοδοξία). With the phrasing, cf. Hor. *Ep.* 2.1.177 *uentoso Gloria curru.* **uentosa:** cf. 7.807 *cursuque pedum praeuertere uentos*; it is tempting to see subtle foreshadowing via the echo of *uentos* in *uentosa* that the Ligurian's plan to speed away on horseback from the dismounted Camilla is doomed, because she on foot is so exceptionally fast. V.'s description of Camilla's swiftness at 7.808–11 derives from *Il.* 20.226–9, on Erichthonius' fast horses. **fraudem:** an apt final word for this trickster; within the narrative, it means 'harm' (cf. 10.72 *quis deus in fraudem* (*egit*)), but the reader understands 'deceit, guile' on a secondary level, as a way of characterising the Ligurian's words as they end. The reading *fraudem* is preferable to *laudem* (which would change *gloria*, 'vainglory', to *gloria*, 'glory', with *uentosa* then seemingly 'fickle', as a way of indicating that Camilla's heroic run in the battle is about to end), not only for its aptness as the Ligurian's final word but also as the *lectio difficilior*: *fraudem* is more likely to have been changed in transmission to *laudem* than vice versa, since *laudem* yields a known phrase in V. (see 791–2, 12.321–2 *quis* *tantam Rutilis laudem . . . | attulerit*). For an argument in favour of *laudem*, see Henry ad loc., vehement and prolix even by his standards.

709 furens: of fury caused by and directed at the Ligurian specifically. **acrique accensa dolore:** *accensa* signals a loss of rational control; Camilla, her pride stung, is in a mad frenzy. Cf. 4.203 *amens animi et rumore accensus amaro*, 7.392 *furiisque accensas pectore matres*, 12.946 *furiis accensus. dolor* = 'indignation'. For *acrique . . . dolore*, cf. 7.291 (Juno) *acri fixa dolore.*

710 The holodactylic line reflects the speed with which Camilla responds to the Ligurian. **tradit equum:** cf. Liv. 6.24.10 *optimum uisum est . . . tradi equos et pedestri pugna inuadere hostem.*

711 Cf. 9.548 *ense leuis nudo parmaque inglorius alba.* **ense . . . nudo:** *nudus* in connection with a sword might be expected to mean 'unsheathed'. But context suggests that the adj. = 'alone, only'; Camilla meets the Ligurian's challenge boldly, with just a foot soldier's sword (and shield) to balance his. Hardie on 9.548 cites Fordyce on the same line from his unfinished commentary: '*ense nudo* seems to be the equivalent of ψιλῷ ξίφει, "sword without other weapons": cf. X. *Cyr.* 4.5.58 (of hastily armed soldiers) "he ordered that they be given shields and bare daggers τὰς ψιλὰς μαχαίρας"'. **pedes:** in strong contrast to *equum* in the previous line. **puraque . . . parma:** Serv. ad loc. explains by noting that Camilla was fighting in war for the first time (*tunc enim primum in bella descenderat*); Serv. ad 7.796 observes that, among men of yore, the *scuta* of those who were new to war or were idle, worthless fighters were *pura*, unlike the *picta scuta* of brave fighting men. Cf. 9.548, where the *parmaque . . . alba* describes Helenor's shield, plain because he is inexperienced in war. Cf., too, Stat. *Theb.* 4.267–8 (Parthenopaeus, modelled in part on Camilla) *imbelli parma pictus Calydonia matris | proelia*; plausibly, *imbelli parma* picks up on the inexperienced Camilla's shield even as *pictus* reverses V. For a different interpretation of Camilla's shield, see Morello 2008: 46–50. *pura parma* is in significant juxtaposition with *interrita*; although in her first battle, Camilla stands fearless. **interrita:** first found in V. (also at 837, 5.427, 5.863), probably another coined negatived participial adj.

712 uicisse dolo ratus 'thinking that he had prevailed through guile'. Statius imitates at *Theb.* 11.556 *fraterque ratus uicisse*; at 11.554, Eteocles plans for Polyneices a *fraudem supremam.* **ipse** 'for his part'.

713 haud mora: for the litotes in parenthesis, a Virgilian mannerism, cf. 5.140, 6.177. V. also has it for narrative transitions (3.207, 3.548, 5.749, 7.156, *G.* 4.548), a characteristically epic use of the phrase (cf. Stat. *Theb.*

8.277, V. Fl. 5.60, 5.558, Sil. 4.101, Petr. 99.6), although *nec mora* (only once transitionally in V. (5.368)) is the norm in V.'s epic successors. **conuersis . . . habenis:** cf. Sil. 10.55–6 *conuersis – uidi nam flectere – habenis | euasit Varro* (with *euasit* picking up V.'s *euadere* at 703). **fugax:** more than a synonym for *fugiens.* Adjs. in *-ax* indicate tendency or characteristic traits, often negative (Tarrant on 12.364, A–G §251); the suggestion is that the Ligurian is prone to flee in battle (cf. 10.697 *Palmumque fugacem*). The word also implies timidity, as at 9.591, 10.724, and *G.* 3.539, where it is used of timid animals. *fugax* supports the idea that *bellator* at 700 is contemptuously ironic.

714 The rhythm of the first half of the line reflects the galloping movement of the swift horse, while the alliteration of *q*/*c* and *f* conveys energy. **quadrupedemque:** the correct spelling seems to be *quadru-* before *p* and *quadri-* before other letters (Horsfall on 7.500). The use of the word for 'horse' is predominantly poetic (*OLD* 4b); V. has it with that meaning at 875, 8.596, and 10.892. *quadrupes* designates other animals at 3.542, 7.500, and *Ecl.* 5.26. **fatigat:** cf. 1.316–17 *qualis equos Threissa fatigat | Harpalyce.*

715 uane Ligus: *uane* can be understood to mean both 'foolish' (*OLD* 6) in relation to *frustra* later in the line and *nequiquam* in the following line and 'false' (*OLD* 4; cf. 2.879–80 *Sinonem* | . . . *uanum*) in relation to the emphasis on duplicity in the next two lines. *Ligus* is an ethnic voc., scornful like that at 686. **animis elate superbis:** focalised through Camilla, but to be understood as an accurate reflection of the Ligurian's arrogant pride after *uicisse dolo ratus* at 712.

716 patrias . . . artis 'native trickery', but with a sense of 'paternal trickery' in conjunction with *fallaci Auno* in the following line. **temptasti:** cf. *putasti* at 686 for another syncopated perfect form in Camilla's emotional, excited speech. **lubricus:** adverbial, 'shiftily, deceitfully'. This meaning of *lubricus* is rare and occurs first (and only here) in V. (*TLL* VII.2.1689.83–1690.20). Cf. V. Fl. 2.555 *acri lubricus astu* (with *astu* presumably responding to V.'s *astu* at 704).

717 perferet: of carrying or conveying to a person, with the idea of successful delivery (*OLD* 1). **fallaci:** another *-ax* adj. to describe a characteristic quality; see 713n. **Auno:** how Camilla knew the name of the Ligurian's father is a mystery; suspension of disbelief seems in order.

718 pernicibus . . . plantis: cf. 4.180 (*Fama*) *pedibus celerem et pernicibus alis.* The adj. describes Diana at ps.-V. *Cul.* 119. Cf. Catul. 2.11–12 (Atalanta) *puellae | pernici,* Stat. *Theb.* 4.312 (Atalanta) *fugit siluas pernicior* *alite uento,* and Sil. 10.189 (Anna Perenna) *per patulos currit plantis pernicibus agros.* V. plausibly has in mind the Amazons, who were depicted fighting on foot more often than on horseback in visual material and, probably, in literature (La Penna 1988: 225). **ignea:** describing speed of movement (*OLD* 3d). There is no need to give the adj. a secondary sense of 'fiery (in spirit)' (Horsfall ad loc.); word order indicates that the reference is to Camilla's swiftness alone, a cardinal trait (see 532n.).

719 transit 'overtakes'. **frenisque . . . prehensis** answers *conuersisque . . . habenis* at 713; the Ligurian had tried to flee by turning his horse in flight, but Camilla seizes the horse by the reins and captures him.

719–20 aduersa . . . | congreditur 'she engages (him) face to face'.

720 poenasque . . . sumit: the motif of death-as-punishment is never purely objective in V. and instead reflects the perspective of a character (Tarrant on 12.949 *poenam scelerato ex sanguine sumit*). In this case, it reflects Camilla's anger at the deceit of the Ligurian and her accompanying sense that his deed deserves the ultimate punishment. **inimico:** adj. for gen., as at 84.

721–4 The motif of the hawk and dove is conventional (cf. e.g. *Il.* 21.493–4, A. *Pr.* 857, E. *Andr.* 1140–1, A.R. 4.485–6, Lucr. 3.751–2, Hor. *Carm.* 1.37.17–18, Ov. *Fast.* 2.90, Sil. 4.105–14); this particular simile, however, takes its point of departure from *Il.* 22.139–42 (Achilles chasing Hector), 'as a hawk in the mountains, swiftest of birds, swoops effortlessly after a trembling dove, which flees out of reach, while (the hawk) hard at hand continually rushes at it, and his heart bids him to seize it' (ἠΰτε κίρκος ὄρεσφιν, ἐλαφρότατος πετεηνῶν, | ῥηϊδίως οἴμησε μετὰ τρήρωνα πέλειαν, | ἡ δε θ' ὕπαιθα φοβεῖται, ὁ δ' ἐγγύθεν ὀξὺ λεληκὼς | ταρφέ' ἐπαΐσσει, ἑλέειν τέ ἑ θυμὸς ἀνώγει). Its second two lines then incorporate details from *Od.* 15.525–7, 'as he spoke, a bird flew towards him on the right, a hawk, swift messenger of Apollo; it tore feathers from the dove it held in its claws, and the feathers fell to the ground' (ὣς ἄρα οἱ εἰπόντι ἐπέπτατο δεξιὸς ὄρνις, | κίρκος, Ἀπόλλωνος ταχὺς ἄγγελος· ἐν δὲ πόδεσσι | τίλλε πέλειαν ἔχων, κατὰ δὲ πτερὰ χεῦεν ἔραζε). Operative is the dove's association with fear and cowardice (cf. *Il.* 22.140, 23.874, Var. *R.* 3.7.4 *nihil . . . timidius columba,* N–H on Hor. *Carm.* 1.37.18), given the Ligurian's terrified attempt at flight. The ruthlessness of the predatory hawk stands out by implied contrast. There is perhaps also an implicit reversal of expected gender roles, which Serv. ad 722 notes (*ipsa etiam comparatio sumpta ex contrario est: nam aequius uir accipitri, Camilla compararetur columbae*). This works well after the Ligurian's taunting *femina* at 705; in a kind of *lex talionis,* he is now feminised as he learns how wrong, and how dangerous, it was to taunt Camilla as a woman, and how powerful she is in the male world of warfare. On the *accipiter*, see Capponi, *EV* v*.350, Fratantuono ad loc. (who resists the gendered reading of the simile); on the *columba*, see Capponi, *EV* v*.348. Cf. Hor. *Carm.* 1.37.17–18, where the feminised dove corresponds to Cleopatra and the hawk to Augustus. Quintus of Smyrna compares Achilles to a hawk and Penthesilea to a dove at *Post.* 1.572. This reworks *Il.* 22.139–42; it is uncertain if Quintus also responds to V. and reverses his comparison of the hawk with Camilla (see 868–95n.).

721 sacer ales: cf. Ἀπόλλωνος . . . ἄγγελος at *Od.* 15.526. Serv. ad loc. and O'Hara 2017: 232 propose play on the resemblance between ἱέραξ, 'hawk, falcon' (Homeric ἴρηξ), to which *accipiter* corresponds, and ἱερεύς, 'priest'; Mackail ad loc. argues similarly based on the link between ἱέραξ and ἱερός, 'holy'.

722 consequitur pinnis 'overtakes in flight'; the instrumental *pinnis* = *uolando. consequitur* corresponds to *transit* at 719. **sublimem in nube columbam:** cf. 5.516 *nigra figit sub nube columbam.*

723–4 The lines are significantly more violent and gorier than *Od.* 15.526–7. Rather than narrate Camilla's killing of the Ligurian, V. implies through the simile that she dispatched him with ruthless brutality.

723 comprensamque corresponds to *prehensis* at 719. **euiscerat:** poetic since Ennius (*trag.* 296 Jocelyn); cf. Cic. *Tusc.* 2.21 (translating S. *Tr.* 1077–80) *miserandum aspice | euisceratum corpus lacerati | patris.* Cf. Sil. 13.847 (Orthrus punishes a Vestal Virgin) *polluto euiscerat ungue.*

725–67 TARCHON RALLIES THE ETRUSCANS

Watching the cavalry battle unfold and Camilla fight successfully, Jupiter stirs the Etruscan leader Tarchon, who both rallies his troops and advances against the enemy, killing the Latin Venulus (742–58). This is the lone appearance of Jupiter in *Aen.* 11. He is a fully realised, intervening divinity, rather than a projection of a person's psychology and impulses, a personification of an emotion (Heinze 1993: 244; for the distinction, cf. 9.184–5, with Hardie's and Dingel's notes). The prompting god (which has Homeric precedent; cf. e.g. *Il.* 8.218–19, 21.544–9) stands in contrast to Diana: whereas she cannot alter events so that Camilla might live, he intervenes to keep Camilla from victory and sets in motion a counterattack that leads to her death and, subsequently, to Latin defeat. Jupiter's intervention is thus integral to the action and a decisive moment in the battle (see, further, Feeney 1991: 145–6).

For Tarchon's rallying speech during the battle (*cohortatio*), cf. 9.781–7 (Mnestheus rallies the Trojans) and 10.369–78 (Pallas rallies the Arcadians); see also 14–28n. and 376–444n. As was conventional in *cohortationes*, Tarchon, Mnestheus, and Pallas all appeal to shame to spur their troops. Yet Tarchon is significantly more vituperative than Mnestheus and Pallas, as he reviles the Etruscans for allowing a woman to get the better of them and faults them for being soft and decadent; this is to question their manhood in the face of the female warrior's onslaught. The Homeric model for the vituperation is *Il.* 4.338–48, where Agamemnon rallies Menestheus and Odysseus; see 738–40n. Cf., too, *Il.* 7.96, where Menelaus chides the Greeks for not volunteering to fight Hector by calling them 'women of Achaea, no longer men' (Ἀχαιΐδες, οὐκέτ' Ἀχαιοί); that phrase also occurs at *Il.* 2.235 (Thersites impugns the Greek commanders). For other rallying speeches in Homer, see *Il.* 13.95–124 and 15.733–41. Tarchon's criticism also resembles Numanus' abuse of the Trojans for their eastern decadence at 9.614–20.

Effeminacy and decadence, including in the areas of food and sex, were stereotypical traits of the Etruscans (e.g. Farney 2007: 133–44); V. incorporates the stereotypes into the *cohortatio*, but has Tarchon and his troops belie them by mounting a vigorous attack. This restores some gender norms in the battle – although it will take something other than Etruscan military *uirtus*, i.e. masculine displays of fighting valour and strength, to defeat Camilla.

In narrative terms, the scene lends variety by opening a new perspective on the fight, and it builds tension for Camilla's death by delaying it.

725–6 non . . . nullis . . . | . . . oculis: emphatic litotes; Jupiter has been keeping a very close eye on the battle. Commentators compare *Il.* 10.515 'nor did Apollo of the silver bow keep a blind watch' (οὐδ' ἀλαοσκοπιὴν εἶχ' ἀργυρότοξος Ἀπόλλων). Cf., too, *Il.* 16.644–5 'nor did Zeus ever turn his bright eyes from the fierce combat' (οὐδέ ποτε Ζεὺς | τρέψεν ἀπὸ κρατερῆς ὑσμίνης ὄσσε φαεινώ).

725 hominum sator atque deorum = 1.254. Unelided *atque* (see 183n.) lends solemnity and gives the feel of an archaic formula, although the phrasing might well originate with V.

726 Cf. 836–7, 10.3–4 (Jupiter) *terras unde arduus omnis | castraque Dardanidum aspectat populosque Latinos.*

727 Tarchonem: see 184n.

728 suscitat: of stirring to action in battle. Cf. 2.618 (Jupiter) *ipse deos in Dardana suscitat arma*, 9.463 *Turnus in arma uiros, armis circumdatus ipse, |*

suscitat. **inicit** 'instils' (*OLD* 8a). Preferable to the reading *incitat*, which is jangling after *suscitat. incitat* is possibly a corruption from 10.263 *suscitat iras*, with the verb substituted for the echoing *suscitat.*

729 inter caedes cedentiaque agmina 'amid the slaughter and collapsing ranks'; Camilla's *aristeia* has pushed the Etruscans to the edge of defeat. The sound-play in *caed-* and *ced-* links the two words and emphasises the direness of the situation.

730 fertur: middle voice; Tarchon propels himself on his horse through the mayhem. **uariisque instigat uocibus:** cf. 10.368 (Pallas stirs the retreating Arcadians to fight) *nunc prece, nunc dictis uirtutem accendit amaris. uariisque . . . uocibus* indicates that Tarchon similarly varies his words and shifts from entreaty to harsh rebuke (although 732–40 shows only the last) to rally his fighters.

731 Macrobius (6.1.34) identifies Furius Bibaculus (fr. 13–14 Courtney) as the model for the line: *nomine quemque ciet* | . . . | . . . *exsuscitat acris* | *ad bellandum animos reficitque ad proelia mentes.* **nomine quemque uocans:** also at 12.759, where Turnus upbraids the Rutulians when calling on them to fight. Cf. *Il.* 10.68 (Agamemnon tells Menelaus to rouse his men) 'calling each man by his line and father's name' (πατρόθεν ἐκ γενεῆς ὀνομάζων ἄνδρα ἕκαστον). The motif of calling soldiers by name when rallying them, especially just before a battle, is common in historiography (see Oakley on Liv. 8.39.4).

732 dolituri refers to the sense of shame that should attend cowardice and military defeat, and that should be especially acute here because of Camilla's gender. Cf. *G.* 3.102 *quis cuique dolor uicto.* **inertes:** the adj. is used of a lack of fighting, manly spirit; *ignauia* in the next line reinforces the idea. Cf. 414, 9.55 *Teucrum mirantur inertia corda.*

733 quae tanta . . . ignauia: imitated at Stat. *Theb.* 3.607 (Capaneus exhorting his soldiers to fight) *quae tanta ignauia*; Statius then imitates 738–40 at *Theb.* 3.614–15.

734 The line is better taken as an indignant, incredulous rhetorical question (C–N, Gransden) than as an exclamation (Mynors, Horsfall, Conte). Rallying speeches typically begin with rhetorical questions (see 10.369, *Il.* 4.338–40; Mnestheus' speech at 9.781–7 is comprised entirely of questions). It would be awkward to break up the typical questions at 732–3 and 735 by inserting an exclamation between them. **femina** follows up on *inertes* and *ignauia* in the previous lines to sharpen the critique of the Etruscans; their lack of manly, martial spirit allows a woman to rout them. Tarchon is also incredulous that they are falling to just a single woman (so Tib. ad loc. *obtrectationem sumpsit a numero et sexu*); cf. 9.783–5, where Mnestheus rebukes the Trojans for failing to resist 'one man' (*unus homo*, 783), Turnus. **palantis** 'scattering'; of bested troops also at 5.265, 9.780, 10.674, 12.615, and 12.738.

735 quo 'to what purpose'. **tela inrita:** the phrase recalls Homeric ἄλιον βέλος, 'useless spear' (*Il.* 4.498, 5.18, 11.376, 11.380, 15.575, 16.480). Cf. 2.459 *tela manu miseri iactabant inrita Teucri*, 10.229–31 *tela* | . . . | *inrita.*

736 in Venerem 'when it comes to love'. Cf. *G.* 3.97 *frigidus in Venerem senior.* **segnes:** Tarchon implies, of course, that the Etruscans are *in Martem segnes.* Cf. 9.787 (Mnestheus exhorts the Trojans to fight) *et magni Aeneae, segnes, miseretque pudetque.* **nocturnaque bella:** battle/warfare as a metaphor for sex is very common (Adams 1982: 158–9) and best known from love elegy. Cf. Catul. 66.13 *nocturnae rixae*, Ov. *Am.* 1.9.45–6 *nocturnaque bella*, *Ars* 3.71, *Rem.* 31 *nocturna . . . rixa*, Prop. 1.16.5 *nocturnis . . . rixis.* The irony is very cutting: the Etruscans will not fight the woman-soldier Camilla, but will engage in these other 'battles' with women as part of the *militia amoris.* Military battles were normally not fought at night, which lends still more point to the irony.

737 I follow Williams, Mynors, and Horsfall ad loc. in placing a period at the end of the line (Gransden has a comma, while Conte has a colon). **curua . . . tibia:** a Phrygian pipe, in line with Bacchus' connections to Phrygia (e.g. E. *Bac.* 58–9, 78–9, Apollod. 3.5.1); cf. Tib. 2.1.86 *Phrygio tibia curua sono.* The taunt recalls Numanus' mockery of the Trojans at 9.617–18 *o uere Phrygiae, neque enim Phryges, ite per alta* | *Dindyma, ubi adsuetis biforem dat tibia cantum.*

738–40 V. varies *Il.* 4.343–6 'You two [Menestheus and Odysseus] first hear my call to the feast, whenever we Achaeans prepare a feast for the elders. Then you are happy to eat roast meat and drink cups of honeyed wine, so long as you want' (πρώτω γὰρ καὶ δαιτὸς ἀκουάζεσθον ἐμεῖο, | ὁππότε δαῖτα γέρουσιν ἐφοπλίζωμεν Ἀχαιοί. | ἔνθα φίλ' ὀπταλέα κρέα ἔδμεναι ἠδὲ κύπελλα | οἴνου πινέμεναι μελιηδέος, ὄφρ' ἐθέλητον). Etruscans were stereotypically gluttonous (cf. *G.* 2.193 *pinguis Tyrrhenus*, Catul. 39.11 *obesus Etruscus*).

738 exspectate 'await in expectation' (*OLD* 4). The imperative is derisive.

739–40 The preponderance of dactyls and coincidence of ictus and accent in the second halves of the lines is perhaps meant to be suggestive of ease and languor (Gransden ad loc.).

739 hic amor, hoc studium: for the anaphora of *hic* in different forms and asyndeton, cf. 4.347 *hic amor, haec patria est,* 6.129 *hoc opus, hic labor est,* 7.122 *hic domus, haec patria est.* Ovid reuses V.'s phrase at *Met.* 14.634, on the nymph Pomona who cares only for cultivating her garden (and not for love). **dum** 'until', with the subjunctive to imply expectancy, as commonly after *exspecto* (A–G §553). **secundus haruspex:** the *haruspex* is 'favourable' because he proclaims favourable, propitious omens from the entrails he observes. *secundus* is thus in part a transferred epithet (for *sacra secunda*), but is also applied to the *haruspex* who interprets the omens in an extension of the use of the adj. for people or deities who give support and are encouraging (*OLD* 3). The *haruspex* was intimately associated with the Etruscans; 'divination by this means [haruspicy] was *the* characteristic part of the *disciplina Etrusca*' (Eden on 8.498). Cf. the Etruscan *haruspex* at 8.498 and the Etruscan Asilas (see 620n.). In Etruscan lore, Tarchon was closely linked to the development of haruspicy, via the prophet Tages (de Grummond 2006: 28–31, Muse 2007: 587–8).

740 hostia pinguis: the sacrificial victim is to be eaten after the *haruspex* inspects the entrails and declares the offering favourable. This was familiar practice at Rome (Beard, North, and Price 1998: I.36). *pinguis* is sardonic, in that it describes a victim that will please not only the gods but also, of course, the gluttonous Etruscans.

741–56 Tarchon boldly joins the fray after his hortatory speech. Cf. 10.379 (Pallas after encouraging his men) *haec ait et medius densos prorumpit in hostis, Il.* 17.342 (A. after encouraging his men) 'so he spoke, and he leapt far to the front of the lines and took his position' (ὣς φάτο, καί ῥα πολὺ προμάχων ἐξάλμενος ἔστη). Leading by example in battle was a regular mark of a good general in Rome; cf. e.g. Sal. *Cat.* 60.4, Caes. *Gal.* 5.35, 7.87–8, Liv. 2.19.6, 4.41.4, Plu. *Marius* 20.6.

741 moriturus: not foreshadowing, because Tarchon does not die (see 758n.). The participle instead appears to capture Tarchon's thoughts (so Serv. ad loc. *moriturus animo*); he shows bravery by rushing into the fight while (mistakenly) thinking he was going to die and prepared for that outcome. Cf. 2.408 (Coroebus) *sese medium ineicit periturus in agmen,* 9.554 (Helenor) *iuuenis medios moriturus in hostis* (*inruit*); in both cases, the future participles seem to reflect the characters' consciousness.

742 Venulo: the spokesman who reported to Latinus and his council Diomedes' response to their embassy. **se . . . infert:** the reflexive is used of an attacking advance (*OLD* 2c); cf. 9.53 (= *G.* 2.145) (Turnus) *campo sese arduus infert,* 10.575 *interea biiugis infert se Lucagus albis,* 10.768 *se uastis* *infert Mezentius armis.* **turbidus:** a weather-metaphor; see *OLD* 1, 2; Cf. 10.763 (Mezentius) *turbidus ingreditur campo.*

743 Cf. Liv. 22.47.3 *stantibus ac confertis postremo turba equis uir uirum amplexus detrahebat equo.* Serv. ad loc. links V.'s description to the story in Julius Caesar's diary (*in ephemeride sua*) that Caesar was seized from his horse by a Gallic enemy; he was then saved when another Gaul called him by name, which his captor mistook for the command in the Gallic language to release him. The story has every appearance of fanciful fiction, and the cited Caesarian text is a mystery and is perhaps made up by Servius (see Horsfall ad loc.). **complectitur hostem:** cf. Luc. 3.694 *saeuus complectitur hostem,* Sil. 4.589 *hic hostem, orbatus telo, complectitur ulnis.*

744 'with all his might he carries him off at a gallop (holding him) in front of his own lap'. **aufert** answers (*se*) *infert* at 742: *infert* describes the attack on Venulus and *aufert* the result of that attack.

745 **tollitur in caelum clamor:** Ennian (*Ann.* 428 Sk.). For the hyperbole, see 192n. **cunctique:** strong alliteration with *caelum clamor.* The sound effect, reinforcing the description of loud, excited noise, extends back to *concitus* in the previous line and ahead to *conuertere* in the following.

746 **igneus aequore Tarchon:** the rhythm and the coincidence of ictus and accent (see 638n.) convey galloping speed. For *igneus,* see 718n. *aequore* = 'over the plain'. Cf. Sil. 16.510–11 *tollit sese aequore Theron | igneus.*

747 **arma uirumque:** as at 696, V. reuses his epic *incipit* at a moment of charged epic combat. **ipsius:** i.e. of Venulus.

748 **partis rimatur apertas** 'he casts about for an exposed/unprotected place'. The probable model is *Il.* 22.321 (Achilles poised to strike Hector) 'surveying his fair body, to see where it was especially open (to a blow)' (εἰσορόων χρόα καλόν, ὅπῃ εἴξειε μάλιστα). This indicates that *rimatur* = 'casts about (with his eyes)' (*OLD* 2b); sitting behind Venulus, Tarchon presumably scans his back, neck, and sides for a place to strike (although we could imagine Tarchon sitting erect and Venulus held in a slightly reclining position, in which case Tarchon could probably see Venulus' front). Cf. *Il. Lat.* 591 *partesque oculis rimantur apertas.*

749 **qua uulnus letale ferat** 'where he may administer a deadly wound'; a purpose clause introduced by a relative adv., as at *Il.* 22.321. Cf. 9.580 *letali uulnere;* the adj. (also at 4.73) is first securely attested in V. (The variant *letalibus* should very likely not be read for *uitalibus* at Lucr. 3.820

uitalibus ab rebus munita tenetur; see Kenney ad loc.) *ferat* seems to be *simplex pro composito* for *adferat*; cf. 10.77 *uim ferre*, 10.797 *plagamque ferentis*. For *adfero* meaning 'administer', see *OLD* 9.

750 sustinet a iugulo dextram: *sustinet* = 'holds back'. Cf. Stat. *Theb.* 2.648 *a iugulo nitentem sustinet hastam.* **uim uiribus exit** 'he escapes force with force'. *exeo*, normally intransitive, is used transitively; cf. 5.438 *tela . . . exit*, Lucr. 5.1330 (battle horses trying to escape boars) *feros exibant dentis adactus*, and see *TLL* v.2.1367.53–65, Görler, *EV* II.267. There is no distinction in meaning between the singular and plural forms of *uis* in the battle polyptoton; the plural is a poetic variation and metrically convenient.

751–6 Another bird-simile after that at 721–4. It is based on *Il.* 12.200–9, a narrative passage rather than a simile. Homer describes an eagle that struggles with a monstrous snake in flight, but drops it in pain amid a Trojan crowd, including Hector and Polydamas; the latter interprets this as a portent warning the Trojans of great casualties and disarray if they should attack the Greek ships (12.211–29). By contrast, in V. the eagle (Tarchon) holds tight to the struggling snake (Venulus) and carries it off in victory. The Homeric intertext implies that the snake is a portent of defeat, which extends beyond Venulus and to the Latin side as a whole. Before V., Cicero imitated *Il.* 12.200–9 in his poem *Marius* (Courtney 17.1–8), quoted at *Div.* 1.106.

751 uolans alte corresponds to ὑψιπέτης (αἰετός) ('high-flying eagle') at *Il.* 12.201. Cicero loosely translates the Homeric epithet with *altisonus* (fr. 17.1 Courtney). **draconem:** V. only has *draco* for a regular snake here, echoing δράκοντα at *Il.* 12.202. Elsewhere in V., the word is used of the monstrous, portentous serpents that kill Laocoön and his sons (2.225), the dragon that guards the golden apples of the Hesperides (4.484), and the serpent into which Proteus turns (*G.* 4.408, after δράκων at *Od.* 4.457). V. echoes δράκων at *Il.* 12.202 presumably because *draco* carries a sense of monstrosity, awe, and portentousness beyond that of *serpens, anguis*, or *coluber* and, thus, captures on its own the quality of the Homeric creature ('a blood-red, prodigious snake' (φοινήεντα δράκοντα . . . πέλωρον), *Il.* 12.202). Cicero uses *serpens* (fr. 17.2 Courtney) and *anguis* (fr. 17.3 Courtney) when recasting Homer.

751–2 fulua . . . | . . . aquila: the golden eagle. V. chooses the bird because of its association with Jupiter (cf. 12.247 *fuluus Iouis ales*, Cic. fr. 16 Courtney *nuntia fulua Iouis*), who stirred Tarchon to attack. At *Il.* 12.209, the writhing snake is a 'portent of aegis-bearing Zeus' (Διὸς τέρας αἰγιόχοιο). Homer describes the colour of the snake (φοινήεντα δράκοντα), and V. the colour of the eagle.

752 unguibus haesit: cf. *Il.* 12.202 φέρων ὀνύχεσσι, 'bearing in its claws', Cic. fr. 17.3 Courtney *transfigens unguibus.*

753 Marked alliteration of the *s* sound, which continues with *squamis et sibilat* in the following line, suggests the hissing of snakes, as at 12.848 *serpentum spiris* (with Tarrant's note). **sinuosa uolumina uersat:** cf. 2.208 (the Laocoönian serpents) *sinuatque immensa uolumine terga. sinuosus* is first attested at *G.* 1.244 *flexu sinuoso elabitur Anguis,* its only other appearance in V. Statius imitates V. at *Theb.* 1.562 (Python) *caerulei sinuosa uolumina monstri.*

754 arrectisque horret squamis 'and bristles with raised scales'. A sign of fear, as at *G.* 3.545 *attoniti squamis adstantibus hydri,* mixed with aggression.

755 arduus insurgens: the snake rises to attack the eagle; cf. 5.277–8 (a wounded but defiant snake) *sibila colla | arduus attollens.* **obunco** 'hooked'. The adj. also occurs at 6.597 (of a vulture's beak); it is first found in V. and is thereafter rare (*TLL* IX.326.21–42). *obunco* is the *lectio difficilior* over the more common adj. *adunco.* Cf. Ov. *Met.* 6.516 (of an eagle's talons) *pedibus praedator obuncis.*

756 luctantem: probably *simplex* for *reluctantem.* Cf. Hor. *Carm.* 4.4.11–12 (an eagle) *nunc in reluctantes dracones | egit amor dapis atque pugnae,* ps.-V. *Cul.* 195–6 (a snake, killed by a shepherd) *horrida squamosi uoluentia membra draconis, | atque reluctantis,* Claud. *in Gild.* 470–1 (a golden eagle snatches a snake) *dumque reluctantem morsu partitur obunco, | haesit in ungue caput.* **aethera uerberat alis:** for the coincidence of ictus and accent in the last three feet, see 638n. and 746n. The dactylic rhythm seems to reflect the rapid and sustained beating of wings. Cf. 5.377 (the shadow-boxing Dares) *uerberat ictibus auras,* which has the same prosody.

757 praedam 'prey', thus extending the animal imagery of the simile, but also with the suggestion of spoils, which Tarchon will take from his defeated foe. **Tiburtum ex agmine:** that Venulus fights in the Tiburtine ranks implies that he was from Tibur.

758 ouans: a clear sign that Tarchon is the victor in this encounter, even though the simile breaks off mid-struggle; see, too, *euentum* later in the line. Tarchon's joy at his success is not premature (*pace* Tarrant on 12.479), but is an early manifestation of how the tide of battle has shifted against the Latins/Volscians and in favour of the Trojans and their allies. This is the last appearance of Tarchon in *Aen.* He exits in high style, stirred to exemplary bravery by Jupiter and carrying off a bested foe. **ducis exemplum euentumque** 'the successful model of (their) leader'; hendiadys.

For *euentus* meaning 'success', see *OLD* 2. The unusual rhythm, with no third-foot caesura and, due to the elision, no fourth-foot caesura to match that in the second foot, emphasises the pair *exemplum euentumque.*

759 Maeonidae: Maeonia = Lydia, from which the Etruscans were said to have originated (see 184n.). Cf. 8.499 (addressing Etruscan warriors) *o Maeoniae delecta iuuentus.* **fatis debitus Arruns:** the man who will kill Camilla; he is owed to fate because, according to Diana's will and command (590–2), he is destined to be killed after killing Camilla. The flow of the narrative makes it evident that Arruns is one of the *Maeonidae* who follow Tarchon's successful lead; he is part of the Etruscan counter-attack. The view that he is a traitorous ally of Camilla goes back to antiquity but is unfounded; see, further, 762–5n., 785n., and Miller 1994: 172 n. 5. The name Arruns is identifiably Etruscan; cf. Liv. 1.34.2, 1.42.1 (son of Tarquinius Priscus), 1.46.4 (Tarquinius Superbus' brother, husband of Servia), 1.56.7, 2.6.6, 2.6.7 (son of Tarquinius Superbus, slayer of Brutus), 2.14.5 and 2.14.6 (son of Lars Porsena), 5.33.3 (of the Etruscan city Clusium). Cf., too, the Etruscan soothsayer Arruns at Luc. 1.584–638. V. would not have wanted to connect Arruns to the Roman family of the Arruntii and to Lucius Arruntius, consul in 22 BCE (*pace* Trundle 2003: 185–6); the connection would have been hardly flattering, and thus hardly appropriate, given the negative portrayal of Arruns (see 767n., 836–67n.).

760 uelocem . . . Camillam: the epithet refers to a cardinal trait of Camilla (see 532n.); here, however, she rides on her swift horse (see 827), having remounted after her encounter with the Ligurian (cf. Heinze 1993: 159). **iaculo et multa prior arte:** *prior* is difficult. I take it to mean 'superior' in his spear and his great cunning (with *iaculo* and *multa . . . arte* thus abls. of specification with *prior*). This resembles Homer's description of Euphorbus at *Il.* 16.808–9, 'he who surpassed all men of his age in the spear' (ὅς ἡλικίην ἐκέκαστο | ἔγχεϊ); Euphorbus is a model for Arruns (see 806–8n.). Cf. 292 *pietate prior.* Others understand *prior* as 'taking the initiative' with his spear and his great cunning (Page, Horsfall ad loc.). Arruns' *ars* links him with the trickster Ligurian at 699–720.

761 circuit 'circles around'. **fortuna** 'opportunity, favourable chance/occasion' (*OLD* 6). **temptat** 'investigates, probes'.

762–5 qua . . . cumque . . . | hac . . . | qua . . . | hac: the correlatives show how Arruns coordinates his movements with those of Camilla, stalking her to find the moment to kill. Serv. ad 762 suggests, following Aelius Donatus, that only if Arruns fought on Camilla's side would he be able to retreat with her; cf. Fratantuono 2007: 344–5. But although Camilla's movements are rather obscure, V. does not say that she returns to her ranks, and it is easy to imagine her making forays *in medium agmen* (762) and then withdrawing, at most, to the edge of the fighting, but still within range of the enemy Arruns. At the very least, nothing in the account of Arruns' shadowing of Camilla is enough to counter the overwhelming sense given at 759 that he fights as an Etruscan with Tarchon.

762 furens: of battle-rage. Cf. 1.491 *Penthesilea furens mediisque in milibus ardet.*

763 subit 'approaches'. The verb is in the same metrical *sedes* as *redit* in the following line; the matching positions reinforce the sense of shadowed movements. **tacitus uestigia lustrat** 'silently tracks her steps'. Cf. 12.467 *uestigat lustrans, Ecl.* 2.12 *uestigia lustro.* The phrase suggests hunting; Camilla has again (see 694n.) become the hunted (see, further, Kayachev 2018: 101–3). For *lustro* used of hunting, see *Ecl.* 10.55 *mixtis lustrabo Maenala Nymphis,* with Clausen's note.

764 uictrix: predicative, 'as victor'.

765 celeris detorquet habenas 'he turns his swift reins'; Arruns changes his horse's direction to follow Camilla as she moves from attack to retreat. Cf. 12.373 *ora citatorum dextra detorsit equorum.* The transferred epithet *celeris* indicates that Arruns is a match for Camilla (see 760n.).

766 Cf. 5.441–2 (Dares searches for an opening in his boxing match against Entellus) *nunc hos, nunc illos aditus omnemque pererrat | arte locum.* **hos aditus iamque hos aditus:** *aditus* = 'opening to attack' (*OLD* 7). The repetition emphasises the doggedness of Arruns.

767 certam 'unerring'. The adj. foreshadows the fatal throw, as at 12.267–8 *stridula cornus et auras | certa secat*; it implies not that Arruns' spear always hit its mark, but that this one is destined to do so. **improbus:** the adj. has a dark moral tint, as at 512; Arruns goes beyond what is fair and right in his relentless, covert stalking of Camilla. Although Arruns is a Trojan ally who kills a major enemy, sympathies do not lie with him, and he is presented in villainous terms (*pace* Rosenmeyer 1960: 164).

768–93 CAMILLA APPROACHES DEATH

Attention now turns to Camilla and Chloreus, a priest of the goddess Cybele marked by exoticism and effeminacy. His extravagant dress and equipment, which V. describes in detail (769–77), seduce and distract

Camilla; she wants them as spoils, either to dedicate in a temple or to wear in the hunt. This lapse of focus makes her vulnerable to Arruns, who prays to Apollo to allow him to kill Camilla. Arruns succeeds in doing so before Camilla can slay Chloreus (*pace* Macr. 5.15.12, Horsfall 2016: 94), who dies by Turnus' hand at 12.363.

A desire for spoils belongs to the male heroic ethos in ancient epic and Roman warfare. But V. recurrently links that desire to disaster and death, especially when it results in the donning of spoils; cf. the Nisus and Euryalus episode (esp. 9.359–73) and Turnus' despoliation of Pallas (10.496–505). Camilla's attraction to Chloreus' gear is a variation on the theme. This complicates her portrayal. Although someone who violates Roman norms first as a virgin huntress and later as a female fighter, Camilla nevertheless embodies Roman norms and ideals of masculine warfare with her bravery and fighting skill. At the same time, her desire for Chloreus' spoils aligns her with that Other: she and Chloreus share tastes, and she is capable of being seduced by his eastern effeminacy and gaudy splendour. Camilla and Chloreus are closer than they might at first appear, with resemblances to balance their differences. Binaries (Italian/eastern, masculine female warrior/effeminate male warrior) define the relationship between them. But these are not absolute, and the two are both opposites and reflections of each other (Hardie 2007: 138–9). This is another way in which V. complicates Camilla's identity, so that tidy binaries are insufficient (see also 648–63n.).

The masculine/feminine binary is also complicated by the phrase *femineo praedae et spoliorum . . . amore* at 782. *femineo* ascribes to Camilla a woman's passion, which leads to her ceasing effectively to operate in a male role. See, further, Intro. pp. 23–4.

The divinity upon whom Arruns calls to aid him in the killing of the incautious Camilla is Apollo Soranus, in whose wolf-cult Arruns serves as a priest. This reintroduces the wolf-leitmotif, which V. will develop further (see 792n.).

768 Cybelo: Mt Cybelus, the sacred mountain of Cybele in Phrygia. Cf. 3.111 *mater cultrix Cybeli.* **Chloreus:** the name is probably derived from Gk χλωρός, 'greenish-yellow'. The Galli, or eunuch priests of Cybele (see e.g. Catul. 63, Lucr. 2.610–43, Juv. 6.513–16; cf. Apul. *Met.* 8.26–8), dressed extravagantly (and, to critics, outlandishly), including in robes 'mainly yellow or many-coloured' (Vermaseren 1977: 97). The name Chloreus for a priest of Cybele seems meant to conjure the Galli's colourful dress, although it tended to be golden-yellow or saffron. At the very least, it implies effeminacy, with which yellow was associated (Horsfall ad loc.). **olimque sacerdos:** it is uncertain whether *olim* means 'formerly' or 'since long ago'. As a priest of Cybele, whether past or current,

Chloreus is implicitly a eunuch (Anderson 1999: 206–7). While warrior-priests appear in epic (in *Aen.*, see Arruns at 6.484, 9.327, and 10.537), Chloreus is an outré version of the type. Chloreus, at least, confirms Numanus Remulus' taunts about the effeminacy of the Trojans (9.614–20); at 9.619–20, Numanus insults them as followers of Cybele.

769 insignis 'conspicuous'. **Phrygiis . . . armis:** *Phrygiis* conjures eastern effeminacy and decadence, as at 403. Hence the phrase is not simply synonymous with *arma* | *Troia* at 778–9.

770–1 quem . . . | . . . tegebat 'which a skin with bronze scales, like plumage, and golden clasps covered'. Chloreus rides as a richly ornamented *catafractus*, or mail-clad cavalry fighter; this identifies him as eastern (cf. Sal. *Hist.* 4.64, Liv. 35.48.3, 37.40.5, 37.40.6, 37.42.7, Prop. 3.12.12). *in plumam* indicates that the bronze plates were laid 'featherwise', viz. one on another to look like feathers.

772 peregrina ferrugine clarus: *ferrugo* describes a deep blue colour, close to purple (Serv. ad 9.582 *uicinus purpurae subnigrae,* Edgeworth 1992: 126–7); Chloreus wears clothing dyed in that colour. *ferrugo* is Spanish at 9.582 *ferrugine clarus Hibera* and probably here as well (see 775–6n.); Chloreus is an eastern figure, but he owes his rich appearance to different parts of the world. *clarus* = 'remarkable, striking'; yet the word, 'which commonly means "bright", is *para prosdokian* after a word for a dark colour' (Hardie on 9.582). **ostro:** more than a metrically convenient alternative to *purpurae,* the word conveys a sense of eastern opulence, given the connection between the dye *ostrum* and Tyre; see 72n. Camilla herself wears a cloak of *ostrum* at 7.814.

773 spicula . . . Lycio Gortynia cornu: Gortyna was a city on Crete. The island and Lycia were noted for archers; hence *Lycius* and Cretan place-name adjs. were both common archery epithets (for *Lycius,* see 7.816, 8.166; for Crete's associations with archery, see 4.70, 5.306–7, Hor. *Carm.* 1.15.17, 4.9.17–18, Prop. 3.3.10, Ov. *Met.* 8.22). The adjs. are not just conventional, but are an indication that Chloreus possesses first-rate gear. Camilla has a Lycian quiver (*Lyciam . . . pharetram*) at 7.816; on this, see Boyd 1992: 218 n. 16.

774–6 V. repeatedly has triple forms of *aurum* and *aureus* (see Wills 1996: 286–7). Cf. 4.137–9 (Dido) *Sidoniam picto chlamydem circumdata limbo; | cui pharetra ex auro, crines nodantur in aurum, | aurea purpuream subnectit fibula uestem,* with 780 below. Cf. *Il.* 2.872–3 (probably the Carian Amphimachus, but perhaps Nastes) 'and he came to the war wearing gold, just like a girl, the fool' (ὃς καὶ χρυσὸν ἔχων πόλεμόνδ' ἴεν ἠΰτε κούρη | νήπιος). Cf., too, Atalanta, distracted in her race with Hippomanes by three golden apples (e.g. Ov. *Met.* 10.649–80; see Alessio 1993: 123).

774 aureus ex umeris erat arcus: cf. 652 *aureus ex umero sonat arcus*; V. establishes clear links between the equipment of Chloreus and Camilla here and in the previous two lines. The *arcus* is presumably the same bow as at 773. Perhaps V. imagines it made of horn and then gilded or inlaid with gold, although *cornu* could describe a bow made of some other substance besides horn (*OLD* 4, Horsfall on 7.497).

775 cassida: an alternative nom. for *cassis*, also at Prop. 3.11.15 (Penthesilea) *aurea cui postquam nudauit cassida frontem*; the noun, instead of standard *galea*, seems designed to mark unusual gear.

775–6 croceam chlamydemque sinusque crepantis | carbaseos 'a saffron cloak of rustling linen folds'; hendiadys. The *chlamys* is a sumptuous item, as always in V. (3.484, 4.137, 5.250, 8.167, 9.582). Its colour suggests effeminacy and is probably meant to recall the dress of the Galli (see 768n.). Cf. 9.614 (Numanus Remulus on the Trojans) *uobis picta croco et fulgenti murice uestis*. With *carbaseos*, cf. Catul. 64.227 *carbasus obscurata dicet ferrugine Hibera*. V.'s echo of *carbasus* here and of *ferrugine* at 772 is solid evidence for his debt to Catullus (and, concomitantly, for supposing that he was thinking of Spanish *ferrugo*). *carbaseus* is rare in Latin literature (*TLL* III.428.45–51); it occurs before V. at Cic. *Ver.* 5.30. Statius derives the adj. from V. at *Theb.* 7.658 *carbaseique sinus*, on Eunaeus, a priest of Bacchus who has come to war.

777 pictus 'embroidered'. Cf. 9.582 *pictus acu chlamydem*. A middle participle, 'referring to an action effected by the subject in his own interest through another agent' (Fordyce on 7.796) – 'having had [his tunic and pants] embroidered'. See Courtney 2004: 428. **barbara tegmina crurum:** a final marker of Chloreus' Otherness; Romans did not wear trousers, which were seen as barbarian clothing. Cybele's consort Attis was commonly depicted wearing trousers. Cf. *pictoque . . . subtegmine bracae* at V. Fl. 6.227, in a passage heavily indebted to V. (6.225–7 *tenuia non illum candentis carbasa lini, | non auro depicta chlamys, non flaua galeri | caesaries pictoque iuuant subtegmine bracae*). Cf., too, Tac. *Hist.* 2.20.1 (Gallic trousers) *bracas, barbarum tegumen*.

778–80 siue . . . | . . . | uenatrix: V. leaves the question of Camilla's intentions unresolved. That she might have wished to don what she took from Chloreus, even as a hunter rather than as a fighter, lends a sense of doom, since in V. 'the wearing, or even the desire to wear, another man's armour ends badly' (Horsfall 1995: 176), in accordance with Roman usage (see 2–11n.); cf. 9.365–6, 9.373–4, 10.501–5, 12.941–52. Hanging spoils in a temple, meanwhile, is correct piety (cf. e.g. 2.504–5, 3.286–8, 5.393, 8.721–2).

778 templis: presumably a temple of Diana.

779 captiuo . . . auro: for *captiuus* of spoils, cf. 2.765 *captiua uestis,* 7.184 *captiui . . . currus.* **se ferret** 'flaunt herself'. **in** 'wearing' (*OLD* 36).

780 uenatrix: the strong enjambment echoes that of *Troia* at 779; C–N, Page, and Mackail ad loc. misunderstand when they place a comma after 779 and take *uenatrix* as the subject of *sequebatur* rather than of *se ferret.* With Chloreus' spoils, Camilla would resemble the hunting Dido at 4.137–9, quoted at 774–6n. The dress is impractical for serious hunting, but that is precisely the point: Camilla is so seduced by what Chloreus wears that she ignores how wrong it is for the hunt. **unum** 'alone'. The adj. agrees with *hunc* at 778 and is emphasised by hyperbaton. Camilla's single-minded focus on Chloreus mirrors that of Arruns on her, although her blind incaution distinguishes her actions from his. Cf. 9.438–9 (Nisus) *solumque per omnis | Volcentem petit, in solo Volcente moratur.* **ex omni certamine pugnae** 'out of all the battle-strife'. Cf. 12.598 *pugnae . . . in certamine,* Lucr. 4.843 *certamina pugnae.* A variation on *certamina belli,* which is probably Ennian (see Harrison on 10.146). Cf. Homeric νεῖκος πολέμοιο ('strife of war', *Il.* 13.271), ἔριδος μέγα νεῖκος ('great battle-strife', *Il.* 17.384).

781 caeca: adverbial, like *incauta* later in the line. It describes impaired judgement, owing to the influence of overwhelming emotion (see Tarrant on 12.279 *caecique ruunt*). Camilla runs to foolish excess in her pursuit of the spoils, which causes her to become incautious and unaware of the danger around her and of the consequences of her actions; cf. Hardie, Intro. p. 26. V. perhaps recasts *Il.* 16.789–90, where Patroclus does not see the approach in battle of Apollo, who is hidden in a mist (ὃ μὲν τὸν ἰόντα κατὰ κλόνον οὐκ ἐνόησεν | ἠέρι γὰρ πολλῇ κεκαλυμμένος ἀντεβόλησε). **sequebatur:** suggestive of hunting (see 674n.).

782 The line 'recalls and redefines Diana's earlier description' of Camilla at 583 (*aeternum telorum et uirginitatis amorem*) (Egan 2012: 46–7). **femineo:** *inpatienti, inrationabili, ut* [7.345] *femineae ardentem iraeque curaeque coquebant* (Serv. ad loc.). Ovid appears to immitate at *Am.* 3.2.40 *femineus pectora torret amor.* Cf. Liv. 34.7.8 (on women) *non magistratus nec sacerdotia nec triumphi nec insignia nec dona aut spolia bellica iis contingere possunt:*

munditiae et ornatus et cultus, haec feminarum insignia sunt, his gaudent et gloriantur, hunc mundum muliebrem appellarunt maiores nostri; Camilla confounds the distinctions drawn in Livy as a woman who could win spoils, but who is also attracted to sumptuous attire. **ardebat amore:** the phrase combines epic and erotic imagery (Gildenhard and Henderson ad loc.); the latter anticipates the sexualised imagery of 804.

783–4 Hysteron proteron (the reversal of temporal order), although the actions are nearly simultaneous.

783 telum: V. creates tension by revealing only gradually the person to whom the weapon belongs; *ex insidiis* and *tandem* hint at Arruns, who the reader knows has been secretly stalking Camilla for some time, but it is only in the next line that he is named. **cum:** a *cum inuersum* construction, in which the *cum*-clause comes after the main clause and expresses the principal action. It is used here, as commonly, for dramatic effect; the action of the *cum*-clause interrupts what had been occurring (often described in the imperfect) and constitutes a critical turn of events (Tarrant on 12.249). **tempore capto** 'seizing the moment'; *tempus* = Gk καιρός, 'the right moment', as at 459 *arrepto tempore.* Cf. Liv. 3.9.7 *insidiatum eum et tempore capto adortum rem publicam.*

784 sic uoce precatur: a formula in V. to introduce prayers, also at 9.403; cf. 6.186 *sic forte precatur,* 10.420 *quem sic Pallas petit ante precatus.* Cf. Homeric ὣς ἔφατ' εὐχόμενος, which concludes prayers, including the model for Arruns' (*Il.* 16.249; see the following note). For prayers before discharging a missile in battle, see 9.404–9, 10.421–3, 10.773–6; the convention goes back to Homer (e.g. *Il.* 3.351–4, 4.119–21, *Od.* 24.521).

785–93 The prayer of Arruns reworks parts of Achilles' prayer to Zeus of Dodona at *Il.* 16.233–48 to grant Patroclus success in battle and return him safely from it.

785 summe deum: the address calls Jupiter to mind; thus Achilles opens his prayer at *Il.* 16.233 with Ζεῦ ἄνα, 'Zeus, the king'. The phrasing points to the close correspondence between Apollo and Jupiter here, as throughout the *Aen.* (see Miller 1994: 174–5, 2009: 167). In allowing Arruns to kill Camilla, Apollo ensures the reversal in the battle that Jupiter had initiated through Tarchon. **sancti custos Soractis Apollo:** Mt Soracte (cf. Hor. *Carm.* 1.9), modern Soratte, roughly 25 miles north of Rome, was the seat of worship of the Italian deity Soranus, later subsumed by Apollo. The god was worshipped in Faliscan territory (on the Etruscan side of the Tiber), in a cult whose priests were called the Hirpi. Serv. ad loc.

gives an account of the origin of the cult. At rites for Dis Pater, wolves stole the sacrificial *exta*. Shepherds pursued the animals to a cave, from which a pestilence was emitted. Apollo's oracle then stated from the cave that the deadly exhalation would cease only if the men would imitate wolves, viz. would live by plunder. The Hirpi are themselves 'Wolf-Men'; the name comes from the Oscan word for 'wolf'. For more on Apollo Soranus and the Hirpi, see Rissanen 2012. On Apollo's broader connections with the wolf, see Gershenson 1991 and Graf 2008: 120–2, 132, and 155. Arruns need not be allied with Turnus (and, thus, Camilla), even though men of Soracte fight on the Latin side (cf. 7.696). V. could have distinguished the Hirpi from those men of Soracte, or this could be a moment of inconsistency. *sanctus* seems to be only applied to Apollo and to Hercules in extant pre-Augustan literature (Brenk 1999: 128).

786 quem primi colimus: it is natural in prayers to emphasise the worshipper's proven devotion (so Tarrant on 12.778). *primi* presumably means that Arruns and his fellows stand above all others in their devotion, although 'earliest' cannot be ruled out, to show the antiquity of the Hirpi's worship at Soracte. With the first person plural here and at 788, Arruns identifies himself as one of the Hirpi.

786–7 cui pineus ardor aceruo | pascitur 'for whom the pinewood blaze feeds on the pile'. *pineus* is a transferred epithet (for *pineo . . . aceruo*); this *-eus* adj. occurs in poetry before V. at Catul. 61.15 and 64.10 and Lucr. 4.587 (in prose at Cato *Agr.* 18.8 and 48.3).

787–8 The Hirpi are counterparts to the Selli at *Il.* 16.234–5, who were priests at the sanctuary of Zeus at Dodona: 'Around you dwell the Selli, your prophets, with unwashed feet and sleeping on the ground' (ἀμφὶ δὲ Σελλοὶ | σοὶ ναιουσ' ὑποφῆται ἀνιπτόποδες χαμαιεῦναι). Whereas the Selli have dirty feet, the Hirpi use their feet to walk through fire; on this aspect of their cult, see Plin. *Nat.* 7.19, Str. 5.2.9, Sil. 5.175–8. According to Serv. ad loc., Varro contended that the Hirpi did not rely on *pietas* alone when fire-walking and, in fact, anointed their feet with a *medicamentum* to protect them. *Pace* Alessio 1993: 140, there is no sign that V. wished to activate that demystifying explanation and to suggest thereby that Arruns, as a member of the Hirpi, was a trickster. Arruns' stealth is enough on its own to make him a second devious fighter, after the Ligurian, who faces Camilla.

788 multa . . . pruna 'in the deep hot ash'.

789 da, pater . . . aboleri: for the solemn prayer formula *da, pater* in V., cf. 2.691, 3.89, 10.62, and 10.421. For the infinitive with *do* in prayers, cf. 6.66–7 (A. prays to the Sibyl) *da . . . | . . . Latio considere Teucros*, 5.689 (A. prays to Jupiter) *da flammam euadere classi*, and 10.61–2 (Venus prays to Jupiter) *iterumque reuoluere casus | da, pater, Iliacos Teucris*, with Görler, *EV* II.271; cf. Gk δός + inf. in prayers, with Norden on 6.66f. On *do* + inf. generally, an apparent Grecism (although a blend of Latin inheritance cannot be ruled out), see Mayer 1999: 165–6, 173–4, Penney 1999: 255–6. **dedecus:** an emotional word of archaic flavour, also at 10.681 (where see Harrison's note) and 12.641. Arruns understands the success of the female warrior Camilla to be a source of shame, much like Tarchon before him. Contrast Turnus' *decus Italiae uirgo* at 508.

790 omnipotens: with *pater* in the previous line, a word more appropriate to Jupiter; see 785n. Emphatic by position.

790–1 non exuuias . . . | . . . peto: a contrastive echo of the beginning of the book (7); Arruns departs from the heroic norm of seeking spoils. His stated lack of interest in spoils distinguishes him from Camilla. Arruns disingenuously masks his cowardice: he plans to kill Camilla stealthily from afar to avoid facing her openly and to save himself, but spins this as a lack of concern for winning spoils.

791–2 mihi cetera laudem | facta ferent: the underlying idea is that killing Camilla, a woman and, as such, a source of *dedecus*, is not the stuff of *laus*. Cf. 2.583–4 *etsi nullum memorabile nomen | feminea in poena est nec habet uictoria laudem*, Prop. 4.6.65–6 (Cleopatra, unsuitable for a triumph) *quantus mulier foret una triumphus, | ductus erat per quas ante Iugurtha uias.* Arruns could sincerely believe this while also being disingenuous about his actions; he would think that killing a woman brings no fame, and he would imply that he accordingly will stay hidden and seek no recognition, even though fear also – and even principally – motivates that behaviour. Arruns shows arrogant confidence that glory will later come his way; the contrast with what soon happens to him (see 863–6) is sharp.

792 dira: the word suggests hellish destructiveness. **meo . . . uulnere:** *meo* = 'inflicted by me'; cf. 12.51 *nostro sequitur de uulnere sanguis.* **dum** introduces a proviso clause. **pestis** carries the sense of 'pestilence/plague' as well as of 'instrument of death/ruin'. There is an allusion to the cult of Apollo Soranus and the Hirpi, who drive off a pestilence connected to thieving wolves (see 785n.); Arruns suggests that he will vary his apotropaic role as wolf-priest of Apollo and drive off a different kind of plague. Camilla is not objectively a lycanthrope, a destructive she-wolf that needs to be slain (*pace* Fratantuono 2007: 349–50). Rather, it is Arruns who connects her to wolves; while there is a possible link between Camilla and, through the Amazons, wolves (see 680–1n.), and while Camilla resembles Harpalyce (cf. 1.316–17), whose name means 'Snatcher She-Wolf', she is a baneful wolf-figure only in his hostile enemy eyes. Arruns' *pestis* is part of a thematic frame for Camilla's *aristeia*: one of her first victims was a kind of wolf, and now a wolf-priest, who equates her with a wolf-pestilence, ends her *aristeia* and her life. *pestis* is used elsewhere in *Aen.* of the Harpies (3.215), Polyphemus (3.620), Allecto (7.505), and the Dirae (12.845).

793 remeabo: the verb is more common with a preposition (*ad* or *in*); cf. e.g. Luc. 1.690 *patriae sedes remeamus in urbis.* **inglorius:** Arruns extends his claim at 790–2. Arruns' stated indifference to glory reverses Achilles' prayer to Zeus at *Il.* 16.241 to 'send forth glory' with Patroclus (τῷ κῦδος ἅμα πρόες).

794–835 THE DEATH OF CAMILLA

Arruns' prayer to Apollo is (partly) answered, and Camilla falls unawares to his spear-throw. V. adapts several elements from the death of Patroclus in *Il.* 16, thus continuing the intertextual engagement with Homer begun at 785–93; see 794–8n., 806–8n., 815n., 831n., and Knauer 1964: 308–15, 423. In addition, V. recasts a wolf-simile from *Il.* 15 (see 809–13n.) to describe Arruns after he kills Camilla, thereby extending the wolf-leitmotif in the Camilla passage.

As Camilla is fatally struck, V. returns to the theme of gender: he ties the theme to sexuality by equating her death to the deflowering of a virgin and by figuring the deadly spear as a nursing child. The image of lost virginity links her to Pallas (see 68–71n., Intro p. 28). Camilla is not the erotic object in death that the Amazon Penthesilea is, with whom Achilles falls in love after he kills her. Yet she is unable to escape eroticised male violence, which violates her body, contradicts her earlier life as a virgin huntress and makes a return to it impossible, and ends this female warrior's striking and successful stint in the masculine theatre of war.

Several verbal echoes connect Camilla to Dido; although Camilla's gender identity is complicated, V. ties her as a major female death in the second half of *Aen.* to a major female death in the first half (Intro. pp. 26–7).

Camilla's final thoughts and words are on how to defeat the Trojans. The orders she gives to bring that about, however, are wrong-headed. Camilla is a brave, skilled, and powerful warrior, and she demonstrates the care of a good military commander. Yet she is also a deficient leader in that she does not understand the best way to prosecute the battle (see 823–7n.). In this, she resembles Turnus (see 896–915n.). Camilla and

Turnus are also linked because the same line describes their moments of death (831 and 12.952); see Intro. p. 29.

794–8 Modelled closely on *Il.* 16.249–52 (Zeus responds to Achilles' prayer for Patroclus): 'Zeus the counsellor heard him. The father granted him one part, but denied the other. He granted him to drive back war and battle from the ships, but denied that he returns safe from the battle' (τοῦ δ᾽ ἔκλυε μητίετα Ζεύς. | τῷ δ᾽ ἕτερον μὲν δῶκε πατήρ, ἕτερον δ᾽ ἀνένευσε· | νηῶν μέν οἱ ἀπώσασθαι πόλεμον τε μάχην τε | δῶκε, σόον δ᾽ ἀνένευσε μάχης ἒξ ἀπονέεσθαι). For Apollo's granting of Arruns' prayer to kill Camilla, cf., too, *Il.* 16.788–804, where Apollo strikes Patroclus before he is further injured, and then killed, by Euphorbus and Hector.

795 mente dedit 'granted by his will'. Cf. 10.629 (Juno to Jupiter) *mente dares.* **uolucris dispersit in auras:** the image is a commonplace in Greco-Roman poetry (Hardie on 9.312–13, Quinn on Catul. 30.10, N–H on Hor. *Carm.* 1.26.2, McKeown on Ov. *Am.* 1.4.11–12). That Apollo grants only half of his priest's prayer means that Diana will be able to avenge Camilla's killer (cf. 590–2); while there is no sign of divine cooperation between the sibling gods, Apollo's actions accord with his sister's intentions.

796 The *ut*-clause is to be construed not with *oranti* but with *adnuit* in the next line, an unusual construction (*TLL* 1.1.792.41–3), to balance *non dedit* + *ut* at 797–8. **subita turbatam morte Camillam:** neat interlocking word order. Camilla is confounded by the arrival of surprise death.

797 reducem . . . uideret: Arruns does not in fact pray to get back home; but there is an assumed prayer to that effect in his statement that he will return to his paternal city *inglorius* if Apollo grants him the killing of Camilla.

798 inque Notos: virtually *in se* with *procellae*; on such alternative expressions for the reflexive, see Housman on Man. 1.539, Kenney on ps.-V. *Mor.* 61. For *Notus,* the South Wind, in the topos of winds bearing words away, cf. e.g. Ov. *Am.* 1.1.14, 1.7.16, 2.6.44, 2.8.20, Tib. 1.5.36.

799 ergo ut 'and so when'. *ergo* is transitional and resumes the account of the spear-throw at 783–4.

800 acris 'intent'. In this reaction shot to the spear-throw, the Volscians focus with keen dread on Camilla, recognising as she does not the danger she is in. The adj. is to be taken with both *animos* and *oculos*; the line is arranged chiastically (verb–object–object–verb), with the adj. in the middle agreeing with both words that flank it.

801 cuncti . . . nihil ipsa: an asyndetic, quick-cut contrast to intensify the drama.

801–2 nihil . . . nec . . . | nec . . . aut: for the accumulation of negatives, cf. 9.428–9 *nihil iste nec ausus nec potuit*, with Hardie's note; for the negatives with a final *aut*, an unusual sequence, cf. 12.135 *neque nomen erat neque honos aut gloria monti.* **aurae | . . . sonitus:** hendiadys, 'sounding air'.

802 memor 'mindful'.

803–4 The language strongly suggests the deflowering of a virgin; the *hasta*, which was a metaphor for the penis (Adams 1982: 19–20), pierces Camilla (albeit in the breast) and draws virgin blood. By implication, this renders her a bride on her wedding night. The further suggestion is that this is the first experience of battle for her as it was for Pallas, deflowered in death at 68–71; both are new to war, as a virgin is new to sex. But the spear is not only a penetrating penis; it is also a monstrous version of a nursing child. 'The spear that pierces Camilla's nipple and drinks her blood . . . figures a grotesquely accelerated sexual maturation, from virgin to bride to nursing mother' (Oliensis 1997: 308). See Intro. p. 28.

803 exsertam . . . papillam: Amazonian imagery; see 649n. Cf. 1.492 (Penthesilea) *exsertae . . . mammae.*

804 The suggestion of defloration was recognised by Ausonius, who reuses the line in his *Cento Nuptialis* (118) to describe a penis (*hasta* in Ausonius (117)) taking a bride's virginity. **haesit:** emphasised as an unelided spondee at the start of the line (see 48n.); the pause is expressive of the action described. **uirgineumque . . . cruorem:** cf. Claud. *Fesc.* 26–7 (on the imperial bride Maria's loss of virginity) *uestes Tyrio sanguine fulgidas | alter uirgineus nobilitet cruor.* **alte . . . acta** 'driven deep'. Cf. 10.850 *alte uulnus adactum.* **bibit:** with *papilla*, suggestive of nursing, but cf. the use of *haurio* ('drink to the full') for deep and fatal wounds (2.600, 10.313–14).

805–6 dominamque ruentem | suscipiunt: cf. 4.391 (Dido's maids hold up the swooning queen) *suscipiunt famulae.*

806–8 Arruns' response to his killing of Camilla is modelled on *Il.* 16.813–15 (on Euphorbus after injuring Patroclus) 'but he ran back and mingled with the throng, when he had snatched the ashen spear from the body, and he did not await Patroclus, unarmed though he was, in the battle' (ὁ μὲν αὖτις ἀνέδραμε, μίκτο δ' ὁμίλῳ, | ἐκ χροὸς ἁρπάξας δόρυ μείλινον, οὐδ' ὑπέμεινε | Πάτροκλον γυμνόν περ ἐόντ' ἐν δηϊοτῆτι).

806 fugit: juxtaposed with *suscipiunt* to highlight the two different reactions to the fatal shot. **ante omnis:** to be taken with *fugit* (rather than with *exterritus*), with *ante* in a temporal sense. V. emphasises how Arruns at once fled the battle, as soon as he saw what he had done; cf. *continuo . . . abdidit* at 810, which corresponds to Arruns' flight from the scene. *omnis* in that case includes Camilla's *comites*; he flees before they all run up to help her, as well as before they can try to avenge her (cf. 809 *prius quam tela inimica sequantur*). V. would have had in mind the gathering crowd at *Il.* 15.588, quoted at 809–13n.

806–7 exterritus Arruns | laetitia mixtoque metu: *exterritus* is here used of strong emotion that includes but is not confined to terror, 'stunned', 'overwhelmed'. Cf. 3.307–8 (Andromache on seeing A. approaching) *magnis exterrita monstris* | *deriguit*, Hor. *Ep.* 1.6.11 *improuisa species exterret utrumque*, with *TLL* v.2.2027.31–7. For the mix of fear and happiness, cf. 1.513–14 *percussus Achates* | *laetitiaque metuque*, 2.99–100 *mixtoque ingens exorta tumultu* | *laetitia.*

807 iam: for the elision, see 564n.

809–13 The wolf-priest Arruns is likened to a wolf that hides in agitated fear after a brazen killing. V. adapts the simile from *Il.* 15.586–8: the swift Antilochus, spotted by Hector as he, Antilochus, leapt to strip the fallen Melanippus, 'fled like a wild animal that has done some wrong – one that has killed a dog or herdsman beside his kine, and flees before a crowd of men gather' (ἔτρεσε θηρὶ κακὸν ῥέξαντι ἐοικώς, | ὅς τε κύνα κτείνας ἢ βουκόλον ἀμφὶ βόεσσι | φεύγει πρίν περ ὅμιλον ἀολλισθήμεναι ἀνδρῶν). A crucial change is that of Homer's θήρ, 'wild animal', to *lupus.* Wolf-similes are recurrent in *Aen.* (2.355–8, 9.59–64, 9.565–6). Elsewhere, they illustrate ferocity in battle, whereas here the comparison underscores Arruns' fear and cowardice. There is a further reference to the Hirpi and the cult of Apollo Soranus. Arruns had likened his killing of Camilla to eliminating a pestilence and, therefore, claimed the apotropaic role of wolf-priest. But now, after slaying her, he becomes a hunted wolf, like the creatures that fled to the cave after stealing sacrifices in the origin story of the Apollo cult (785n.). This implies what the simile itself indicates, that Arruns was a wrongdoer, despite his self-perception.

809 ille: deictic, anticipating the subject. The hyperbaton with *lupus* 'adds to the impression of immediacy: the reader registers details . . . and only gradually takes in the whole scene' (Tarrant on 12.5). For similar use of the pronoun with a postponed subject in a simile, cf. 10.707–8 *ac uelut ille* . . . | . . . *aper* and 12.5–6 *saucius ille* . . . | . . . *leo*; for the pattern in narrative, see Fordyce on 7.787 and Harrison on 10.707–8. Cf. 494n. **sequantur:** in classical Latin, the subjunctive and indicative are equally common in *priusquam*-clauses (*NLS* §227). V. has the subjunctive at 1.192, 1.472, and *G.* 3.468 and the indicative at 6.328 and *G.* 1.50.

810 auius abdidit altos: the dactylic rhythm, assonance, and correspondence of ictus and accent seem designed to suggest the speed with which the wolf (and, thus, Arruns) hid himself away. Cf. 638n., 746n., and 756n. The tense of *abdidit*, as of *subiecit* and *petiuit* at 813, is difficult to explain; the present is customary in epic similes. Page and C–N ad loc. suggest that *abdidit* is a perfect of instantaneous result after *continuo*, to convey the speed with which the action was performed. This would seem to demand at 813 the same uses of the tense, in theme and variation with *in montis sese auius abdidit altos* (i.e. the wolf immediately hides his tail beneath his belly and seeks the woods). Page also proposes a gnomic perfect for *abdidit*, as did Heyne ad loc.; but the simile is dealing with a particular action, not in general truths about wolves. Homer sometimes uses the aorist in similes, including in a wolf-simile at *Il.* 16.352 (ἐπέχραον) and 16.354 (διέτμαγεν).

811 occiso pastore: cf. *Il.* 15.587 κτείνας . . . βουκόλον. For *occiso*, see 193n. **magnoue iuuenco:** V. adapts Homer's κύων; the large bullock is powerful and formidable (cf. *G.* 2.237 *ualidis . . . iuuencis*, 3.50 *fortis . . . iuuencos*), like the corresponding Camilla.

812 conscius audacis facti: V. ascribes to the wolf a motivation for fleeing into the woods, which is only implicit in Homer; he is aware that he has committed an act of rash boldness (though he feels no guilt over it). This further psychologises the corresponding Arruns after 806–7. While the deed is not *malum* to answer κακὸν at *Il.* 15.586, *audax* gives it negative colouring (*OLD* 2). Statius imitates at *Theb.* 4.368 (a wolf) *magnique fugit non inscius ausi.* **remulcens** 'curling down' (*OLD* 1b).

813 pauitantem: transferred, for *pauitans lupus.*

814 ex oculis se . . . abstulit: cf. 4.389 *seque ex oculis auertit et aufert.* **turbidus** 'frantic, disordered in mind or judgement' (*OLD* 5).

815 contentusque fuga 'satisfied with flight'. This fits exactly with Arruns' prayer at 790–1; he is content with escaping and seeks no plunder. Cf. 582 *sola contenta Diana*, 5.314 *galea contentus*, 7.736–7 *patriis sed* *non et filius aruis* | *contentus.* Other commentators, including Page and Fratantuono ad loc., understand *contentus* from *contendo* and render 'in eager/strained flight'. Ovid appears to imitate at *Met.* 5.169 *contentusque fuga est,* on Perseus, content with the flight of his wounded adversary Molpeus. **mediis se immiscuit armis:** cf. *Il.* 16.813 μίκτο δ' ὁμίλῳ; another echo linking Arruns, via the wolf, to Euphorbus (see 806–8n.). *se immiscuit armis* also occurs at line-end at *G.* 4.245 *asper crabro imparibus se immiscuit armis,* although there it describes hornets joining battle with bees, not shrinking from it like Arruns; cf. 10.796 (Lausus joins the fray) *seseque immiscuit armis.* See 278n. on the elision of *se.*

816 trahit 'pulls at', with *manu* emphasising the effort Camilla makes.

817 ferreus . . . mucro 'iron point'. **stat:** of a weapon, 'sticks/holds fast' (*OLD* 6).

818–19 Cf. 3.308–9 (Andromache) *calor ossa reliquit,* | *labitur.*

818 labitur . . . labuntur: anaphora for pathos. *labitur* describes Camilla slipping from her mount; she falls from it at 828. **frigida:** the cold of death, as at 828. A bold variation on how the body grows cold in death. The adj. can be understood to do double duty and to function also as a transferred epithet with *leto.*

819 purpureus: used of the glow and vitality of youth, as at 1.590–1 *lumenque iuuentae* | *purpureum,* which has faded as Camilla nears death; it is in contrast to *exsanguis* in the previous line. The adj. recalls the flower-simile for the death of Euryalus at 9.435–6 *purpureus ueluti cum flos succisus aratro* | *languescit moriens* and, by extension, the corresponding flower-simile for the death of Pallas at 68–71; cf. the *uiola* there, a purple flower (Edgeworth 1992: 28). (On the *hyacinthus* in the simile, see 69n.) After 803–4, a suggestive echo of passages that equate death with the loss of virginity. **quondam:** with *purpureus,* 'once radiant'. A pathetic use of the adv., as at 72 and 105; in reality, of course, Camilla's face was very recently radiant.

820 exspirans 'breathing her last'. **Accam:** not a name among Camilla's *lectae comites* at 655–6. It is tempting to identify her with Larina, which would support her association with Acca Larentia/Larentina (see 655n.). V. seems also to choose the name in order to recall Anna, the sister of Dido (see 822n., 823n.).

821–2 fida . . . | . . . curas 'who, faithful before others to Camilla, was the only one with whom she [Camilla] was accustomed to share her cares'. Sc. *erat* in the rel. clause introduced by *quae*; *quicum* is then a second rel.

clause within the first. *quicum* is an archaic abl., of all genders (cf. Catul. 2.2 *quicum ludere*); its antecedent is (Acca) *sola. partiri* is a historic infinitive of repeated or customary action; cf. 2.98–9, 4.422 (with Austin's n.), 7.15, *G.* 1.199–200. Only here in V. is a historic infinitive in a relative clause; such infs. in subordinate clauses are generally rare (A–G §463).

822 quicum partiri curas: the role of confidant links Acca and Dido's Anna. Statius imitates at *Theb.* 8.279–81 (Thiodamas) *quicum ipse arcana deorum | partiri et uisas uni sociare solebat | Amphiaraus aues.*

823–7 Camilla's final speech is brief and simple. She shows poignant pride and a soldier's stoicism in the face of death, and her last thoughts are not for herself, but for what needs to be done in the battle. Camilla thinks that her death, as commander and leading warrior, will turn the tide of the cavalry battle in favour of the Trojans (and she is correct in this; see 834–5, 868–90), and she concludes that Turnus' leadership and more troops are needed to try to stem this. But hers is the wrong advice. Like Turnus, Camilla does not see that his proper move was to remain in ambush, and that this was his last, best chance for victory.

823 hactenus 'up to this point in time' (and no more). **Acca soror:** *soror* can be used of unrelated female friends (Dickey 2002: 125); here it indicates a close bond. Cf. 4.9 *Anna soror.* **potui:** better understood as a reference to Camilla's ability to fight (i.e. this is as far as her success in battle goes, but now she can do no more), rather than to her ability to bear her wound; the former is more suitably grand and heroic. So Tib. ad loc.: *a commemoratione superioris temporis quo potens in certaminibus et nobilis fuit transit ad praesentem casum quo urgebatur in finem.* Cf. Dido's valedictory words at 4.653 *uixi et quem dederat cursum Fortuna peregi.* **acerbum:** of premature death, as at 28 and 587.

824 conficit 'subdues', in the sense of finishing off an enemy (*OLD* 16b). Sc. *me.* **nigrescunt:** black, the colour of death, closes all around. The verb also occurs at 4.454, its first appearance in extant literature. **circum:** adverbial; V., however, often likes the word at line-end as a preposition in anastrophe with an immediately preceding dactylic neuter plural that it governs (Pease on 4.145).

825 mandata nouissima: *mandata* need not be sent to a subordinate; cf. 176 and 7.267. Still, a final glimpse of Camilla's self-assurance vis-à-vis Turnus; with her dying words, she issues orders to him, and she thereby demonstrates the same direct, confident forcefulness that she did when approaching him at 502–6. With *nouissima,* 'last', cf. 4.650 (Dido speaks for the last time before her suicide) *dixitque nouissima uerba.* The language also hints at the use of *mandata* for one's dying words/wishes; on this use of the word, see Cairns 1972: 90, Courtney 209.

826 The spondaic rhythm seems to reflect both the gravity of the command and Camilla's laboured effort to speak. **succedat pugnae:** *succedo* is commonly used of military replacement or relief (*OLD* 4). For the phrasing, cf. 10.689–90 *Mezentius ardens* | *succedit pugnae.* The subjunctive (like *arceat*) is in indirect command after *mandata* in the previous line.

827 iamque uale: the speech concludes within the line, lending special emphasis to Camilla's last words for dramatic and pathetic effect (see 98n.). V. restricts *iamque uale* to farewells from the dead and dying; cf. 2.789 (the ghost Creusa to A.), 5.738 (the ghost Anchises to A.), and *G.* 4.497 (Eurydice to Orpheus). **simul:** preposition; with *his dictis* also at 5.357.

827–8 simul . . . | . . . fluens: cf. M. Furius Bibaculus (fr. 8 Courtney) *ille graui subito deuinctus uulnere habenas* | *misit equi lapsusque in humum defluxit.* Camilla entered at 499–500 by dismounting (501 *defluxit*) from her horse when calling on Turnus to send her to face the enemy cavalry; she now departs by slipping slowly from her horse in death. With *simul his dictis,* the imperfect in *linquebat* conveys that Camilla gradually dropped the reins while speaking to Acca.

828 non sponte indicates Camilla's lack of agency as, in the throes of death, she slips from the horse.

829 exsoluit se corpore: cf. 4.703 (Iris to the dead Dido) *teque isto corpore soluo.*

829–30 lentaque colla | . . . caput: cf. 9.436–7 *lassoque papauera collo* | *demisere caput,* with 819n.

830 captum 'overcome', with *leto* an abl. of means; see *TLL* III.340.21–2. **relinquens:** preferable to *relinquunt,* which Conte and Horsfall print, even though *relinquunt* is the *lectio difficilior.* There seems to be an echo of *linquebat habenas* at 827; the dying Camilla first drops the reins and then, at the moment she dies, leaves behind her arms. *linquebat* and *relinquens,* with Camilla as the subject, thus provide a frame for 827–30. Cf. 6.444 *curae non ipsa in morte relinquunt;* but *arma relinquunt* does not make the sense that *curae non . . . relinquunt* does. For discussion of the textual problem, see Courtney 1981: 25–6 and Timpanaro 2001: 73–5. The reference to arms as the death scene draws to a close underlines Camilla's identity as a warrior; appropriately and poignantly for this *bellatrix*, they are the last thing she leaves before her life departs. Cf. Grat. 125 (on the bow and arrow, associated with Diana, as hunting weapons) *ne tela relinquite diuae*, with Kayachev 2018: 125.

831 Cf. 12.952, and see 794–835n. The Homeric source is *Il.* 16.856–7 (the death of Patroclus) = 22.362–3 (the death of Hector) 'and his soul taking flight from his limbs was gone to Hades, lamenting its fate, leaving manhood and youth' (ψυχὴ δ' ἐκ ῥεθέων πταμένη Ἄϊδόσδε βεβήκει, | ὃν πότμον γοόωσα, λιποῦσ' ἀνδροτῆτα καὶ ἥβην). V.'s repetition of the line parallels that in Homer (although in V. the second death is of course not in retribution for the first, as it is in the *Iliad*). **indignata:** Camilla's soul protests its fate; comparison with Homer's ὃν πότμον γοόωσα, λιποῦσ' ἀνδροτῆτα καὶ ἥβην, just quoted, implies the complaint that she has died young (so Serv. ad loc. *seruat hoc ubique, ut iuuenum animas a corporibus dicat cum dolore discedere, quod adhuc esse superstites poterant*, ad 12.952 *'indignata' . . . uel quia, ut supra . . . de Camilla, discedebat a iuuene*). Traina on 12.952 compares *indigne* in funerary epigraphic texts, on those who die before their time; cf. Catul. 101.6 *heu miser indigne frater adempte mihi*, Plin. *Ep.* 6.6.7 *illum immatura morte indignissime raptum.*

832 tum uero: see 633n.

832–3 ferit aurea clamor | sidera: also at 2.488, where the night-time stars shine serenely over the devastation of Troy. It is less integrated here, since it is not yet night, although it creates a similar contrast to that at 2.488 between 'the patines of bright gold in the serene heaven and the horror upon earth' (Austin on 2.488). The bright stars also contrast with the darkness of death and the *umbrae* in the previous line. Perhaps, too, a bitterly ironic allusion to the golden spoils coveted by Camilla, which led to her doom.

833 deiecta: in effective contrast with *surgens . . . clamor* in the previous line. **crudescit** 'grows bloodier'; cf. 7.788 *effuso crudescunt sanguine pugnae.* Cf. Stat. *Theb.* 9.670–1 *pugna ereptis maior crudescit utrimque | regibus*, Corippus, *In laudem Iustini minoris* 4.885 *fracto crudescit pugna tumultu.*

834–5 With the death of Camilla, the battle decisively turns, and the Trojans and their allies rush forward as a unified, overwhelming force (Intro. pp. 28–9).

834 densi simul: the repetition of the syllable *si* (which is then reversed, at word-end, in *omnis*) conveys excitement and is perhaps designed to represent iconically the packed ranks marching together (Dainotti 2015: 78 n. 254). Cf. 453(n.) *arma manu. densi* = Gk πυκνοί. Cf. 12.280–1 *densi rursus inundant* | *Troes Agyllinique et pictis Arcades armis.*

835 Euandrique Arcades alae: also at line-end at 12.551 *Tuscorum phalanx Euandrique Arcades alae.*

836–67 THE DEATH OF ARRUNS

Opis avenges the death of Camilla, as Diana had commanded (590–2), with deep compassion for the fallen. The passage creates with Diana's speech at 532–96 a frame for the story of Camilla; it brings closure to the account of her in battle, but also emphasises the divine concern for her.

Opis assures Camilla of wide fame as a favourite of Diana. Camilla's renown creates a sharp contrast with her killer Arruns, who is forgotten and abandoned at the moment of death. V. continues to paint Arruns as a contemptible figure, and totally unequal to his victim; the contrast between Camilla's divinely promoted fame and his oblivion indicates how beneath her he is.

Arruns has points of comparison with A. (listed by Alessio 1993: 144–5, who, however, overstates matters and fails to account for narrative context). But the two are hardly parallel figures; whatever the ambiguities in V.'s treatment of A., he is of course not the furtive, cowardly, and odious figure that Arruns is. Plausibly V. sought to contrast the killers of Camilla and of Turnus: she is brought down by the unworthy Arruns, while Turnus dies at the hand of a hero who possesses superior strength and enjoys greater divine favour.

836 Triuiae: see 566n. **custos:** in the sense of *speculatrix* (Barchiesi, *EV* 1.967); Opis is Diana's sentinel, observing the activities on the battlefield and looking out for Camilla's death. Cf. 4.186–7 (*Fama*) *luce sedet custos aut summi culmine tecti* | *turribus aut altis.* **iamdudum** 'for a long while', i.e. since Opis received her command from Diana at 587–94.

837 interrita: used of Camilla at 711, although Opis is unshaken for a different reason: she is beyond the dangers of battle as an immortal who observes the fighting from a great and faraway height. *exterritus Arruns* at 806 contrasts with both Camilla and Opis.

838 procul medio: significant juxtaposition, underscoring the distance between the divine realm and the welter of mortal battle. **iuuenum in clamore furentum:** *furentum* is used of battle-rage. Cf. 12.409–10 *clamor* | *bellantum iuuenum.*

839 prospexit: Opis spots Camilla dead on the battlefield, which indicates that Diana has not yet removed her body from the fray and delivered it home. This is consistent with 593–4, where Diana states that she will take the body away after Opis avenges Camilla's death; hence that act of divine concern is still coming. **tristi . . . morte:** cf. 534 *tristis Latonia* and 589 *tristis . . . pugna.* As the following lines indicate, *tristi* is focalised through Opis, who shares Diana's perspective on Camilla's death. **multatam** 'punished', the preferable reading to *mulcatam* ('beaten, defeated'). The verb fits well with *luisti* at 841, since both refer to punishment. The combination of *multo* and instrumental *morte* is attested elsewhere (Cic. *Scaur.* 3 *qui se ipse morte multauit, Orat.* 1.194 *uitia . . . hominum . . . morte multantur,* Apul. *Met.* 3.26 *morte multata Photide*). Camilla is punished for her attempt to challenge the Trojans in war (see 842).

840 imo pectore: see 377n.

841–9 Opis' speech (along with the close of Diana's story at 586–94) strongly influences V. Fl. 6.497–502 (Hecate laments that Medea will be led away from her, states that she will not abandon her, and promises vengeance on Jason).

841 heu nimium . . . nimium: *heu nimium* is not found before V.; it occurs also at 4.657 and 6.189. V. has the interjection *heu* thirty-four times in *Aen.*, against five times in *G.* and six times in *Ecl.* (twice as double *heu heu,* in imitation of Theoc. 4.26 φεῦ φεῦ). Conversely, he has *a* nine times in *Ecl.*, twice in *G.* (including *a nimium* at 2.252, an idiom at least as old as Plautus), and never in *Aen.* exclamatory *a* was colloquial, but was taken up by Catullus and the Neoterics (Ross 1969: 51–3). Repeated *nimium* is emotional; cf. ps.-V. *Cir.* 161 *heu nimium certo, nimium.* Cf., too, Stat. *Silv.* 5.5.59 *o nimium felix, nimium crudelis,* which combines imitation of this line and of *Aen.* 4.657 (Dido's dying words) *felix, heu nimium felix.* Opis recognises that Camilla paid the price for taking up arms against the Trojans, but views her punishment with sympathy; she does not doubt that Camilla's actions were misguided, but does lament the cruelty of the penalty. **crudele** echoes (*bellum*) *crudele* at 535. Perhaps also a nod to *Aen.* 4.661 (the dying Dido of A.) *crudelis,* given the presence of *heu nimium* here and at 4.657.

842 Teucros conata lacessere bello: also at 585. Opis again (after *crudele* in the previous line) recalls Diana's speech on Camilla. The repetitions characterise Opis as a faithful adherent echoing her revered mistress and affirming her words (Moskalew 1982: 110).

843 desertae in dumis . . . Dianam: emotional alliteration. *desertae* = 'alone, solitary'. A neutral reference to Camilla's life in the woods, although *desertus* usually has a negative colouring when applied to people ('left alone, lonely, forsaken'; see *OLD* 2, and cf. 2.562, 2.572, 4.330, 4.677). The meaning 'abandoned/forsaken' (by Diana)', entertained by C–N and Fratantuono ad loc., can be rejected: Diana of course never abandoned Camilla, but rather lamented that Camilla had left her service to go to war. The notion of abandonment also clashes with 845 *non . . . regina reliquit.*

844 profuit: cf. *Il.* 5.53–4, on the great hunter Scamandrius, taught to hunt by Artemis, and cut down in battle by Menelaus: 'but in no way did the archer Artemis give protection now, nor did his skill in archery, in which before he excelled' (ἀλλ' οὔ οἱ τότε γε χραῖσμ' Ἄρτεμις ἰοχέαιρα, | οὐδὲ ἑκηβολίαι, ᾗσιν τὸ πρίν γ' ἐκέκαστο). **nostras umero gessisse pharetras:** cf. 536 *nostris . . . armis,* with 652n.

845 tua te regina reliquit: further marked alliteration, to convey emotion and perhaps to underscore the connection between Diana and Camilla. The juxtaposition of *tua* and *te* is likewise expressive of a close bond; cf. 9.486–7 *nec te tua funere mater | produxi* and 12.872 *te tua, Turne, potest germana iuuare.* For *relinquo* meaning 'leave (in a particular condition)' with a predicate adj. (*indecorem*), see *OLD* 6b.

846 extrema iam in morte: also at 2.447. Cf. Catul. 76.18 *extremam iam ipsa in morte*; like Catullus, V. elides the monosyllable *iam.*

846–7 neque . . . | . . . erit: the suggestion is that Diana will convey Camilla home and to a commemorating burial mound (cf. 594), which will preserve her *nomen.* Her fame, however, will extend beyond her homeland and through the nations; Camilla's *tumulus* is only one of the things that will perpetuate her name, and Diana will spread her renown wider in a sign of her great favour. Camilla's repute will be more extensive than that of her model, Sarpedon (see 532–96n., 593–4n., 594n.), who will be celebrated in his home of Lycia (*Il.* 16.673–5).

847 famam patieris inultae '(nor) will you endure the ignominy of one unavenged'. Cf. 590 *ultricem . . . sagittam.*

848 Cf. 591, with Diana's *uiola(ue)rit* in that line necessarily changed to *uiolauit.*

849 morte luet merita: the speech ends mid-line, for dramatic and pathetic effect. **fuit** introduces a geographical ecphrasis, like *est* at 522.

850 regis Dercenni: this king of Laurentum is entirely obscure to us; see Guaitoli, *EV* II.27 for discussion. Dercennus is one of 'several names of legendary figures in *Aen.* . . . [that] appear to belong not to ingenious fantasy but to some older stratum of tradition of which V. knew little – and we nothing' (Horsfall ad loc.). **terreno ex aggere bustum:** the commemorative *bustum*, ominous for Arruns, anticipates the gravesite of Camilla, suggested by Opis' statement that her death will not be *sine nomine*, and contrasts with the abandonment of Arruns' body at 865–6. Cf. Catul. 64.363 *excelso coaceruatum aggere bustum.*

851 opacaque ilice recalls the Roman custom of planting trees around tombs; cf. Petr. 71.7 *omne genus enim uolo sint circa cinerum mearum et uinearum largiter*, Mart. 1.88.5 *faciles buxos et opacas palmitis umbras.* The darkness of the ilex (i.e. of its leaves) makes it suitable for the setting. The ilex is used for pyres at 4.505 and 6.180. *opaca ilice* also occurs at 6.208–9.

852 rapido . . . nisu 'with swift advance'. **pulcherrima:** the superlative is not merely ornamental, but creates an effective visual contrast between Opis and the shadowy burial-spot (Fratantuono ad loc.).

853 sistit: with *se* in the previous line, 'comes to a stop', 'halts', with a possible military undercurrent suggesting the stationing of a soldier (*OLD* 4). **speculatur:** of watching from a distance and looking for an object (*OLD* 3); Opis then locates Arruns in the next line. The verb seems to have a military tone (Horsfall on 7.477, Harrison on 10.290); V. is the first to use it in high poetry.

854 fulgentem armis: MS authority is strong for this reading over *laetantem animis*, which Conte prints. While *laetantem animis* corresponds nicely in meaning with *uana tumentem*, such balance between the two participial phrases is no sure goal. With *fulgentem armis*, V. indicates how Opis spotted Arruns. The phrase also recalls 769 *fulgebat in armis*, perhaps meaningfully: Arruns, for whom Opis looks so that she might avenge Camilla, resembles Chloreus, whom Camilla sought when Arruns killed her. **uana tumentem** 'groundlessly swelling with pride'. Cf. DServ. ad loc. *plenum falsae gloriae, quam Graeci* κενοδοξίαν *dicunt. uana* is an internal acc. The description of Arruns is focalised through Opis; she sees the detested enemy as a man puffed up with empty pride. But there is no reason to doubt that Opis' perception matches reality; the ugly Arruns combines cravenness when stealthily pursuing Camilla and after killing her with, now, vain conceit.

855 Cf. 5.162 *quo tantum mihi dexter abis? huc derige gressum* (although Conte prints *cursum* for *gressum*) and 5.166 *quo diuersus abis? derige gressum* also occurs at 1.401. **diuersus** 'in another direction'.

856–7 huc . . . | praemia: cf. *Il.* 20.429 (Achilles to Hector) 'come near, so that you may sooner arrive at the coming of destruction' (ἆσσον ἴθ', ὥς κεν θᾶσσον ὀλέθρου πείραθ' ἵκηαι).

856 periture expresses purpose, 'to die'; cf. 2.675 *si periturus abis.* A simple voc., as the addressee of the imperative; Fordyce on 7.425 and Görler, *EV* II.265 wrongly include it among the instances where a predicative adj. or participle normally agreeing with the subject in the nom. is attracted into agreement with a voc.

856–7 digna Camillae | praemia 'a reward due Camilla'. *Camillae* is gen. with *digna,* a Grecism in use from the first century BCE (H–S 79).

857 tune . . . Dianae? deeply acerbic and disdainful; Opis feels that Arruns is unworthy of dying by Diana's weapons. Cf. Stat. *Theb.* 10.910 (a contemptuous Jupiter to Capaneus) *tune etiam feriendus?*

858–62 A close description of Opis preparing to shoot, modelled on *Il.* 4.116–26, where Pandarus readies his bow and launches an arrow at Menelaus. Pandarus is similar to Arruns in that he prays to Apollo, called the 'wolf-born god' (Ἀπόλλωνι Λυκηγενέϊ, 4.119); like Arruns, too, he refers in his prayer to his return home to his native land (the city of Zeleia, 4.120–1). V. thus takes as his model for Opis, who prepares to kill Arruns, a Homeric character that resembles Arruns.

858 aurata: with *pharetra* at 859 in hyperbaton. The quiver is Diana's (see 590); as a divine weapon, it is appropriately golden (see 652n.). **Threissa:** V. places Opis in Thrace perhaps as a reference to Hyperborean Oupis (532n.) and to connect Opis with the Amazons as she avenges the Amazonian Camilla. Cf. 1.315–16 *Threissa . . . | Harpalyce.*

859 deprompsit pharetra: see 590n. **infensa:** adverbial. The adverbial use is common in connection with hostile, aggressive troops (*OLD* 1); here it implies that Opis is like a soldier on the attack. Cf. 5.587 *spicula uertunt infensi.*

860 et duxit longe 'and she drew (the bow) far'. **curuata coirent:** cf. *Il.* 4.124 '(Pandarus) drew the great bow into a semi-circle' (αὐτὰρ ἐπεὶ δὴ κυκλοτερὲς μέγα τόξον ἔτεινε). *coirent* is subjunctive with *donec* to indicate intention (A–G §552 n. 1, *NLS* §224).

861 capita: the ends or tips of the bow. **manibus . . . aequis:** i.e. Opis' left hand was stretched out as far as her right hand was drawn back.

862 '[until she touched] the steel's point with her left hand and her breast with her right and the bow-string'. Cf. *Il.* 4.123 '(Pandarus) brought the string to his breast and the iron arrowhead to the bow' (νευρὴν μὲν μαζῷ πέλασεν, τόξῳ δε σίδηρον). **laeua:** the elision of long *a* before short *a* is extremely unusual in V.; the only other probable instance is at 1.642 *antiqua ab origine gentis*, although some MSS have *antiquae*. See Gransden ad loc., Winbolt 1903: 168. **papillam:** Horsfall ad loc. notes that Opis employs the 'Cretan' draw, as against the 'Scythian' (to the shoulder). But V. is not interested in technique as such. Rather, he recalls 803; a shot from Opis' breast will avenge the shot to Camilla's breast. Details in the next three lines further link Arruns' killing of Camilla and his death; these underscore that the latter is punishment for the former. *papillam* also calls to mind the Amazons.

863 teli . . . sonantis: cf. 801–2 *aurae* | *nec sonitus . . . teli.*

864 una . . . haesitque: *una* with *-que* indicates that the two actions took place at the same time: the moment Arruns heard the arrow, he was struck by it. *haesitque* echoes *haesit* at 804. Although Arruns hears the arrow shot at him while Camilla did not hear Arruns' spear, he is as defenceless against it as Camilla was against his weapon, and he is surely as shocked, because of the simultaneity of sound and shot, as she was when struck.

865 illum exspirantem: cf. *exspirans* at 820. **socii** sets up the expectation that Arruns' comrades will tend to him as Camilla's *comites* had tended to her after his spear-shot (805–6); this adds point when things turn out very differently. **extrema gementem:** cf. *multa gemens* at 4.395, 5.869, 12.886, and *G.* 3.226. The image is in sharp contrast with what follows: Arruns is ignored and abandoned when he might have elicited sympathy and care as he groans his last.

866 Variation on the 'death in an unknown land' motif in epic, on which see Harrison on 10.705–6; for the motif in Homer, see Griffin 1980: 106–12. A reversal, too, of epic scenes in which comrades in battle fight to keep a fallen fighter's corpse (e.g. *Il.* 18.155–64). **obliti:** Arruns is very newly dead but already forgotten. This mocks his willingness to forgo glory in his prayer to Apollo (790–2): he is consigned to oblivion and, thus, to an anonymity far beyond what he (disingenuously) welcomed for killing Camilla, and he has no hope of future heroic *laus*. Arruns' fate lies in pointed contrast with Camilla's wide posthumous *nomen* (846–7). **ignoto . . . in puluere:** cf. *ignota . . . harena* at 5.871 *nudus in ignota, Palinure, iacebis harena* and *terra ignota* at 9.485 *terra ignota canibus data praeda Latinis.* **linquuunt:** used of abandoning bodies without burial, as at 10.559 *alitibus linquere feris.* Cf. Hor. *Carm.* 1.28.33 (the ghost of a shipwrecked man) *precibus non linquar inultis,* with N–H's note. It is a natural assumption that Arruns was left to birds of prey or to dogs, 'the standard epic (and tragic) indignity for the unburied corpse' (Hardie on 9.485–6; cf *Il.* 1.4–5, Catul. 64.152–3).

867 aetherium . . . Olympum: the adj.–noun pair is also found at 6.579, 8.319, and 10.621. The adj. is predominantly poetic (*TLL* I.1152.68–1154.23). **pinnis aufertur:** cf. 3.258 (Celaeno) *pinnis ablata,* another rounding-off line.

868–95 THE ROUT OF THE ITALIAN FORCES

The death of Camilla brings sudden panicked upheaval among the troops, beginning with the Volscians and then spreading among the Italian forces, who flee from the battle and make for the city, seeking refuge. Homeric precedents for soliders' flight after the death of a leader appear at *Il.* 11.744–6 and 16.290–2. There is also a parallel at Quintus of Smyrna 1.630–2, on the reaction to the death of the Amazon Penthesilea: 'When the Trojans saw her struck down in battle, in full force they trembled with fear and rushed to the city, endlessly pained in spirit with great grief' (Τρῶες δ' ὡς ἐσίδοντο δαϊκταμένην ἐνὶ χάρμῃ, | πανσυδίῃ τρομέοντες ἐπὶ πτόλιν ἐσσεύοντο | ἄσπετ' ἀκηχέμενοι μεγάλῳ περὶ πένθει θυμόν). It is tempting to suppose that Quintus adapted V. on the Amazonian Camilla when dealing with the Amazon queen; but the question of how much, and even whether, Quintus imitated V. remains unsettled (despite e.g. Gärtner 2005, James 2007, and Fratantuono 2016). See 892n., 895n. Cf. Dares Phrygius 36 (the Trojan response after Neoptolemus (*sic*) kills Penthesilea) *eo facto totum exercitum Troianorum in urbem fugat.* For historiographical accounts of soldiers' flight after the death of a commander, see Liv. 4.19.5, 24.7.7, 26.6.5, and 30.18.13.

For the flight of the Italian army to the city, cf. *Il.* 21.537–43 and 21.606–11, where the fleeing Trojans enter their city whose gates have been left open. The Italian soldiers initially find open gates, but then have the *portae* closed to them; the fear is that the Trojans will also enter the city. This leads to hideous slaughter, which V. describes in pathetic detail (see 884–6, 887). The scene compares with passages in Livy (5.13.13, 5.25.14–16, 44.28.13) on fleeing armies killed before closed gates. Cf., too, *Aen.* 9.723–30, where Pandarus closes the gate to the Trojan camp, leaving many Trojans outside, but does not see that Turnus has got in.

At the end of the scene, women take up arms to defend the city, inspired by Camilla (891–5). This is a final moment in the book where V. blurs gender roles and places women in the male theatre of combat. Camilla's challenge to gender norms does not end with her death but continues on after it in how she motivates the Latin mothers to defend their city.

868–9 fugit . . . | . . . fugiunt . . . fugit: for the shift between singular and plural in examples of triple repetition, cf. 12.826–7 *sit . . . sint . . . | sit, Ecl.* 10.19–20 *uenit . . . uenere . . . | . . . uenit, G.* 1.77–8 *urit . . . urit . . . | urunt.* The repetition highlights how widely and quickly the rout spread after Camilla's forces took flight.

869 turbati conveys disorder and confusion, and signals the outbreak of flight; see 618n. **acer Atinas:** also at line-end at 12.661, where Atinas and Messapus alone hold out before the gates of Latinus' city against the Trojans. Atinas is not otherwise found in *Aen.*; he is probably to be connected with the Volscian town Atina, mentioned at 7.630. *acer* is not simply conventional (see 518n.), but rather is in significant juxtaposition with *fugit,* to suggest how total the rout is: even a fierce, vehement warrior has taken flight.

870 A four-word line (see 700n.), for weight and gravity, and with alliteration for dramatic, emotional effect. **desolatique manipli:** V. turns from commanders to common (cavalry) soldiers, who are abandoned by their fleeing leaders; cf. Stat. *Theb.* 9.672–3 *desolatumque magistro | agmen.* For *manip(u)lus* used of cavalry units rather than infantry, see *TLL* VIII.318.6–7.

871 auersi: used in a reflexive sense (*OLD* 1b), 'having turned themselves/wheeled'.

873 sustentare 'to hold back', 'to check'. Cf. 12.662 *sustentant acies* (where one of the subjects is *acer Atinas*). **sistere contra** 'stand firm in opposition'.

874 laxos . . . arcus: the slack bows reiterate what the previous two lines have shown: Italian forces have given up the fight against the Trojans. Cf. Hor. *Carm.* 3.8.23–4 *iam Scythae laxo meditantur arcu | cedere campis,*

Antip. Thess. *Anth. Pal.* 9.297.3 'bows broken in fear' (φόβῳ κεχαλασμένα τόξα). **umeris languentibus** 'on drooping shoulders'.

875 Onomatopoetic; the alliteration and predominant dactyls convey the sound and rush of the galloping horses. The rhythm contrasts with the spondees at 872; the Trojan side bears down heavily, and the Italian side takes rapid flight. **quadrupedumque:** see 714n. **cursu:** recurrent in alliterative combinations; cf. 879, 3.200, 4.154, 5.291, 9.91, 12.751, 12.902, and *G.* 3.132. The running horses shake the ground; cf. 8.596 *quadrupedente putrem sonitu quatit ungula campum*, Lucr. 2.330 (*equites*) *ualido quatientes impete campos.* **quatit ungula campum** varies Ennian phrasing; cf. *Ann.* 242, 263 (quoted at 513n.), 431 Sk. *concutit ungula terram.*

876–7 caligine turbidus atra | puluis 'a swirling black cloud of dust'. Cf. 9.36 (the Trojan Caicus on the advancing enemy army) *quis globus, o ciues, caligine uoluitur atra? atra* has customary strong emotional force and indicates that the cloud is not just dark but 'dreadful', 'ominous'.

877 e speculis . . . matres: cf. 4.586 *regina e speculis*, 7.511 *saeua e speculis tempus dea nacta nocendi.* The watchtowers are on the walls; V. describes dust rolling to the *muri* followed by the response of the women who stand upon them. The line is strikingly Christianised by the fourth-century poet Juvencus, who echoes it twice when describing the mothers who watched over the tomb of Jesus (4.714 *e speculis matres miracula tanta tuentur*, 4.726 *e speculis seruant matres et cuncta tuentur*). **percussae pectora:** emotional alliteration, picking up on *puluis* (and the *p*-sound in *speculis*). Alliteration continues in the next two lines. For the phrase, cf. 4.589 *pectus percussa decorum*, 7.503 *percussa lacertos. pectora* is a retained acc. with the middle participle.

878 femineum: cf. *femineo* at 782. Camilla was a masculine fighter who succumbed to a feminine emotion; the *matres* lament in a woman-like manner but will later (891–6) battle like soldiers, inspired by Camilla. **clamorem . . . tollunt:** cf. 37(n.).

879 cursu 'at rushing speed'. Cf. 2.321 *cursuque amens ad limina tendit.* **primi inrupere:** *primi* = the first of the Italian forces. The verb is often used of meeting military objectives by forcing a way into a place (*OLD* 1b), as at 9.683 *inrumpunt aditus Rutuli*, 9.729 (Turnus) *inrumpentem.* Here the situation is quite the opposite; the defeated troops rush suddenly (*OLD* 1c) into the city in an attempt to take refuge, having been overcome in battle. Elision in *primi inrupere* underscores the forceful rapidity of the action. The fast movement depicted in the narrative contrasts with the spondaic rhythm; the metre creates a heavy, baleful mood.

880 'hard on them the enemy host presses, their ranks mingled'.

881 miseram . . . mortem: cf. 10.829 *miseram solabere mortem.* V. likes to use the adj. to describe the dead, the act of dying, the grieving, and the circumstances surrounding death (63, 119, 156, 182, 203, 215, 885, 2.140, 2.215, 3.622, 4.697, 6.21, 8.488, 12.636, 12.646, 12.881); for the broader use of the adj. in the context of death, see *TLL* VIII.1103.81–1104.24. **limine in ipso:** strong drama and pathos, which continues through the next line: the soldiers are cut down while right on the verge of finding refuge in their city and houses. Cf. 9.687 *ipso portae posuere in limine uitam.*

882 inter: having arrived at the *moenia patria,* the soldiers stand 'among' their houses in the sense that they are in close proximity to them; *inter* exaggerates for emotional effect. The alternative reading *intra* would exaggerate too much. **tuta domorum:** the use of the neuter plural substantive adj. followed by a gen. is originally a Grecism (though fairly rare in Gk); is poetic since Ennius (*Ann.* 84 Sk. *infera noctis*); is something of a mannerism in Lucretius; and is common in Augustan poetry (Fordyce on 8.221) as well as in Sallust, Livy, and post-Augustan prose. Metrical convenience no doubt promoted the use of the construction in the hexameter. See, further, Austin on 3.332, Thomas on *G.* 4.159. V. has it repeatedly (Görler, *EV* II.265), including at 513 *ardua montis.* The gen. is partitive, although as the idiom develops, often the partitive sense either is faint or disappears altogether. Here the phrase = *tutas domos* (the neuter expresses the quality, like *ardua* at 513), not 'the safe part of the house'.

883 exspirant animas 'breathe out their (last) breath'. Cf. 820 and 865, with Serv. ad 1.96 *possumus autem uti hoc sermone, ut et per se plenus sit et recipiat adiectionem. ergo dicimus . . . et exspirat et animam exspirat.* **claudere:** a historic infinitive in excited narration, unusual in being used singly (see 142n.).

883–5 pars . . . | . . . | . . . orantis: cf. 9.725–6 (Pandarus) *multosque suorum | moenibus exclusos duro in certamine linquit.*

884 aperire uiam: a choice variation on the use of the phrase for opening a way by military force, as at 10.864 *aperit si nulla uiam uis*; cf. Sal. *Cat.* 58.7 *ferro iter aperiendum est,* Liv. 7.33.9 *nec posse aperire in hostes uiam,* Tac.

Ann. 2.21.1 *uiamque strage hostium aperiret.* Variation, too, on *aperio* used of making a breach in walls (*OLD* 2).

885 oriturque miserrima caedes: also at 2.411, where A. and his comrades, disguised as Greeks, are set upon by Trojans. An analogous situation here: in the desperate mayhem, men are killed by those on their side. Hence the superlative *miserrima*; the slaughter is 'most pitiable' because soldiers are killed by their own people in a kind of momentary Latin civil war (DServ. ad loc.).

886 defendentum . . . ruentum: a striking frame, showing vividly the two sides in the fight; the chiastic pattern and the polyptotonic *armis* . . . *arma* (cf. 293n.) further underline the sense of oppositional forces. The sound effect produced by paired participial *-um* endings continues in the following line with *lacrimantumque* . . . *parentum*; it adds to the gloom of the account.

887–9 exclusi . . . | pars . . . | . . . pars: cf. 12.277–8 *fratres* . . . | *pars* . . . *pars.*

887 ante oculos lacrimantumque ora parentum: the scene grows darker still; the deaths of the soldiers are 'exacerbated by the religious pollution of seeing one's own children die' (Harrison on 10.443 *cuperem ipse parens spectator adesset*; see also Sullivan 2009). Cf. 1.94–6 *o terque quaterque beati, | quis ante ora patrum Troiae sub moenibus altis | contigit oppetere*, 2.531–2 *ante oculos euasit et ora parentum | concidit ac multo uitam cum sanguine fudit*, 6.308 (= *G.* 4.477) *impositique rogis iuuenes ante ora parentum.* The parents who grieve over the deaths of their children recall Evander and the dead Pallas (cf. 150 *lacrimansque*). Cf., too, the suffering fathers at 454.

888–9 pars . . . | . . . pars: V. divides the crowd to depict diverse but simultaneous action. An approach to creating narrative vividness (*enargeia*) with parallels in historiography (see 468–97n.), where it is 'especially frequent in scenes of disorder and confusion' (Walsh 1961: 186).

888 praecipitis 'sheer', but also with a suggestion of *in praeceps*, describing the troops falling 'headlong' into the deep ditches.

889 immissis . . . frenis 'with loosened reins'. **caeca:** the soldiers are blind with panicked desperation. The adj. is pointed after *ante oculos* at 887.

890 Cf. Sil. 4.149 (an *ala*) *arietat in primos obicitque immania membra.* **arietat:** the verb is suggestive of a battering ram (*aries*). It scans as a dactyl, with consonantal *i*, like *ariete* at 2.492, 7.175, and 12.706; cf., too, *abiete* at

667. **duros obice postis** 'strongly barred doors', lit. 'doors strong with their barrier'. 'By a characteristic variation of the ordinary Latin usage in which an ablative noun and adjective are attached to another noun as a quasi-adverbial phrase, Virgil frequently attaches the adjective syntactically to the latter noun. This is one of his habitual innovations' (Mackail, App. A.4, p. 514). On the construction, see, too, Fordyce on 7.639.

891 summo certamine 'with utmost zeal'. Cf. 5.197 *olli certamine summo* (*procumbunt*). Servius ad loc. misunderstands the phrase to mean *in extremo discrimine*, comparing it to 476 *uocat labor ultimus omnis.* **matres:** cf. 475–6; the Latin women who mounted the walls as a last line of defence now join the fight that has come to the city.

892 monstrat: probably used intransitively and absolutely, 'shows (the way)' (*OLD* 6). Perhaps, however, with *conferre manum* implied, as at 9.44 *conferre manum pudor iraque monstrat*; this is retrospectively understood once 893–5 are read. **amor uerus patriae:** cf. 6.823 *uincet amor patriae. patriae* is juxtaposed with *matres* in the previous line: mothers overcome their feminine emotion (see 877–8) and, inspired by Camilla, become (masculine) warriors for the fatherland. **ut uidere Camillam:** not to be taken with the preceding parenthetical statement (Mynors and Horsfall extend the parenthesis to the end of the line). The women's patriotic zeal does not come and stir them just when they see Camilla; rather, their *amor patriae* is its own discrete force and motivation. Did the women literally see Camilla, or did they see her *exemplum uirtutis*, i.e. the example of her bravery in their minds' eyes, which inspired them to fight? V. implies that, from their high vantage point on the walls, the women saw Camilla lying dead, which drove them, in turn, to burn for death while fighting (see 895); and it is not necessarily inconsistent with *post* at 593 that the body remained on the battlefield immediately after Arruns was killed, when the soldiers were in flight, because of the temporal uncertainty of the preposition. From the sight of the dead Camilla, the mothers then drew an example of fighting courage and resolve. For thorough discussion of this matter, see Arrigoni 1982: 118–23. Cf. Quintus of Smyrna 1.403–46, where the Trojan Tisiphone is inspired upon seeing the Amazon Penthesilea in battle and stirs other women to join the fight. Another suggestive parallel between the Greek poet and V. (see 868–95n.).

893 tela manu . . . iaciunt: *manu* stresses the forceful effort behind the throw, as at 650, 676, and 799; cf. 10.264 *tela manu iaciunt*, 10.886 *tela manu iaciens.* Cf. Liv. 5.21.10 (women and slaves of Veii hurl rocks and tiles at Roman soldiers from roofs) *cum ex tectis saxa tegulaeque a mulieribus* *ac seruitiis iacerentur.* **trepidae** suggests a mix of fear and excitement (see 300n.): although afraid, the *matres* show an eagerness to fight.

893–4 robore duro | stipitibus 'with stakes made of hard oak'.

894 The women extemporise with hard billets and seared (and, thus, hardened) stakes, which imitate proper weapons. Cf. the improvised and rustic arms at 7.506–7 *hic torre armatus obusto, | stipites hic grauidi nodis,* 7.524 *stipitibus duris agitur sudibusue praeustis.* **sudibusque . . . obustis:** cf. Ov. *Met.* 12.299 *sude . . . obusta.*

895 primaeque . . . pro moenibus: *pro* is best understood as 'a forward position on/at the edge of' (*OLD* 1b) with *primae*, 'in the forefront'. Cf. Sal. *Jug.* 67.1 *mulieres puerique pro tectis aedificiorum saxa . . . certatim mittere.* V. suggests that the *matres*, in their zeal, long to stand up front upon the walls and to die there defending their city. Others (C–N, Horsfall) take *pro* to mean 'for (i.e. in defence of)'. Cf. Quintus of Smyrna 1.437–9 (the Trojan women, inflamed by Tisiphone) 'they eagerly stirred to go before the wall in arms, keen to aid their city and people' (ἐσσυμένως δὲ πρὸ τείχεος ὁρμαίνεσκον | βήμεναι ἐν τεύχεσσιν ἀρηγέμεναι μεμαυῖαι | ἄστεϊ καὶ λαοῖσιν). **mori . . . ardent:** *ardeo* takes the infinitive as a verb of wishing. The construction occurs repeatedly in V. (1.515, 1.581, 2.315–16, 4.281, and 8.163–4); it is found before him at Sal. *Jug.* 39.5 *persequi . . . mederi . . . ardebat,* and is rare after him (although Statius has it six times, presumably on V.'s model; *TLL* II.1.486.61–74).

896–915 TURNUS' RETURN TO ACTION

Acca makes her way to Turnus' concealed position and gives him the grim news about Camilla and the Trojan advance. Hearing this, Turnus immediately leaves the place of ambush to return to battle. V. does not report that Acca repeated Camilla's command at 826; it is a reasonable supposition that she did not need to do so, and that Turnus headed for battle immediately upon hearing of the Italian plight – an act in accordance with Jupiter's will (see 901). Turnus' move is self-defeating. He acts too quickly, without suitable strategic judgement, and this causes him to lose by the narrowest margin a great and final opportunity for military victory by surprising and routing A. and the Trojans (so Otis 1964: 368). Turnus' actions are understandable. Yet V. indicates that his is not the right response at this particular moment. Turnus fails to exercise needed self-control and to recognise the chance before him to alter the course of the battle; while Jupiter demands that Turnus proceed as he does, Turnus himself is partly responsible for his departure (see 901n.), and how he reacts reveals his shortcomings as a general. In his lack of foresight, restraint, and self-possession, Turnus contrasts with *pater* A. (see 904n.).

The book opened with daybreak and closes with sunset (the only example in *Aen.* of such a close to a book), which ends the day that opened with the Latin council (see 445–67n.), and which keeps A. and Turnus from (climactic) fighting. The gentle, pretty description of nightfall contrasts with the horrors of the day's fighting, the slaughter at the walls, and the violence that threatened to continue (Williams ad 912f.).

897 nuntius 'message', as at 447 above (also with *implet*), rather than 'messenger'; V. refers to the news that fills Turnus and then, with Acca, to the bearer of the news. **ingentem fert Acca tumultum:** a compressed phrase; Acca brings news of (*OLD* s.v. fero 26) the great outbreak of violent disorder that necessitates an emergency measure (*OLD* s.v. tumultus 2), but also brings great alarm (*OLD* s.v. tumultus 3) to Turnus with that news.

898–900 Abbreviated reported speech is characteristic of V. (Highet 1972: 342; cf. 11.227–30, 11.449–50). Here, however, concision is entirely realistic and, indeed, necessary, since Acca knew that immediate action was demanded.

898 deletas: an extreme word ('obliterated'), occurring in V. only here and at 9.248. While the Volscians have been routed, Acca is hyperbolic about what they have suffered; her exaggerated report reflects her frightened despair. Cf. Tib. ad loc. *hic uerus tumultus, qui sine falsitate esse non poterat; non enim reuera omnis Volscos dimicationis aduersus euentus absumpserat.*

899 ingruere: a military term, appearing four other times in *Aen.* (2.301, 8.535, 12.284, 12.628; also in a non-military sense at *G.* 2.410): 'fall menacingly on', with the idea of threat or actual attack dependent on context (Austin on 2.301). The verb is found before V. at Pl. *Am.* 236 *hostes crebri cadunt; nostri contra ingruunt,* a parody of a military dispatch. *ingruo* occurs first in extant prose in Livy; it is later a favourite of Tacitus. **Marte secundo:** probably 'in successful battle' (with *Marte* a metonymy) rather than 'with Mars favouring (them)'. There is latent water-imagery in *secundo*; the adj. suggests a favourable following current (cf. 7.494 *fluuio . . . secundo,* 10.687 *fluctuque . . . secundo, G.* 3.447 *secundo . . . amni*). Cf. the river-imagery in 10.21–2 (Turnus) *tumidusque secundo | Marte ruat. Marte secundo* also occurs at line-end at 12.497.

900 corripuisse suggests a torrent (*OLD* 4) in conjunction with water-imagery in *secundo* in the previous line.

901 furens: Acca's report provokes battle-rage in Turnus (see 486n.). Included in that emotion is (self-)destructive irrationality. Turnus rages when he needs to think strategically and to realise that staying in ambush is the right course of action and his only chance of victory. Cf. 9.756–61, where Turnus misses an opportunity to win the war, overcome by battle-rage (9.760–1 *sed furor ardentem caedisque insana cupido | egit in aduersos*); 'forethought and precaution, not *furor*, mark the successful general' (Hardie on 9.757). **et saeua Iouis sic numina poscunt:** cf. 4.614 *et sic fata Iouis poscunt,* 8.512 *quem numina poscunt.* V. ascribes double motivation (i.e. human and divine causes for an action; the term originates with Lesky 1961) to Turnus' departure from his place of ambush; his own rage and Jupiter's will drive him from the spot. Jupiter is *saeuus* in relation to Turnus; his will causes Turnus to miss his opportunity to ambush the Trojans, and he has destined Turnus to be defeated and to die. Cf. 12.849 (Jupiter sends a Dira as an omen of doom to Juturna and Turnus) *saeui . . . regis. saeua* picks up on *saeuissimus* at 896; Turnus is beset by terrible news and by an implacable divinity.

902 deserit: cf. 9.694–5 (Turnus) *deserit inceptum atque immani concitus ira | Dardaniam ruit ad portam.* **obsessos collis, nemora aspera:** neat chiasmus. With *obsessos,* cf. 516(n.) *obsidam.* **linquit:** *simplex* for *relinquit.*

903–5 'The conjunction of the pluperfect and imperfect brings out the "near-miss" quality of Turnus' departure and its folly. When it is just too late – when Turnus has already left and is in the plain – Aeneas with the greatest ease (present tense) sails through the abandoned ambush' (Mack 1978: 47).

904 pater Aeneas: as at 184, *pater* signals A.'s responsibility, now as the leader of his army in the field. There is an implied distinction between A. and the young Turnus, for whom *furor* overwhelms responsible, reasoned thought and action in a crisis. **apertos** 'open', in the sense of affording safe passage. *apertos* is opposed to *obsessos* at 902.

906–7 totoque . . . | agmine 'in full force'.

906 feruntur: middle voice.

907 nec longis inter se passibus absunt 'and are at no long distance from each other'.

908 ac simul 'and at the same moment'. **fumantis puluere campos** 'the field clouded with dust'. For this unusual use of *fumo,* see *OLD*

3. V. was perhaps thinking of Lucr. 6.460–1 (dust-coloured clouds) *tanto magis edita fument | adsidue fuluae nubis caligine crassa.*

909 prospexit longe: cf. 838–9 *procul . . . | prospexit,* 12.353 (Turnus spots Eumedes) *hunc procul ut campo Turnus prospexit aperto.* A. sees the battlefield from a distance, where Turnus and his troops had just arrived (903), at the same time as Turnus spots him. A moment of high tension, resolved by the end of the day's fighting rather than by a confrontation in battle. *prospexit longe* is difficult with *nec longis . . . passibus absunt* at 907; A. looks upon the field and Turnus at a distance even though A.'s and Turnus' forces march near each other.

910 saeuum Aenean: the adj. is focalised through Turnus, but also has objective force and links A. to Jupiter at 901 as a figure 'savage' to Turnus; the suggestion is that A., like the god, is Turnus' implacable opponent. *saeuus* is applied to A. a handful of other times after the death of Pallas (10.813, 10.878, 12.107, 12.498). Here and in those instances, it marks him as a ferocious warrior; *pietas* and *saeuitia* coexist in him, a hero who both desires peace and battles with a savage brutality that abides to the end of the poem. Serv. ad loc. glosses *saeuum* with *fortem,* because he is uncomfortable with the meaning 'savage'; see Thomas 2001: 96, Murgia 2004: 197–8. **in armis** 'mobilised, under arms'. Word order points decisively against taking *saeuum* with *in armis,* 'savage in arms', as at 12.107 (A.) *maternis saeuus in armis.*

911 Cf. 607. V. very likely follows the pattern of that line and refers to infantry in the first half of the verse (*pedum*) and cavalry in the second (*equorum*); Horsfall ad loc., by contrast, maintains that *pedum* refers to hooves. We are apparently to suppose that a body of allied cavalry has joined up with the infantry as A. marches out of the hills. An effective turn from sight in 909–11 to sound.

912–14 ineant . . . temptent | . . . | tingat . . . reducat: present subjunctives used in a past contrary-to-fact conditional for vividness. The construction is found in early Latin; it survives more frequently in poetry than in prose (A–G §517e nn. 1–2, *NLS* §197–8). For other examples in *Aen.*, see 1.58–9, 2.599, 5.325–6, 6.293–4, and 12.733.

912 ineant pugnas: for *ineo* used of embarking upon/beginning a battle, see *OLD* 7. **proelia temptent:** cf. 505, 2.334 *proelia temptant,* 3.240 *noua proelia temptant.*

913 roseus implies a delicate, warm glow (Austin on 1.402). The adj. is used elsewhere in V. of dawn (6.535 *roseis Aurora quadrigis,* 7.26 *Aurora in* *roseis fulgebat lutea bigis*), as commonly. Its presence is a way of linking the opening and close of the book, in that it evokes dawn while describing the setting sun. **gurgite . . . Hibero:** the western ocean. Cf. Ov. *Met.* 7.324 *ter iuga Phoebus equis in Hibero flumine mersis,* Auson. *Ep.* 17.1–2 Green *condiderat iam solis equos Tartesia Calpe | stridebatque freto Titanius ignis Hibero. gurges* is used properly of a swirling or seething mass of water (as at 298), but is regular in poetry for the waters of the ocean/sea. Cf. 12.114–15 (on dawn) *cum primum alto ab gurgite tollunt | Solis equi.*

914 tingat equos: cf. 1.745–6 (= *G.* 2.481–2) *quid tantum Oceano properent se tinguere soles | hiberni,* Ov. *Met.* 15.418–19 *in alto Phoebus anhelos | aequore tinguet equos.* Phoebus' horses are a conventional image (cf. 12.115 *Solis equi*), but are also evocative of the cavalry fighting that is so prominent in the book. **die labente:** also of the waning day at 4.77 *nunc eadem labente die conuiuia quaerit.* An extension of the use of *labor* for the setting sun and for the movement of stars through the sky (cf. 3.515 *sidera . . . tacito labentia caelo*); see *TLL* VII.2.781.6–43.

915 It is more plausible that both sides camp in front of the walls, rather than that *considunt* refers to the Trojans and *uallant* to Turnus' forces, who retire within the city and fortify its walls (so DServ., Page, Williams ad loc.), particularly given the closed gates and the mayhem at them. *moenia* in that case refers to the walls of the temporary camps (cf. 9.676 and 10.22), which both sides fortify with palisades. The action that opens *Aen.* 12 seems to occur in Latinus' palace (although the setting is vague; see Tarrant on 12.1–80). We are left to wonder how Turnus got there from his camp *ante urbem.*

BIBLIOGRAPHY

EDITIONS AND COMMENTARIES

Works included in this section are cited throughout by author's surname only.

All of Aeneid

C–N = Conington, J. and H. Nettleship, *Works of Virgil*, 3 vols. (London 1858–83)

Conte, G. B., *P. Vergilius Maro: Aeneis* (Berlin and New York 2009)

Geymonat, M., *Vergili Maronis opera* (Turin 1973)

Goold, G. P., *Virgil*, 2 vols. (Cambridge, MA 1999–2000)

Henry, J., *Aeneidea*, 4 vols. (London and Dublin 1873–92)

Heyne, C. G., *P. Vergilii Maronis opera*, 4th edn, rev. by G. P. E. Wagner, 5 vols. (Leipzig 1830–41)

Mackail, J. W., *The Aeneid of Virgil* (Oxford 1930)

Mynors, R. A. B., *P. Vergili Maronis opera* (Oxford 1969)

Page, T. E., *The Aeneid*, 2 vols. (London 1894, 1900)

Paratore, E., *Eneide*, 6 vols. (Milan 1978–83)

Perret, J., *Enéide*, 2nd edn, 3 vols. (Paris 1981–7)

Ribbeck, O., *P. Vergili Maronis opera* (Leipzig 1859–68)

Williams, R. D., *The Aeneid of Virgil*, 2 vols. (London 1973)

Individual Books of the Aeneid

Aeneid I, ed. R. S. Conway (Cambridge 1935)
ed. R. G. Austin (Oxford 1971)

Aeneid II, ed. R. G. Austin (Oxford 1964)
ed. N. M. Horsfall (Leiden 2008)

Aeneid III, ed. R. D. Williams (Oxford 1962)
ed. N. M. Horsfall (Leiden 2006)

Aeneid IV, ed. A. S. Pease (Cambridge, MA 1935)
ed. R. G. Austin (Oxford 1955)

Aeneid V, ed. R. D. Williams (Oxford 1960)
ed. L. M. Fratantuono and R. A. Smith (Leiden 2015)

Aeneid VI, ed. E. Norden, 3rd edn (Leipzig 1927)
ed. R. G. Austin (Oxford 1977)
ed. N. M. Horsfall (Leiden 2013)

Aeneid VII, ed. C. J. Fordyce (Oxford 1977)
ed. N. M. Horsfall (Leiden 2000)

Aeneid VIII, ed. P. T. Eden (Leiden 1975)
ed. C. J. Fordyce (Oxford 1977)
ed. K. W. Gransden (Cambridge 1976)
ed. L. M. Fratantuono and R. A. Smith (Leiden 2018)
Aeneid IX, ed. P. R. Hardie (Cambridge 1994)
ed. J. Dingel (Heidelberg 1997)
Aeneid X, ed. S. J. Harrison (Oxford 1991)
Aeneid XI, ed. K. W. Gransden (Cambridge 1991)
ed. N. M. Horsfall (Leiden 2003)
ed. L. Fratantuono (Brussels 2009)
Selections, ed. I. Gildenhard and J. Henderson (Cambridge 2018)
Aeneid XII, ed. W. S. Maguinness (London 1953; reprint 2002)
ed. A. Traina (Turin 1997, rev. edn 2004)
ed. R. J. Tarrant (Cambridge 2012)

Cited Editions Commentaries on Other Works

Bömer, F., *P. Ovidius Naso: Metamorphosen*, 7 vols. (Heidelberg 1969–86)
Clausen, W., *Virgil: Eclogues* (Oxford 1994)
Coleman, R., *Vergil: Eclogues* (Cambridge 1977)
Courtney, E. *The fragmentary Latin poets* (Oxford 1993)
Fordyce, C. J., *Catullus* (Oxford 1961)
Frank, M., *Seneca's Phoenissae* (Leiden 1995)
Hollis, A. S., *Ovid: Metamorphoses Book VIII* (Oxford 1970)
Hornblower, S., *Lykophron: Alexandria* (Oxford 2015)
Housman, A. E., *Manilius: Astronomica*, 5 vols. (London 1903–30)
Hutchinson, G., *Propertius: Elegies Book IV* (Cambridge 2006)
Kenney, E. J., *Lucretius: De rerum natura Book III* (Cambridge 1971)
Moretum: A Poem Ascribed to Virgil (Bristol 1984)
Kraus, C. S., *Livy: Ab urbe condita Book VI* (Cambridge 1994)
Leonard, W. E. and S. B. Smith, *T. Lucreti Cari De rerum natura libri sex* (Madison, WI 1942)
Lyne, R. O. A. M., *Ciris: A Poem Attributed to Vergil* (Cambridge 1978)
McKeown, J. C., *Ovid: Amores*, 3 vols. (Leeds 1987–98)
Myers, K. S., *Ovid: Metamorphoses Book XIV* (Cambridge 2009)
Mynors, R. A. B., *Virgil: Georgics* (Oxford 1990)
N–H = Nisbet, R. G. M. and M. Hubbard, *A Commentary on Horace: Odes Book 1, Book 2*, 2 vols. (Oxford 1970–8)
N–R = Nisbet, R. G. M. and N. Rudd, *A Commentary on Horace: Odes Book 3* (Oxford 2004)
Oakley, S. P., *A Commentary on Livy, Books VI–X*, 4 vols. (Oxford 1997–2005)
Ogilvie, R. M., *Livy Books 1–5* (Oxford 1965)
Quinn, K., *Catullus: The Poems* (New York 1971)

Skutsch, O., *The Annals of Ennius* (Oxford 1985)

Thomas, R. F., *Virgil: Georgics*, 2 vols. (Cambridge 1988)

Horace: Odes Book IV and Carmen saeculare (Cambridge 2011)

OTHER WORKS CITED

Adams, J. N. (1982) *The Latin sexual vocabulary*. London

(2013) *Social variation and the Latin language*. Cambridge

Adkin, N. (2010) 'Further Virgilian etymologizing: *Privernum* and *Privernus*', *Invigilata Lucernis* 32: 7–11

Adler, E. (2003) *Vergil's empire: political thought in the Aeneid*. Lanham, MD

Ahl, F., trans. (2007) *Virgil: Aeneid*. Oxford

Alessio, M. (1993) *Studies in Vergil: Aeneid eleven. An allegorical approach*. Laval, Quebec

Alexander, W. H. (1945) 'War in Aeneid', *CJ* 40: 261–73

Allen, W. H. (1973) *Accent and rhythm: prosodic features of Latin and Greek. A study in theory and reconstruction*. Cambridge

Anderson, W. S. (1990) 'Vergil's second *Iliad*', in Harrison (1990): 239–52

(1999) '*Aeneid* 11: the saddest book', in C. Perkell, ed., *Reading Vergil's Aeneid: an interpretive guide* (Norman, OK): 195–209

André, J. (1967) *Les noms d'oiseaux en latin*. Paris

Arnott, W. G. (2007) *Birds in the ancient world from A to Z*. London and New York

Arrigoni, G. (1982) *Camilla: Amazzone e sacerdotessa di Diana*. Milan

Axelson, B. (1945) *Unpoetische Wörter: Ein Beitrag zur Kenntnis der lateinischen Dichtersprache*. Lund

Badian, E. (1958) *Foreign clientelae 264–70 BC*. Oxford

Barchiesi, A. (1999) 'Representations of suffering and interpretation in the *Aeneid*', in P. Hardie, ed., *Virgil: critical assessments of classical authors*, vol. III (London and New York): 324–44

(2015) *Homeric effects in Vergil's narrative*, trans. I. Marchesi and M. Fox. Princeton

Basson, W. P. (1984) 'Vergil's Mezentius: a pivotal personality', *Acta Classica* 27: 57–70

(1986) 'Vergil's Camilla: a paradoxical character', *Acta Classica* 29: 57–68

Beard, M. (2007) *The Roman triumph*. Cambridge, MA

Beard, M., J. North, and S. Price (1998) *Religions of Rome*, 2 vols. Cambridge

Bell, A. J. (1923) *The Latin dual and poetic diction*. London and Toronto

Bowra, C. M. (1990) 'Aeneas and the Stoic ideal', in Harrison (1990): 363–77

Boyd, B. W. (1992) 'Virgil's Camilla and the traditions of catalogue and ecphrasis', *AJPh* 113: 213–34

Bremmer, J. N. and N. M. Horsfall (1987) *Roman myth and mythography.* London

Brenk, F. E. (1999) *Clothed in purple light: studies in Vergil and in Latin literature, including aspects of philosophy, religion, magic, Judaism, and the New Testament background.* Stuttgart

Brill, A. (1972) *Die Gestalt der Camilla bei Vergil.* Diss. Heidelberg

Bruère, R. (1971) 'Some recollections of Virgil's Drances in later epic', *CP* 66: 30–4

Burke, P. F. (1974) 'The role of Mezentius in the *Aeneid*', *CJ* 69: 202–9

(1978) '*Drances infensus*: a study in Vergilian character portrayal', *TAPhA* 108: 15–20

Burton, P. F. (2011) *Friendship and empire: Roman diplomacy and imperialism in the Middle Republic.* Cambridge

Cairns, F. (1972) *Generic composition in Greek and Roman poetry.* Edinburgh

(1989) *Virgil's Augustan epic.* Cambridge

(2006) 'The nomenclature of the Tiber in Virgil's *Aeneid*', in J. Booth and R. Maltby, eds., *What's in a name? The significance of proper names in classical Latin Literature* (Swansea): 65–82

Canfora, L. (2006) 'Immagine tardoantica di Cicerone', in E. Narducci, ed., *Cicerone nella tradizione europea: dalla tarda antichità al settecento* (Florence): 3–15

Carstairs-McCarthy, A. (2015) 'Does Aeneas violate the truce in *Aeneid* 11?', *CQ* 65: 704–13

Catrein, C. (2003) *Vertauschte Sinne: Untersuchungen zur Synästhesie in der römischen Dichtung.* Munich and Leipzig

Chaudhuri, P. (2014) *The war with god: theomachy in Roman imperial poetry.* Oxford

Cilliers, L. and F. P. Retief (2005) 'Burial customs and the pollution of death in ancient Rome: procedures and paradoxes', *Acta Theologica* 7: 128–46

Clausen, W. (2002) *Virgil's Aeneid: decorum, allusion, and ideology.* Munich and Leipzig

Combellack, F. M. (1948) 'Speakers and scepters in Homer', *CJ* 43: 209–17

Conte, G. B. (2007) *The poetry of pathos: studies in Virgilian epic*, ed. S. J. Harrison. Oxford

(2016) *Critical notes on Virgil.* Berlin and Boston

Courtney, E. (1981) 'The formation of the text of Virgil', *BICS* 28: 13–29

(2004) 'The "Greek" accusative', *CJ* 99: 425–31
Currie, H. M., ed. (1985) *Silver Latin epic.* Bristol and Chicago
Dainotti, P. (2015) *Word order and expressiveness in the Aeneid.* Berlin and Boston
de Grummond, N. T. (2006) *The religion of the Etruscans.* Austin, TX
Della Corte, F. (1972) *La mappa dell'Eneide.* Florence
Dickey, E. (2002) *Latin forms of address from Plautus to Apuleius.* Oxford
Dionisotti, C. (2007) '*Ecce*', *BICS* 50: 75–91
Duckworth, G. E. (1969) *Vergil and classical hexameter poetry.* Ann Arbor, MI
Dué, C. and M. Ebbott (2010) *Iliad 10 and the poetics of ambush: a multitext edition with essays and commentary.* Washington, DC.
Dunkle, J. R. (1973) 'The hunter and hunting in the *Aeneid*', *Ramus* 2: 127–42
Edgeworth, R. J. (1992) *The colors of the Aeneid.* Frankfurt
Egan, R. B. (1983) 'Arms and etymology in *Aeneid* 11', *Vergilius* 29: 19–26
(2012) '*Insignes pietate et armis*: the two Camilli of the *Aeneid*', *Vergilius* 58: 21–52
Esposito, J. (2016) 'Who kills Turnus? "Pallas" and what Aeneas sees, says and does in *Aeneid* 12.939–52', *CJ* 111: 463–81
Fantham, E. (1999) 'Fighting words: Turnus at bay in the Latin council', *AJPh* 120: 259–80
Farney, G. D. (2007) *Ethnic Identity and Aristocratic Competition in Republican Rome.* Cambridge
Farron, S. (1985) 'Aeneas' human sacrifice', *Acta Classica* 28: 21–33
Feeney, D. C. (1990) 'The taciturnity of Aeneas', in Harrison (1990): 167–90
(1991) *The gods in epic: poets and critics of the classical tradition.* Oxford
Fletcher, K. F. B. (2006) 'Vergil's Italian Diomedes', *AJPh* 127: 219–59
(2014) *Finding Italy: travel, nation, and colonization in Vergil's Aeneid.* Ann Arbor, MI
Flower, H. I. (1996) *Ancestor masks and aristocratic power in Roman culture.* Oxford
Forbes Irving, P. M. C. (1990) *Metamorphosis in Greek myth.* Oxford
Fowler, D. (1987) 'Vergil on killing virgins', in P. Hardie, Mary Whitby, and Michael Whitby, eds., *Homo viator: classical essays for John Bramble.* Bristol: 185–98
Fraenkel, E. (1916) 'Zur Geschichte des Wortes Fides', *RhM* 71: 187–99 (repr. in *Kleine Beiträge zur klassichen Philologie*, 2 vols. (Rome 1964): II.583–98)
Fratantuno, L. (2005) '*Posse putes*: Virgil's Camilla and Ovid's Atalanta', *Collection Latomus: Studies in Latin literature and history* XII, 185–93
(2007) *Madness unchained: a reading of Vergil's Aeneid.* Lanham, MD

(2016) 'The Penthesilead of Quintus Smyrnaeus: a study in epic reversal', *Wiener Studien* 129: 207–31
Galinsky, G. K. (1988) 'The Anger of Aeneas', *AJPh* 109: 321–48
Gärtner, U. (2005) *Quintus Smyrnaeus und die Aeneis: Zur Nachwirkung Vergils in der griechischen Literatur der Kaiserzeit* (Zetemata 123). Munich
Gaskin, R. 'Aeneas *ultor* and the problem of *pietas*', *Erene* 30: 70–96
Gershenson, D. E. (1991) *Apollo the wolf-god.* Washington, DC.
Gladhill, B. (2016) *Rethinking Roman alliance: a study in poetics and society.* Cambridge
Gotoff, H. C. (1984) 'The transformation of Mezentius', *TAPhA* 114: 191–218
Graf, F. (2008) *Apollo.* London and New York
Gransden, K. W. (1984) *Virgil's Iliad: an essay on epic narrative.* Cambridge
Green, C. M. C. (2007) *Roman religion and the cult of Diana at Aricia.* Cambridge
Griffin, J. (1980) *Homer on life and death.* Oxford
Gross, N. P. (2003–4) 'Mantles woven with gold: Pallas' shroud and the end of the *Aeneid*', *CJ* 99: 135–56
Hansen, M. H. (1993) 'The battle exhortation in ancient historiography: fact or fiction?', *Historia* 45: 22–38
Hardie, P. (1986) *Virgil's Aeneid: cosmos and imperium.* Oxford
(2007) 'Images of the Persian Wars in Rome', in E. Bridges, E. Hall, and P. J. Rhodes, eds., *Cultural responses to the Persian Wars* (Oxford): 127–43
(2012) *Rumour and Renown: representations of Fama in western literature.* Cambridge
Hardie, W. R. (1920) *Res metrica: an introduction to the study of Greek & Roman versification.* Oxford
Harrison, S. J., ed. (1990) *Oxford Readings in Vergil's Aeneid.* Oxford
Heinze, R. (1993) *Virgil's epic technique,* trans. D. and H. Harvey and F. Robertson. Berkeley and Los Angeles
Hellegouarc'h, J. (1963) *Le vocabulaire latin des relations et des partis politiques sous la République.* Paris
Henry, E. (1989) *The vigour of prophecy: a study of Virgil's Aeneid.* Carbondale and Edwardsville, IL
Heuzé, P. (1985) *L'image du corps dans l'oeuvre de Virgile* (Collection de l'école française de Rome 86). Rome
Highet, G. (1972) *The speeches in Vergil's Aeneid.* Princeton, NJ
Hölkeskamp, K.-J. (2004) *Senatus populusque Romanus: Die politische Kultur der Republik. Dimensionen und Deutungen.* Wiesbaden
Horsfall, N. M. (1985) 'Illusion and reality in Latin topographical writing', *G&R* 32: 197–208

(1988) 'Camilla, o i limiti dell'invenzione', *Athenaeum* 66: 31–51
(1991) *Virgilio: l'epopea in alambicco.* Naples
(1995) *A companion to the study of Virgil.* Leiden, New York, and Cologne
(2016) *The epic distilled: studies in the composition of the Aeneid.* Oxford
Hough, J. W. (1975) 'Monosyllabic verse-endings in the *Aeneid*', *CJ* 71: 16–24
Housman, A. E. (1926) *M. Annaei Lucani Belli ciuilis libri decem.* Oxford
Hubbard, T. K. (1998) *The pipes of Pan: intertextuality & literary filiation in the pastoral tradition from Theocritus to Milton.* Ann Arbor, MI
Jackson Knight, W. F. (1944) *Roman Vergil.* London
James, A. W. (2007) 'Quintus of Smyrna and Virgil – a matter of prejudice', in M. Baumbach and S. Bär, eds., *Quintus Smyrnaeus: transforming Homer in the second Sophistic* (Berlin and New York): 145–57
Johnson, W. R. (1976) *Darkness visible: a study of Vergil's Aeneid.* Berkeley, Los Angeles, and London
Karakasis, E. (2005) *Terence and the language of Roman comedy.* Cambridge
Kayachev, B. (2018) 'Hunt as war and war as hunt', in S. J. Green, ed., *Grattius: hunting an Augustan poet* (Oxford): 97–114
Keith, A. M. (2000) *Engendering epic: women in Latin epic.* Cambridge
Kenney, E. J. (1967) Review of J. Soubiran, *L'élision dans la poésie latine, CR* 17: 325–8
Kinsey, T. (1979) 'The meaning of *interea* in Virgil's *Aeneid*', *Glotta* 57.3/4: 259–65
Knauer, G. (1964) *Die Aeneis und Homer: Studien zur poetischen Technik Vergils mit Listen der Homerzitate in der Aeneis* (Hypomnemata 7). Göttingen
Kraggerud, E. (2012–13) 'On Vergil, *Aeneid* 11.256: a conjecture', *Eranos* 107: 21–3
(2017) *Vergiliana: critical studies on the texts of Publius Vergilius Maro.* London and New York
Kronenberg, L. (2005) 'Mezentius the Epicurean', *TAPhA* 135: 403–31
Kroon, C. (2011) 'Latin particles and the grammar of discourse', in J. Clackson, ed., *A companion to the Latin language* (Malden, MA): 176–95
Kühn, W. (1957) 'Rüstungsszenen bei Virgil', *Gymnasium* 64: 28–59
La Penna, A. (1979) 'Spunti sociologici per l'interpretazione dell'Eneide', in *Fra teatro, poesia e politica romana* (Turin): 153–65 (= H. Bardon and R. Verdière, eds., *Vergiliana: recherches sur Virgile* (Leiden 1971): 283–93)
(1988) 'Gli archetipi epici di Camilla', *Maia* 40: 221–50
Lausberg, H. (1997) *Handbook of literary rhetoric: a foundation for literary study,* ed. D. E. Orton and R. D. Anderson, trans. M. T. Bliss and A. Jansen. Leiden

Lee, M. O. (1979) *Fathers and sons in Virgil's Aeneid: tum genitor natum.* Albany, NY
Leigh, M. (1993) 'Hopelessly devoted to you: traces of the Decii in Virgil's *Aeneid*', *PVS* 21: 89–110
Lesky, A. (1961) *Göttliche und menschliche Motivation im homerischen Epos.* Heidelberg
Lintott, A. W. (1968) *Violence in republican Rome.* Oxford
Löfstedt, E. (1956) *Syntactica: Studien und Beiträge zur historischen Syntax des Lateins.* Lund
Lovatt, H. (2013) *The epic gaze: vision, gender, and narrative in ancient epic.* Cambridge
Lyne, R. O. A. M. (1987) *Further voices in Vergil's Aeneid.* Oxford
(1989) *Words and the poet: characteristic techniques of style in Vergil's Aeneid.* Oxford
Mack, S. (1978) *Patterns of Time in Vergil.* Hamden, CT
Malkin, I. (1998) *The returns of Odysseus: colonization and ethnicity.* Berkeley, Los Angeles, and London
Maltby, R. (1991) *A lexicon of ancient Latin etymologies.* Leeds
Man, J. (2018) *Searching for the Amazons: the real warrior women of the ancient world.* New York
Martindale, C., ed. (1997) *The Cambridge companion to Virgil.* Cambridge
Mayer, R. G. (1999) 'Grecism', *Proceedings of the British academy* 93: 157–82
Mayor, A. (2014) *The Amazons: lives & legends of warrior women across the ancient world.* Princeton, NJ
McDermott, W. C. (1980) 'Drances-Cicero', *Vergilius* 26: 34–8
Miller, J. F. (1994) 'Arruns, Ascanius, and the Virgilian Apollo', *Colby Quarterly* 30: 171–8
(2009) *Apollo, Augustus, and the poets.* Cambridge
Mitchell, R. N. (1992) 'The violence of virginity in the *Aeneid*', *Arethusa* 24: 219–38
Morello, R. (2008) '*Segregem eam efficit*: Vergil's Camilla and the scholiasts', in S. Casali and F. Stok, eds., *Servio: stratificazioni esegetiche e modelli culturali* (Brussels): 38–57
Moskalew, W. (1982) *Formular language and poetic design in the Aeneid* (Mnemosyne Suppl. 73). Leiden
Murgia, C. (2004) 'The truth about Vergil's commentators', in R. Rees, ed., *Romane memento: Vergil in the fourth century* (London): 189–200
Muse, K. (2007) 'Sergestus and Tarchon in the *Aeneid*', *CQ* 57: 586–605
Nelis, D. (2001) *Vergil's Aeneid and the Argonautica of Apollonius Rhodius.* Leeds
Nielson, K. P. (1983) 'The *tropaion* in the *Aeneid*', *Vergilius* 29: 27–33

Nisbet, R. G. M. (1990) '*Aeneas imperator*: Roman generalship in an epic context', in Harrison (1990): 378–89

O'Hara, J. J. (1997) 'Virgil's style', in Martindale (1997): 241–58

(2017) *True names: Vergil and the Alexandrian tradition of etymological wordplay*, new edn. Ann Arbor, MI

Oliensis, E. (1997) 'Sons and lovers: sexuality and gender in Virgil's poetry', in Martindale (1997): 294–311

(2004) 'Sibylline syllables: the intratextual *Aeneid*', *PCPhS* 50: 29–45

Opelt, I. (1965) *Die lateinischen Schimpfwörter und verwandte sprachliche Erscheinungen*. Heidelberg

Otis, B. (1964) *Virgil: a study in civilized poetry*. Oxford

Panoussi, V. (2009) *Greek tragedy in Vergil's Aeneid: ritual, empire, and intertext*. Cambridge

Papaioannou, S. (2000) 'Vergilian Diomedes revisited: the re-evaluation of the *Iliad*', *Mnemosyne* 53: 193–217

Pascal, C. B. (1990) 'The dubious *deuotio* of Turnus', *TAPhA* 120: 251–68

Paschalis, M. (1997) *Virgil's Aeneid: semantic relations and proper names*. Oxford

Peirano Garrison, I. (forthcoming) *Eloquentia: Persuasion, Rhetoric and Roman Poetry*. Cambridge

Penney, J. H. W. (1999) 'Archaism and innovation in Latin poetic syntax', *Proceedings of the British Academy* 93: 249–68

Petrini, M. (1997) *The child and the hero: coming of age in Catullus and Virgil*. Ann Arbor, MI

Pöschl, V. (1962) *The art of Vergil: image and symbol in the Aeneid*, trans. G. Seligson. Ann Arbor, MI

Powell, A. (2008) *Virgil the partisan: a study in the re-integration of classics*. Swansea

Putnam, M. C. J. (1965) *The poetry of the Aeneid*. Cambridge, MA

(1995) *Virgil's Aeneid: interpretation and influence*. Chapel Hill, NC and London

(2012) *The humanness of heroes: studies in the conclusion of Virgil's Aeneid*. Amsterdam

Pyy, E. (2010) '*Decus Italiae uirgo*: Virgil's Camilla and the formation of *Romanitas*', *Arctos* 44: 181–203

Quartarone, L. (2011) 'Quantity, quality, tension, and transition: the dimensions of Vergil's *ingens*', *Vergilius* 57: 3–34

Quinn, K. F. (1968) *Virgil's Aeneid: a critical description*. London

Quint, D. (1993) *Epic and empire: politics and generic form from Virgil to Milton*. Princeton, NJ

(2018) *Virgil's double cross: design and meaning in the Aeneid*. Princeton, NJ

Ramsby, T. (2010) 'Juxtaposing Dido and Camilla in the *Aeneid*', *Classical Outlook* 88: 13–17
Reed, J. D. (2007) *Virgil's gaze: nation and poetry in the Aeneid.* Princeton, NJ
Rissanen, M. (2012) 'The Hirpi Sorani and the wolf cults of central Italy', *Arctos* 46: 115–36
Rogerson, A. (2017) *Virgil's Ascanius: imagining the future in the Aeneid.* Cambridge
Rosenmeyer, T. G. (1960) 'Virgil and heroism: *Aeneid* XI', *CJ* 55: 159–64
Ross, D. O. (1969) *Style and Tradition in Catullus.* Cambridge, MA
(2007) *Virgil's Aeneid: a reader's guide.* Malden, MA
Rossi, A. (2004) *Contexts of war: manipulation of genre in Virgilian battle narrative.* Ann Arbor, MI
Sargeaunt, J. (1920) *The trees, shrubs, and plants of Virgil.* New York
Saunders, C. (1940) 'Sources of the names of Trojans and Latins in Vergil's *Aeneid*', *TAPhA* 71: 537–55
Schenk, P. (1984) *Die Gestalt des Turnus in Vergil's Aeneis* (Beiträge zur klassischen Philologie 164). Königstein
Schlunk, R. R. (1974) *The Homeric scholia and the Aeneid.* Ann Arbor, MI
Scholz, U. W. (1999) 'Drances', *Hermes* 127: 455–66
Schultz, C. (2010) 'The Romans and ritual murder', *Journal of the American Academy of Religion* 78: 516–41
Seelentag, S., ed. (2012) *Der pseudovergilische Culex.* Stuttgart
Sharrock, A. (2015) 'Warrior women in Roman epic', in J. Fabre-Serris and A. Keith, eds., *Women & war in antiquity* (Baltimore, MD): 157–78
Small, S. G. P. (1959) 'Virgil, Dante, and Camilla', *CJ* 54: 295–301
Soubiran, J. (1966) *L'élision dans la poésie latine.* Paris
Sparrow, J. (1931) *Half-lines and repetitions in Virgil.* Oxford
Stahl, H.-P. (1990) 'The death of Turnus: Augustan Virgil and the political rival', in K. A. Raaflaub and M. Toher, eds., *Between Republic and Empire: interpretations of Augustus and his empire* (Berkeley, Los Angeles, and London): 174–211
(2015) *Poetry underpinning power: Vergil's Aeneid. The epic for the emperor Augustus.* Swansea
Stephens, V. G. (1990) 'Like a wolf in the fold: animal imagery in Vergil' *ICS* 15: 107–30
Sullivan, T. M. (2009) 'Death *ante ora parentum* in the *Aeneid*', *TAPhA* 139: 447–86
Sumi, G. S. (2005) *Ceremony and power: performing politics in Rome between Republic and Empire.* Ann Arbor, MI
Tarrant, R. J. (1998) 'Parenthetically speaking (in Virgil and other poets)', in P. Knox and C. Foss, eds., *Style and tradition: studies in honor of Wendell Clausen* (Stuttgart and Leipzig): 141–57

Thomas, R. F. (1982) *Lands and peoples in Roman poetry: the ethnographical tradition* (*PCPhS* Suppl. 7)
(1998) 'The isolation of Turnus (*Aeneid*, book 12)', in H.-P. Stahl, ed., *Vergil's Aeneid: Augustan epic and political context* (London): 271–302
(2001) *Virgil and the Augustan reception*. Cambridge
Timpanaro, S. (2001) *Virgilianisti antichi e tradizione indiretta*. Florence
Tissol, G. (1992) 'An allusion to Callimachus' *Aetia* 3 in Vergil's *Aeneid* 11', *HSCP* 94: 263–8
Toynbee, J. M. C. (1971) *Death and burial in the Roman world*. Ithaca, NY
Tränkle, H. (1960) *Die Sprachkunst des Properz und die Tradition der lateinischen Dichtersprache* (Hermes Einzelschriften 15). Wiesbaden
Trappes-Lomax, J. (2004) 'Hiatus in Vergil and in Horace's *Odes*', *PCPhS* 50: 141–58
Trundle, M. (2003) 'Camilla and the Volscians: historical images in *Aeneid* 11', in J. Davidson and A. Pomeroy, eds., *Theatres of action: papers for Chris Dearden* (Auckland): 165–86
Unruh, D. (2011) '*Skeptouchoi*: a new look at the Homeric scepter', *CW* 104: 279–94
Vermaseren, M. J. (1977) *Cybele and Attis: the myth and the cult*. London
Versnel, H. S. (1970) *Triumphus: an inquiry into the origin, development, and meaning of the Roman triumph*. Leiden
Viparelli, V. (2008) 'Camilla: a queen undefeated, even in death', *Vergilius* 54: 9–23
von Albrecht, M. (2006) *Vergil: Bucolica, Georgica, Aeneis. Eine Einführung*. Heidelberg
Walsh, P. G. (1961) *Livy: his historical aims and methods*. Cambridge
Weber, C. (1969) 'The diction for death in Latin epic', *Agon* 3: 45–68
West, D. A. (1990) 'Multiple-correspondence similes in the *Aeneid*', in Harrison (1990): 429–44
West, G. S. (1985) 'Chloreus and Camilla', *Vergilius* 31: 22–9
Wigodsky M. (1972) *Vergil and early Latin poetry* (Hermes Einzelschriften 24). Wiesbaden
Wilhelm, M. P. (1987) 'Venus, Diana, Dido, and Camilla in the *Aeneid*', *Vergilius* 33: 43–8
Williams, G. (1968) *Tradition and originality in Roman poetry*. Oxford
(1983) *Techniques and ideas in the Aeneid*. New Haven, CT and London
Wills, J. (1996) *Repetition in Latin poetry: figures of allusion*. Oxford
Wiltshire, S. F. (1989) *Public and private in Vergil's Aeneid*. Amherst, MA
Winbolt, S. E. (1903) *Latin hexameter verse: an aid to composition*. London
Wiseman, T. P. (1971) *New men in the Roman senate, 130 BC – AD 14*. Oxford
Wofford, S. L. (1992) *The choice of Achilles: the ideology of figure in the epic*. Stanford, CA

INDEXES

Italic numbers refer to pages of the Introduction; non-italic numbers refer to line numbers in the Commentary.

1. SUBJECTS (INCLUDING LATIN WORDS OF THEMATIC INTEREST)

2. LATIN WORDS